# Edmund Husserl

# Edmund Husserl

## Founder of Phenomenology

**Dermot Moran**

polity

First published in 2005 by Polity Press

Reprinted in 2008

Polity Press
65 Bridge Street
Cambridge CB2 1UR, UK.

Polity Press
350 Main Street
Malden, MA 02148, USA

ISBN: 978-0-7456-2121-0
ISBN: 978-0-7456-2122-7 (pb)

A catalogue record for this book is available from the British Library and has been applied for from the Library of Congress.

Typeset in 10 on 11.5 pt Palatino
by SNP Best-set Typesetter Ltd, Hong Kong
Printed and bound in the United States by Odyssey Press Inc.,
Gonic, New Hampshire

For further information on Polity, visit our website: *www.polity.co.uk*

To Loretta, Katie, Eoin and Hannah

# Contents

# Acknowledgements

Edmund Husserl (1859–1938) is best known as the founder of phenomenology, the descriptive science of consciousness and its objects as they are experienced. In his mature works, he also developed and radicalized the post-Kantian tradition of transcendental idealism. He published few books in his lifetime, but he left behind a corpus of philosophical writing that is vast, complex and varied, ranging from lecture notes to bundles of private research writings organized thematically. As this *Nachlass* continues to be edited and published, the overall picture of Husserl as a philosopher is undergoing rapid change. In this book I hope to introduce Husserl's thought as it appears across the range of his works and from within, recognizing the originality and power of his descriptive analyses of the life of consciousness as well as his original approach to transcendental philosophy. I want to present Husserl in a way that will entice readers to seek out his original works. For this reason, I have tried as far as possible to present his project *from within*, in terms of its own motivations rather than in comparison and contrast with other philosophers (which would require a quite different book). I do not intend to address his critical legacy (the work of Heidegger, Merleau-Ponty, Levinas, Sartre or Derrida, etc.); rather, my aim is Husserl *par lui-même*, in his own words. I want to explicate Husserl's achievement primarily for those coming to him for the first time; so I have tried as far as possible to avoid unnecessary philosophical jargon and to explain Husserlian terms as they are introduced. I have not engaged in lengthy critique of his positions, but rather I have sought to present them in the most charitable and sympathetic light. Nevertheless, while I aim this book at the neophyte, I also hope, that my interpretative reading of Husserl has sufficient originality to interest and challenge more advanced students and scholars.

While the final responsibility for the interpretation of Husserl in the pages following rests with me alone, I would like here to record my thanks to some of the scholars who have assisted me over the four years it has taken me to research and write this book. First, I want to thank the Husserl Archive in the Katholieke Universiteit Leuven, Belgium, for accommodating me during several visits, especially its director, Rudolf Bernet, secretary, Ingrid Lombaerts, as well as Roland Breeur, Ullrich Melle and Robin Rollinger. Thanks also to William Desmond and Carlos Steel of the Higher Institute of Philosophy in Leuven. I would especially like to record my appreciation of the scholarship of the late Karl Schuhmann of the University of Utrecht, who gently and generously corrected some of my misconceptions about Husserl. I would also like to record the influence of the following scholars: in France, Jocelyn Benoist, Jean-François Courtine, Natalie Depraz, Claire Ortiz Hill and Jean-Luc Marion. In Germany, I would like to mention specifically the work of Klaus Held, Dieter Lohmar and Olav Wiegand. In Switzerland, Eduard Marbach, Kevin Mulligan and Gianfranco Soldati have been extraordinarily generous with their time and knowledge. In the UK, Michael Beaney, David Bell, Sir Michael Dummett and Peter Simons have all assisted me in understanding the relationship between Frege and Husserl.

Among US scholars, I have learned a great deal from Lester Embree of the Center for Advanced Research in Phenomenology, David Woodruff Smith and Donn Welton. I have benefited greatly from conversations with members of the Husserl Circle, especially Betsy Behnke, Marcus Brainard, John Brough, Richard Cobb Stevens, Steve Crowell, John Drummond, Burt Hopkins, Len Lawlor, Nam-In Lee, Sebastian Luft, William McKenna, James Mensch, Tom Nenon, Rosemary Rizo-Padron Lerner, John Scanlon, Robert Sokolowski and Dallas Willard. In Ireland, Jim Levine of Trinity College Dublin offered helpful comments on Frege's philosophy of mathematics. I would also like to thank my colleagues at UCD, and especially Richard Kearney for stimulating conversations and insights, and my Head of Department Gerard Casey for facilitating my research leave. I am grateful to graduate students at UCD and Rice University (in particular Irene McMullin) for their comments on draft chapters of this book.

This book could not have been written without institutional support. I would like to thank the Irish Research Council for the Humanities and Social Sciences (IRCHSS) for a Senior Fellowship in the Humanities in 2002–3, and University College Dublin for the President's Fellowship for 2003–4. Thanks to Professor Steven Crowell and the Philosophy Faculty at Rice University for hosting me as Lynette S. Autry Visiting Professor in the Humanities (Fall 2003). A special word of thanks to Professor Arthur Few, Master, and his wife, Joan Few, for making me welcome as Visiting Scholar at Martel College. I thank Dan

Zahavi for accommodating me at the Center for Subjectivity Research, University of Copenhagen. I am grateful to the Publications Committee of University College Dublin and to the National University of Ireland for their support. I want also to thank the Humanities Institute of Ireland for providing me with a research office to complete writing the book. Last, but not least, I would like to thank my family for their support, especially my wife Loretta and our three children, Katie, Eoin and Hannah.

University College Dublin

# Abbreviations

| | |
|---|---|
| *APS* | Husserl, *Analysen zur passiven Synthesis*, Hua 11 (*Analyses Concerning Passive and Active Synthesis*, trans. A. J. Steinbock; English translation also includes selections from Hua 14, 17 and 31) |
| *Bedeutungslehre* | Husserl, *Vorlesungen über Bedeutungslehre: Sommersemester 1908*, Hua 26 |
| *Briefwechsel* | Husserl, *Briefwechsel*, ed. K. and E. Schuhmann, Husserliana Dokumente, vol. 3, 10 vols |
| *Chronik* | *Husserl-Chronik*, ed. K. Schuhmann |
| *CM* | Husserl, *Cartesianische Meditationen*, Hua 1 (*Cartesian Meditations*, trans. D. Cairns) |
| *CPR* | Kant, *Critique of Pure Reason*, trans. P. Guyer and A. Wood |
| *CW* | Husserl, *Collected Works* |
| *DP* | Brentano, *Deskriptive Psychologie*, ed. R. Chisholm and W. Baumgartner (*Descriptive Psychology*, trans. B. Müller) |
| *DR* | Husserl, *Ding und Raum*, Hua 16 (*Thing and Space: Lectures of 1907*, trans. R. Rojcewicz) |
| *EB* | *Encyclopaedia Britannica* article, Hua 9 (*Psychological and Transcendental Phenomenology*, trans. T. Sheehan and R. E. Palmer) |
| *ELE* | Husserl, *Einleitung in die Logik und Erkenntnistheorie: Vorlesungen 1906/1907*, Hua 24 |
| *EP* I | Husserl, *Erste Philosophie (1923/4)*, Erster Teil: *Kritische Ideengeschichte*, Hua 7 |
| *EP* II | Husserl, *Erste Philosophie (1923/4)*. Zweiter Teil: *Theorie der phänomenologischen Reduktion*, Hua 8 |

| | |
|---|---|
| *EU* | Husserl, *Erfahrung und Urteil*, ed. L. Landgrebe (*Experience and Judgment*, trans. J. Churchill and K. Ameriks) |
| EV | Husserl, 'Entwurf einer "Vorrede" zu den *Logischen Untersuchungen* (1913)', ed. Eugen Fink, *Tijdschrift voor Filosofie*, 1, 1 and 2 (May 1939), pp. 319–39 (*Draft Introduction to Logical Investigations*, ed. E. Fink, trans. P. J. Bossert and C. H. Peters); Hua 20/1: 272–329 |
| *EW* | Husserl, *Early Writings in the Philosophy of Logic and Mathematics*, in *Collected Works*, vol. 5, trans. D. Willard |
| *FTL* | Husserl, *Formale und transzendentale Logik*, Hua 17 (*Formal and Transcendental Logic*, trans. D. Cairns) |
| *GA* | Frege, *Die Grundlagen der Arithmetik* (1884) (*Foundations of Arithmetic*, trans. J. L. Austin) |
| *GPP* | Husserl, *Grundprobleme der Phänomenologie* (1910/11), Hua 13 |
| *HSW* | *Husserl, Shorter Works*, trans. and ed. Frederick Elliston and Peter McCormick |
| Hua | Husserliana, Kluwer (now Springer) publishers, 1950– |
| *Ideen* I | Husserl, *Ideen zu einer reinen Phänomenologie und phänomenologischen Philosophie. Erstes Buch*, Hua 3 (*Ideas Pertaining to a Pure Phenomenology and to a Phenomenological Philosophy, First Book*, trans. F. Kersten) |
| *Ideen* II | Husserl, *Ideen zu einer reinen Phänomenologie und phänomenologischen Philosophie. Zweites Buch: Phänomenologische Untersuchungen zur Konstitution*, Hua 4 (*Ideas Pertaining to a Pure Phenomenology and to a Phenomenological Philosophy, Second Book*, trans. R. Rojcewicz and A. Schuwer) |
| *Ideen* III | Husserl, *Ideen zu einer reinen Phänomenologie und phänomenologischen Philosophie. Drittes Buch: Die Phänomenologie und die Fundamente der Wissenschaften*, Hua 5 (*Ideas Pertaining to a Pure Phenomenology and to a Phenomenological Philosophy, Third Book*, trans. T. E. Klein and W. E. Pohl) |
| *IG* | Twardowski, *Zur Lehre vom Inhalt und Gegenstand der Vorstellungen: Eine psychologische Untersuchung* (*On the Content and Object of Presentations*, trans. R. Grossmann) |
| *Intersubjektivität* | Husserl, *Zur Phänomenologie der Intersubjektivität. Texte aus dem Nachlass*. Hua 13–15 |
| *IP* | Husserl, *Die Idee der Phänomenologie*, Hua 2 (*Idea of Phenomenology*, trans. L. Hardy) |

| | |
|---|---|
| Krisis | Husserl, *Die Krisis der europäischen Wissenschaften und die transzendentale Phänomenologie*, Hua 6 (*The Crisis of European Sciences*, trans. D. Carr) |
| LU | Husserl, *Logische Untersuchungen* Hua 18, 19/1 and 19/2 (*Logical Investigations*, trans. J. N. Findlay, ed. D. Moran, 2001) |
| LV | Husserl, *Londoner Vorträge*, Hua 35 |
| PA | Husserl, *Philosophie der Arithmetik*, Hua 12 (*Philosophy of Arithmetic*, trans. Dallas Willard) |
| PES | Brentano, *Psychologie vom empirischen Standpunkt*, 3 vols. (*Psychology from an Empirical Standpoint*, trans. A. C. Rancurello, D. B. Terrell and L. L. McAlister) |
| Phän. Psych. | Husserl, *Phänomenologische Psychologie. Vorlesungen Sommersemester* 1925, Hua 9 (*Phenomenological Psychology*, trans. J. Scanlon) |
| PP | Merleau-Ponty, *Phénoménologie de la perception*, 1945 (*Phenomenology of Perception*, trans. C. Smith) |
| Prol. | Husserl, *Prolegomena, Logische Untersuchungen* (*Prolegomena, Logical Investigations*, trans. J. N. Findlay) |
| PSW | Husserl, 'Philosophie als strenge Wissenschaft', Hua 25 ('Philosophy as a Rigorous Science', trans. Q. Lauer) |
| PV | *Pariser Vorträge*, Hua 1 (*Paris Lectures*, trans. P. Koestenbaum) |
| Rezension | Frege's review of Husserl's *Philosophy of Arithmetic* |
| SZ | Heidegger, *Sein und Zeit* (*Being and Time*, trans. J. Macquarrie and E. Robinson) |
| TE | Sartre, *La Transcendence de l'égo. Esquisse d'une déscription phénoménologique* (*Transcendence of the Ego*, trans. F. Williams and Robert Kirkpatrick) |
| Trans. Phen. | Husserl, *Psychological and Transcendental Phenomenology and the Confrontation with Heidegger (1927–1931)*, trans. and ed. R. E. Palmer and T. Sheehan |
| Wiss. | Bolzano *Wissenschaftslehre* (*Theory of Science*, trans. R. George) |
| ZB | Husserl, *Zur Phänomenologie des inneren Zeitbewusstseins (1893–1917)*, Hua 10 (*On the Phenomenology of the Consciousness of Internal Time*, trans. J. Brough) |

In general, citations of Husserl give the English translation pagination (if any) followed by the Husserliana volume number and pagination. In the case of *Ideen* I, the German pagination is that of the original published edition of 1913, printed in the margin of the Husserliana edition. For *Erfahrung and Urteil*, the English pagination is followed directly by the German pagination of the Meiner edition. For the English translation of Husserl's *Logical Investigations*, I am using the revised edition of J. Findlay's translation (London and New York: Routledge, 2001). Volumes 1 and 2 are indicated by **I** and **II** respectively, followed by page number.

# Introduction

My mission is science alone.[1]

There is only one philosophy, one actual and genuine science . . .
the all embracing science of transcendental subjectivity. (FTL §103)

## Husserl: Phenomenologist and Transcendental Philosopher

Edmund Husserl (1859–1938) is a serious, difficult – often inaccessible
– thinker, yet his work also exhibits extraordinary originality, range,
depth, vitality and relevance. His unique contribution, *phenomenology*
(the careful description of what appears to consciousness precisely
in the manner of its appearing), was highly influential on twentieth-
century European philosophy, but he also offers an interesting and
challenging programme for a radicalized transcendental philosophy. In
this book I propose to read Husserl as both phenomenologist and transcendental philosopher.

Despite his historical prominence, Husserl is today quite neglected,
usually approached as a precursor to Heidegger and contemporary
European philosophy rather than as a systematic philosopher in his
own right. Indeed, he attracted the best minds among several generations of European philosophy students, including Heidegger, Gadamer,
Arendt, Marcuse and Levinas, who studied with him, as well as Sartre,
Merleau-Ponty, Ricoeur, Derrida, Habermas, Adorno and others, who,
while they did not personally study with him, engaged creatively with
his thought, to such an extent that the contemporary French philosopher Jean-Luc Marion has characterized phenomenology as assuming
in the twentieth century the 'the very role of philosophy itself'.[2]
Nevertheless, students of European philosophy tend to be more

directly familiar with Martin Heidegger (even though he acknowledged that it was his mentor Husserl who first gave him 'eyes' to see),
or with Levinas or Derrida, than with Husserl.

Analytic philosophy has similarly neglected Husserl in favour of
Frege as the founding father of its movement. There is some recognition, largely due to the work of Michael Dummett, of Husserl's significance for the history of early analytic philosophy, but recent
Anglophone discussions,[3] while illuminating for their close focus on
his pre-transcendental writings, have tended to downplay or dispar-
age what Husserl himself regarded as his real 'breakthrough': namely,
his development of *transcendental phenomenology*, reached through
the consistent application of the *epoché* and reductions. His deepening
exploration of phenomenology led him to embrace a radicalized form
of the Kantian project of transcendental philosophy and to recover transcendental idealism (in the spirit of Fichte). Husserl believed that consciousness must be conceived anti-naturalistically – as *transcendental*,
as a condition for the possibility of the objective world in all its appearing forms. Because of the re-emergence of an anti-naturalistic, transcendental tradition in recent analytic philosophy, there is need to
revisit Husserl with fresh eyes.

## Consciousness: The Mystery of Mysteries

Building on the insights of his teacher, Franz Brentano (1838–1917),
Husserl envisaged *phenomenology* as the descriptive, non-reductive
science of whatever appears, in the manner of its appearing, in the *subjective* and *intersubjective* life of consciousness. He was fascinated
by what he regarded as the 'mystery of mysteries': namely, the *life of
consciousness* (*Bewusstseinsleben*), with its unique, inner temporal flow
and its ability to gain objective knowledge of what transcends it. His
account of the essential forms, structures and complex interlacings and
layerings of this 'stream of consciousness' (*Bewusstseinsstrom*),[4] is considerably richer and more subtle than those of his contemporaries
William James (1842–1910) and Henri Bergson (1859–1941). Of course,
the nature of consciousness is now of intense interest to the cognitive
sciences, philosophy of mind and psychology, but Husserl, under
the name of 'phenomenology', offers an original and astonishingly
thorough and systematic way of approaching these problems that
still has considerable scientific relevance.[5]

The achievement of knowledge cannot be understood without consciousness. Husserl stresses that consciousness is presupposed in all
our dealings with the world. It is the medium through which everything objective – the whole world with all its layers and horizons – is
made manifest (Hua 9: 326). As he put it in his *Idea of Phenomenology*

lectures of 1907, the 'riddle' of epistemology is how to explain how transcendent knowledge is possible (*IP*, p. 30; Hua 2: 38). Phenomenology solves this riddle by side-stepping it. It accepts what is given *purely as given*, excluding all positing of 'non-immanent reality' (2: 45), grasping transcendent entities as revealed in immanence, i.e. how they are 'constituted' *as* transcendent. In this way Husserl focuses attention not just on the conditions for the possibility of objective knowledge, but also on the conditions for the very appearing or manifestation of the interminable and inexhaustible world itself.

At one point in the Twenties, Husserl characterized this project as specifying the 'ABC of consciousness'. As he wrote in the visitor's book of the psychiatrist Ludwig Binswanger at the latter's home in Kreuzlingen:

> Unless we become as children, we shall not enter the longed-for heavenly kingdom of a pure psychology. We must search out the ABC of consciousness (*das ABC des Bewusstseins*), and so become true elementary learners (*ABC-Schütze*). The path that leads to the ABC of consciousness and thence upwards to elemental grammar and, through a gradual ascent, to the universal a priori of concrete formations is that path that makes possible true science and knowledge of the All.[6]

In pursuit of this objective, throughout his writings Husserl offers detailed descriptive analyses of the complex structure and contents of our perceptual experience, memory, imagination, judgement and other cognitive and affective acts – the entire inventory of psychic life. Moreover, he offers not just isolated studies of individual cognitive acts, but a subtle account of what must belong to the whole complex yet unified 'interconnected complex of consciousness' (*Bewusstseinszusammenhang*),[7] a philosophical account of the cognitive architecture of conscious cognition, including the complex manner in which environmental backgrounds and horizons are involved in even the most simple conscious experiences. This led him to recognize that human experience is always temporal and finite, and always takes place within the broader context that he calls 'world'. Indeed, although Kant had already recognized the essential components of sensuousness and finitude in human knowledge, Husserl is the first modern philosopher to make the theme of *embodiment* central to his analysis of consciousness.

Husserl began his phenomenological researches into consciousness from the standpoint of the individual, an approach he characterized as '*egological*'. But he always regarded this as an abstraction from our concrete social world, and he developed profound analyses of the encounter with the other through 'empathy' (*Einfühlung*; lit. 'feeling-into') and of the whole network of intersubjective sociality, influencing a range of European thinkers, including Schutz, Sartre, Merleau-Ponty and Levinas, among many others. Husserl radically rethought the nature of subjectivity and its relationship to all forms of objectivity or 'otherness', including human others or persons, leading to his recognition of the manner in which the objective world is in fact always experienced as an intersubjective, public, communal world.

On Husserl's view, phenomenology is not just a science of consciousness and subjectivity, a science of 'objective subjectivity' as he puts it in *CM* (§13); rather, it also seeks to identify and catalogue the *objectifying* structures that allow consciousness to come to knowledge of 'what is', i.e. what philosophers – including Husserl – have called 'being'. Phenomenology, then, takes over the role that previous philosophers since Aristotle have assigned to 'first philosophy' (*protē philosophia*). Husserl regarded phenomenology as laying the only solid basis for metaphysics and ontology, thereby stimulating his younger colleague Martin Heidegger (1889–1976) in his inquiries into fundamental ontology.[8]

Finally, Husserl is also of interest for his challenging vision of the practice of philosophy (including metaphysics) as a rigorous, strict science, which tries to institute human life as a life of grounded and responsible rationality, constantly on guard against the dangers of prejudice and ungrounded speculative thinking. His work is testimony to his belief in the role of philosophy in the preservation and renewal of the scientific and cultural achievement of humankind. Indeed, there is a genuine sense in which Husserl is *par excellence* the philosopher's philosopher. His thought and writing, like that of the later Ludwig Wittgenstein (1889–1951), is fractured and sporadic. It encapsulates the very *experience* of philosophical thinking itself, probing, encountering uncertainties, difficulties and blockages (*aporiai*, 'dead-ends', from *aporos* = 'without passage', 'having no way through') searching for 'solid ground', for 'clarity'. There is no last word, only evolving thought. He constantly made new beginnings, and indeed, at the end of his life, claimed that he had at last earned the right to call himself a 'true beginner' in philosophy. As he put it, he had won the right to live a philosophical life.

## The Emergence of Phenomenology

Originally trained as a mathematician, Husserl's philosophical career began when he applied Brentanian descriptive psychology to the clarification of basic mathematical concepts. He was soon forced to pursue deeper foundational inquiries into the nature and status of logical concepts and ideal objects, and into the framework of cognitive acts (e.g. judgements) that constituted the subjective side of the accomplishment

or 'achievement' (*Leistung*) of knowledge. This led to the epistemological inquiries of *Logische Untersuchungen* (*Logical Investigations*, 1900/1),
in which he offers a devastating critique of psychologism. He is
an energetic critic of the representationalist account of knowledge in
classical empiricism. He went on to criticize naturalism (the view that
everything belongs to nature and can be studied using the natural
sciences; see *PSW*; Hua 25: 8), positivism (the resolution of physical
nature into complexes of sensations; 25: 9), biologism, historicism and
scientism. In his Freiburg years (e.g. in *First Philosophy*), he was a
creative and insightful reader of Descartes, Hume and Kant.

Husserl's approach in *LU* owes its fruitfulness to the far-reaching
and profound consequences he drew from the fundamental phenomenon of the *intentionality* ('directedness' or 'aboutness') of conscious experiences. Brentano provided Husserl with his key insight:
namely, that the 'essential character' (*Grundcharakter*) or 'universal
fundamental property' (*CM* §14) of our mental life is *intentionality*. In
his *Psychology from an Empirical Standpoint* (1874), Brentano states:

> Every mental phenomenon is characterized by what the Scholastics of
> the Middle Ages called the intentional (or mental) inexistence of an
> object, and what we might call, though not wholly unambiguously, ref-
> erence to a content, direction towards an object (which is not to be under-
> stood here as meaning a thing), or immanent objectivity. (*PES*, p. 88)

Every mental act is directed at an object.[9] Consciousness is constantly
stretching out or reaching beyond itself towards something else. The
manner of this reaching out and the manner in which the object comes
into view are both matters that can be considered from the phenomenological point of view. Phenomenology, then, considers every object
in so far as it is an object-for-a-subject. For Husserl, intentionality
became the 'indispensable fundamental concept' for phenomenology
(*Ideen* I §84).

Using intentionality, Husserl explored and documented the *essential*
(or 'eidetic', *eidetisch* – a word Husserl coined from the Greek *eidos*
meaning 'essence' or 'form'; see *Ideen* I §2)[10] structures of the whole 'life
of consciousness' with its contents, objects, backgrounds, horizons and
sense of world-involvement (what Husserl often called 'world-having',
*Welthabe*), all described according to their unique modes of givenness.
His slogan from *LU* onwards was 'back to the things themselves'. These
'things' include not just the immediate perceptual objects of our
sensuous experience, but also so-called *ideal* and *categorial* objects and
'objectivities' (*Gegenstandlichkeiten*), such as the states of affairs of the
cat-being-on-the-mat. We are conscious not just of physical things, but
also of ideal objects such as numbers, propositions, essences, possibilities and so on. Phenomenological reflection, furthermore, can turn

back towards consciousness itself, and explore the essences of conscious acts (perceivings, judgings, imaginings, rememberings and so
on). If scientific, philosophical knowledge is to be clarified, then
the ineliminable role of subjectivity in knowledge needs to be truly
grasped.

Husserl refers to this early phenomenology as a 'method for the
analysis of origins' (7: 230), according to which, as he insisted in a letter
to the German philosopher Hans Cornelius, *origin* signifies 'the exhi-
bition (*Aufweisung*) of the intuitive sense of the genuine meaning' (24:
441; see also *Ideen* I §1n.). Phenomenology wants to clarify concepts in
terms of the original intuitions in which they are experienced in a living
way. In a sense, the eighteenth-century empiricists had tried to do this
when they sought to characterize the concept of solidity in terms of
resistance or to explain the perception of distance in terms of experiences of movements in the eyes. Husserl too wanted to locate the concrete intuitions underlying key cognitive concepts, and so he regards
phenomenology as a radicalized empiricism. Soon after the publication
of *LU*, however, he realized that it had been a mistake to cast phenomenology in terms of descriptive *psychology* (where psychology is
understood as an *empirical* science), when what was at stake was in fact
'essential analysis' (*Wesensanalyse*) or the a priori 'intuitive viewing of
essences' (*Wesenserschauen*). From 1902 onwards, he sought strenuously
to correct the mistaken impression that he was doing psychology in
any sense; rather, he was pursuing ideal, a priori, *eidetic* description
which in no way related to the individuality (or *haeccitas*, 'thisness') of
real experiences (24: 426).

This led Husserl to re-conceive phenomenology in terms of the *transcendental idealist* tradition of philosophy, which he traces not just to
Kant (with whom he acknowledges his 'basic affinity', *Ideen* I §16), but,
more importantly and controversially, especially given the later reception of his thought, to Descartes' discovery of an egological subjectivity that cannot be thought away even in the most radical doubt. Husserl
offers a demythologized version of transcendental idealism: there is
no such thing as the 'thing in itself'; all being and objectivity must be
understood as the product of subjective accomplishments, and cannot
be thought without them. As he put it in 1908, 'Transcendental phenomenology is the phenomenology of constituting consciousness' (24:
425). Thus in his 1924 address to the Kant Commemoration held in
Freiburg on the bicentennial of Kant's birth, he says that, 'despite all
remoteness from Kant's fundamental presuppositions, guiding problems and methods', there is a 'manifest essential kinship' (7: 230)
between his philosophy and that of Kant, from whom he had taken the
term 'transcendental'. He sees himself as radicalizing Kant, challenging the typical nineteenth-century reading of him as a *psychologist* of
the a priori forms of human consciousness. Indeed, Husserl believes he

has taken a step beyond Kant and Hume by clarifying the true meaning of the a priori as having nothing to do with inner mental structures, but referring to the domain of essence (Hua 2: 51), to what necessarily belongs to the nature of something as the very kind of thing it is.

In similar vein, Husserl wants to recover what he perceives to be the ground-breaking *transcendental* insights of René Descartes (1599–1650), especially in the latter's *Meditations on First Philosophy* (1641/2), insights that had subsequently been covered up and lost in the naturalism of John Locke and his successors. Husserl's emulation of Descartes is explicitly brought to the fore in his *Paris Lectures* of 1929, where he characterizes his programme as almost a 'new Cartesianism' (*PV*, p. 3; Hua 1: 3).

In his mature work, Husserl explicitly defended a radicalized version of transcendental idealism whereby all 'being and sense' are produced by the transcendental ego, or, more precisely, by a plurality of embodied, intersubjectively related egos which both produce the world and are incarnated in it. The life of knowing is to be approached as a life of *meaning*, of *intending*; it is always in its very essence object-directed. But there are different ways in which objects present themselves to the experiencer, different modes of 'object-having' (as Husserl puts it) *correlated with* the different cognitive 'attitudes' (*Einstellungen*) such as believing, judging, knowing.[11] He explicitly characterizes phenomenology as the systematic study of the essential correlation of subjectivity with objectivity (24: 441). It is essentially 'correlation-research'.

## The Phenomenological *Epoché* and Reduction

In his mature work, from 1905 onwards, Husserl distinguished between the 'philosophical' or 'transcendental' attitude and the 'natural attitude' (*IP*, p. 15; Hua 2: 17), according to which we accept the world and its forms of givenness as simply *there*, 'on hand' (*vorhanden*; Hua 3/1: 53) for us. The philosophical attitude arises when we recognize the natural attitude as one of naïveté. Borrowing from the Greek sceptics, Husserl terms this disruption or break with the natural attitude, *epoché* (literally 'check' or 'suspension', but used by ancient Greek philosophers to mean 'suspension of judgement'). He characterizes it as a 'certain refraining from judgement' (*Ideen* I §32; Hua 3/1: 55),[12] an 'abstention' (*Enthaltung*), 'bracketing' (*Einklammerung*) or 'putting out of play' (*ausser Spiel zu setzen*). According to this *epoché*, the objects and contents of our experience are now treated simply as phenomena: '*Thus to every psychological experience there corresponds, by way of the phenomenological reduction, a pure phenomenon that exhibits its immanent essence* (taken individually) *as an absolute givenness*' (*IP*, p. 34; Hua 2: 45).

In *Ideen* I, Husserl speaks of *epoché* as a decision, produced by a free act of the mind, to suspend the belief component or commitment of our intentional experiences, to remove or bracket what he calls the 'general thesis' (*Generalthesis*) that assumes the existence of the world, so that we can focus solely on what is given as it is given 'immanently', and are not seduced by our naïve belief in its extantness or 'on-hand-ness' (*Vorhandenheit*).[13] This procedure is similar to that performed by Descartes with his methodic doubt, but Husserl maintains that his version has an entirely different purpose and, furthermore, that he is not interested in doubt *per se*, but only in the particular exercise of *epoché* as refraining from judgement and modifying its thetic function. The new attitude arrived at, Husserl terms 'transcendental'. This putting of the very 'obviousness' (*Selbstverständlichkeit*) of the world in question highlights what Husserl calls the 'being-sense' (*Seinssinn*) of the world, its being and meaning, what it *means to be* an entity, in whatever way, and in so doing it also brings the function of our normal, naïve world-acceptance or 'world-belief' (*Weltglaube*) into relief. But it also has the significant effect of bringing our consciousness to bear on consciousness itself, leading to a kind of 'doubling' of the ego, with one side of it acting as a non-participating spectator towards the ongoing activity of natural, conscious life. When we thus grasp experiences and objects in their 'self-givenness' or 'immanence' (in Husserl's sense), we have arrived, he says, at 'the shore of phenomenology' (Hua 2: 45). Entities still have, as it were, a reference to transcendence. Our perceptual objects still carry as it were a 'made in the transcendent world' label on them: 'The relating-itself-to-something-transcendent . . . is an inner characteristic of the phenomenon' (*IP*, p. 35; Hua 2: 46). We are led into a world of the pure phenomenon, of what is self-given, and hence into the domain of the 'evident'.

## The Crisis of the Sciences and the Discovery of the Life-World

One of the most exciting aspects of Husserl's contribution is his critical account of the emergence of scientific rationality in European thought. This theme found published expression quite late in his *Crisis of the European Sciences* (1936),[14] but had been a preoccupation in his work since his essay *Philosophy as a Rigorous Science* (1910/11). Husserl emphasizes the importance of understanding that original breakthrough to systematic science that occurred in ancient Greece with the discovery of the essential and universal, and in modern Europe, in Galileo and Descartes, with the development towards mathematical formalization that led to the transformation of European and Western culture. Unless the essential form of scientific thought can be understood, and its origin grasped and clarified, the nature of its current crises cannot be understood.

Husserl's investigation into the meaning of modern science aims to recover its 'hidden, innermost motivation' (*Krisis* §5, p. 11; Hua 6: 9) through intellectual reconstruction using a 'genetic' or 'critical historical inquiry' into the 'primal foundations' (*Urstiftungen*) of original scientific breakthroughs. In *Krisis* he shows how it is possible to remain rigorously scientific while divesting oneself of the Cartesian dualist picture of the world that necessarily leads to a reductive scientism. This intellectual reconstruction (he uses the word 'hermeneutics' in his 1931 Frankfurt lecture (Hua 27: 177)) must recover not only the scientist's own motivations but also other forces which were at work on him, even if he did not sense them. Husserl writes:

> In order to clarify the formation of Galileo's thought we must accordingly reconstruct (*rekonstruieren*) not only what consciously motivated him. It will also be instructive to bring to light what was implicitly included in his guiding model (*Leitbild*) of mathematics, even though, because of the direction of his interest, it was kept from his view: as a hidden, presupposed meaning it naturally had to enter into his physics along with everything else. (*Krisis* §9a, pp. 24–5; Hua 6: 21–2)

This reconstruction helps remove distortions that threaten the meaning of science: for instance, the danger of substituting the formalized version of objects and the world found in the mathematical-experimental sciences for the real living world in which humans flourish.

Husserl wants to recognize the primacy of our life-world (*Lebenswelt*) which founds all scientific inquiry.[15] This notion of 'world' as the 'horizon of horizons' emerged in *Ideen* I in connection with the consideration of life in the natural attitude. As conscious beings, we always inhabit – *in a pre-theoretical manner* – an experiential world (3/1: 73), given in advance (*vorgegeben*), on hand (*vorhanden*), and always experienced as a unity. It is the universal framework of human endeavour, including our scientific endeavours. It is the general structure that enables objectivity and thinghood to emerge in their different ways in different cultures. Husserl sometimes speaks as if the structure of the life-world is invariant for all; but according to his more differentiated account, there is not one single life-world, rather there is a set of intersecting or overlapping worlds, beginning from the world which is closest to us, the 'home world' (*Heimwelt*), and extending to other worlds which are farther away, 'foreign' or 'alien worlds', the worlds of other cultures, and so on.[16] Husserl even projected a new science of this much-disparaged world of opinion, or *doxa* (*Crisis* §44, p. 155; Hua 6: 158).

## Husserl's Achievement

Husserl has, at various times, been characterized as caught in Cartesian metaphysical presuppositions (by Heidegger), as a bourgeois
rationalist (by Theodor Adorno and Max Horkheimer), an epistemological foundationalist (by Richard Rorty) and so on. Indeed, on the
basis of a casual and superficial reading, it is relatively easy to detect
strains of introspectionism, foundationalism, Cartesian solipsism and
so on in his work. But the true Husserl is a much more complex and
compelling thinker. While he does believe in beginning one's philosophical meditations from the standpoint of oneself, he is by no means
a philosopher of the isolated, solipsistic, 'Cartesian' consciousness.
Indeed, he has a deep understanding of the essentially communal and
intersubjective nature of human experience. Similarly, there is a fairly
standard view of Husserl that his search for a priori essential ('eidetic')
structures failed to recognize the brute facticity, historicity and finitude
of human existence that Heidegger and later French existentialist
thinkers have emphasized as central to the human condition. To invoke
Hans-Georg Gadamer's vignette, Husserl somehow 'forgot' history.
But in fact, he recognizes the essentially temporal character of consciousness and subjectivity, and while emphasizing its transcendental
role as producer of 'being and meaning', also insists on its necessary
embodiment, historicity and finitude. Furthermore, Husserl, especially
in his later years, not only had a deep interest in the history of modern
philosophy as the explicit working-out of the ideal of self-knowledge,
he had a poignant awareness of the fragility of the scientific project in
the face of the growing scepticism, relativism and irrationalism of the
age, and sought, notably in *Krisis*, to mount a spirited defence of self-
critical universal rationality as the only way to combat the descent into
barbarism so visible in the Germany of the 1930s.

Fortunately, a number of important studies have helped to overcome
these stereotypes by offering much fuller and more nuanced accounts
of Husserl's *œuvre*.[17] Nevertheless, there is still considerable ignorance
about the meaning of his achievement. In this book, therefore, I want
as far as possible to provide a more balanced picture of Husserl's philosophical achievements, to read through all his work and not just his
early books, and to free him from the accumulated layers of post-
Heideggerian interpretation, to recover him as an exciting and original
philosopher in his own right.[18]

## Difficulties in Reading Husserl

One should not underestimate the difficulties involved in attempting
an overview of Husserl's achievement. His work is complex and, even

with growing English translations, relatively inaccessible. As even the most casual encounter will confirm, he is a difficult – even tortuous – thinker, beset by constant doubts about the nature and legitimacy of his project, struggling to overcome periods of mental despondency and inability to move forward, incessantly revising his position and advocating a plurality of approaches to his transcendental 'first philosophy'. He wrote incessantly, mostly for himself. As his former student, the Polish philosopher Roman Ingarden (1893–1970) remarked, 'Husserl wrote because writing was his manner of thinking.'[19] The result is a vast, untidy range of unpublished writings, ranging from short private notes in shorthand to relatively complete book manuscripts, brought almost to the point of publication and then abandoned by their frustrated author.

There are also genuine difficulties with his published books, not only because they range over many complex, technical areas – from the meaning of signs and the nature of the forms of judgement to the arcane areas of the ego's self-constitution in time (its 'self-temporalization') and its co-operation with the 'community of monads' to constitute the objective world – but also because their publication dates do not necessarily correspond in any straightforward way to stages of his own development. It is now clear from the ongoing publication of his research manuscripts by Husserl Archives teams that he often pursued several avenues of approach more or less in parallel, and his 'zig-zag' method of referring backwards and forwards defeats any simplistic concept of progression. Moreover, his published books – just six in his lifetime – were usually occasioned by external circumstances, and do not adequately reflect his thought as a whole. In most of these books (e.g. *Ideen* I, *CM*, *Krisis*) his focus is mostly procedural; he labours to set out and justify the theoretical foundations of phenomenology as a distinct science and as providing intellectual clarification for all scientific knowledge. These publications at best should be considered like the visible tip of an iceberg, the vast bulk of which lies 'under water', i.e. in his manuscripts. These private research writings often contain much more detailed analyses of phenomena than those found in the published works: for instance, his detailed analyses of memory, fantasy, image- or picture-consciousness (*Bildbewusstsein*), judgement, empathy, intersubjectivity, time-consciousness and so on. Fortunately, this 'hidden' Husserl is now coming to light in the critical Husserliana edition, now extending towards forty volumes. Undoubtedly, there are still many twists and turns in his progress to be uncovered and understood; nevertheless, we are now beginning to see the overall shape and extent of his lifelong meditations on the nature of consciousness, cognition, embodiment and communal rational life. His voluminous correspondence (now available in a ten-volume critical edition[20]), includes illuminating exchanges with other prominent philosophers of his day, offering considerable insight into his motivations.

## The Approach of this Book

Despite these difficulties, I hope here, by drawing selectively from his *oeuvre* as a whole, to introduce readers to the living texture of Husserl's thought through his research life, showing the main themes of his thinking and attempting as far as possible to show how they emerge and develop. I want to emphasize the continuity of Husserl's thought and the manner in which his transcendental philosophy is already prefigured in his descriptive phenomenology. Despite the variety of themes and approaches, there is only *one* Husserl.

I shall draw both from the published books, all of which have been translated into English, and the extensive *Nachlass*, which is mostly not available in English aside from his *On the Phenomenology of the Consciousness of Internal Time*, his *Analyses of Active and Passive Synthesis*[21] and some other works. I shall also refer to works not available in English, e.g. *Phantasie, Bildbewusstsein, Erinnerung*,[22] and *Erste Philosophie* ('First Philosophy', *EP* I and *EP II*), an extremely rich source of material on Husserl's conception of the history of modern philosophy (and his own position in relation to it). *EP* I, with its 'critical history of ideas' involving extensive discussions of Descartes, Locke, Berkeley, Hume, Leibniz and Kant, gives the lie to the popular opinion that Husserl, as a trained scientist, was not well versed in philosophy. *EP* II marks an important transition in Husserl's work, in that it focuses on the theory of the phenomenological reduction, the theme he took to be vital to the whole phenomenological project. It attempts to explicate the sense in which phenomenology as an 'ultimately grounded' science must investigate its own conditions of possibility, in terms of its own possibility of reflecting on its own operations. Iso Kern's three-volume edition of Husserl's research on intersubjectivity, *Zur Phänomenologie der Intersubjektivität: Texte aus dem Nachlass* (*On the Phenomenology of Intersubjectivity: Texts from the Posthumous Works*), Hua 13–15, has been extensively commented on by German and French philosophers, but is hardly known in the Anglophone world, apart from Husserl specialists. These volumes offer extensive discussions both of Husserl's account of the intuition of others in 'empathy' as well as analyses of social acts and communal forms of intentionality.[23] Volume 15, especially, contains many of Husserl's late reflections on time, the transcendental ego, transcendental intersubjectivity, the community of monads and the Absolute, showing that Husserl was capable of entering into the most complex of metaphysical discussions. This dense and difficult speculation in the mid-Thirties is all the more surprising when one puts it beside the wonderfully clear and penetrating discussions of science and philosophy in the Vienna Lecture and *Krisis* texts of the same period. In these texts Husserl struggled to explicate the full sense of his transcendental problematic.

Thanks to recent publication of Hua 34 and 35, I have been able to make use of Husserl's writings from the Twenties, works composed in that long period between the publication of *Ideen* I (in 1913 and *FTL* in 1929. The recent publication of Husserl's 1922/3 lectures, *Einleitung in die Philosophie* (*Introduction to Philosophy*) and the London Lectures of 1922 (both in Hua 35), also provides significant new insight into Husserl's explication of phenomenology in terms of a particular reading of the history of modern philosophy, and especially his attempt to rethink and revive Descartes' project in the *Meditations*.

My approach in the book is both chronological and thematic. In chapter 1, I describe Husserl's life and intellectual development. He began as a theorist of knowledge, interested specifically in mathematics and logic as modes of knowledge to be investigated by descriptive psychology, which he broadened into, first, eidetic and, later, transcendental phenomenology. In chapter 2, I offer an overview of his conception of philosophy as sense-clarification. Chapter 3 charts Husserl's development from his first 'psychological' investigations into the nature of number to his 'breakthrough' to phenomenology in *LU*. Chapter 4 offers a relatively detailed tour through *LU*, with particular attention paid to the emergence of phenomenology in that work. Chapter 5 departs from the chronological approach to explore the essential structures of consciousness in a more composite way, drawing from across Husserl's *oeuvre*, emphasizing the consistency of his descriptions of conscious acts throughout his career. Here I give a brief exposition of his understanding of the noema, the object as intended, or sense, but I shall not dwell on it because, despite the extensive commentary it has generated, it does not play a great role in his writing after *Ideen* I. His late work took an idealist turn and focused more on the transcendental ego, intersubjectivity and the life-world, and so chapter 6 focuses on central themes of Husserl's mature philosophy: namely, his transcendental idealism.

More and more in his mature writings, Husserl made the philosophizing self a major theme: not just the self of everyday 'natural' experiences, not just the anonymous transcendental ego that functions to give the world its 'being-sense' (*Seinssinn*), but also the self who deliberately philosophizes, the 'detached spectator' whose self-critical self-awareness marks a new and higher possibility for humankind. Chapter 7 attempts to disentangle the various strands of his complex approach to the transcendental ego and to capture the sense of Husserl's growing attachment to transcendental idealism in his late metaphysical musings about the community of 'monads' (his term for the whole individual person's life) as well as his critical analysis of the meaning of the natural attitude and the 'life-world' (*Lebenswelt*) in which humans always live and find themselves. Finally, I conclude with a brief overview and assessment of Husserl's achievement and influence.

For reasons of space, I have had to forgo treatment of Husserl's reflections on ethics and value theory, subjects he pursued for decades, primarily in his lectures (see, e.g., Hua 28 and 37).

# 1

# *Edmund Husserl (1859–1938):*
# *Life and Writings*

Edmund Husserl was a serious, somewhat distracted academic, although 'not without charm and a certain sense of humour',[1] who lived his professional life within the confines of the German university system. He published only sporadically, and generally avoided philosophical conferences (since, in his view, they did not produce genuine philosophizing), and made few trips outside Germany. Even his most devoted students considered his lectures to be interminable monologues, lost in intricate detail (he reminded one hearer of a mad watchmaker[2]), although he obviously had charisma and conveyed authority such that, as his Freiburg student Gerda Walther (1897–1977) recalls, at the lecture podium he seemed like an Old Testament prophet.[3] While he could write clearly and fluently (as in *Krisis*), much of his output consists of notes – complicated, private musings not intended for publication. As we shall see in chapter 2, he had a profound, even grandiose sense of the mission of philosophy, and sought always to lead 'the philosophical life'. But he also had constantly to struggle against deep uncertainty and depression to gain the longed-for 'clarity' that obsessed him.

## Husserl's Early Education and his First Mentor, Karl Weierstrass

Edmund was born into comfortable, bourgeois circumstances on 8 April 1859, in Prossnitz, Moravia, then part of the Austrian Empire, now Prostejov in the Czech Republic.[4] His father, Adolf Abraham (1827–84), owned a draper's store, and his family belonged among the assimilated Jews in what was the largest and most liberal Jewish community in Moravia at that time. Edmund was brought up in the Jewish religion in a liberal manner.[5] He attended a local school for three years (1865–8), and then transferred to the Leopoldstädter Realgymnasium in Vienna and, a year later, to the Deutsches Staatsgymnasium in Olmütz (now Olomouc in the Czech Republic). He was an unexceptional student, albeit with an aptitude for mathematics,[6] and he graduated in June 1876 with solid but unspectacular results. Indeed, his own classmates were somewhat surprised when he announced his intention to study astronomy at university.[7]

Husserl enrolled in the University of Leipzig that autumn, and for the next three semesters attended lectures in mathematics, physics and astronomy. He took philosophy lectures from the renowned philosopher and psychologist Wilhelm Wundt (1832–1920), lectures that, at the time, made little impression.[8] However, encouraged by another philosophy student, Thomas Masaryk (1850–1937), he began reading the British empiricists, especially Berkeley, who held a lifelong fascination for him.[9] In the summer of 1878 he moved to Berlin, where he spent six semesters studying mathematics, attending the lectures of Karl Weierstrass (1815–97),[10] renowned for his success in arithmetizing analysis, and Leopold Kronecker (1823–1891). He also attended philosophy lectures, given by Friedrich Paulsen (1846–1908) and Johann Eduard Erdmann (1805–92) – but again they made no great impression.[11] Weierstrass, on the other hand, was inspirational, instilling in the young Husserl the 'ethos for scientific striving'.[12] His lectures on the theory of functions awoke Husserl's interest in the foundations of mathematics such that he would later write that he hoped to do for philosophy what Weierstrass had done for arithmetic: that is, set it on a single foundation.[13]

In the belief that an Austrian degree might improve his chances of employment,[14] at the beginning of the summer semester of 1881 Husserl transferred to Vienna to study mathematics. He earned his doctoral degree in 1882 with a purely mathematical dissertation on differential calculus, '*Beiträge zur Theorie der Variationsrechnung*' ('*Contributions to the Theory of the Calculus of Variations*'), supervised by Leopold Königsberger (1837–1921), a disciple of Weierstrass. In the summer of 1883 he returned to Berlin to assist the ailing Weierstrass, but soon became restless, and in October began a year's military service. On his discharge from the army, he moved to Vienna, where his friend Masaryk was now *Privatdozent*. Masaryk recommended that Husserl attend the lectures of the former Catholic priest Franz Brentano, who was causing quite a stir with his new approach to psychology. Masaryk, a committed Christian, also encouraged him to read the New Testament, leading to Husserl's baptism in the Lutheran church in Vienna on 26 April 1886 (*Chronik*, p. 15). Thereafter he remained a committed if non-confessional Christian, reading the New Testament daily.[15] Although his phenomenological approach was 'atheological' (*Briefwechsel*, 7: 237),[16] in that it bracketed the results of all positive sciences, including theology, nevertheless he was deeply religious, and even saw phenomenology as progressing ultimately to theological questions and treating scientifically what had previously been symbolized in religion. A close confidante of his final years, Sr Adelgundis Jaegerschmidt records him as saying: 'In my phenomenological reduction I simply want to gather all philosophies and religions by means of a universally valid method of cognition.'[17] His aim was, as he put it, to reach 'God without God'. Husserl had converted from his lapsed Judaism to Christianity for genuinely religious reasons; however, he always rejected the traditional conception of the divine attributes as absurd: for example, he denies that God has the kind of immediate, non-inferential and complete intuition of entities that has been traditionally attributed to him.[18] His mature conception of the divine was expressed in terms of quasi-Hegelian 'absolute spirit', in the form of a 'community of monads' in a teleological project of absolute reason, or as an absolute ego that temporalizes itself, pluralizes itself in individual egos, and requires expression in the world (15: 381).[19]

## With Brentano in Vienna

Husserl spent but two years (1884 to 1886) with Brentano, attending his lectures and absorbing the latter's distaste for German Idealism and his admiration for British empiricism, notably Hume.[20] Brentano was also part of the German neo-scholastic 'return to Aristotle'. He wanted philosophy to emulate the kind of exact description practised by empiricists from Aristotle to Mill. In *Psychology from an Empirical Standpoint* (1874) he proposed a new strict science of psychology – *descriptive psychology* – as a classificatory science of mental acts and their contents based on the apodictic self-evidence of inner perception. From the Scholastics, he took over the concept of intentionality, 'directedness to an object' (*die Richtung auf ein Objekt*; *PES* 88), as the chief characteristic of 'mental phenomena'.

Brentano's vision inspired Husserl to become a philosopher: 'Brentano's lectures gave me for the first time the conviction that encouraged me to choose philosophy as my life's work, the conviction that philosophy too was a serious discipline which also could be and must be dealt with in the spirit of the strictest science.'[21] In particular, Husserl cites Brentano's attempts to trace every concept back to its intuitive sources. As he later claimed, he was also particularly stimulated by Brentano's attempted reform of Aristotelian logic,[22] proposed in his 1884–5 lecture course. Husserl remained in contact with Brentano even after he left Vienna. He diligently collected Brentano's lecture transcripts, e.g. his *Descriptive Psychology* lectures of 1887–91, his investigation of the senses, as well as his studies of fantasy, memory and judgement. Husserl always acknowledged the fundamental importance of Brentano.[23] They remained friends and engaged in correspondence on technical issues in mathematics and geometry until Brentano's death in 1917.[24] Husserl initially followed Brentano's concept of *descriptive psychology* in his first publication, *Philosophy of Arithmetic* (1891), which aimed at the clarification of arithmetical concepts by elucidating their 'psychological origin'. For example, in his late *Krisis* he could write:

> This is the place to recall the extraordinary debt we owe to Brentano for the fact that he began his attempt to reform psychology with an investigation of the peculiar characteristics of the psychic (in contrast to the physical) and showed intentionality to be one of these characteristics; the science of "psychic phenomena", then, has to do everywhere with conscious experiences. (*Krisis* §68, pp. 233–4; Hua 6: 236)

But, crucially, Husserl continues: 'Unfortunately, in the most essential matters he remained bound to the prejudices of the naturalistic tradition (*Krisis*, §68, p. 234; Hua 6: 236). In fact, it took Husserl many years to extract himself from the shadow of his teacher. As he wrote to his American student Marvin Farber:

> Even though I began in my youth as an enthusiastic admirer of Brentano, I must admit that I deluded myself, for too long, and in a way hard to understand now, into believing that I was a co-worker on his philosophy, especially, his psychology. But in truth, my way of thinking was a totally different one from that of Brentano, already in my first work, namely the *Habilitation* work of 1887.[25]

In *LU* Husserl was already marking off his differences from his teacher, rejecting his psychophysical dualism, his representationalism and his account of the distinction between inner and outer perception. Many years later he would point to the deficiency in Brentano's conception of intentionality:

> ... Brentano's discovery of intentionality never led to seeing in it a complex of performances (*Zusammenhang von Leistungen*), which are included as *sedimented history* in the currently constituted intentional unity and its current manners of givenness – a history *that one can always uncover following a strict method*. (FTL §97, p. 245; Hua 17: 252)

Husserl's own breakthrough insight concerning intentionality came in 1898 (as he later recalled in *Krisis*), when he realized that there was a 'universal a priori of correlation between experienced object and manners of givenness' (*Krisis* §48, p. 166n. Hua 6: 169 n. 1). In other words, that intentionality really encapsulated the entire set of relations between subjectivity and every form of objectivity. Anything that is – whatever region it belongs to – must be understood as 'an index of a subjective system of correlations' (*Krisis* §48, p. 165; Hua 6: 168).

Inspired by Brentano and Weierstrass, Husserl became increasingly conscious of the need for a clarification of the fundamental concepts of mathematics and logic. An important influence on Husserl at this time was the four-volume *Wissenschaftslehre* (*Theory of Science*, 1837) by the neglected Austrian thinker Bernard Bolzano (1781–1848),[26] which contained new approaches to semantics and logic, and, in particular, defended the objective validity of logical meanings.[27] Bolzano carefully distinguished between thoughts as psychic occurrences, their expression in linguistic sentences, the statements made, and the abstract propositions they stood for, 'propositions-in-themselves' (*Sätze an sich*) which have existence but not actuality, thus anticipating Frege's critique of psychologism by some fifty years.[28] Husserl was drawn to Bolzano's account of pure logic as the 'theory of science'; his conception of science as a coherent intermeshing system of theoretical truths; his account of 'presentations' and 'truths-in-themselves' (*Wahrheiten an sich*), a conception later defended in the *Prolegomena* (1900). He adopted and developed Bolzano's accounts of analyticity, logical consequence (*Abfolge*) and the distinction between the *judgement* itself (*Satz an sich*) – the content or proposition judged – and the *act* of judging (see *ELE*; Hua 24: §49c; see also 26: §8a), a distinction crucial for the development of pure logic, distinct from psychology.[29] On the other hand, it is clear from the Draft Preface to the second edition of *LU* that Husserl resented the claim (made by Rickert among others) that he was merely reviving Bolzano (EV, p. 37; Fink 130; 20/1: 298).[30]

Brentano recommended that Husserl continue his studies with a former student, Carl Stumpf (1848–1936),[31] who was actively developing descriptive psychology, in particular in concrete analyses of sense perception and spatial awareness.[32] In 1886 Husserl moved to Halle, where he attended Stumpf's psychology lectures, and in 1887 completed his *Habilitation* thesis, *Über den Begriff der Zahl, Psychologische Analysen* (*On the Concept of Number, Psychological Analyses*, Hua 12). The mathematician Georg Cantor (1845–1918), another former student of Weierstrass, was a member of the examination committee. Meanwhile, on 6 August 1887, he married Malvine Charlotte Steinschneider, who had also grown up in Prossnitz, the daughter of the schoolteacher and leading Jewish scholar of his day, Sigismund Steinschneider. Malvine followed Husserl into the Christian religion, being baptised on 8 July 1887 (*Chronik*, p. 20), shortly before their marriage. Their three children – a daughter, Elizabeth (Elli, b. 1892), and two sons, Gerhart (b. 1893) and Wolfgang (b. 1895) – were all born in Halle.

## Husserl's Difficult Years at Halle (1887–1901)

In autumn 1887 Husserl took up duties as *Privatdozent* in the Philosophy Department at Halle. He would spend the following fourteen years there with no public salary, only lecture fees and fellowships,[33] without promotion, isolated and exceptionally lonely, and, as he later confirmed to Dorion Cairns, suffering from a kind of intellectual depression.[34] He did form friendships with colleagues: notably Cantor;[35] with Erdmann, his former Berlin professor now at Halle; and with the philologist Hans von Arnim. But in the main he immersed himself in his work, putting great stress on family life, according to his wife Malvine. He lectured on a broad variety of topics.[36] He read widely in logic and in the history of philosophy. In fact, he was well versed in modern philosophy, although he called himself an 'autodidact' in this subject and depended heavily on secondary sources (including Windelband and Cassirer).

Husserl's first book, an expanded version of his *Habilitation* thesis, *Philosophie der Arithmetik: Psychologische und logische Untersuchungen*, appeared in 1891. He was already changing his mind about the view of mathematics expressed therein, and he abandoned the planned second volume on the nature of the calculus, even as the first volume was being printed. He eventually renounced the project in 1894,[37] confessing to Stumpf that he had come to realize that the negative, irrational and imaginary numbers were not based on the cardinal numbers, and that he could no longer explain the whole of arithmetic in the manner originally intended, since he now understood that arithmetic was really a segment of formal logic.[38] His focus now shifted from mathematics to more fundamental problems in the foundations of logic and epistemology. Part of his liberation came, as he himself records in his *Personal Notes*, when he was required to lecture on psychology in 1891–2. He read extensively in descriptive psychology, including dipping into the work of William James (a personal friend of Stumpf), which 'yielded a few flashes of insight' (*EW*, p. 491; Hua 24: 443). His copy of James's *Principles of Psychology* is closely annotated, especially chapters in volume 1 such as 'The Stream of Thought', 'Attention' and 'The Perception of Space'.[39] During the Nineties, Husserl poured all his energies into logic, reading critically the works of contemporary logicians such as Mill, Boole, Bolzano, Schröder, Lotze and Frege, and publishing a number of detailed review articles criticizing prevailing conceptions. His target was not just psychologistic logic, but also formal mathematical approaches, including that of Ernst Schröder, whose *Vorlesungen über die Algebra der Logik* (1890–5), synthesizing the work of Boole, E. J. Jevons (1835–1882) and others, had sought to develop an extensionalist logic based on the emerging set theory.

Schröder sought to develop a common calculus for reasoning in different areas, but Husserl thought that this approach misunderstood the essential character of logic.

In 1891 Husserl began corresponding with Gottlob Frege on various logical problems, including their different understandings of the relationship between concepts and objects. In *PA* he had already discussed Frege's account of definition and identity in a critical manner, and in 1894 Frege in turn reviewed Husserl's *PA* in a penetrating but somewhat intemperate manner. Frege's searching criticisms were partly responsible for Husserl's change of focus, leading to his critique of psychologism in the *Prolegomena* (1900), the first volume of *LU*, but Frege's influence on Husserl should not be exaggerated, for Husserl was an extremely independent thinker, advancing along a similar path, as his letters to Frege make clear).[40]

Husserl's developing philosophical ability may be seen in his draft writings in the Nineties: for example, his article, 'Intentional Objects', probably written in 1894 and reworked up to 1898, but never published.[41] This essay sets out his views on the nature of the intentional object, and specifically tackles the problem of so-called objectless presentations (e.g. the thought of 'nothing', a 'centaur', a 'round square', a 'green virtue' or a 'gold mountain', 'the present King of France'), originally discussed by Bolzano in his *Wissenschaftslehre*, book I, §67, and subsequently taken up by Brentano, Twardowski, Marty, Meinong and Russell, among others.[42] Here Husserl begins by rejecting the common manner of treating the problem – that is, to claim that we can *represent* such non-existent objects to ourselves because we can form an idea or picture of them in our heads. He also rejects Twardowski's solution: namely, that we must distinguish between a content with mental or intentional existence and an object, because again we have a false duplication of the object (whether I merely think of Berlin or think of it as existing, it is the same Berlin to which I am referring, *EW*, p. 350; Hua 22: 308; see *IG*). In this article, as in his unpublished review of Twardowski's book, dating from the same period (*EW*, pp. 388–95; Hua 22: 349–56), Husserl introduces a crucial distinction between the '*real* psychological content' and the '*ideal* logical content' (*idealer Gehalt*; 22: 350n.) or meaning, of the act, which is always identical and unchanging. In the 'Intentional Objects' essay, Husserl already argues that 'truths, propositions and concepts are also objects' and can be said to exist in the full sense, although not in the sense of 'real' or spatiotemporal existence (22: 326). He distinguished the *psychological* components of a mental process (part of the proper object of the empirical science of psychology) from the unchanging, timeless, identical, ideal meanings and their intended objects, which are the focus of logic and ontology, respectively. Gradually, he came to recognize further phenomenological features of a lived experience, e.g. what he called the

act-quality as opposed to its matter, intentional essence, temporal structure and so on.

An important problem that preoccupied him in the 1890s (and laid
the basis of all his subsequent research) was the issue of the relationship between two basic kinds of experience that seemed to divide up
all mental life: namely, between those 'intuitions' (*Anschauungen*) that
are fully 'filled' by the presence of the intuited object and what he
initially called 'representations' (*Repräsentationen*; 22: 351n.), thoughts
where the intended object is absent. In *PA*, following Brentano, he
had already distinguished between so-called authentic or genuine
presentations (the lower numbers) and inauthentic or symbolic
presentations of the higher concepts of arithmetic. Science is
impossible without 'inauthentic' representations, the problem is:
how are they grounded? In part, the answer must involve the careful
study of the nature of genuine intuitions whose object is given directly,
immediately and 'fully', as opposed to those representations (*Vergegenwärtigungen*) where the objects are given mediately, indirectly and
'emptily'.

*Logische Untersuchungen* (*Logical Investigations*) – the title echoes the
subtitle of his first book – 'born of distress, of unspeakable mental distress, of a complete "collapse" ' was the result of this decade of hard,
lonely work. The first volume *Prolegomena zur reinen Logik* (*Prolegomena
to Pure Logic*) was published independently in July 1900,[43] followed by
a second volume of six Investigations, subtitled *Investigations in Phenomenology and the Theory of Knowledge*, published in two parts in 1901.
Husserl records that the *Prolegomena* originated from two lecture series
given in Halle in the summer and autumn of 1896 (Hua 18: 12; 24: 57);[44]
this was a devastating critique of logical psychologism and a defence
of logic as a theory of science, reviving the Leibnizian notion of a *mathesis universalis*. In his 1896 lectures he had already developed the insight
that 'The first and principal foundation of all logic is the objective, that
is, non-psychological theory of dependency relationships between sentences'.[45] Husserl had written to Paul Natorp on 21 January 1897 about
the work he was composing against the 'subjective-psychologising
logic of our time', a tendency to which he himself, as a student of
Brentano, had once subscribed (*Briefwechsel*, 5: 43). In the Foreword to
*LU*, he ruefully invokes Goethe's remark: 'One opposes nothing more
strongly than errors one has just abandoned' (*LU*, Foreword, **I** 3; Hua
18: 7, trans. modified). In fact, it had been Hermann Lotze (1817–81),
and specifically his interpretation of Platonic Ideas, that had helped
Husserl understand Bolzano's 'propositions in themselves' (*Sätze an
sich*) as the senses of statements and not as mysterious kinds of things,
and thus led him out of psychologism.[46] He later noted that Natorp had
subscribed to the same view of mathematics and logic as based on ideal
entities and as ultimately forming a unity (24: 57). Husserl's conver-

sion from psychologism, then, had been motivated by his reading of Bolzano and Lotze rather than Frege (whose work he criticized for other reasons, e.g. its treatment of identity). We shall return to this topic in chapter 3.

The *Prolegomena* was enthusiastically received. Established German philosophers – Wilhelm Dilthey, Wilhelm Wundt and Paul Natorp[47] – commented favourably on it. Natorp reviewed it favourably in *Kant-Studien*, but opined that neo-Kantians would find little in it to be surprised about.[48] Wundt gave it a strange review, to which Husserl reacted badly and which he severely criticized. Wundt accepted the *Prolegomena*'s arguments against psychologism, but criticized Husserl's second volume as proposing an extreme 'logicism' and demanding a complete reform of psychology. Husserl, for his part, rejected Wundt's criticism as a complete misunderstanding of the work, saying that he neither advocated logicism (in Wundt's sense) nor said a word about the reform of psychology.[49] Reviewers of the second volume assumed either that Husserl, with all his talk of 'lived experiences' (*Erlebnisse*), had relapsed back into psychologism, or that he was merely substituting a rationalistic, scholastic account of ideal meanings (EV, p. 22; Fink, p. 115; 22/1: 279). Husserl was sensitive to the widespread misunderstanding of his second volume. Not all comment was negative, however. The Munich philosopher-psychologist Theodor Lipps, himself criticized in the *Prolegomena* (*LU*, Prol. §17) as psychologistic, began to send students to Husserl. In his Draft Preface (1913) Husserl boasts that he has practised phenomenological seeing for over two decades, with the result that:

> I see phenomenological differences, especially differences of intentionality, as well as I see the difference between this white and that red as pure data of colour. If someone can absolutely not see differences of the latter kind, one would say that he is blind; if someone cannot see differences of the former sort, so I cannot help myself and I must once more say that he is blind, albeit employing blindness in a wider sense. (20/1: 321; my translation)

## The Development of Phenomenology: Göttingen 1901–1916

Husserl claimed that writing *LU* 'cured' him from the depression of his Halle years (*Chronik*, p. 22); it also enabled his escape to Göttingen, which, since the time of Johann Carl Friedrich Gauss (1777–1855), had been a world-renowned centre of mathematics. In September 1901 he was appointed Professor Extraordinarius at Göttingen University, against the wishes of its Philosophy Faculty.[50] In contrast with the isolation at Halle, his Göttingen years would be extremely productive. Husserl joined a renowned circle of scientists that included the mathematicians Felix Klein (1848–1925), David Hilbert (1862–1943), Richard Courant (1888–1972), Erhard Schmidt (1876–1959), the function theorist Ernst Hellinger (1883–1950) and the physicist Max Born (1882–1970). Hilbert,[51] who had already formulated his axiom of completeness for arithmetic and had published his hugely influential *Grundlagen der Geometrie* (1899), which organized geometry as a formal axiomatic system, had envisaged Husserl as playing a vital role in advancing the cause of *formalism* in mathematics and logic. Husserl himself already suspected that the imaginary numbers would prove an obstacle to such completeness.[52] Hilbert's students attended Husserl's seminars, including Ernst Zermelo (1871–1953), who also worked on set theory, Paul Bernays (1888–1977) and the physicist Herman Weyl (1885–1955),[53] who later attempted to integrate phenomenology into mathematics and physics.[54]

Despite being surrounded by mathematicians, Husserl's own inquiries drew him towards *epistemological* problems and the *phenomenology* of cognitive states. He was developing phenomenological descriptions of conscious awareness in its specific forms, including perception of things in space, memory, fantasy (*Phantasie*), image-consciousness or 'pictorial awareness' (*Bildbewusstsein*), and awareness of time (see Hua 23). He began to lecture on the 'phenomenology of inner time-consciousness' in the winter semester of 1904/5, criticizing Brentano (who related temporal awareness to the imagination), and continued these lectures in later years (Hua 10). It was Natorp who, in his review of the *Prolegomena*, suggested that any attempt to understand how the real psychological was connected with the ideal logical forms would need to examine the concept of time itself. Husserl began to examine the manner in which consciousness is framed by temporal experience.

At the same time, he was also clarifying the chief differences between phenomenology as an *eidetic* science of 'pure' consciousness, studied in 'immanence', and psychology as an empirical, factual science of psychophysical states of animals. This led him inexorably to an overall critique of *naturalism*, expressed in his 1906–7 ELE lectures (Hua 24). Around this time too, Husserl began also to reconceive his relationship to Descartes and Kant, and, with the discovery of the *epoché* and reduction, eventually made the decisive breakthrough into transcendental philosophy. His attempts to penetrate the complexities of time-consciousness appear to have been one of the triggers that propelled him to try to isolate the intentional relationship between meaning-giving and the meant objectivity, by bracketing existential concerns about the transcendent world. But clearly it is an extension of the 'principle of presuppositionlessness' introduced in *LU*. As he would put it in 1913, the chief function of the *epoché* is to exclude all appeal to existing sciences. Phenomenology, as an eidetic science, '*necessarily precludes any incorporation of cognitional results yielded by the empirical sciences*' (*Ideen* I §8, p. 17; Hua 3/1: 18).

Around the same time, he also began his first reflections on the experience of the other person in what he called 'empathy' (*Einfühlung*), following Theodor Lipps (1851–1914) and the German psychological tradition. Lipps is usually credited with coining the term from the Greek *empatheia*, 'feeling into'.[55] *Einfühlung* thus refers to the phenomenon of feeling (or thinking) one's way into the experiential life of another. How do we perceive another person's body as a living body, as a centre of consciousness and of feelings? How do I constitute another as an *alter ego* with its own 'centre' and 'ego-pole' (*Ichpol*) of psychic experiences, affections and performances?

At Göttingen, with his fame spreading due to the reception of *LU*, Husserl began to attract a following of devoted and gifted students. First, Johannes Daubert (1877–1947), a student of Lipps, visited him in Göttingen (*Chronik*, p. 72).[56] Through Lipps and Daubert, an informal 'school' of Husserlian phenomenologists formed in Munich, which included Alexander Pfänder (1870–1941), Adolf Reinach (1883–1917) and, from 1906, Max Scheler. Husserl addressed this group in Munich in 1904, and, the following year, some of Lipps's Munich students travelled to Göttingen to see him. Reinach, in particular, was highly regarded by Husserl, writing his *Habilitation* under him and acting as a teaching assistant to Husserl at Göttingen. When Reinach lost his life in the Great War in 1917, Husserl wrote several moving obituaries.[57] In 1907 a group of Husserl's students founded the Göttingen Philosophy Society, led by Theodor Conrad and including Hedwig Conrad-Martius, the French student Jean Héring,[58] Fritz Kaufmann, the Canadian Winthrop Bell and the Russian Alexandre Koyré. Later Edith Stein and Roman Ingarden joined this group. This 'old Munich' school saw phenomenology as a realist philosophy of pure description of objects and emphasized the objective rather than the subjective side of description.[59] These students did not follow Husserl in his reductions and transcendental idealism, a position Husserl later characterized as 'empirical phenomenology' as opposed to his own 'transcendental' phenomenology (*Ideen* II, p. 374; Hua 4: 364).

In 1905 Hilbert recommended Husserl for promotion, but the Ministry rejected his application on the grounds that his work lacked scientific merit (*Chronik*, p. 90). Husserl travelled to Berlin to enlist Dilthey's support, and eventually, in 1906, he was elevated to a full professorship. Yet he continued to suffer from self-doubt and depression, as he recorded in his 1906 diary.

# The Transcendental Turn and the Discovery
# of the Reduction

Husserl's change of direction came in his research manuscripts (known as the *Seefelder Blätter*) of the summer of 1905 while on vacation at Seefeld, near Innsbruck, Austria. In this 1905 manuscript he used the term 'phenomenological reduction' (10: 237) for the first time. It was first publicly revealed in lectures given at Göttingen in 1906–7 (Hua 24, as Husserl acknowledges, *Briefwechsel*, 6: 277),[60] subsequently in lectures delivered in 1907 – later published as *Die Idee der Phänomenologie* (*The Idea of Phenomenology*) – on the reduction as a way of moving from the psychological to the truly epistemological domain. He now began to characterize his phenomenology in transcendental terms (see 24: 240) and embarked on a serious rereading of Kant. A whole series of problems emerge together in these notes, problems with which Husserl continued to wrestle for the rest of his life: problems concerning the constitution of temporal experiences in consciousness, the enduring unity of the 'I' across different acts and experiences and the nature of its 'sense-giving' (*Sinngebung*), the problem of the recognition of the other person in empathy, and, perhaps most importantly, the intersubjective constitution of objectivity, a theme that received public expression only in later books such as *FTL* and *Krisis*.

Husserl's researches on time-consciousness made him realize that he had neglected the structural features that unified conscious acts over time, allowing them to be acts that intended the same enduring object. In particular, he realized that the ego had a temporal structure, and that his earlier treatment of it in *LU* had been seriously inadequate. He had originally accepted the Brentanian view that the ego as the source of psychic acts could be bracketed, but he came to realize that the ego played a crucial role not only in generating these acts and stamping its unifying syntheses upon them but also in structuring the meaning-constituting functions of the acts themselves. Scheler, Dilthey and Natorp had all criticized his thin Humean account of the ego in *LU*, and gradually he recognized the need for a concept of a 'pure', or 'transcendental', ego.

For the rest of his life Husserl struggled to articulate the nature of the breakthrough afforded by the phenomenological reduction and what he also called 'eidetic' and 'transcendental' reductions. Husserl felt that the nature of consciousness could only be grasped properly if persistent *naturalistic distortions* could be removed. These distortions are produced not just by our incorrect *theories* about the nature of the world, but also by the very object-positing or 'thetic' structure of consciousness itself. Thus he wanted to 'put out of action', or 'put out of play', the 'natural attitude' (*die natürliche Einstellung*), bracket it, with the aim of purifying consciousness of all intrusion from 'objective actualities' – including 'the actuality of all material nature' and of psychic experiences. The metaphor of 'bracketing' is clearly derived from Husserl's mathematical training. The aim of the initial 'phenomenological' reduction is to individuate correctly the domain of pure consciousness as the domain of meaning-constitution, but he quickly realized that it must also be complemented by an eidetic reduction that moves from fact to essence. Husserl always maintains that bracketing objects does not alter experience for us in any way; nothing is lost, but the domain of subjectivity and knowledge is properly brought into view, purged of the presuppositions imposed on it by the natural attitude. He was soon articulating his new conception of phenomenology with considerable confidence, for example, in his 1910–11 lectures on *Grundprobleme der Phänomenologie* (now in Hua 13) (*Fundamental Problems of Phenomenology*)[61] which recognize the role of the 'living body' (*Leib*) and intersubjectivity, themes that continued in his draft *Ideen* II manuscript.

An indication of Husserl's growing stature was that he was invited by the Southwest neo-Kantian Heinrich Rickert (1863–1936) to contribute an essay to Rickert's new journal *Logos* in 1910–11. This programmatic essay, 'Philosophie als strenge Wissenschaft' ('Philosophy as a Rigorous Science', PSW), offered a sustained critique of naturalism and historicism as leading to relativism. Husserl's critique of *psychologism* was extended to all varieties of *naturalism*, including the naturalistic psychology of Wilhelm Wundt. But he also found a new target in the increasingly influential historical hermeneutics of Wilhelm Dilthey, which he viewed as a historicism leading to relativism, and hence to the collapse of the mission for science. In particular, Husserl singled out Dilthey's 'philosophy of world-views' (*Weltanschauungsphilosophie*) for its denial of the objective validity of cultural formations. The elderly Dilthey was upset by Husserl's attack, and wrote to him denying the charge of relativism. It was not until years later that Husserl made amends, acknowledging Dilthey's contribution to descriptive psychology (*Phän. Psych.*).

In 1913 Husserl, in collaboration with Reinach, Scheler, Geiger and Pfänder, founded his yearbook, *Jahrbuch für Philosophie und phänomenologische Forschung* (*Yearbook for Philosophy and Phenomenological Research*). He had been planning such a journal since 1907 (see his letter to Daubert, 26 August 1907, Hua 25: p. xv), but the plan was revived in 1911.[62] The *Jahrbuch* quickly became a repository of brilliant phenomenological studies, including Husserl's *Ideen* I, which appeared in the first issue, alongside a major work by Scheler, *Formalism in Ethics*, and later, Heidegger's *Sein und Zeit* (*Being and Time*, 1927). The *Jahrbuch* was not meant simply to be an outlet for orthodox Husserlian phenomenology, but to promote the new science in all its range (draft letter to August Messer, 1914; Hua 25: 249). Moreover, it was to be a journal not only of phenomenology but also of 'phenomenologically founded philosophy' (25: 63). In the Foreword to the first volume, he wrote: 'This journal is intended . . . to unite those in shared work who hope for a fundamental reform (*Umgestaltung*) of philosophy by means of the pure and rigorous execution of phenomenological method, on the way towards a securely founded, self-standing, forwardly developing science' (25: 63 my trans.). Its founders have 'the shared conviction that only through a return to the original sources of intuition, and to the eidetic insights to be drawn from it, can the concepts and the problems of the great traditions of philosophy be evaluated, that only on this path can concepts be intuitively clarified and problems framed anew on an intuitive basis and then solved in principle' (ibid.).

## *Ideen* I (1913) and the Programme for Phenomenological Philosophy

In 1913, some twelve years after *LU*, Husserl published *Ideen zu einer reinen Phänomenologie und phänomenologischen Philosophie*, Erstes Buch: *Allgemeine Einführung in die reine Phänomenologie*, written in a single feverish burst over eight weeks in the summer of 1912. *Ideen* I was originally planned to replace the now out-of-print *LU*, but instead Husserl decided to bring out a revised version of *LU* to accompany the new book. This second revision of *LU* was, however, incomplete, as Husserl found revising the Sixth Investigation too daunting a task. Over the next decade, and again in retirement, he worked on revising the Sixth Investigation without ever completing it.

*Ideen* I is extraordinarily ambitious; it is Husserl's first systematic effort to lay the groundwork for phenomenology as a science ranging over topics from the 'general doctrine of phenomenological reductions' (*Ideen* I, p. xxi; Hua 3/1: 5) to the analysis of pure consciousness and even an outline for the phenomenology of reason. It aims to promote phenomenology as an a priori science of essences, as a 'new eidetics'. Husserl wants to replace the misleading term 'a priori' with the term 'eidetic'; the a priori is to be understood as based on what necessarily belongs to the essence of something. A major innovation of *Ideen* I is its analysis of the natural attitude and of normal sciences as carried out in this attitude and in its theoretical complement ('the natural theoretical attitude', *Ideas* I §1). Here Husserl emphasizes the 'worldly' nature of the sciences of the natural attitude and their dogmatic nature, which must now be confronted by a critical turn, activated by an *epoché*, or 'suspension', which puts out of play all worldly positings of consciousness in order to grasp its very essence. *Ideen* I was widely read as idealist, although, strictly speaking, that term does not appear in the book; nevertheless it was included in Gerda Walther's thematic index (*Sachregister*) produced for the second printing.

Immediately after *Ideen* I, Husserl hurriedly scribbled a further draft, or 'pencil manuscript', in three months. Reworked and edited by Edith Stein, it would eventually be posthumously published in 1952 as *Ideen* II and *Ideen* III. At various times, from 1915 until 1928, he revisited this manuscript, but finally abandoned it, in part because he felt he had not worked out the problem of constitution. As Husserl later explained to Schütz, he felt that the problem of intersubjectivity had not been properly addressed.[63] Edith Stein, who herself was interested in the phenomenology of intersubjective empathy and personal embodiment, collaborated closely with Husserl on the drafting and organization of the work, and indeed it has been suggested that the smooth prose of this work is testimony to Stein's activity as editor and co-writer. Stein acted as Husserl's unpaid assistant from 1916 until 1918.[64] Her task was to learn Gabelsberger shorthand in order to transcribe and arrange Husserl's research manuscripts. Besides *Ideen* II, she also laboured on Husserl's time manuscripts (1905–17), and was actually present in Bernau as he was composing some of them. This edition was eventually published in 1928, edited by Martin Heidegger, with only the slightest reference to Stein's labours. Her letters to her friend and fellow student at Freiburg, Roman Ingarden, show that she found this work frustrating, as she was unable to interest Husserl in her revisions of his manuscripts, including the draft revision of the sixth Investigation. According to her letter to Ingarden of 19 February 1918, Husserl was giving her impossible instructions for arranging the manuscripts, and she also felt stifled because she had no time to carry out creative research of her own, so she tendered her resignation. She was not someone who could simply 'obey' Husserl: 'And if Husserl will not accustom himself once more to treat me as a collaborator in the work – as I have always considered my situation to be and he, in theory, did likewise – then we shall have to part company.'[65] In 28 February 1918 she wrote to Ingarden that 'The Master has graciously accepted my resignation. His letter was most friendly – though not without a somewhat reproachful undertone.'[66] She complained to another philosophy student, Fritz Kaufmann, in a letter of 10 March of the same year, that 'putting manuscripts in order, which was all my work consisted of for months, was gradually getting to be unbearable for me'. Her own interest at the time was in the 'analysis of the person',[67] whereas she had come to regard Husserl as someone who had 'sacrificed his humanity to his science'.[68]

Despite its unfinished state, *Ideen* II, a set of studies in 'the phenomenology of constitution', is one of Husserl's most original and successful works. In its unpublished draft form, it had an enormous influence on Stein, on Heidegger (who refers to it in *SZ* §10, 47 n. ii;

489) and, most famously, on the young Merleau-Ponty, who read it in typescript in the newly founded Husserl Archive in Leuven, while researching his *thèse d'état* (second doctoral thesis), published as *Phénoménologie de la perception* in 1945.[69] Perhaps the most influential themes of *Ideen* II are its account of the nature of the body, which can be grasped both as physical object (*Körper*) and animate organism or lived body (*Leib*), and its account of the nature of the 'surrounding world', which is 'not the physicalistic world but the thematic world of my and our intentional life' (*Ideen* II §55, p. 230; Hua 4: 218).

    *Ideen* II begins with a discussion of the 'idea of nature' in general, as the correlate to the *attitude* of the scientific inquirer. In other words, the whole work is conceived as a study of noetic-noematic *constitution*, and from that point of view it assumes the results of *Ideen* I, although it does not explicitly discuss theoretical issues concerning the reduction (which term does not even appear in the Index) or the methodology of phenomenology as a transcendental science of pure consciousness. Rather, the aim of the work is to identify and describe the various levels or 'strata' involved in the constitution of entities in the world as material, animal and human natures, including the realms of personhood and communal and cultural life, which Husserl, following German tradition generally, calls 'spirit' (*Geist*). The spiritual world is the world of cultural products, practices and institutions. It is a world that is explicable not in terms of causation that governs the natural world, but rather in terms of 'motivation', a conception discussed originally by Dilthey but which Husserl (and following him, Stein) had made central to the intentional life of persons (and indeed higher animals). We do not just causally interact with objects in the world; we deliberately turn our attention towards them, they 'motivate' our interest: 'The room's stale air (which I experience as such) stimulates me to open the window' (*Ideen* II §55, p. 229; Hua 4: 218).

    In the first section, developing his account in his *Thing and Space* lectures of 1907, Husserl gives a new and more rigorous phenomenological foundation to the notion of a material extended thing, what Descartes called a *res extensa*, and how it grows out of the constitution of the sense object and the object as consistent substrate of varying and invariant properties. In dealing with the objects of the senses, he is revisiting age-old philosophical debates concerning the proper objects of the senses, primary and secondary qualities, and so on; but he proceeds without reference to these philosophical debates, bracketing them, in order to get back to the fundamental nature of intuited objects. In this respect he carefully distinguishes the 'sense object', the 'phantom' (*Ideen* II §10), and the mere 'sense datum' with all spatial and other factors removed. He gives his favourite example of a tone played on a violin. One can distinguish the sensory object located in space, which can be heard more loudly or more faintly as one moves towards or away from the sound, and the purely 'aural phantom', which still has spatial reference (a certain 'spread'), and then there is the sense datum, the tone as considered the same in all circumstances, which may be thought with even its spatial element removed. Husserl discusses how spatial objects come to be 'grasped'. They are given through what he calls 'kinaesthetic sensations', the sensations connected with bodily movement (turning the head, focusing the eyes, moving the hands, and so on). It is a constant refrain of Husserl's (found also in his analyses of time-consciousness) that the sensory experiences we undergo are not to be identified directly with the sensory properties that we attribute to objects. The objective properties are constituted out of the stream of our subjective experiences, but we must be careful not to rashly conclude either that the object as such is an ideal construction or that the stream of experiences is purely subjective, errors made by both traditional empiricism and idealism.

A draft third volume, *Ideen* III, subtitled 'Phenomenology and the Foundations of the Sciences', finally published in 1952, was to be a general reflection on the nature of philosophy as first science (*Ideen* I, p. xxii; Hua 3/1: 5), a theme to which he would return in his *First Philosophy* lectures in the Twenties. In these draft volumes of *Ideen* Husserl is exploring the manner in which natural and cultural entities are constituted in consciousness. For him, there is a fundamental intuitive division of the world into material things, animate beings and psychological entities. In *Ideen* III he hints at an essentially new science, one never before conceived, never mind realized: namely, 'somatology' (Hua 5: §2) – the science of the perception and experience of animate organisms. This is an a priori science of the manner in which animate body comes to be constituted on material body. Human corporeality is only one realization of this science, as he sees it.

The intensive labour involved in producing the various manuscripts of *Ideen* and re-editing the *LU* left Husserl psychologically drained, and the advent of the First World War dispirited him further. He progressed little in phenomenology of logic or epistemology, and instead concentrated on 'the most general philosophical reflections', focusing mainly on the idea of a phenomenological philosophy as such (see his remarks in the 1920 Foreword to the second edition of the Sixth Logical Investigation, *LU* VI, **II** 177; Hua 19/2: 533) and on ethical matters. Despite the horrors of war, the spirit of resilience and common purpose of the German people impressed Husserl initially. As he wrote in 1915 to the German psychologist Hugo Münsterberg, who had emigrated to the USA:

> Everyone experiences concentrated in himself the life of the whole nation, and this gives to every experience its tremendous momentum. ... We believed at first that we should break down; and yet we have

learned to bear it. A magnificent stream of national will to win floods through every one of us and gives us an undreamt of strength of will in this terrible national loneliness.[70]

His two sons had 'gone out to fight this war in the Fichtean spirit as a truly sacred war'; God was on Germany's side (*Briefwechsel*, 3: 402).[71] Germany had been abandoned, and the world's nations had formed an international league to destroy it (25: 268). Indeed, right to the end of his life, he associated himself proudly with the great accomplishments of German culture, from Copernicus and Kepler to Beethoven, Herder, Schiller, Goethe and Kant (see Fichte Lectures, 25: 267, and *Briefwechsel*, 7: 27). He even saw phenomenology as part of this German contribution to world culture.

As the war went on, Husserl became deeply depressed by the loss of so many of his students, including the gifted Reinach. His sons were mobilized, and his daughter Elli volunteered to work in a field hospital (as Edith Stein also did). On 8 March 1916 his 20-year-old younger son Wolfgang, bearer of the Iron Cross, was killed at Verdun, and his eldest son Gerhart was badly wounded. As late as 1918, according to Malvine (*Briefwechsel*, 9: 348), he was still predicting a German victory. After the war, however, he came to the view that the old idea of a just war was now without ethical force (*Briefwechsel*, 10: 20).

## Lectures on Fichte and the Creation of Universal Humanity

The extent of Husserl's commitment to transcendental idealism, which had been emerging steadily from around 1907, has become clearer with the publication of Husserliana 36, but it is especially evident in his Fichte Lectures (1917/18), a series of three lectures delivered in Freiburg in the last months of the Great War on *Fichtes Menschheitsideal* (*Fichte's Ideal of Humanity*),[72] lectures that earned him the Iron Cross for his assistance to the military effort. German Idealism, 'indigenous to our people' (25: 268), once fully understood but now fallen into neglect and misunderstanding, will return now that this 'one-sided naturalistic mode of thinking and feeling is losing its power' (25: 269). Husserl draws a historical parallel with the situation in Germany after Napoleon's victory at Jena. It was Fichte who was able to find spiritual resources in that defeat. Fichte offers more than theoretical philosophy, as 'the great man of praxis' (25: 271); he provides the true critique of practical reason, putting Kant's philosophy on a secure footing by genuinely uniting theory and practice and ridding it of obscure 'things in themselves'. Husserl briefly sketches how Descartes and Kant overturned naive belief in the world, by showing that the 'world is posited by us in our thought' (25: 272), and that space, time and causality are 'the basic forms of a thinking which belong inseparably to our kind of mind' (ibid.), leading to the Kantian view that 'subjectivity is world-creative, shaping the world from out of the pre-given materials of sensation in accordance with its firm laws' (25: 273).

According to Husserl, 'Kant's results are the points of departure for Fichte' (25: 274). Kant had, unfortunately, maintained that the transcendent things in themselves affect our sensibility even if we cannot know anything about them. Fichte sweeps away this remnant of dogmatism, and, along with it, Kant's assumption that sensibility must be passively stimulated from without before it can be active. For Fichte, human subjectivity is itself not fact (*Tatsache*) but action (*Tathandlung*), action that brings the experience of world into being: 'The Fichtean I . . . is the self-positing action out of which in infinite succession ever new actions originate' (25: 275). Moreover, these actions are teleological or goal-oriented, and thus: 'To write the history of the I, of the absolute intelligence, is therefore to write the history of the necessary teleology in which the world as phenomenal comes to progressive creation, comes to creation in this intelligence' (25: 276). This absolute 'I' splits itself into individual humans. It is a fundamental principle for Fichte, as for Husserl, that every 'I' has its 'You'. Philosophy consists in grasping the world as the product of this self-splitting ego through immersion in the essence of the 'I' and bringing the world to progressive reconstruction (25: 276). Furthermore, Fichte's particular genius was to have identified the moral dimension of this idealism. The ego has a drive towards reason, towards the Ideal of a moral world order (another name for God). Husserl himself, looking to a universal moral community beyond any narrow national self-interest, cites Fichte's hope for a 'total rebirth of humanity' (25: 279). Finally, for Fichte, human self-understanding is the self-revelation of God. Husserl's description of Fichte's idealism is everywhere positive and endorsing: 'How elevating is this philosophy for the noble self-consciousness of the human being and the dignity of his existence when it proves that the entire world-creation is achieved in the absolute intelligence for his sake' (25: 279). Like Husserl himself, Fichte is an optimist seeking a reformation of Germany and humanity in dark times.

## Developing Phenomenology as a System: Freiburg (1916–1928)

In the middle of the war, and shortly after the death of his son, on 1 April 1916, Husserl took up the Chair of Philosophy at Freiburg, a centre of neo-Kantianism through Windelband and Rickert. Husserl's exchanges with Natorp had led him to appreciate neo-Kantianism, and

*Ideen* I had effectively confirmed his philosophy as transcendental idealism.

The War created difficulties for the university as the male students enlisted and student numbers dwindled. Only two of his Göttingen students followed him: Roman Ingarden, a Pole exempt from military service, and Edith Stein. He had to build up a new following, chief among whom would be the young *Privatdozent* Martin Heidegger. On 3 May 1917, he delivered his inaugural lecture, 'Pure Phenomenology: Its Research Domain and Method', (HSW, pp. 9–17; Hua 25: 68–81), which called for reconstruction in science and philosophy: 'Most recently, the need for an utterly original philosophy has re-emerged, the need of a philosophy that . . . seeks by radically clarifying the sense and the motifs of philosophical problems to penetrate to that primal ground on whose basis those problems must find whatever solution is genuinely scientific' (HSW 10; 25: 69). The mission of philosophy is to protect and promote the 'spiritual life of mankind' (*das Geistesleben der Menschheit*). Philosophy, however, is possible only as a rigorous science, and this is achievable only through phenomenology: 'all philosophical disciplines are rooted in pure phenomenology' (HSW 10; 25: 69). Phenomenology, 'the science of every kind of object', recognizes the correlative domain of subjectivity: 'To every object there corresponds an ideally closed system of truths that are true of it and, on the other hand, an ideal system of possible cognitive processes by virtue of which the object and the truths about it would be given to any cognitive subject' (HSW 10–11; 25: 69). In the lecture Husserl speaks of Descartes, who had been poised on the point of discovering the genuinely phenomenological domain.

Husserl quickly gathered a group of students around him in Freiburg. Gerda Walther, who arrived in 1917, recalls in her autobiography that his class grew from only 30–40 students in the War years to 200 after the War.[73] He would have them round to his house for evening-long discussions, where his students would sit on an old sofa that had followed him from Halle.[74] Walther recalls Husserl's love of coffee, extremely hard to get during the War, but which her father could obtain from Denmark. Husserl would proclaim: 'Give me my coffee so that I can make phenomenology out of it' (*Geben sie mir Kaffee, dann mache ich Phänomenologie daraus*; p. 212). According to Walther, he was not exactly a feminist. He proposed starting a phenomenological society at Freiburg (as Rickert had previously done), but sought to exclude women (p. 213). Eventually, it was founded, with women admitted. Walther was prevailed on (by Carl Löwith) to speak. She posed the question: if the pure ego is really empty, how can it intend anything?

Husserl had met Heidegger, who had recently received his *Habilitation*, soon after his own arrival in Freiburg. Husserl requested a copy of Heidegger's thesis and was instrumental in getting it published in 1916 (he is thanked in the dedication). The two kept in contact after Heidegger was called up for military service, and on his return from the War, he became a salaried assistant in the Philosophy Department beginning in January 1919 (*Chronik*, p. 231), and closely collaborated with Husserl (who became Dean in 1919), until a position came up in Marburg in 1923.

Shaken by the War, students were turning towards philosophy of life and existentialism. Husserl's response was to develop a philosophical 'system', as he acknowledged in 1921 (in his revised Sixth Investigation, *LU* VI, **II** 177; Hua 19/2: 533), an all-encompassing phenomenological philosophy, that would answer the cognitive and spiritual need of humanity.[75] He believed in building phenomenology 'from below', as he wrote to Ingarden (Nov. 1921; *Briefwechsel*, 3: 213). Since 1917 he had also been making attempts in his lectures to explore the transcendental constitution of logic from a genetic point of view (he speaks of *Urkonstitution*), in particular focusing on the earliest pre-predicative 'passive syntheses' of conscious experience, recognizing that the flow of experience already presents itself as internally organized. The fruits of these researches were later published as *Formale und transzendentale Logik* (*Formal and Transcendental Logic*) (*FTL*, 1929) and in his last work *Erfahrung und Urteil* (*Experience and Judgment*), edited by Ludwig Landgrebe, largely derived from his logic lectures of the late Teens and Twenties. In these published works he is concerned to analyse how categoriality (the essence of judgement and hence of knowledge) is already anticipated in pre-conceptual experience. He studies the layers by which this comes about; how already in perception there are syntheses of anticipation. He goes much deeper into the kind of sustained perceiving that actually distinguishes characteristics of an object, a sustained observation that is driven by the desire for confirmation. Since 1912 (*Ideen* III) Husserl had been characterizing this new approach as 'genetic', and he broadly distinguishes 'genetic' from constitutive phenomenology.[76]

As part of his intention to establish phenomenology as an international movement, Husserl visited England (the first German philosopher to visit after the War). From 6 to 12 June 1922, he gave a series of four lectures at University College, London, 'in this great place of English science', entitled 'The Phenomenological Method and Phenomenological Philosophy'.[77] These lectures represented an attempt to sketch the outline of a system of transcendental first philosophy, a rigorous science that would have universal impact and play a role in the development of new universal humanity. These lectures laid the basis for his later Paris Lectures (1929),[78] by presenting the 'Cartesian way' of entering into transcendental phenomenology. Phenomenology, as he would say in the first draft of the *Encyclopaedia Britannica* article, must begin with self-experience by performing the 'egological reduction' (*Trans. Psych.*, p. 93; Hua 9: 246) as first preliminary indicated by the Cartesian *ego cogito*. His major focus in the years between 1922 and 1929 was on articulating the stages of this Cartesian way.

In 1923/4 Husserl contributed three articles on the theme of *renewal* (*Erneuerung*) to a Japanese intellectual journal, *The Kaizo* ('Renewal'), to which Rickert, Einstein and Russell, among others, also contributed.[79] His theme was the renewal of philosophy and science through the creation of a universal moral order, and through a surpassing of narrow nationalisms in order to found true community in shared interests. Here, echoing the mood of many Germans, he bemoaned the appalling state of affairs in the Weimar Republic, where 'psychological tortures' and economic humiliation had replaced war. Husserl saw the only hope for overcoming *Realpolitik* and rebuilding the confidence of a people was through a spiritual retrieval of the human sense of purpose, a renewal of the ideals of the European Enlightenment (which culture, in his opinion, Japan had recently joined). Of course, this renewal consisted in philosophy as a rigorous science; but now a science of the human spirit was needed to complement and give moral purpose to the exact sciences. Husserl proposes 'the a priori science of the essence of human spirituality' (*HSW* 329; Hua 27: 9). Human beings are in essence rational animals:

> The human being is called *animal rationale* not merely because he has the capacity of reason and then only occasionally regulates and justifies his life according to the insights of reason, but because the human being proceeds always and everywhere in his entire, active life in this way. (27: 33)

This rationality emerges in practical striving that has given itself the goal of reason, which, in its ideal limit, is also the idea of God (27: 34). 'All specifically personal life is active life and stands as such under the essential norms of reason' (27: 41). Essentially, in these years Husserl was developing his philosophy as a kind of 'higher humanism', a vision he would develop in his last work, *Krisis* (1936).

Husserl delivered an important series of lectures, *Erste Philosophie* (*First Philosophy*), in two parts in 1923/4. Here he gives an extremely rich and sophisticated account of his own philosophy in relation to a 'critical history of ideas', from ancient scepticism to Kant. Husserl is beginning to think of the genesis and historical shaping of the idea of philosophy itself, something that emerged fully in *Krisis*. *EP* II offers a 'theory' of the phenomenological reduction, and rehearses themes that would later appear in the highly condensed form of *CM*. In 1925 he gave an important set of lectures on *Phenomenological Psychology*, in which he returned to his favourite theme of the need to distinguish between phenomenology and psychology, and the need for a phenomenological clarification of basic concepts in psychology. These lectures provide a valuable rethinking of *LU* and a restatement of his own position regarding the descriptive psychologies of Brentano and Dilthey and the empirical psychology of Wundt. In these lectures he also develops the need for an intentional phenomenological psychology parallel to transcendental phenomenology, a theme that occupies his later work generally. Indeed, one of the ways into the transcendental is precisely through a radical rethinking of the results of phenomenological psychology in the light of the 'sense-bestowal' (*Sinngebung*) of the ego (e.g. *Krisis* §59), whereby I realize that my natural outlook is really the reverse side of my transcendental outlook.

## Husserl's Retirement and the Critique of Heidegger

Through the Twenties Husserl had continued to support Heidegger, inviting him on holidays, assisting him in securing a post at Marburg (writing references), securing a publisher for *Sein und Zeit*, even helping him with the page proofs of that book, and promoting him as his successor in the Freiburg Chair that Husserl would vacate in 1928. In a spirit of intellectual co-operation, in 1927 he invited Heidegger to work with him on the 'Phenomenology' article for the 14th edition of the *Encyclopaedia Britannica*. They worked through several drafts together from September 1927 to February 1928, but their views diverged radically, and in the submitted version, Husserl excised much of Heidegger's contribution, especially the latter's introductory paragraph locating phenomenology within fundamental ontology.[80] Similarly, Husserl was initially satisfied with the version of his *Lectures on Internal Time Consciousness* published by Heidegger in 1928, but he quickly came to find fault with the truncated form in which they were presented, for which he blamed Heidegger.

Husserl retired on 31 March 1928, and a *Festschrift* was prepared for his seventieth birthday as a special issue of the *Jahrbuch* (1929). In 1929 Heidegger presented him with copies of *Being and Time* and *Kant and the Problem of Metaphysics*. When he finally found time to read these works, Husserl was shocked by the extent of Heidegger's departure from his own vision of transcendental phenomenology.[81] In a letter to Pfänder in 1931, he admits his 'blindness' in not seeing through Heidegger.[82] He entirely disapproved of the existential starting point of *Being and Time*, which he saw as an anthropology written from within the natural attitude. As a result, he wrote in 1931: 'A philosophy that takes its start from human existence falls back into that naiveté the overcoming of which has, in our opinion, been the whole meaning of modernity' (*Trans. Phen.*, p. 499; Hua 27: 179). Husserl felt the need to go on the offensive to defend his life's work. Now in retirement he embarked on another burst of frenetic writing: 'since September last I live in a fever of work,' he wrote to Georg Misch on 27 June 1929 (*Briefwechsel*, 6: 275). In the space of some months, he wrote *FTL*, published in the *Jahrbuch* (1929), essentially a sustained rethinking of the issues first discussed in *LU*: namely, the objectivity of truth and meaning and the phenomenological structures which constitute it. He travelled to Amsterdam in April 1928 to deliver two public lectures on 'Phenomenology and Psychology', a development of his views as laid out in the recently completed *Encyclopaedia Britannica* article (Hua 9: 302–49; trans. *Trans. Phen.*, pp. 213–53).

The Lithuanian-born but French domiciled philosopher Emmanuel Levinas attended Husserl's and Heidegger's seminars in the summer semester of 1928 and the winter semester of 1928–9, and actually assisted Husserl's wife, Malvine, with French lessons in preparation for their forthcoming trip to Paris and Strasbourg.[83] Over the course of two days, 23 and 25 February 1929, in Paris, Husserl delivered two two-hour lectures entitled 'Introduction to Transcendental Phenomenology' (later published as the Paris Lectures) at the Descartes Amphitheatre of the Sorbonne, invited by the German Institute of the Sorbonne. In attendance were Levinas, Lucien Lévy-Bruhl, Jean Cavaillès, Jean Héring, Alexandre Koyré, Gabriel Marcel and, according to Maurice de Gandillac, Maurice Merleau-Ponty. In 1931, a French translation of these lectures was published, translated by Levinas and Gabrielle Peiffer, assisted by Alexandre Koyré, entitled *Méditations Cartésiennes* (*Cartesian Meditations*). This French edition of *CM* was enormously influential, but Husserl felt that he had run into problems concerning the constitution of intersubjective experience and held back the German edition for further revision.[84] He saw the lectures as merely offering a sketch of the breadth of transcendental life, the domain of transcendental phenomenology; but due to their broad circulation, they have been seen as a canonical expression of his mature transcendental philosophy. Indeed, Husserl himself seems to have held them in high regard, referring to them as his 'great work, his life's work' in a letter to Dorion Cairns (21 March 1930). *CM* offers canonical expression to the Cartesian way into phenomenology, yet in the Fifth Meditation Husserl carries out a detailed exploration of the experience of the other and intersubjectivity, ending with some speculations on the nature of a future metaphysics.[85] Later, his assistant Eugen Fink sought to develop, with Husserl's encouragement, what he would call a *Sixth Cartesian Meditation* which laid down the conditions which made it possible to undertake transcendental inquiry in the first place and proposed Husserl's work as a continuation of Kant's transcendental philosophy, with both a 'transcendental aesthetic' and a 'transcendental doctrine of method'.[86] Fink's interesting speculation develops Husserl in a Heideggerian direction, and although publicly endorsed by Husserl, it represents a significant shift away from Husserl's own work.

In 1931 Husserl gave an invited talk to the Kant Society in Frankfurt on 'Phenomenology and Anthropology', and gave further lectures in Berlin and Halle to huge audiences. In 1934 he was invited to the Eighth International Congress of Philosophy in Prague, to speak on the topic of 'the mission of philosophy in our time'. He sent a letter (*Briefwechsel*, 8: 91–5; also Hua 27: 240–4), the so-called Prague Letter, which was read out at the conference, and an accompanying manuscript on his vision of the nature of philosophy (27: 184–221) that praised the singular breakthrough of Descartes. Here he speaks of philosophy, from its 'primary founding' (*Urstiftung*) in Greece, as the great cultural product of Europe, its gift to the world, the challenge of philosophy being to live a life of self-answerability or responsibility (*Selbstverantwortung*): 'Philosophy is the organ for a new kind of historical existence (*Dasein*) of humankind, that of existing out of a spirit of autonomy' (27: 240). In fact, the more adverse the political situation in Europe became, the more Husserl emphasized that its salvation could only come about through radical philosophical reflection, a theme he would continue in *Krisis*.

## The Rise of National Socialism

In January 1933, Hitler's National Socialist Party came to power in Germany, and, in keeping with that party's promises, on 7 April of the same year, a new law on 'the re-establishment of a permanent civil service' was promulgated prohibiting non-Aryans from holding positions in the state service. Indeed, Heidegger, now Rektor of Freiburg University, counter-signed this official decree of enforced leave of absence that affected emeritus professor Edmund Husserl.[87] Husserl was devastated, having always considered himself a German nationalist, whose sons had served in the German army and whose daughter had worked in a field hospital in the Great War (*Chronik*, p. 428), and he sought to have himself excluded on those grounds. The initial decree against non-Aryans in public service was rescinded on 28 April 1933 (Husserl was exempted because of his sons' military contribution to the Great War), but not before his surviving son Gerhart had lost his position in the Law Faculty at Kiel (a university at the forefront of the Nazification process). One extraordinarily poignant testimony of the distance that had come to separate Husserl and Heidegger is a document now held in the Husserl Archive in Leuven as part of Husserl's papers. Husserl never wasted paper, and would make use of any spare scraps that were lying around. One such page contains a draft of a letter Husserl wrote, seeking to get an appointment for his son. The reverse of this page shows it to be a circular letter, numbered 6210 and dated 26 June 1933, sent by Heidegger as Rektor to all teaching faculty, stating that a short anti-Versailles protest would be made by the university after the 'military sports exercises' (*Wehrsportübungen*) in the exercise arena. All staff were urged to attend. Signed 'Heidegger'.[88]

In April 1935, in a letter to Landgrebe, Husserl expressed the hope that he might not after all be relegated to the 'non-Aryan dung heap' (*Briefwechsel*, 4: 328), but by September of the same year a new law had been promulgated, and Husserl's teaching licence was withdrawn, and, eventually, his German citizenship was revoked. Husserl's letters from this period witness his attempts to get his son a job, writing to many of his former students, including Dorion Cairns and Marvin Farber, on his son's behalf. Even though Husserl carried a German passport and was a German citizen, he was now deemed under Nazi law to be a non-German, and thus he was refused a place on the official delegation of German philosophers to the conferences in Belgrade in 1936 and the Ninth International Philosophy Congress in Paris in 1937. From 1936 his name was dropped from the Freiburg faculty lists (*Chronik*, p. 472), and though his published works were not banned, he was not allowed to publish anything else in Germany. The National Socialists denounced his philosophy for promoting an ideal of universal rationality for all men, since this meant including 'Unmenschen' such as Jews and Negroes. For the Nazis, Husserl represented 'a barren spirit without blood lineage or race' which did not understand 'the attachment to the soil of genuine spirituality' (*Erdverbundenheit echter Geistigkeit*).[89] The Nazi philosopher Ernst Krieck, for instance, wrote an article condemning Husserl.[90]

## The Crisis of the European Sciences

In spite of these official restrictions, Husserl continued his research work, focusing increasingly on the crisis of the sciences and the nature of rationality, and also on issues concerning genetic phenomenology. He lived in increasing isolation, visited only by a few loyal friends, notably Eugen Fink and Ludwig Landgrebe. Life became increasingly difficult for him and his family, but, though he was offered a professorship at the University of Southern California, he did not take it up, partly because he could not secure a place for Fink or for his young American student Dorion Cairns, and partly because, at his advanced age, he could not see himself as a professor in another country; he was German and would live and die there.

Yet, despite these set-backs, Husserl felt he had achieved a new plateau of philosophical clarity. The year 1935 was marked by a remarkable burst of activity. He delivered his famous lecture 'Philosophy in the Crisis of European Humanity' (*Die Philosophie in der Krisis der europäischen Menschheit*), in Vienna on 7 and 10 May 1935 (generally referred to as the Vienna Lecture, and later intended as an introduction to the German edition of *CM*). In November 1935, at the invitation of the Philosophy Circle in Prague, he gave two lectures, entitled 'The Crisis of European Science and Psychology' (*Die Krisis der europäischen Wissenschaft und die Psychologie*), later to be incorporated in the *Crisis of European Sciences*. Landgrebe, Schütz, Felix Kaufmann and Jan Patočka, among others, were in attendance. While these lectures focused on the revolution in modern philosophy and science, Alfred Schütz recalled that, at a separate invited seminar, Husserl talked of the importance of the Greek breakthrough in philosophy and the emergence of the purely theoretical attitude, themes he had been developing since the Twenties.[91] During his Prague visit, on 18 November, Husserl also addressed the Brentano Society, and, at the invitation of Roman Jakobson, the *Cercle linguistique*.

Husserl published the first part of this planned book (§§1–27 of the present edition of *Krisis*) in Belgrade in the yearbook *Philosophia*, founded in 1936 by the exiled German, neo-Kantian philosopher Arthur Liebert.[92] *Krisis* is not a unified book, but rather a set of reflections on different aspects of a huge problematic, which Husserl had been busily sketching through the mid-1930s, and which were originally presented as a series of lectures, but remained an unfinished work-in-progress.

In March 1936 he fell ill. The following year, he was forced for racial reasons to leave his home in Lorettostrasse. He was bedridden from August 1937, and died on 27 April 1938, soon after his seventy-ninth birthday. No one from the Freiburg Philosophy Faculty, except Gerhard Ritter, attended his funeral; Heidegger was in bed, sick with the flu, as he protested later. On 15 August 1938, some months after Husserl's death, a Belgian Franciscan priest, Fr Hermann Van Breda, who had just completed his licentiate in philosophy at the Catholic University of Leuven, arrived in Freiburg with the intention of researching Husserl's unpublished manuscripts. Husserl left some 40,000 manuscript pages written in Gabelbergerschrift shorthand, and another 10,000 pages of typescripts made by his assistants Stein, Landgrebe and Fink. Van Breda met with Husserl's widow, Malvine, and Husserl's assistant, Eugen Fink, and they soon embarked together on a plan to secure the future of the extensive *Nachlass*, which they feared the Nazis planned to destroy. Husserl had spent his last years trying to order his manuscripts with the help of his assistants. After some unsuccessful attempts, Fr Van Breda managed to use the Belgian diplomatic courier service to send the *Nachlass* to Leuven,[93] where they now form part of the Husserl Archive there. Merleau-Ponty was one of the first to use the Archive in April 1939, being particularly interested in the typescript of *Ideen* II.[94] Fr Van Breda also arranged for Husserl's widow to move to safety in Belgium, where she hid in a convent during the Nazi years, eventually travelling to the USA in 1946 to join her two surviving children, who had emigrated there in 1933–4. Husserl's remains were later returned to Germany, and he is buried with his wife in the cemetery of the Franciscan Friary in the village of Günterstal a few kilometres outside Freiburg.

Husserl had asked Landgrebe to compile a book from his manuscripts on transcendental logic, some dating from his work on genetic logic from 1919/20.[95] This eventually appeared as *Erfahrung und Urteil*, printed in Prague in late 1938, but the Nazi annexation of Czechoslovakia closed the press, and the only copies of the work that actually circulated were those that had been sent to London, and thence to the United States. The work shows Husserl's attention to the 'genealogy' of logic, which was emphatically not history of logic, but rather an exploration of the manner in which predicative judgements, which Husserl took to be the central core of all reasoning and logic, come to be formed from 'pre-predicative' lower levels. Husserl claims that traditional logic has focused on self-evident judgements and not examined the manner in which objects come to be given in self-evidence – that is, the manner in which the object is given prior to its being judged explicitly in the judgement. This is what Husserl calls the 'pregiven' object and reflects his growing interest in the area of passive receptivity, or what he called 'passive synthesis'. Landgrebe's edition draws extensively on Husserl's own words and may be regarded as a genuine work of Husserlian philosophy. Since 1950 a large number of Husserl's manuscripts have been published in the Husserliana edition, so that his influence continues in new publications well beyond his death.

# 2

# *Husserl's Conception of Philosophy*

## Philosophy as a Rigorous Science

In this chapter I shall give an overview of Husserl's conception of philosophy. As we saw in chapter 1, his initial schooling in the subject was conventional, but he went on to develop a profound and challenging vision of the task of philosophy, recovering its classical position as the most fundamental science. For Husserl, philosophy stands for 'pure and absolute knowledge'; its vocation is 'to teach us how to carry on the eternal work of humanity' (PSW, pp. 72–3; Hua 25: 4). He accepted the critical turn of modern philosophy since Descartes, and saw the chief question of philosophy as how to comprehend and safeguard the meaning of our scientific achievement. He strongly identified with the project exemplified in Descartes' *Meditations* to set scientific knowledge on a secure foundation and banish scepticism, which he regarded as threatening to lead to irrationalism. Indeed, for Husserl, scepticism was the great enemy, leading ultimately to the very breakdown of the scientific outlook itself. His oft-repeated problematic was: how to arrive at 'solid ground' (*fester Boden*)?

From the beginning Husserl was captivated by Descartes' project of securing science on the basis of evident cognitions, cognitions given 'clearly and distinctly' (*clare et distincte*), the project of founding all deductions in intuitions. Indeed, he often invokes Descartes' twin criteria of truth: namely, 'clarity and distinctness' (19/1: 10) in our concepts. Central to the Cartesian way, then, is the account of evidence. However, for Husserl, neither Descartes nor the modern philosophical tradition had grasped the real meaning of evidence: 'Descartes lacked, as did all modernity, any intentional explication of evidence as the achievement of self-presentation (*Selbstdarstellung*), in which the currently meant comes to original self-givenness'. (34: 409, my trans.).

Evidence has to be construed as correlated with *givenness*. Following the empirical tradition of Aristotle (as revived by Brentano), Berkeley and Hume, Husserl maintains that knowledge begins from experience: 'living is . . . in a certain sense, an experiencing' (*So zu leben ist . . . in gewissem Sinn ein Erleben*, Hua 25: 144). Evidence is experience. He always claims that it is folly to deny the intuitive nature of genuine knowledge. He accepted from Descartes (cf. *Regulae*) that knowledge must ultimately relate back to evident intuitions; and he clearly distinguished between what is genuinely intuited and what is established by inference and deduction. Modern empiricism, however, had a false notion of what is given in experience, and denied the possibility of directly intuiting high-order ideal and categorial objectivities (universals, abstract objects, propositions and so on; *Ideen* I §§19–20). Husserlian phenomenology, by contrast, recognizes the multiplicity of evident forms of givenness. Indeed, he criticizes both Descartes and modern empiricism for their dogmatic restriction in advance (and for theoretical reasons) of the legitimate intuitive forms.

From the outset, Husserl sought to institute philosophy on a strictly scientific basis, adopting Brentano's slogan 'philosophy as rigorous science' (*Philosophie als strenge Wissenschaft*). Brentano had promulgated the theory that philosophy progressed through alternating phases of abundance and different stages of decline,[1] and had diagnosed his own age as a period of decline; hence he advocated a renewal of philosophy as rigorous science. According to his periodization, all great periods of growth in philosophy are characterized by the preponderance of a *purely theoretical interest*. Following Brentano, Husserl too criticized previous philosophy for failing to be scientific, and for having become enmeshed in prejudices, groundless speculation or irrational 'gushing' (*Schwärmerei*).

Reflection on scientific knowledge had originally been the task of philosophy, but philosophy in Husserl's – as in Kant's – day was beset by endless quarrelling, engendering doubt and scepticism. His inquiry into the grounds of science, then, is at the same time an attempt to revitalize philosophy as a science in its own right. Husserl believed that the principles that drove scientific inquiry (including the fundamental principles of logic and mathematics) were not understood, and had not been subject to proper critical scrutiny. Indeed, he had been first drawn to philosophy by the 'crisis of foundation' in contemporary mathematics and logic that threatened to introduce scepticism and relativism into knowledge. In a strong sense, and from very early in his career, he felt that scientific crises were at the heart of wider cultural problems of his age; for crises in the self-conception of the nature of the sciences led to confusion in human self-understanding. For the mature Husserl, the driving idea of philosophy (its 'teleological idea') should be precisely 'a thorough-going, highest and final "self-reflection" (*Selbstbesinnung*), "self-understanding" (*Selbstverständigung*) and "self-justification" (*Selbstverantwortung*) of the achievements of knowledge' (*EP* II; Hua 8: 3).

To become a genuine, autonomous, 'self-responsible' science, philosophy had to free itself from ungrounded assumptions and accept only what can be grasped with rational insight. But instead of being responsible, philosophy had itself become a source of prejudices. The values once attested by philosophy now have little to offer to the positivistic scientific enterprise, which had swept ahead precisely because it was value-free. But science too was in trouble. The sciences of his day had also succumbed to prejudice, specifically to *positivism* (which too narrowly restricted the data of evidence to the date of sensation, 25: 9) and thus lacked 'the philosophical spirit' (*APS*, p. 6; Hua 11: 355). An exclusively positivistic approach distorted science in a disastrous way. As he would put it in *Krisis*: merely fact-minded sciences make merely 'fact-minded people' (*Tatsachenmenschen*; *Krisis* §2, p. 6; Hua 6: 4).

Other dominant nineteenth-century trends, e.g. psychologism (which interpreted ideal laws of formal validity in terms of the psychological laws governing empirical human minds; see *LU, Prol.* §17), naturalism (PSW; Hua 25: 8–9) and biologism (the understanding of psychological laws in terms of evolutionary adaptation, see Hua 2: 3), also threatened genuine science, in that they distorted both the meaning of objectivity and the essential role played by consciousness and subjectivity in the achievement of objective knowledge: 'to follow the model of the natural sciences almost inevitably means to reify consciousness' (PSW, p. 103; Hua 25: 26). This scientific spirit of unquestioning (and naive) acceptance of the world has led to a kind of 'reification' (*Verdinglichung*), a 'philosophical absolutizing of the world' (*philosophische Verabsolutierung der Welt*; *Ideen* I §55, p. 129; Hua 3/1: 107), that was the opposite of a true understanding of the nature of the objective world and its relation to inquiring subjects.

Against this blind trust in science (scientism) and naive realism, philosophy was required to revisit scientific achievement and bring it to self-consciousness regarding its own nature. Philosophy would thus effect a 'complete personal transformation' (*Krisis* §35, p. 137; 6: 140), leading to a kind of transparent rational *self-responsibility* that runs through all our human lives and actions. Philosophers, in this respect, must become the 'functionaries' or 'civil servants' of humankind (*Funktionäre der Menschheit*; 6: 15), defending what Husserl calls 'genuine humanness' (*echtes Menschentum*; *Krisis* §3, p. 6; Hua 6: 3–4).[2]

In his later work, Husserl highlighted philosophy's specific responsibility to address the 'breakdown situation of our time' (*Krisis* §9), including not only the deep spiritual and political *crises* (a recurrent theme in his late work) that had befallen Germany under the National Socialists, but also the wider collapse of critical rationality into calculative thinking. Addressing these problems with an exactness and attention to intuitive evidential clarification had, for him, the character of an ethical demand. As his Polish student Roman Ingarden wrote: 'Husserl could not treat them in any other way, guided as he was by his great sense of responsibility and his ethical approach to his whole philosophical activity.'[3]

Contrary to what many believe, Husserl never gave up the dream of philosophy as a rigorous science. At the end of his life, faced with the fact that German philosophy (i.e. Jaspers, Heidegger, the followers of Nietzsche and Kierkegaard) had turned to existentialism and life philosophy pursued in what he regarded as an unsystematic manner (as a world-view or a form of poetry), he lamented that 'the dream is over' (*der Traum ist ausgeträumt, Krisis*, p. 389; 6: 508), but at the same time maintained that clarification was never more urgently needed, and that scientific philosophizing was ever more important.

## The Greek Breakthrough to Genuine Science

As part of his inquiry into the meaning of scientific knowledge, Husserl wrote a good deal on the emergence of the scientific spirit of the West and the role of philosophy in that first 'breakthrough'. In his lectures on the history of philosophy in the Twenties, as well as in later works such as *Krisis*, he reflected deeply on the emergence of the 'theoretical attitude', the attitude of wondering (Greek: *thaumazein*; Hua 6: 331) that inaugurated philosophy (and made it vigorous, according to Brentano), a new attitude first identified by the ancient Greeks, specifically by 'a few Greek eccentrics' (*ein Paar griechischen Sonderlingen; Krisis*, p. 289; Hua 6: 336) as *theoria*. The theoretical attitude is that of the impartial, distinterested, 'non-participating spectator' (*unbeteiligter Zuschauer*; Hua 6: 331; see also 35: 79), or what he came to refer to in short as the *transcendental attitude*, or simply *theoria*. This true philosophical attitude could only be reached by a certain 'alteration of attitude' (*Einstellungänderung*), breaking out from our normal world-accepting 'natural attitude', which simply takes the world as already existing and goes on to investigate its properties (Hua 2: 18). Moreover, a constant vigilance is required to safeguard against falling back into the old *naïvetés*.

Husserl reflected deeply on the inner meaning of the cumulative history of philosophy. According to his reading of that history, Socrates and Plato stand for the possibility of true knowledge, *epistēmē*, facing down the dogmatic scepticism and relativism of Gorgias and Protagoras (see *EP* I; Hua 7: 8, and *Krisis* §17).[4] Socrates' response to the sceptic paradoxes had been to propose reform of moral life, such that the genuinely human life is to be the life of reason (7: 9), where evidence replaces opinion (*doxa*). No philosopher can renounce this commitment to the goal of reason. The ideal of scientific philosophy received its 'primal institution' (*Urstiftung*) in Plato (*LV*; Hua 35: 313), who systematized the Socratic demand for essential definition in opposition to the destructive *skepsis* of the Greek Sophists, especially Gorgias (*ELE*; Hua 24: 147). For Husserl, Socrates' decisive step was to recognize essences (7: 11) and to conceive of knowledge in terms of justification; Plato subsequently systematically defended knowledge of essences, thereby inaugurating Western scientific culture, which has in recent centuries expanded to become the global culture (Hua 7: 11–16). Furthermore, Husserl embraces the Delphic oracle's injunction to Socrates (as reported in the *Apology*), *gnóthi seauthon* (35: 476), as the motto for the philosophical enterprise itself. Philosophy, the paradigm of grounded knowledge, begins with 'self-experience' (*Selbsterfahrung*) and self-knowledge. It is through self-conscious reflection and clarification that philosophy carries out its task to be a rigorous science.

In general, as in his so-called Vienna Lecture (1935) and *Krisis*, Husserl maintains (in a somewhat Hegelian manner, but undoubtedly without much direct familiarity with Hegelianism, which was in disrepute in German academia at the time, certainly in the Brentanian and neo-Kantian circles in which Husserl moved) that philosophy encapsulates the very essence of European rationality. Somewhat controversially (given the documented technological and scientific achievements of other civilizations), he sees the theoretical attitude as a specific contribution of Greece, rather than Egypt, India or China. Whereas one might speak of Indian or Chinese 'philosophy' in a loose sense, their systems of thought do not break through to the concepts of *idealization* and the *discovery of infinity* that mark out Greek philosophy and make it truly universal. Indeed, the decisive 'breaking into' (*Einbruch*; 6: 331) the theoretical attitude in Greece is to be contrasted with the various 'mytho-practical attitudes' (*mythisch-praktische Einstellungen*) that emerged elsewhere. Greek philosophy gave humanity a 'revolutionary' change of attitude and a reorientation (*Umstellung*) through the promotion of the ideas of *abstraction* and *infinity*:

> But with the appearance of Greek philosophy and its first formulation, through consistent idealization, of the new sense of infinity, there is accomplished in this respect a thoroughgoing transformation (*Umwandlung*) which finally draws all ideas of finitude and with them all spiritual culture and its [concept of] mankind into its sphere. (*Vienna Lecture*, *Krisis*, p. 279; Hua 7: 325, trans. modified)

According to Husserl, this emergence of the idea of infinity through idealization is revolutionary, and cuts off scientific culture from all pre-scientific culture, moving human culture from limited to unlimited goals:

> Scientific culture under the guidance of ideas of infinity means, then, a revolutionization (*Revolutionierung*) of the whole culture, a revolution-ization of the whole manner in which mankind creates culture. It also means a revolutionization of historicity, which is now the history of the cutting-off (*Entwerden*) of finite mankind's development as it becomes mankind with infinite tasks. (Vienna Lecture, *Krisis*, p. 279; Hua 6: 325).

For Husserl, science, and specifically modern post-Galilean science, which has now been universalized as science, is a product of a specif-ically European rationality, first formulated in Greek philosophy. Crises in the sciences, then, have to be traced back to confusions latent in the articulation of this theoretical attitude itself.

The interrogation of the theoretical attitude requires a 'questioning back' (*Rückfrage*), to grasp what Husserl refers to as the original 'primary institutings' that found our knowledge achievements. Knowl-edge consists not in passive acquisition of facts, but in our capacity to revitalize and repeat these institutings: 'In all cases it is based on self-activity, on an inner reproduction . . . of the rational insights gained by creative spirits' (PSW, p. 73; 25: 4). This intellectual revitalization of foundational moments leads to a reflective 'deepening' of sense, and thence to 'responsible critique' (*Krisis* §15, p. 72; Hua 6: 73). The inquirer is looking for the dimensions of 'sense-bestowal', 'sense formation' and 'sense-sedimentation' in the history of philosophy itself (e.g. *Krisis*, p. 372; 6: 381). This includes rethinking the historical evolution of philosophy itself, seeking its essential inner meaning – 'the unitary meaning which is inborn in this history from its origin' (*Krisis* §5).

> What is clearly necessary . . . is that we *reflect back*, in a thorough *histori-cal* and *critical* fashion, in order to provide, *before all decisions*, for a radical self-understanding: we must inquire back into what was originally and always sought in philosophy . . . We shall attempt to strike through the crust of the externalised 'historical facts' of philosophical history, inter-rogating, exhibiting, and testing their inner meaning and hidden teleol-ogy. Gradually . . . possibilities for wholly new, complete reorientations of view will make themselves felt, pointing to new dimensions. (*Krisis* §7, pp. 17–18; Hua 6: 16, trans. modified)

One can see how Heidegger's conception of the 'destruction' (*Destruktion, Abbau*) of the history of philosophy in *Being and Time* (1927) parallels Husserl's radical revitalization of the legacy of the philosophical tradition, on which he was lecturing throughout the Twenties.

# The Philosophical Attitude and Philosophy as 'Correlation Research'

According to Husserl, philosophy begins with what has been 'taken for granted' as 'obvious' (*selbstverständlich*), in order to make it truly understood. As he put it in 1906–7, 'it is the destiny of philosophy that it must find the greatest problems in the greatest trivialities' (Hua 24: 150). The 'obviousness' of the world, its 'acceptance' by us, has to be made explicitly thematic, a phenomenon to be studied, and this requires putting in question the natural attitude correlated with this 'obviousness'. The very manifest appearance of the world – its modes of givenness – has to be explicated in relation to the productive activity of consciousness. As he will claim in his mature works, this very 'obviousness' (*Selbstverständlichkeit*) of the world in its givenness to common sense covers up the mystery of its being constituted by anonymous, functioning subjectivity (*Krisis* §53; also Hua 34: 397). It is necessary to dig beneath the obviousness of the world to uncover this mystery.

Husserl accepted the traditional definition of philosophy as the knowledge of what is, as 'universal science of the world' (*Krisis* §73; 6: 269), but realized that in modern times the focus had to be on what he called 'the *enigma of all enigmas*': namely, 'the essential correlation between reason and what is in general' (*Krisis* §5). Often, as in *IP* (1907) or PSW (1910/11; e.g. 25: 14), Husserl puts the problem in apparently straightforward Kantian terms: how is it that the mind can transcend its own experiences to gain a foothold in objectivity? What accounts for the 'validity' (*Triftigkeit*, 2: 37) of knowledge, for its ability to hit the mark? His answer is to suspend existential questions concerning the factual world transcendent to us in order to examine the *givenness* inherent in the phenomena themselves as they are found present or 'immanent' in our experience, thereby giving a new sense to the notion of immanence, moving away from the Kantian conception. This, of course, involves the *epoché* and reduction (see Hua 2: 44–5). Phenomenology solves (or dissolves) the 'riddle' of knowledge by redefining the relation between 'inner' or 'immanent' subjectivity and 'outer' or 'transcendent' objectivity, such that one attends only to what is transcendent-within-immanence.

Husserl's critique of knowledge is driven by his recognition that the truly human dimension – that is, the dimension of *knowing subjectivity* (*erkennende Subjektivität*) – had been excluded for reasons of method by the positive sciences. The interconnecting web of human cognitive performances – the whole architecture of cognizing subjectivity – depends on the essential *correlation* between a knowing subjectivity and an object known. As he writes in *Krisis*: 'The first breakthrough of this universal a priori of correlation between experienced object and manners of givenness (which occurred during my work on the *Logical Investigations* around 1898) affected me so deeply that my whole subsequent life-work has been dominated by the task of systematically elaborating on this a priori of correlation' (*Krisis* §48, p. 166n.; Hua 6: 169n.). From *LU* onwards, Husserl's mission was to do justice to what he terms the essential 'two-sidedness' of knowledge. As he writes in 1910/11: 'The field of knowledge is infinite in two directions: on the one hand, the totality of objects (*der Inbegriff der Gegenstände*) that we call nature; on the other, the totality of objects that we call consciousness, *cogitatio*, phenomenological given' (Hua 13: 172, my trans.). His concern for both sides of knowledge led him to a critique of any objectivism that denied or excluded subjectivity, on the one hand, and to develop a phenomenology of the essential structures of consciousness, on the other. Instead of positing naive objectivity, phenomenology would always approach objectivity as *correlated* to a corresponding subjectivity: 'Further: if knowledge theory will nevertheless investigate the problems of the relationship between consciousness and being, it can have before its eyes only being as the correlate of consciousness . . . (*nur Sein als correlatum von Bewusstsein*' PSW, p. 89; Hua 25: 15). Phenomenology would become a transcendental *science of subjectivity*, which seeks overall to bring the whole of human rational life to transparency. As he would write in 1925:

> Finally, the possibility of a boundlessly all-inclusive, purely subjective mode of consideration (*Betrachtungsweise*) must be clarified, one which consistently recognizes as subjective *all* producings (*Leistungen*) carried out in subjectivity, including the objectivizing ones – by means of the inseparable unity of producing (*Einheit des Leistens*) with the produced formations – a mode of consideration which thereby includes in ultimately encompassing subjectivity (*in die letztumspannende Subjektivität*) all objectivity precisely as a product to be shaped in subjectivity. (*Phän. Psych.*, §27, p. 115; Hua 9: 150)

This is a project of astonishing scope and range. He is interested not just in individual subjective accomplishments, but social, cultural and collective achievements – the 'entire socio-historical living and producing beyond individual persons' (Hua 9: 130). Moreover, for Husserl, objectivity as such 'resolves into' intersubjectivity (as he puts it in *Krisis* §53).

For Husserl, philosophy gave birth to the very ideal of objectivity that drives the sciences in their pursuit of objective knowledge, but these sciences have lost the essential truth that objectivity is precisely an *achievement* (*Leistung*) of subjectivity, and hence are ignorant of their foundation, and hence uncertain of their final validity. He therefore was seeking that most difficult and basic science, for which he borrowed the Cartesian and Aristotelian term 'first philosophy' (see 24: 95), the science of being as such, the 'science of original sources' (*Urquellenwissenschaft*; Hua 8: 4) that would clarify once and for all how subjectivity comes to objective knowledge not just of the world but also of itself as transcendental subject. First philosophy is 'a philosophy of beginnings instituting itself in the most radical philosophical self-consciousness' (*EP* I; Hua 7: 6), to arrive at the 'universal doctrine of science'. In other words, the most self-aware, most self-critical knowledge of being would in fact be the science of transcendental subjectivity. For Husserl, the study of objectivity led inexorably to subjectivity, and the study of subjectivity itself required a fundamentally new attitude and a transcendental turn. First philosophy can presuppose no other established form of cognition; it must justify its claim to knowledge by a return to what is given, precisely in the manner in which it is given. The nature of this knowing activity has not been understood. Indeed, modern philosophy has misconstrued it naturalistically as a problem for *psychology*. Overcoming this 'psychologization' of subjectivity (a major theme of Husserl's *LU*) is one of the first steps towards a true science of subjectivity. There is, therefore, as he himself believed, a smooth path from Husserl's phenomenology of consciousness to his transcendental idealism.

## Sense-Clarification and Sense-Bestowal

Husserl has a very particular understanding of philosophy as the project of making sense, clarification (*Aufklärung*, *Klarlegung*) or 'illumination' (*Erhellung*), casting critical light on the achievements of cognition (*Erkenntnis*), understood in the broadest sense to include the whole human encounter with the world. Philosophy is clarification of the *sense* of all the forms of givenness, including those that resist objectification and remain in some sense 'other'. The goal of philosophy is 'final' or 'ultimate clarification' (*Letztklärung*) or 'ultimate grounding' (*Letztbegründung*) of the sense of our entire cognitive accomplishment. He frequently speaks of grasping the 'being-sense' (*Seinssinn*). Sense-clarification means grasping how the established sense or meaning of any object is in fact a product of subjective constitutional processes, of 'sense-bestowal' (*Sinngebung*). He believes that the true understanding of any object, situation or region means understanding how sense gets conferred or bestowed on that particular object or region, a sense that can be recovered in a kind of 'reflection' (*Besinnung*). As he writes in *FTL* (1929), this clarification is a matter of moving from vaguely grasped ideas to fully informed concepts: '*Sense-investigation* [*Besinnung*] signifies nothing but the attempt actually to produce the sense "itself" . . . it is the attempt to convert the "intentive sense" [as it was called in the *Logical Investigations*], the sense "vaguely floating before us" in our unclear aiming, into the fulfilled, the clear, sense, and thus to procure for it the evidence of its clear possibility' (*FTL*, p. 9; Hua 17: 13). This sense investigation aims at grasping the 'rootedness' (*Verwurzelung*) of the whole objective world in the transcendental subjectivity (*CM* §59, p. 137; Hua 1: 164). Or, as he puts it in *Krisis*: 'The only true way to explain is to make transcendentally understandable' (§55, p. 189; Hua 6: 193).

The Brentanian doctrine of the intentionality of consciousness allowed Husserl to consider cognition as already object-directed, as already in internal relations to the object of knowledge. He opposed what he called the 'experimental fanatics' (*PSW*, p. 95; Hua 25: 20) who misunderstood it and 'reified consciousness' (25: 26). He protested strongly against the traditional empiricist approach to consciousness:

> Consciousness is not the name for 'psychic complexes,' for 'contents' fused together, for 'bundles' or streams of 'sensations' which, without sense in themselves, also cannot lend any 'sense' to whatever mixture; it is rather through and through 'consciousness,' the source of all reason and unreason, all legitimacy and illegitimacy, all reality and fiction, all value and disvalue, all deed and misdeed. Consciousness is therefore *toto coelo* different from what sensualism alone will see, from what in fact is irrational stuff without sense – but which is, of course, accessible to rationalization. (*Ideen* I §86, pp. 207–8; Hua 3/1: 176)

Consciousness is not a blank slate or a piece of white paper on which signs are written (34: 229). It cannot be treated in a naturalistic way. Indeed, the 'naturalization of consciousness' (*PSW*; 25: 12) is for him one of the greatest errors of contemporary philosophy. Thus, for instance, in a letter dated 20 December 1915 addressed to the leading neo-Kantian Heinrich Rickert, Husserl commented that he found himself in alliance with German Idealism against the common enemy: 'the naturalism of our time'.[5] The seamless whole of consciousness and its constituting achievements needed a new approach, and Husserl found this approach in his radical interpretation of the Brentanian doctrine of intentionality.

## The Basic Character of the Mental: Intentionality

While beginning from Brentano's concept of intentionality, Husserl thinks talk of 'immanent' objectivity is misleading. As he writes with regard to perception (and by extension, his claim holds for all modes of cognition): 'Perception does not consist in staring blankly at some-

thing lodged in consciousness, inserted there by some strange wonder
. . . Rather for every imaginable ego-subject, every objectlike existence
with a specific content of sense is an accomplishment of consciousness.
It is an accomplishment that must be new for every novel object' (*APS*,
p. 57; Hua 11: 19). Husserl insists that all objects of thought – including the objects of fantasy and memory – are *mind-transcendent*; they are
objects with identity conditions. Even when I am imagining something
non-existent – e.g., if I am thinking of the mythical god Jupiter – the
god Jupiter is not *inside* my thought in any sense, it is not a real element
or real part of the experience (*LU* V §11). Rather, even fictional objects
*transcend* our mental experiences. The object *transcends* the act of perceiving it. As Husserl puts it in his 1910/11 lectures: 'Now, it belongs
properly to the essence of the intentional relation (that is, precisely, the
relation between consciousness and object of consciousness), that the
consciousness, i.e. the specific *cogitatio*, is conscious of something that
it itself is not' (*GPP*; Hua 13: 170 my trans.). Intentional experience
always transcends itself towards the object; its character is a 'pointing
beyond itself towards' (*über sich hinausweisen*) something. Every conscious experiencing is 'consciousness *of* something' (*Bewusstsein von
Etwas*; 25: 144), or, in the quasi-Cartesian language Husserl frequently
adopts: 'Each *cogito*, each conscious process, we may also say, "*means*"
*something or other* and bears in itself, in this manner peculiar to the
*meant*, its particular *cogitatum*. Each does this, moreover, in its own
fashion' (*CM* §14, p. 33; Hua 1: 71). For Husserl, the main value of
Brentano's account is that it called attention to the fact that there are
essentially different kinds of psychic relatings, different modes of
intending, depending on whether we are judging, willing, perceiving
and so on (*LU* V §10). Husserl is precisely interested in investigating
these modes of 'intentional relating' (*die intentionale Beziehung*): there
are essentially different species of relating.

After *LU*, Husserl progressively re-conceived intentionality in an
entirely non-naturalistic, non-psychologistic manner. It is not any kind
of *psychological* relation between a mental act and its immanent content;
nor is it a relation between a worldly occurrence and something
non-worldly (a proposition or a meaning). Intentionality refers to the
manner in which objects disclose themselves to awareness as transcending the act of awareness itself. In his 1907 *Idea of Phenomenology*
(Hua 2) lectures, he prefers to talk about grasping the true immanence
of the subjective and, within that immanence, attending to the experience of the transcendent intentional object, now understood somewhat
paradoxically as 'immanent transcendence'. The intended object as
such can be grasped in its sense of transcending the act, without reference to its actual worldly existence or non-existence.

In his late works, he went on to treat intentionality much more
broadly as the general name for the *appearing* or manifestation of

objects and of the whole world to consciousness, their 'self-givenness'. He now speaks of 'phenomenality', as he put it in his late Amsterdam Lectures of 1928:

> Whatever becomes accessible to us through reflection has a noteworthy general character: that of being conscious *of* something, of having something as an object of consciousness, or to be aware of it correlatively – we are speaking here of intentionality. This is the essential character (*der Wesenscharakter*) of mental life in the full sense of the word . . . We can also bring in here the language we use in speaking of appearing (*Erscheinen*) or having something appear. Wherever we speak of appearing (*Erscheinung*) we are led back to subjects who appear; at the same time, however, we are also led back to moments of their mental life in which an appearance takes place as the appearing of something, of that which is appearing in it. . . . Accordingly, phenomenality (*Phänomenalität*), as a characteristic that specifically belongs to appearing and to the thing that appears, would, if understood in this broadened sense of the term, be the fundamental characteristic of the mental (*der Grundcharakter des Psychischen*) (*Trans. Phen.*, pp. 217–18; Hua 9: 307)

The fundamental characteristic of conscious, mental or psychic life is intentionality, the characteristic of having something appear to one, what he here calls 'phenomenality'. In emphasizing the phenomenality of the world, Husserl is putting a much greater stress on the role of consciousness in exhibiting the world as such, in lighting the world up, a theme that will be developed by Heidegger in his account of *Dasein* as the lighting up of Being.

## The Natural and the Mundane

In his mature works, Husserl articulates in some detail the meaning of mundane life in the 'natural attitude' (*die natürliche Einstellung* – a term he uses from at least as early as 1906–7), which involves all aspects of human engagement with others and with the world as a whole, the very experience of 'being-in-the-world' that Heidegger later thematizes explicitly in *Being and Time* (1927). Indeed, the natural attitude has to count as one of his greatest and perhaps most misunderstood phenomenological contributions, first set out in detail in published form in *Ideen* I (1913) §§27–30, and continuing as a major theme into his late analysis of 'worldly life' and the 'life-world' (*Lebenswelt*). His insight is that the ordinary, natural world that surrounds us on all sides, in which we live and move and have our being, is actually itself the *correlate* of a very powerful yet also quite specific and particular attitude: the *natural attitude*. Inherent in the natural attitude is a certain conception of reality, truth and validity. The natural attitude has its own forms of verification, reliability and confirmation.[6] In the natural attitude we experience the world as simply *there*. Inherent in it is what Husserl called the 'general thesis' (*Generalthesis*; *Ideen* I §30), a general belief, *doxa*, acceptance involving the universal positing of the world and everything in it as objectively there, 'on hand' (*vorhanden*). Every society begins within the natural attitude or some version of a primordial attitude rooted in the natural attitude:

> We speak in this connection of the natural primordial attitude (*von der natürlichen, urwüchsigen Einstellung*), of the attitude of original natural life, of the first originally natural form of cultures, whether higher or lower, whether developed uninhibitedly or stagnating. All other attitudes are accordingly related back to this natural attitude as reorientations [of it]. (*Vienna Lecture, Krisis*, p. 281; Hua 6: 326–7)

Other attitudes may arise – if specifically motivated – only *within* or *founded on* this natural attitude. It is crucial to recognize that Husserl's lifelong meditations on the nature of science are illuminated by his recognition that the objectivist, scientific attitude and the formal mathematical attitude are both abstractions from the natural attitude and in a sense presuppose it. Similarly, the psychological attitude (Hua 13: §1, 112) belongs to the overall natural attitude. Husserl always characterizes this attitude as 'naive', since we are normally unaware that what we are living in is precisely given to us as the result of a specific 'attitude' (*Einstellung*). Indeed, even to *recognize* and identify the natural attitude as such is in a sense to have moved beyond it. Husserl's meditations on the *epoché* and the reductions are his attempts to explain how the subject can come to awareness of its own role in the achievement which is our normal consciousness of the world. He also emphasizes that normal questioning, doubting and other attitudes themselves do not abrogate from this 'general thesis': 'No doubt about or rejection of data belonging to the natural world alters in any respect the *general positing which characterizes the natural standpoint*' (*Ideen* I §30, p. 57; 3/1: 53). In this sense, the general thesis is not the result of a specific act, but somehow is always 'on' in the background (*Ideen* I §31). It cannot as such be disrupted, but it can be highlighted, or foregrounded, through a special act of attention that Husserl first describes in print as the 'radical alteration' of the natural attitude.

To reflect systematically on the nature of the natural attitude itself requires a kind of 'bracketing' (which Husserl calls the *epoché*) of our commitments to the factual domain, which leads inevitably to a kind of 'splitting of the ego' (*Ichspaltung*). The meditating self leads a double life. On the one hand, I continue to live naturally; yet, at the same time, I become aware of the functioning of world-creating subjectivity within that natural life: 'First the transcendental *epoché* and reduction releases transcendental subjectivity from its self-concealment (*Selbstverborgenheit*) and raises it up to a new position, that of transcendental self-consciousness' (Hua 34: 399, my trans.).

Husserl is fascinated by the fact that, in the natural attitude into which we are born or into which we wake, we encounter not just individual things and indeed an environing 'world of things' (*Dingwelt*; Hua 13: 27 n. 1), but also living organisms, bodies like ours, which we encounter as *persons* (see *GPP* §4, Hua 13: 115), all within the context of an infinite 'surrounding world' (*Umwelt*). Moreover, we recognize that each of these embodied persons has his or her own sensitivity, sphere of free movement, view on the world, with its correlated aspects or object profiles 'over there', his or her stream of conscious experiences, his or her 'slant' on the world (*Weltaspekt*; Hua 14: 10), 'surroundings' or 'environment' (*Umgebung*), and so on. The surrounding world, for Husserl, is not nature as such, but the world in which we encounter other persons, cultural objects, communal, social forms, and so on: ' "Surrounding world" is a term with personal signification' (*Phän. Psych.* §44, p. 168; Hua 9: 220). This is the surrounding world. Life is always 'worldly life' (*Weltleben*; 34: 394–5). We are 'world-children' (*Weltkinder*). As Husserl put it in 1932: 'Whenever I actively am directed to something worldly, the whole world is mediately and implicitly there in co-validity, each individual is an individual out of a total horizon' (Hua 34: 393, my trans.). The world is always there as my 'thematic ground' (34: 391), and included in it are my 'co-subjects' with whom I interact to form joint projects and realize joint intentions, and whose meanings I constitute through empathy. There is extraordinary depth to Husserl's meditations on the 'I–you relation' and on our relationships with one another and with others in general. Indeed, Husserl has been characterized as the very philosopher of 'otherness'. His problem is to understand the encounter with the other (the transcendent thing, other person, the alien, etc.) and the constitution of the public world.

## Transcendental Idealism and Intersubjectivity

No sketch of Husserl's overall attitude to philosophy can avoid discussing his genuine if problematic (and frustrating for followers such as Edith Stein) commitment to a version of transcendental idealism. For him, the problems of transcendental philosophy are the deepest and most difficult of problems (24: 139). Adopting the Kantian critical position, Husserl understood transcendental idealism to mean that there is no such thing as 'being-in-itself' or 'objectivity as such'; every form of objectivity, the constitution of everything, from the natural world to the world of spirit, culture and history is constituted, is given its 'being and meaning' (*Sein und Sinn*) by a constituting *subjectivity* or subjectivities acting in consort. Furthermore, he always insists that his transcendental idealism is not in any sense solipsism, despite his beginning from the single meditating self, the *solus ipse*. In fact, he regarded 'solipsism' as a transcendental illusion. According to him, the true nature of subjectivity is its belonging within an intersubjective nexus. The objective world is constituted not by the individual subject in isolation, but rather by the essential collaboration of a community of subjects, 'the transcendental we-community' (5: 153). The notion of an 'object' is precisely the notion of something publicly accessible, something there 'for everyone' (*für Jedermann*). One of the greatest puzzles, for Husserl, is how nature and world are constituted by separate yet communicating and co-ordinated other subjects, or what he (following Leibniz) calls 'monads', organized into an 'intermonadic community' (*CM* §56). The nature of transcendental subjectivity, the counterpart of natural psychological subjectivity, means that there are plural transcendental subjects co-operating intersubjectively, yet in another quite mysterious sense, they all belong to the *one* transcendental outlook, since there is a *common* world for everyone. How this is possible is one of Husserl's most difficult problems. Indeed, his late work is all about the experience of the *world*. But he has no doubt about the primacy of the intersubjective: 'The intrinsically first being, the being that precedes and bears every worldly objectivity, is transcendental intersubjectivity: the universe of monads, which effects its communion in various forms' (*CM* §64, p. 156; Hua 1: 182).

A radical aspect of his idealism is that Husserl applies constitution not only to every objectivity, but also to every subjectivity. Alongside the constitution of objects and worldhood, there must also be a 'self-constitution' of the subject. The subject itself has to get its 'sense and validity' (*Sinn und Geltung*), in Husserlian parlance, from transcendental subjectivity, which, he says, functions everywhere anonymously, but which can be made visible through the 'non-participating spectator' stance of transcendental phenomenology. How the subject can be both subject *for* the world and object *in* the world is the deepest puzzle of his transcendental philosophy. There are not two subjects for Husserl – a transcendental subject and an empirical subject – but the transcendental subject has, as it were, two aspects: it is both producing and produced. In chapter 7 I shall attempt to untangle Husserl's complicated account of the ego. Here I will simply note that all philosophy is really a kind of self-explication of the life of the transcendental ego. The breakthrough to transcendental philosophy that occurred (for Husserl) with Descartes is not just the dawning of a new phase of philosophy; it marks the enormously significant moment of the transcendental ego coming to recognize itself and its functioning for the first time. For Husserl, as for Hegel, the history of philosophy is not just the empirical history of a science; it somehow mirrors and exemplifies the process of human self-recognition and self-understanding of transcendental subjects living the life of reason. For this very reason, the possibility of the collapse of philosophy meant for Husserl the collapse of the project of universal, rational humanity, and his later work was dedicated to pointing out the disastrousness of such a possibility. In the end, he is seeking nothing less than a descriptive analysis and clarification and critique of the entire life of *reason*: 'All the reflections (*Besinnungen*) that we ourselves carried out in the search for a genuine philosophy or science were reflections on reason' (Introduction to Philosophy Lectures; Hua 35: 266, my trans.).

# 3

# *The* Philosophy of Arithmetic *(1891)*

## The *Philosophy of Arithmetic* as Proto-Phenomenology

The aim of Husserl's first publication, *Philosophie der Arithmetik: Logische und psychologische Untersuchungen* (*Philosophy of Arithmetic: Psychological and Logical Investigations*),[1] was to clarify the nature of number 'independent of any theory of arithmetic' (Hua 12: 12). It therefore provides an opportunity to understand how Husserl originally envisaged the work of 'clarification' of the 'essence and origination' (*das Wesen und Entstehung*; 12: 15) of concepts by examining their 'psychological constitution'). In subsequent works Husserl maintained his interest in theoretical issues concerning set theory, non-Euclidian geometry, and even Russell's paradox (discussed in a brief essay and in his 1906 exchange with Frege).[2] He remained concerned with the nature and origin of formalization in mathematical thinking, as his late essay on *The Origin of Geometry* attests. In *PA* Husserl first critically reviewed Gottlob Frege's work, leading to correspondence between them. Both were interested in clarifying the nature of number; both agreed that numbers were neither purely physical nor purely mental entities; nor were they to be understood as either properties of things or groups of things. Frege is often credited with saving Husserl from psychologism, but the truth is, as I shall show, somewhat more complicated.

Husserl's strategy is to apply Brentano's method of descriptive psychology to vindicate Weierstrass's concept of number. His basic assumption, following Brentano, is that 'no concept can be thought without a foundation (*Fundierung*) in a concrete intuition' (*PA*, p. 83; 12: 79), a view he would continue to maintain throughout his life-work (e.g. see Hua 24: 46–7). He wants to find the 'origin' (*Ursprung; PA*, p. 67; 12: 64), 'genesis' (*Entstehung; PA*, p. 18; 12: 17) or 'source' (*Quelle*;

*PA*, p. 189; 12: 179) of our basic mathematical *concepts* (*Begriffe*), such as 'multiplicity' (*Vielheit*), 'unity' (*Einheit*), 'collective combination' (*kollektive Verbindung*), 'more' and 'less', and so on (*PA*, p. 67; 12: 64), basic concepts employed in the constitution of specifically mathematical concepts. Unfortunately, Husserl explicates his aims in confused manner, operating within the broadly descriptive *psychological* orientation of Brentano, inquiring specifically about the origin (*Ursprung*) or source (*Quelle*) of 'mathematical presentations' (as he puts it in the Foreword to *LU*),[3] and invoking the testimony of 'inner experience' (*die innere Erfahrung*; Hua 12: 66), e.g. with regard to the manner relations are intuited. The very subtitle 'Logical and Psychological Investigations' testifies to his interest in *both* logic and psychology, disciplines not clearly distinguished by him at the time.

From early in his career, Husserl had been conscious of the 'crisis of foundations' (*Grundlagenkrise*)[4] evident in contemporary mathematics and logic. He further knew, as he put it in a 1901 lecture, that 'obscurity on questions of principle finally one day takes revenge' (*PA*, p. 411; Hua 12: 432).[5] He was aware of the stark contrast between the runaway success of the exact sciences and the confusion of competing theories supposedly underpinning them. As he wrote in *CM*, the positive sciences 'after three centuries of brilliant development' were now hampered by 'obscurities in their foundations, in their fundamental concepts and methods' (*CM* §2, p. 4; 1: 45). The solution he suggests in *PA* is for logicians to insist on 'clear, rigorous, consistently defined concepts' (12: 433). A fundamental *clarification* of the key concepts in the disciplines of scientific knowledge was required to set them on the right theoretical foundation. This continued to be his position, as he wrote in *FTL* (1929): 'The truth is that sciences that have paradoxes, that operate with fundamental concepts not produced by the work of originary clarification (*Ursprungsklärung*) and criticism, are not sciences at all, but, with all their ingenious performances, merely theoretical techniques' (*FTL* §71, p. 181; 17: 189).

This quest for clarification would expand into an entire 'critique of reason, a critique of logical and practical reason, of normative reason in general', as he put it in his *Personal Notes* of 1906 (*EW*, p. 493; 24: 445). Furthermore, it was not just the underlying rationale of the existing sciences that needed to be clarified, but also the very possibility or 'idea' of science. The teleological guiding idea of science had to be clarified from the ground up, not taking any existing science for granted, not even mathematics: 'I must create my concepts anew in autonomous thinking through pure intuition' (*Krisis*, p. 303; 6: 281).

Husserl himself regarded the problems he encountered in writing *PA* as decisive for his subsequent development, and he returned again and again to the problem of the nature of mathematical knowledge, e.g. in his 1906/7 *ELE* lectures. Ten years later, in *LU* (1900/1), Husserl explicitly rejected aspects of *PA* as having psychologistic leanings, but he never entirely repudiated it, and later even reinterpreted it as an exercise in *constitutive phenomenology*, although not grasped as such at the time.[6] Indeed, in *PA*, as I shall make clear, Husserl is already attempting a kind of eidetic phenomenology *avant la lettre*, in that he is not so much interested in the purely psychological underpinnings of our acts of numbering, but rather is seeking to identify the necessary cognitive acts (at the time understood misleadingly as psychological operations, but later more accurately conceived as 'categorial acts') required in order to constitute number concepts. Thus, in his *Personal Notes* of 1906, Husserl, looking back on this 'immature . . . naive and almost childlike' work, wrote:

> I was a novice, without a correct understanding of philosophical prob-
> lems . . . And while laboring over projects concerning the logic of math-
> ematical thought . . . I was tormented by those incredibly strange realms:
> the world of the purely logical and the world of actual consciousness –
> or, as I would say now, that of the phenomenological and also the psy-
> chological. I had no idea how to unite them; and yet they had to
> interrelate and form an intrinsic unity.[7]

These areas of the subjective and the objective had somehow to be intertwined, even if, at that time, he had no idea how to express their correlation. Almost forty years later, in his *FTL* (1929), Husserl, having again acknowledged the immaturity of his first work, claimed that it in fact represented a certain approach to the nature of the formal, and

> presented an initial attempt to go back to the spontaneous activities of
> collecting and counting, in which collections ('sums', 'sets') and cardinal
> numbers are given in the manner characteristic of something that is being
> generated *originaliter*, and thereby to gain clarity (*Klarheit*) respecting the
> proper, the authentic, sense of the concepts fundamental to the theory of
> sets and of cardinal numbers. It was therefore, in my later terminology,
> a phenomenologico-constitutional investigation (*eine phänomenologisch-
> konstitutive Untersuchung*); and at the same time it was the first investi-
> gation that sought to make 'categorial objectivities' of the first level and
> of higher levels (sets and cardinal numbers of a higher ordinal level)
> understandable on the basis of the 'constituting' intentional activities.
> (*FTL* §27a, pp. 86–7; 17: 90–1)

The descriptive psychology of *PA* includes emphasis on gaining insight from the experienced phenomena themselves (*PA*, p. 23; 12: 22), a recognition of the complex structure of the temporal flow of psychic experiences (e.g. the distinction between a presentation of a temporal series and a temporal presentation of a series, *PA*, p. 28; 12: 27), and even a quite differentiated account of what is involved in sense perception (drawing on Stumpf's part/whole analysis of sensory consciousness).

For instance, Husserl claims that a representation of a multiplicity involves the recognition that the elements of the multiple are distinct from one another, but that the notion of their difference is not itself fore-grounded in this representation; that is, the differences themselves do not have to be noticed, and so on.

Furthermore, with regard to his later phenomenological break-through in *LU*, Husserl in *PA* already recognizes the importance of the mental act of synthesis which he calls 'collective combination', which plays an important role in many different kinds of mental process, including our emotional experiences (*PA*, p. 78; 12: 75), and is crucial to the understanding of relation in general. He will even acknowledge (a step towards his insights in the Sixth Investigation) that the concepts of multiplicity, entity, unity and so on are actually *categorial* concepts (*PA*, p. 89; 12: 84). Of course, at that time, he had not yet worked out the nature of categorial acts, which emerged only in the late 1890s and which received its first major elaboration in the Sixth Logical Investi-gation. In another hint at what is to come in his own career, already in this early work Husserl refers to the 'psychological constitution' (*Konstitution*; *PA*, p. 14; 12: 13) of basic concepts. Constitution, of course, is a common neo-Kantian term, and the notion of psychological con-stitution is unclear; nevertheless, it does point forward to Husserl's later constitutional analysis. Of more significance, too, is his speaking of acts of collective combination as 'formal' or 'categorial' acts, ulti-mately involved in all mental operations:

> Collective combination plays a highly significant role in our mental life as a whole. Every complex phenomenon which presupposes parts that are separately and specifically noticed, every higher mental and emo-tional activity, requires, in order to be able to arise at all, collective com-binations of partial phenomena. (*PA*, p. 78; 12: 75).

Without collective combination we could never grasp a complex phe-nomenon *as* a complex unity made up of parts. Already in 1913 in his Draft Preface to the second edition of *LU* Husserl reinterprets *PA* in terms of the discovery of categorial intuition:

> Here [in *PA*] for the first time I hit upon the basic form of the syntheti-cally multi-rayed consciousness (*Grundform des synthetisch-vielstrahligen Bewusstseins*) which takes its place among the basic forms of 'categorial' consciousness in the sense of the *Logical Investigations*. And with the ques-tion about the relationship of the collective forms in contrast to these unitary forms, I hit upon the distinction between sensuous and categor-ial unity. (EV, p. 34; Fink 126; 20/1: 294–5; trans. modified)

In *PA* Husserl is already recognizing this special kind of *synthesis* as a vital aspect of intentional consciousness. He is, of course, aware of

Kant's 'extremely momentous' (he is quoting F. A. Lange) account of synthesis, and notes already a certain ambiguity in the term, since it can stand both for the mental activity of gathering and also for the resulting entities that are gathered into a unity (*PA*, p. 39; 12: 38). Husserl accurately reports Kant's view that combination requires acts of synthesis, so understanding the concept requires reflection on these acts.[8] So, besides an account of number, there is also an important philosophical dimension to *PA*: namely, the clarification of central concepts basic to all cognition, concepts such as unity and multiplicity (*PA*, p. 14; 12: 13).

Husserl drew on classic discussions of number in Hume, Mill and contemporary logicians such as Jevons, Lange and Ernst Schröder (1841–1902). He explicitly rejects Mill's concept of numbers as somehow expressing physical facts (*PA*, p. 18; 12: 17). He also rejected nominalist accounts of numbers, found in Berkeley, Helmholtz and even his own teacher Kronecker, according to which numbers are simply ways of grasping real things in particular sequences (see *PA*, pp. 179–81; 12: 170–2). For Husserl, already in *PA*, numbers are genuine ideal objects, even if they originate in a special kind of *reflection* on complexes encountered in experience. What fascinates him is the manner in which the acts that collect items together into a whole are, in the case of number, entirely oblivious to the kind of entity or item being included in that whole. In other words, the specific reflection that gives rise to number is *content-neutral*, and not related to the physical or other properties of the entities in question.

In the second edition of *Prolegomena,* discussing his approach of tracing concepts to their origins in intuition, Husserl substitutes the term 'phenomenological' for 'logical' origins, because he explicitly recognizes that his talk of the 'origin' of concepts has been misleading in so far as it stressed psychological origin, whereas, in fact, he is concerned with 'insight into essence (*Einsicht in das Wesen*) of the concepts involved' (*LU, Prol.* §67, I 153–4; Hua 18: 246). Insight into essence is something which Husserl had already been committed to in *PA*, but in 1900 he had become clearer that by 'origin' of a concept he meant what essentially belongs to it and nothing psychological. He explains: 'We can achieve such an end only by *intuitive representation* (*Vergegenwärtigung*) of the essence in adequate Ideation, or, in the case of complicated concepts, through knowledge of the essentiality of the elementary concepts present in them, and of the concepts of their forms of combination' (*LU, Prol.* §67, I 154; Hua 18: 246). It is clear that even in *PA* Husserl was really seeking a kind of conceptual clarification involving the analysis of concepts into their component parts and showing the necessary relations between parts and the whole, and he was also seeking to justify his assertions by appeal to *intuitive evidence*. Furthermore, he already recognized the need for his account of concept formation and justification to include the *subjective* – first called 'psychological', later 'phenomenological' – components, the so-called acts involved in the combining of parts, for instance. In *PA* this is the 'psychological' approach he defends *against* Frege. In *LU*, he would re-conceive it as *phenomenology*.

## The Nature of Arithmetic and of Mathematics in General

As we saw in chapter 1, Husserl's first mentor, the mathematician Carl Weierstrass, had inspired Husserl to attempt to clarify the nature of arithmetic (*Chronik*, pp. 6–11). Husserl admired his former Berlin professor for the scientific rigour he displayed in attempting to set mathematics on a purely rational basis, avoiding the dependence on arbitrary intuitions which plagued most nineteenth-century accounts. As Husserl records in *LU*, he was perplexed that mathematicians could achieve valid results while apparently employing different intuitions and theoretical accounts of how they arrived at these results. There appeared to be a yawning gulf between their actual mathematical methods and practice and the theoretical expression they assumed:

> The same thinkers who sustain marvellous mathematical methods with such incomparable mastery, and who add new methods to them, often show themselves incapable of accounting satisfactorily for their logical validity and for the limits of their right use. Though the sciences have grown great despite these defects, and have helped us to a formerly undreamt of mastery over nature they cannot satisfy us theoretically. They are, as theories, not crystal-clear: the function of all their concepts and propositions is not fully intelligible, not all of their presuppositions have been exactly analysed, they are not in their entirety raised above all theoretical doubt. (*LU, Prol.* §4 I 15–16; Hua 18: 26)

Weierstrass himself had provided an arithmetical basis for functional analysis (a programme on which Dedekind, Kronecker and Cantor were also working), in the course of which he focused on the concept of the positive whole number as a foundational concept. Kronecker and Helmholtz began from the concept of ordinal number; still others began from the axiomatic construction of arithmetic and assumed a purely formal concept of number (*ELE*; Hua 24: 160). These variations in approach were unproblematic for practising mathematicians – brilliantly skilled artists or 'technologists' in their own domain (*ELE*; Hua 24: 162). Such lack of clarity, however, could not satisfy the completed overall science within which mathematics was located, and wherein it found its meaning. The mathematician is not, and has no need to be, a pure theorist, for Husserl. For the philosopher it is otherwise (*ELE*; Hua 24: 163).

Husserl therefore sought to provide a foundation for arithmetic by clarifying 'the logical and psychological nature' of its basic concepts. Initially, following Weierstrass, Husserl began from the positive whole numbers or cardinal numbers (1, 2, 3, etc.), as the foundation for all other number concepts, including the irrational, imaginary, real numbers, and so on. However, almost as soon as *PA* was written, Husserl departed from that assumption as too limiting, as it could not deal with more complex aspects of mathematics, especially the so-called *imaginary numbers*, which Husserl construes in a broad manner to include negative and irrational numbers (e.g. −1) (see *PA*, p. 412; 12: 432–3). His problem was: how can valid mathematical calculations be performed that admit into their sequence counter-sensical or absurd formations (12: 433; see also *FTL* §31)? Logic as the science of science aims to eliminate contradictions; so how can mathematics utilize them in valid operations? How can this be tolerated? He came to realize that imaginary numbers cannot be explicated from the natural numbers, as he had tried to argue in *PA*. Indeed, one of his reasons for writing to Frege in 1891 was his admiration for the latter's technique for handling imaginary numbers. Ten years later, in 1901, in his address to the renowned Göttingen Mathematical Society, he again stressed the difficulties that imaginary numbers and the 'transition through the imaginary' were causing for number theory in general (see *PA*, p. 412; 12: 432–3).

Between *PA* and *LU*, Husserl developed a more sophisticated and original account of mathematics generally. In the 1901 Göttingen lecture (as in his Foreword to *LU*), he presents mathematics as having totally surpassed its original domain of number and quantity, and now being the 'theory of theories', the 'science of theoretical systems in general', and indeed as belonging within his more general 'science of manifolds' (*Mannigfältigkeitslehre*). While admiring the formalists (Hilbert) for their sophisticated techniques, in fact, he rejected formalism as a *theory* of mathematics. Mathematics is not just about the rules of a game such as chess, where the physical entities – the pieces – do not matter at all, but only their function according to rules ('games-meaning'; *LU* I §20). Rather, mathematical objects have meaning independently of the rules ('original meaning'; *LU* §20). His overall view, maintained in subsequent years, is that mathematics is one part of a universal a priori theory of objects, or *formal ontology*, the 'eidetic science of any object whatever' (*Ideen* I §10; Hua 3/1: 22).[9] Set theory and the theory of cardinal numbers belong to a more general study of the categorial forms of anything whatever, apart from all content or matter (he acknowledged that Natorp independently held a similar view).

## Genuine and Non-Genuine Numbers

According to Husserl in *PA*, arithmetic depends on two fundamental notions: cardinal number (*Anzahl*) and calculus (a formal procedure for making inferences and drawing conclusions), and the book is divided into two parts along these lines. Husserl poses his basic question in a somewhat ambiguous manner: how can one have 'presentations' (*Vorstellungen*) of number? In his descriptive psychology, Brentano had distinguished between what he termed 'genuine' or 'authentic' (*eigentlich*) presentations, where the object is directly given, and non-genuine, 'inauthentic' or 'symbolic' (*uneigentlich, symbolisch*; 12: 193 n. 1) presentations, where the object is referred to in some kind of indirect or symbolic manner. Husserl applies this distinction in *PA* (and indeed in his subsequent work). His problem is how one can move beyond what is given in full presence in intuition to have genuine knowledge of what is not given in full intuition. Authentic or genuine presentations present the object as it appears directly in the intuition (e.g. the house I actually see before me), 'in the flesh', in Husserl's terminology, whereas I have a merely *symbolic* or *inauthentic* intuition of a house described to me as the house on the corner of such and such a street (Hua 12: 193).[10] When I think of the number '5', I can grasp that object in itself directly in an intuition (though the multiplicity I grasp may be real or imagined). Thus, the first part of *PA* is entitled 'The Genuine Concepts of Unity, Plurality, and Number', referring to those smaller numbers that can be grasped immediately on the basis of a sensory presentation of distinct concrete multiplicities (numbers smaller than a dozen). Indeed, in his 1887 dissertation defence Husserl lists among the theses he was willing to defend: 'One can hardly count beyond three in the authentic sense' (*PA*, p. 357; Hua 12: 339). Part 2 deals with the *symbolic* or *inauthentic* intuitions of higher numbers (which include, Husserl believes at this point, more complex numbers, including negative and imaginary numbers; Hua 12: 7) and the operations (addition, subtraction, etc.) performed on them in arithmetic. While we have direct intuitions of the lower numbers, the concepts of higher numbers (normally, numbers above 12 according to Husserl; Hua 12: 192), are based on indirect or symbolic presentations; e.g. I cannot grasp 1,000 or '33 × 26' except in some symbolized form. For these higher numbers, the object itself is not presented directly, but instead is grasped *symbolically* or 'signitively' (Fifth Logical Investigation). Similarly, in thinking of algebraic formulae and so on, we are relating first to a sign and then *through* the sign to the thing signified. Indeed, it is for Husserl, as for Frege, a central feature of knowledge that humans have to transcend the infinite multiplicity of what is immediately given, so that, through symbolization, they can manipulate things not immediately given to intuition. Frege had written in his *Begriffschrift* that the human 'course of ideas' would be limited, as animals are, to reacting to their impressions, were it not that we had the ability to use symbols to 'make present that which is absent, invisible, perhaps even insensible'.[11] Frege says that the discovery of symbols has the same impact on thought that discovering how to harness the wind to sail against the wind had on navigation. Symbols point to concepts.

Similarly, Husserl's important 1894 article, 'Psychological Studies in the Elements of Logic', expresses puzzlement that our thoughts are able to move through the most flimsy of presentations (sounds, letters, signs) to grasp the objects signified or meant. Indeed, for Husserl, this is the central problem of knowledge: 'Scientific knowledge . . . is totally based on the possibility of our being able to abandon ourselves completely to thought that is merely symbolic or is otherwise most removed from intuition' (*EW*, p. 167; 22: 121).[12] Husserl thinks that humans differ from animals (who share with us in some fashion perception, imagination, memory and so on) in their capacity for reason and for science, which operate with symbols. If all intuitions of numbers were genuine, he writes in *PA*, there would be no need for arithmetic, which consists almost entirely of symbolic operations. But we are finite beings with a limited range of genuine intuitions: 'Indeed the whole of arithmetic is . . . nothing other than a sum of artificial devices for overcoming the essential imperfections of our intellect' (*PA*, p. 202; 12: 192).

At the outset of *PA* Husserl articulated the traditional view that these most basic arithmetical concepts cannot be defined as such,[13] since they are required in the definitions of all the more complex concepts (12: 21; 12: 119). One can only point to the 'concrete phenomena' (12: 15) from which these concepts are abstracted. To understand the fundamental concepts required for number, then, one must identify and describe the concrete experiences in which the basic phenomena or 'presentations' are intuited, from which the number concepts are abstracted. This means attending to the *psychological* acts which give rise to them, thereby giving a 'psychological characterisation of the phenomena upon which the abstraction of concepts rests' (12: 21).

It is important to emphasize here that, although Husserl thought that mathematical concepts could best be explained in terms of a study of the psychological acts whereby we grasp them, he is explicitly *not* saying that numbers themselves are purely and simply products of the mind. In *PA* it is clear that Husserl thought of numbers themselves as ideal entities, independent of the mind, and in this sense he never took a psychologistic stance concerning either mathematics or logic.[14] Of course, in *LU* and after (e.g. *ELE*, 1906/7) he emphasizes more clearly that numbers are ideal: 'Numbers are not objects in nature

(*Naturobjekte*). The number series is a world of genuine objectivities – *ideal* not *real* objectivities. The number 2 is no thing (*Ding*), no natural process, it is not located in space or time. It is certainly not an object of possible perception or of possible "experience"', (ELE; Hua 24: 48, my trans.). Husserl's rather crude account of concept formation in *PA* depends heavily on traditional empiricist accounts, found in Berkeley and Locke, of abstraction as a kind of selective attention, an account that Husserl would himself criticize in his Second Logical Investigation.[15]

The problem is that Husserl expresses himself rather ambiguously: e.g. he refers to mathematical 'presentations' (*Vorstellungen*) in the Foreword to the *LU Prolegomena* (Hua 18: 6), when, in fact, he is trying to 'clarify' the *concept* of number and other key concepts of arithmetic. Already in *PA* he had explicitly distinguished between numbers as self-identical objects and 'presentations' or 'concepts' of numbers (the manner in which numbers are cognitively or epistemically grasped), though he does not go further and expressly articulate the *ideality* of numbers or the kind of objectivity of arithmetical judgement. In *PA* he simply *assumes* this ideality and objectivity, though at times his mode of expression is not entirely clear on this point, something he would later regret (Frege will justly criticize Husserl on this point, as we shall see). The problem, more precisely, is that he labels whatever appears in our experience indifferently as a 'presentation' or a 'concept', but the *objectivity* of these presentations is confirmed in their repeatability and identity, in that they can be accessed over and over in different acts, and grasped as the same in different modes of presentation. The same triangle can be understood as equilateral or as equiangular. The problem (as Frege perceptively identified) is his terminological conflation of psychological and logical concepts, but it is not clear, *pace* Frege, that he actually confused the two in his thinking.

## The Intuition of Groups or Multiplicities

In the case of the concept of number, the originally given 'concrete' phenomena are the presentations of 'totalities' (*Inbegriffe*; 12: 15) or 'multiplicities' (*Vielheiten*; 12: 15) or 'wholes' (*Ganze*; 12: 18) – Husserl's terminology is fluid, and indeed his characterization is imprecise – of objects one meets with in the world. He explicitly asserts (12: 14, 95, 139, 147n.) that he will employ the terms 'plurality' (*Mehrheit*), 'totality' (*Inbegriff*), 'aggregate' (*Aggregat*), 'collection' (*Sammlung*) and 'set' (*Menge*) indiscriminately, another point on which he was criticized by Frege, as we shall see. Husserl begins from these undeniable, empirical experiences of *concreta* (12: 16), concrete wholes or totalities. These include not just sense-perceptible objects, but also objects grasped solely in thought or imagination, abstract objects:

For the formation of concrete totalities (*Inbegriffe*) there actually are no restrictions at all with respect to the particular contents to be embraced. Any imaginable object, whether physical or psychical, abstract or concrete, whether given through sensation or phantasy, can be united with any and arbitrarily many others to form a totality, and accordingly can also be counted. For example, certain trees, the Sun, the Moon, Earth and Mars; or a feeling, an angel, the Moon, and Italy, etc. In these examples we can always speak of a totality, a multiplicity, and of a determinate number. The nature of the particular contents therefore makes no difference at all. (*PA*, p. 17; Hua 12: 16)

Husserl emphasizes that he is not restricting the domain to physical contents, unlike some number theorists (e.g. Mill). It is a particular puzzle to Husserl as to how one can see a group of objects as a number (*Zahl*) of things without necessarily being able to put a specific, definite number (*Anzahl*) on it: I see that there is a group of students in the lecture room without necessarily seeing immediately that there are, say, fifteen students. Husserl gives the example of seeing stars: how can I apprehend a group that is potentially infinite? Following his thesis director, Carl Stumpf, Husserl holds that the ability to sensuously intuit concrete multiplicities is fundamental and irreducible (12: 20), and in regard to seeing large groups he draws on certain characteristic features of the elements suggesting that they belong to the same group (cf. his discussion of 'figural moments'). In these cases, we can have a sensuous intuition of a multiplicity without having consciously colligated its elements (see *LU* VI §51; Hua 19/2: 690n.).

Besides intuiting collections of disparate objects arbitrarily collected together, I am also able to intuit groups where the members are 'fused' together in a special way through some kind of internal connection: e.g. a *row* of soldiers, a *pile* of apples, a *colonnade* of trees, a *flock* of sheep, a *swarm* of bees, a *series* of tones, a melody, a *herd* of cows and so on. I have a direct, sensuous 'intuitive presentation' (*anschauliche Vorstellung*) of these multiplicities and intuit them as bound together in a certain way, as 'fused unities', in what Husserl, independently of the founder of Gestalt psychology, Christian von Ehrenfels, calls 'figural moments' (*figurale Momente*; Hua 12: 203; see also *LU* VI §51; Hua 19/2: 690n.). These groups are grasped through a certain sensuously given 'form' or 'structure' (*Gestalt*), which acts as a sign of the whole group, guaranteeing the possibility of being in principle able to enumerate the items of the group, though in fact we cannot do so (12: 213). These 'forms' are central to Gestalt psychology, and indeed, Frege acknowledged Husserl's positive contributions in this regard.[16] In general, when we intuit a whole, we intuit not just the individual elements in some arbitrary manner, but also the relationship between them. For example, a line is grasped in a relation of continuity. A totality unites objects (its parts) according to some specific relation: 'We can likewise say that a totality forms a whole. The representation of a totality of given objects is a *unity* in which the representations of single objects are contained as partial representations (*Teilvorstellungen*)' (*PA*, p. 21; 12: 20).

Husserl will claim that the concept of multiplicity is itself arrived at by abstracting from our intuition of concrete 'groups' (*Mengen*) or 'totalities of determinate objects' (*Inbegriffe bestimmter Objekte*; Hua 12: 15). In grasping a concrete totality, I grasp more than the individual elements of the set, I also grasp the *relation* connecting them:

> It is misleading to say that the totalities consist merely of the particular contents (*Einzelinhalten*). However easy it is to overlook it, there still is present in them something more than the particular contents: a 'something more' which can be noticed, and which is necessarily present in all cases where we speak of a totality or a multiplicity. This is the *combination* (*Verbindung*) of the particular elements into the whole. (*PA*, p. 19; 12: 18)

*Collective combination* (*kollektive Verbindung*) is 'that sort of combination which is characteristic of the totality' (*PA*, p. 21; 12: 20). It is a special psychic act of a higher order, not part of straightforward everyday experience. It is one thing to see a group of students either together or singly; it is quite a special act to count them, to isolate them as a specific group of unities, and then to enumerate the members of this set. For the purposes of enumeration, the actual nature of the items contained in the multiplicity is of no importance:

> It was clear to begin with that the specific nature of the particular objects which are gathered in the form of a multiplicity could contribute nothing to the content of the respective general concept. The only thing that could come into consideration in the formation of these concepts was the *combination* of the objects in the unitary representation of their totality. It was then a question of a more precise characterization of this mode of combination. (*PA*, p. 67; 12: 64)

What matters is the nature of the *synthesis* binding the units into a totality, and, Husserl felt, the nature of this synthesis had been misunderstood by previous philosophers of mathematics, who all sought to determine it on the basis of some aspect of the content. His insight is that number formation precisely has nothing to do with *content relations*.

The intuition of concrete multiplicities, or groups of items, is not yet the intuition of determinate number. Number requires an explicit act of *counting* or colligating. As Husserl says in his 1906/7 lectures, someone who has never counted has no concept of number: 'A number is given only in the act of counting. Whoever has never counted, does not know what a number is, just as whoever has never sensed red, has no genuine presentation of what it is to be red' (*ELE*; 24: 46, my trans.). But, he emphasizes, the fact that numbers emerge *through* counting does not mean that numbers must be reduced to component parts of the *psychological* process of counting. The ideal, identical objects of mathematics arise in psychological acts, but the objects known are *not* psychological, and they preserve their identities across psychological acts understood as temporal occurrences.

## The Intuition of an 'Item'

How does the most basic act of mentally grasping something arise? Here Husserl adopts Brentano's conception of the intentionality of psychic acts, and specifically his general law that all psychical acts are either presentations or based on presentations.[17] All other kinds of mental act – willing, judging, desiring, etc. – depend in part on initially having presentations or ideas – that is, possessing some kind of content about which to judge or desire, and so on. Reflecting on the nature of this content or object that is present in every presentation or 'act of pre-senting' (*Akt des Vorstellens*; 12: 80), the concept of a 'something' emerges. This 'something' (*etwas*) is, as it were, the content of a pre-sentation in general formally considered merely as an 'object':

> Obviously the concept *something* owes its origination (*Entstehung*) to reflexion upon the psychical act of representing (*Akt des Vorstellens*), for which precisely any determinate object may be given as the content. Hence, the 'something' belongs to the content of any concrete object only in that external and non-literal fashion common to any sort of relative or negative attribute. In fact, it itself must be designated as a relative determination. Of course, the concept *something* can never be thought unless some sort of content is present, on the basis of which the reflexion mentioned is carried out. Yet for this purpose any content is as well suited as another: even the mere name 'something.' (*PA*, p. 84; 12: 80)

Reflection on the structure of the intentional act provides our concept of 'something', and reflection on this concept generates the concept of a 'unity' or 'unit', itself a necessary part or meaning-component of the concept of 'multiplicity' (*Vielheit*). The concept of a multiplicity, or, to use specifically mathematical language, the concept of a set (*Menge*), then, requires or involves the more basic concept of a 'unit' or a 'some-thing in general' (*Etwas überhaupt*). Any item can count as an element in a set. In order to be able to entertain a concept of a determinate multiplicity, I need the more basic concept of a 'something' (*ein Etwas*; 12: 80) – what Michael Dummett calls a 'featureless unit'[18] – that abstracts from every attribute of the entity to be considered, except that it is a 'something or other'. Moreover, Husserl is emphatic that the notion of a 'something' should not be understood as meaning something in nature, a *res* or thing (*Ding*). In his 1910/11 *GPP* lectures (Hua 13) he emphasizes the 'existential neutrality' (*Daseinsfreiheit*) of arithmetic, against those who would give an empirical sense to arithmetical propositions: 'The one (*die Eins*) of arithmetic is something in general and what falls under it is not only the thingly, the spatio-temporal, but precisely something in general, which may also be an idea, or even, for example a number' (Hua 13: 128, my trans.).

Now, in order to see concrete groups or multiplicities *as* multiplicities, as *collections* of objects rather than just disparate objects, I need more than the notion of an individual; I have to be able to enumerate the individuals in the group, at least potentially. According to Husserl, here extrapolating from Brentano's conception of our awareness of parts of a whole intuition, the presentation of a concrete multiplicity is a unity which includes within it presentations of the specific elements of the multiplicity (Hua 12: 20). In order to apprehend a group as a group, and not just as a series of individuals, I must be able to run through or 'colligate' the items in the group, and unify them in a special way. The concept of multiplicity, for Husserl, has the form 'a something and a something and a something, etc.' (12: 79); it includes a conception of colligation or collecting. Husserl is emphatic that this 'etc.', or 'and so on' (*und so weiter*), is included in the very notion of a multiplicity (12: 81). The extension of a general concept has to allow for a certain indeterminacy, for being applied over and over again, and the 'etc.' captures this requirement well. Numbers, then, arise through the 'enumeration of multiplicities' (*PA*, p. 192; 12: 182).

I can see different things as part of the same multiplicity by collecting them together and ignoring their properties or 'contents' and concentrating on each one just as an instance of a 'something'. Thus I can see a pen, a table and a lamp as a group of objects, ignoring their differences. What makes this kind of multiplicity exceptional is that it can be a gathering together of *anything* at all – 'physical or psychical, abstract or concrete, whether given through experience or imagination', e.g. an angel, the moon, Italy (12: 16). Numbers do not designate *concepts* as such; rather, they are general names for definite multiplicities or sets (Hua 12: 182). The number 5, for example, does not refer to the *concept* 5, but to any arbitrary set of five items (12: 181). To form a determinate multiplicity, I must *combine* a 'something' with another thing, which gives me the concept of 2, and so on. For example, if I want to count an apple, a book and a colour, I count each one as a 'something', abstracting from the particular characteristics that make it a book, an apple or a colour. I simply count *three* individual things.

The *concept* of a multiplicity as such has a certain indeterminacy or openness built into its very conception (Hua 12: 83).[19] For this reason, since concepts retain a fundamental indeterminacy of extension, Husserl maintains that one cannot treat concepts simply in terms of their extensions, as Frege proposed. According to Husserl's analysis, the concept of number arises when this indeterminate concept of multiplicity is made determinate by specifying its content in terms of an actual number. Numbers, then, are determinations of, or discriminations between, different concepts of multiplicity. The relation between the general concept of multiplicity and a determinate number is the relation between species and instance (12: 82). Every concrete multiplicity falls under a certain determinate number concept. Each number from 2 onwards is a determined collective combination. The concept of number, then, for Husserl, is arrived at by a 'reflection' (*Reflexion*) on the concept of multiplicity and the suppression of the natural indeterminacy in the multiplicity by precisely determining it. When I combine individual things seen only as 'somethings' into a definite multiplicity and reflect on the outcome of these operations of combining, I arrive at the concept of number. In this sense I understand number by a 'reflection' on this mental act of relating objects in a determinate way.

## Physical and Psychical Relations

Number is derived from the concept of 'collective combination' (*kollektive Verbindung*; 12: 20), which for Husserl is a fundamental relation of a new and special type, which he – somewhat unfortunately – calls a 'psychical' relation, thereby leaving himself open to charges of *psychologism*. As Husserl explicitly acknowledges, he is invoking a modified version of Brentano's distinction between the 'physical' and the 'psychical' (Hua 12: 68, 70 n. 1). What is the nature of the 'relation' involved in collective combination? Husserl's conception of a relation here depends on an *act* of relating. He cites Mill approvingly for the view that any two things which can be thought together can be considered to be related (Hua 12: 66). There are different ways in which multiplicities are grasped. In Husserl's terminology (following Brentano), any relation between things that somehow depends on the *contents* of those things is a 'physical' relation, irrespective of the type of things being related. If we think of a rose and of its parts (12: 72), there are definite relations between the parts, relations that belong to the content of the concept of a rose. Similarly, two acts of memory, two psychic events, are related by their contents, hence instantiate a physical relation between them. Relations of identity, gradation, or degree, and so on, all count as *physical* relations for Husserl, because the content of the thing itself is being considered. Even the more abstract kind of relations which Brentano had called 'metaphysical' relations – e.g. the relation of part to whole (Husserl cites Stumpf here) – are classified by Husserl as 'physical' relations. Husserl regards physical relations, then, as 'content relations' (12: 68).

In a short excursus on relations in general, Husserl distinguishes all content relations, which he also calls 'primary relations' (12: 69), from another class that he designates 'psychical relations'. In contrast to *content* relations, which contain the relation itself as part of the content, in the formation of the concept of multiplicity required for number, no element of the content of each term of the relation is involved. Husserl asks himself the question: 'can nothing of a combination be noticed *in* the representation contents themselves, but rather only in the psychical act which encompasses the parts in a unifying manner?' (*PA*, p. 75; Hua 12: 72). For him, the arbitrary contents in the group provide no hint as to the kind of synthesis combining them. I can relate together different contents without any attention to their specific natures: e.g. I can count 'red, the moon and Napoleon' (12: 74). Collective combination, then, is a purely *psychic*, not a *content*, relation, since it relies solely on a specific act of my mind picking out and combining just those objects I wish to include in my group. It has an absolute generality. A pure mental act, rather than any in-built similarities between the elements, determines what I shall include and what I shall exclude from any concrete grouping of objects, such as a pile of apples and other fruit on a table. On one account, which Husserl rejects, a collection of arbitrary objects consists simply of everything currently held in our consciousness: 'What then is given when we speak of a totality of arbitrary objects? Nothing further than the co-presence of those objects in our consciousness. The unity of representations of the totality thus consists only in their belonging to the consciousness which encompasses them' (*PA*, p. 23; 12: 22). But Husserl regards this as obviously wrong. There are many phenomena in my present consciousness which are not included in the totality I am now contemplating. The mental act of identifying the partial contents in the intuition of a concrete totality is driven by my 'interests' (*Interesse*; *PA*; 12: 30). Indeed, all through his career, Husserl emphasized the manner in which our will and our interests determine what we take to be significant. But in the case of grasping a totality, the content relations are absent, and here 'the collective combination appears almost as a case of *un*relatedness (*Relationslosigkeit*), so to speak' (*PA*, p. 76; Hua 12: 72).

In developing his account of collective combination, Husserl opposes various false conceptions of this relation. He rejects the view held by Kantians that number arises from the successive apprehension of contents, or from the simultaneous grasp of different contents which are co-presented (Hua 12: 74). Among the most common approaches to explaining the origin of number was the attempt (following Kant) to relate arithmetical and geometrical concepts to intuitions of space and time. Against F. A. Lange, for instance, who argued that number is based on the primal intuition of space as 'the original form of all synthesis' (*das Urbild aller Synthesis*; *PA*, p. 138; 12: 37), Husserl argues that the notion of a plurality owes nothing to the intuition of spatial or temporal arrangement (12: 41). Number has nothing to do with spatial intuition. Similarly, it has essentially nothing to do with time. From the outset of his career, Husserl opposed the Kantian determination of number in terms of time. His 1887 public defence lists among the theses he will defend: 'The concept of time is not included in the concept of number' (*PA*, p. 357; Hua 12: 339). While he acknowledges that there is a definite connection between time and number – he even cites Aristotle's definition of time in terms of number (12: 32) – in fact he argues that time is at best a *pre-condition* (*Grundlage*) for the concept of number, not a component of it. Time or succession is a pre-condition for our having a concept of number; but then again, Husserl points out, time is a pre-condition for *all* our psychic experiences. Time is undeniably a part of consciousness, but this does not mean that the concept of time forms part of the concept of number as such (12: 28). Thus Husserl regards Kant's analysis of number, which defines it in terms of the intuition of succession, as confused (12: 32–3). Arithmetic does not depend on the intuition of time, and geometry does not depend on the intuition of space. Rather, both sciences, as he will maintain in *LU* and thereafter, belong to *formal ontology*, the study of what belongs to anything as such. Furthermore, all claims that the human mind can grasp individual items only successively, or can grasp only items co-presented at the same time, take an overly restricted view of the nature of consciousness.

Husserl's contemplation of the role of succession in the formation of concepts leads him to distinguish clearly between presentations and concepts, between the concrete phenomena and their sense.

Accordingly, we must also distinguish between the psychological description [*die psychologische Beschreibung*] of a phenomenon and the statement of its *signification* [*Bedeutung*]. The phenomenon is the foundation of the signification, but is not identical with it. If a totality of objects, A, B, C, D, is in our representation, then, in light of the sequential process through which the total representation originates, perhaps finally only D will be given as a sense representation, the remaining contents being then given merely as phantasy representations which are modified temporally and also in other aspects of their content. If, conversely, we pass from D to A, then the phenomenon is obviously a different one. But the logical signification (*die logische Bedeutung*) sets all such distinctions aside. The modified contents serve as signs, as deputies, for the unmodified ones which were there. In forming the representation of the totality we do not attend to the fact that changes in the contents occur as the colligation progresses. Our aim is to actually maintain them in our grasp and to unite them. Consequently the *logical content* of that representation is not, perhaps, D, just passed C, earlier passed B, up to A, which is the most strongly modified. Rather, it is nothing other than (A, B, C, D). The representation takes in every single one of the contents without regard to the temporal differences and the temporal order grounded in those differences. (*PA*, pp. 32–3; 12: 31–2)

Unfortunately, he does not maintain this clear distinction throughout his discussion.

Husserl also opposes those philosophers (he mentions Sigwart and Jevons; Hua 12: 49) who claim that the concept of multiplicity depends on recognizing explicitly the differences between things. In particular, he focuses on the English logician Jevons's claim that number is 'the empty form of difference' (*die leere Form der Verschiedenheit*; Hua 12: 49); in other words, that grasping a collection requires recognizing that the things being collected are different from one another, and that the concept of number requires the recognition of these differences without further attending to the specific kinds of difference between the items involved. Husserl agrees with Jevons that recognition of difference is *necessary* to the concept of multiplicity; but it is not central to the concept. Of course, I must be able to distinguish things in order to be able to see them as a collectivity and to count them, but I do not have to attend to, or specifically notice, these differences between things in order to arrive at the concept of number (12: 57). Moreover, I certainly do not *represent* the differences in my number concept (12: 54). For Husserl, the apprehension of differences belongs to the domain of content relations (12: 56), whereas number concepts relate things in a purely formal way. *Differentiating* and *enumerating* are essentially different mental acts (12: 59). The units in the multiplicity are connected only by the mental act which holds them together, not by any specific differences between the things, and hence not on the basis of any relations holding between them. And seeing things as collected in this way is determined by my specific *interests* (*Interesse*; Hua 12: 74). Collective combination, then, is a formal relation motivated by interest. (Throughout his life, Husserl maintained that knowledge is driven by interests.)

## The Special Case of Zero and One

As we have seen, Husserl follows Aristotle and Euclid in seeing number as related to multiplicities: 'number is a multiplicity of unities' (*PA*, p. 15; 12: 14). Of course, a consequence of this approach is that the number 1 cannot itself be considered a number, since it is required in the definition of number. If numbers are specifications of multiplicities, how do we arrive at the number 1? Husserl does not shrink from the controversial consequences of his definition of number, so concludes that 1 is not actually a cardinal number. For Husserl, controversially, we arrive at this number negatively, by giving a negative answer to the question, 'how many (*Wieviel*)?', because the answer must always refer to a plurality, a 'many' (*Viel*; Hua 12: 131). Similarly, for Husserl, strictly speaking, zero (0) is not a number, since all numbers initially are based on multiplicities. Zero is, like 1, at best a negative answer to the question 'how many?' Frege will lambast Husserl for this claim.

Besides this unusual account of 0 and 1, Husserl also has difficulties accounting for large numbers. Initially he emphasized that numbers were based on any arbitrary collections whatever, so long as we are able to see that they constitute a collection which is colligated as 'a something and a something and a something, etc.'; but his treatment of higher numbers requires that they be grasped as 'fused' groups: e.g. I grasp the number 1,000 not by articulating it as a series of 1's but as a totality by itself. Frege notes this apparent contradiction.[20] In larger numbers I cannot perform the act of running through all the unities which make up the number. Instead, I employ the concepts of 'more' to increase each number ($5 = 4 + 1$, $149 = 148 + 1$), and in this way I can intuitively form the entire series of numbers, though I must retrace the higher numbers back to the genuine experiences of the lower numbers (*PA*, p. 242; Hua 12: 229).

Husserl's youthful account of the genesis of arithmetical concepts contains many problems, some of which he himself later identified. He sees that apprehending a number, a determinate multiplicity, requires an act that grasps things simply as general somethings. This he understands as an act of selective attention motivated by a special 'interest', which he explicates in terms of fairly traditional theories of abstraction. Around 1896, however, he came to the view (articulated for the first time in *LU* VI) that an act of collection is not to be ranked as a sensuous act of perception or intuition in the simple sense, but rather is a different kind of act, a non-sensuous categorial act, an act of categorial intuition. Indeed, in his Draft Preface to *LU* (1913) Husserl later located the discovery of his crucial distinction between the sensuous and the categorial precisely in his distinguishing, in *PA*, between apprehensions of individual contents of consciousness and the acts of collecting them together into unities which transcend what is given in the components taken singly (EV, p. 34; Fink, p. 126; Hua 20/1: 294). Thus, Husserl did think that there was something fundamentally right about seeing number as related to collective combination, and the act of bringing things together will continue to play a role in his account of categorial intuition in the Sixth Investigation (*LU* VI §51).

Husserl's account of abstraction also underwent transformation in the period between *PA* and *LU*, and even within the course of the six investigations themselves. In *PA*, he accepted a relatively naive, empiricist view of abstraction as selective attention, whereby one focuses on a particular property of an object and neglects others (Cantor held a very similar view). In *LU* II he recognizes that abstraction is consideration of an ideal universal, hence an act of a different kind from selective attention. It is an act that apprehends the general or universal as such. As he comments in *LU* VI with regard to the concept of an intuition of universals (as opposed to individuals), which many have thought to be a contradictory concept:

> Naturally I do not here mean 'abstraction' merely in the sense of a setting-in-relief of some non-independent moment in a sensible object, but Ideational Abstraction, where no such non-independent moment, but its 'Idea', its Universal, is brought to consciousness, and achieves *actual givenness*. . . . Talk of an *intuition* and, more precisely, of a *perception of the universal* is in this case, therefore, well-justified. (*LU* VI §52, **II** 292; Hua 19/2: 690–1)

Also problematic in *PA* is his conception of 'reflection' (*Reflexion*). It seems that basic concepts required in arithmetic are formed by reflection on various kinds of psychic acts (acts of presenting, combining, partitioning and so on); but what is the status of this reflection? Clearly, we are not explicitly conscious of this act of reflection when we employ numbers, since we focus straightforwardly on the numbers themselves. Ten years later, in the Sixth Logical Investigation, Husserl explicitly repudiated the traditional Lockean view that concepts (such as *number*) are found in 'inner perception' through reflection on mental acts. He admits that reflection is a vague word, but insists, against Locke, that 'categorial' concepts such as unity, multiplicity, number and being are not found in reflection as the constituents of psychic acts. Rather, he wants to insist that there are categorial objects (states of affairs) corresponding to categorial acts but transcending them, just as there are sensory objects independent of and transcending to sensory acts: 'Not in these *acts as objects* but in the *objects of these acts*, do we have the abstractive basis (*das Abstraktionsfundament*) which enables us to realize the concepts in question' (*LU* VI §44, **II** 279; Hua 19/2: 670). For Husserl, categorial acts correlate with specific objects yielded by these acts themselves. A group or aggregate is given through an act that involves combining the elements of the aggregate (a + b + c . . .), but the *concept* of the aggregate does not arrive through reflection on this act of aggregating, but rather by paying heed to the individual instance of the aggregate and universalizing it. It is clear that Husserl has not essentially changed his mind concerning the origination of number between *PA* and *LU*. What has changed, rather, is his description of what he is doing in so analysing number.

## The Problem of Psychologism
## in the *Philosophy of Arithmetic*

One of the main problems in *PA*, and one upon which Frege fixes in his famous review, as we shall shortly see, is that Husserl, due to his reliance on Brentano's descriptive psychology, has still not taken sufficient care to distinguish between the 'presentations' (*Vorstellungen*) as immanent psychological contents and the ideal objects or objectivities which are the objective correlates of specific mental acts. Husserl has indifferently spoken of concrete multiplicities (and the narrower class of 'sensible groups'; 12: 195), and of the general *concepts* of multiplicity, etc., formed through abstraction, and of numbers as determinations of these multiplicities. Numbers are higher-order objects. The number concepts, then, for Husserl, have a 'psychological origin' (*psychologische Ursprung*) in quite specific acts of the mind: acts of collective combining, selective attention, ignoring differences of content between items, reflection and so on. It is this account that Frege claimed 'shunts everything off into the subjective', and that he condemned as 'psychologistic'. Indeed, it appears as if Husserl accepts Frege's criticism, since he himself adopts an antipsychologistic position in the 1900 *Prolegomena* to *LU*, crediting Frege as he does so: 'I need hardly say that I no longer approve of my own fundamental criticisms of Frege's antipsychologistic position set forth in my *Philosophie der Arithmetik*, I, pp. 129–32 (now *PA*, pp. 123–8; 12: 118–22). I may here take the opportunity, in relation to all of the discussions of these *Prolegomena*, to refer to the Preface of Frege's later work, *Basic Laws of Arithmetic*, vol. 1 (Jena, 1893)'. (*LU, Prol.* §45, I 318 n. 6; Hua 13: 172).

In the *LU Prolegomena*, as we shall see in the next chapter, Husserl set forth the most far-reaching criticisms of psychologism ever offered by a German philosopher, and appears to reject his own earlier formulations. Nevertheless, he never entirely abandoned the approach of *PA*. In fact, in the book itself, Husserl appears to be already moving from his psychologistic position towards numbers as expressed in the 1887 dissertation, and it is clear that his basic intention was to carry out a specific kind of conceptual analysis, making use of part/whole analysis and of the identification through reflection of acts that set up concepts (by isolating contents according to interest, combining them into groups, colligating them, and so on). This was, of course, descriptive psychology, but in *LU* it was also be termed phenomenology. Frege's criticisms, as we shall see, while directly attacking Husserl, do not seem to be on target. Let us briefly review the famous altercation between Frege and Husserl.

# Frege's 1894 Review of Husserl's
## *Philosophy of Arithmetic*

In 1894, Gottlob Frege reviewed Husserl's *Philosophy of Arithmetic* in an acerbic and cranky manner.[21] This was not the first contact between the two logicians. Husserl had been reading Frege since the mid-1880s. They had begun corresponding with each other in 1891, exchanging papers and views in a respectful way (unfortunately, relatively few of their letters have survived). Frege sent Husserl a copy of his 1891 article, 'Sinn und Bedeutung' and other works; Husserl sent Frege a copy of his newly published *PA* and his review of Ernst Schröder's lectures on the algebra of logic. Both logicians had criticized inconsistencies and imprecisions in Schröder's early attempt at the mathematical formalization of logic, which Husserl regarded as technically brilliant but misguided.[22] Frege found Schröder's work defective because his definitions were not drawn sufficiently sharply. In his letter to Frege of 18 July 1891, Husserl looks for guidance on the treatment of imaginary numbers, which were rendering problematic his attempt to found arithmetic on the positive whole numbers.

In the course of a letter of 24 May 1891, Frege draws attention to the difference between Husserl and himself regarding their understanding of sense and reference with respect to concept words (common names). According to Frege, Husserl operates with a triadic scheme:

concept-word
↓
sense of the concept-word (concept)
↓
object which falls under the concept

Frege, on the other hand, has a more complex scheme, depending on whether he is talking about sentences, proper names or common names, and in the latter case his schema has four levels:

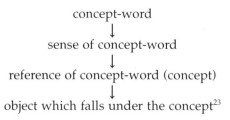

concept-word
↓
sense of concept-word
↓
reference of concept-word (concept)
↓
object which falls under the concept[23]

Frege believes this fourth step is necessary because there are concepts under which no objects fall (empty concepts), while the concept itself remains valid. This step, for Frege, helps to make clear the difference between proper names and concepts, whereas in Husserl's scheme the only difference is that proper names refer to only one thing, whereas concepts to more than one. Indeed, Frege himself admits that he had not been clear on the distinction between sense and reference in his own treatment of content in *Die Grundlagen der Arithmetik (Foundations of Arithmetic,* 1884): 'When I wrote my *Grundlagen der Arithmetik,* I had not yet made the distinction between sense and reference, and so, under the expression "judgeable content", I was combining what I now designate by the distinctive words "thought" and "truth value"'.[24]

In *PA* chapter 7 (12: 118–22), Husserl had been somewhat critical of Frege's 'oft cited and ingenious book' (*geistreiches Buch: PA,* p. 124; 12: 118) – GA – for engaging in overly subtle analyses without positive result (*PA,* p. 125, 12: 120). Husserl had been, along with Cantor,[25] one of very few mathematicians to notice Frege's work at this time, and many of his own analyses in *PA* are in accord with Frege, and indeed probably influenced by his reading of *GA.* Husserl had not made use of Frege's work in his 1887 *Habilitation,* but in *PA* Frege is quoted more than any other author. In general, Husserl admired Frege's clear and precise writing, as evidenced by his letter to Frege of 18 July 1891: 'First of all, I may be permitted to mention the great stimulation and challenge that I have derived from your *Grundlagen.* Amongst the many works that were before me during the preparation of my book, I could not name any one which I studied with nearly as much pleasure as yours'.[26] Frege had written *GA* in deliberately anti-Kantian vein, to prove that number statements were, *contra* Kant, purely *analytic truths,* and that arithmetic could be reduced to logic. As he put it, he wanted to show that propositions that extend knowledge may be analytic (*GA* §88). Logic too is entirely analytic.

Despite his genuine admiration for Frege, Husserl devotes specific sections of *PA* to a critique of *GA.* He is particularly critical of Frege's anti-psychologistic account of numbers, citing the fact that his own work offers precisely the kind of psychological grounding of arithmetic concepts that Frege repudiates (12: 119). Frege's goal is 'chimerical' (12: 120). In an important discussion, Husserl criticizes Frege's reliance on Leibniz's account of identity (those things are the same, of which one can be substituted for the other without loss of truth: *eadem sunt, quorum unum potest substitui alteri salva veritate*) in order to arrive at the definition of numbers in terms of equivalence of classes. He criticizes Frege for assuming that equality and identity are the same.[27] Husserl thinks that Frege has merely discussed the extensions (*Umfänge*) of concepts, not their 'content' (*Inhalt; PA,* p. 128; 12: 122) or intension. Frege had given an example (which Husserl takes up) whereby the statement that 'a is parallel to b', written as

$$a//b,$$

can be interpreted as stating that

'the direction of line a is the same as the direction of line b',

and this can be understood assuming the law of identity

$$a = b.$$

For Frege, definitions were a matter of utility and convenience, and mathematicians may simply choose among equivalent definitions the one best suited to their needs (e.g. definitions of a conic section). Definitions work if they pick out the referent; their sense need not be attended to. Husserl is unhappy with Frege's cavalier treatment of definitions, which for him, have to pick out essence, and hence are contentful. Sense is uppermost for Husserl.

Husserl also rejects Frege's view that a statement about number is a statement about a concept. He summarizes Frege's view as follows: 'The number accrues neither to an individual object nor to a group of objects but rather to the concept under which the objects enumerated fall. When we judge: Jupiter has four moons, then the number four is assigned to the concept *moon of Jupiter*' (PA, p. 126; 12: 120). In agreement with Georg Cantor, Husserl criticized Frege's assumption that a concept determines a precise set, since concepts are more indeterminate in extension than sets. Concepts, for Husserl, embody an 'and so on' (*und so weiter*).

Given these collegial exchanges in 1891, the tone of Frege's review of 1894 is surprisingly caustic.[28] Frege accuses Husserl of making fundamental errors; but, above all, he sees Husserl's book as general evidence of 'the devastation caused by the influence of psychology on logic' (*Rezension*, p. 192; 324). Frege determines Husserl's intention as aiming to 'provide a naive conception of number with a scientific justification' (*Rezension*, p. 180; 315). A view of numbers is 'naive', for Frege, if it treats numbers either as 'heaps' of things or as 'properties' of those heaps. He judges Husserl's version to be naive because it treats numbers as the counting of things from which their properties have been removed, rather than as the set of sets with the same extension, as Frege's *Foundations of Arithmetic* maintained. Frege's view of the relation between number and set is complex. Statements about numbers are statements about extension, but numbers themselves are not extensions *tout court*. Frege offers the following definition of number:

The Number which belongs to the concept F is the extension of the concept 'equal to the concept F' (*GA*, pp. 79–80)

Number is then an extension of a concept of concepts. For Frege, numbers are a certain specific kind of extension of concepts – that is, a certain specific kind of class. For example, let us take a concept (to adapt Frege's own example, say, 'plates on the table') under which concept three plates are included. The number 3 here is not itself the *extension* of that concept, since the extension is actually a set of objects (plates). Rather, the number *three* is a set whose members are *all* such three-membered sets (including the three forks, three knives, etc., of the laid table). Thus, it is a set one of whose members is the set whose members are the plates on the table. So, in terms of extensions of concepts, the number 3, for Frege, is the extension of the concept 'equinumerous with a [given] three-membered class'. For Frege, therefore, we do not need numbers to explain extensions of concepts; thus, for example, the fact that the concept 'plates on the table' determines an extension which includes just these plates as members does not, for Frege, presuppose anything about numbers. Of course, for Frege, each concept does determine a precise extension, even if we do not know what that is. He quite explicitly distinguishes concepts from sets.

Husserl clearly distinguishes between a concept as an abstract thought, an intention, and a concept as a general name for the things that fall under it. Thus he carefully distinguishes between using the term 'colour' to refer to the concept Colour (using capitals to mark out the concept) and using the name 'colour' simply to refer indifferently to different kinds of colours, red, green, etc. (*PA*, p. 82; 12: 78). Thus, we speak of Colour to refer to the concept and 'a colour' or 'colours' to refer to the individuals collected under the concept.

Husserl thinks that no one ordinarily thinks of numbers in the manner in which Frege defines them. Of course, he could have retorted that Frege simply assumed that concepts do organize objects into groups, whereas he himself is interested in addressing how they are so organized by acts of the mind ('psychological acts').[29] Frege also criticizes Husserl for having no clear definition of 'multiplicity' (*Vielheit*), and for using several terms more or less synonymously ('plurality', 'totality', 'aggregate', 'collection' and 'set'), though Husserl did this intentionally, as we have seen.[30] Frege thinks that Husserl has not distinguished adequately between a multiplicity and a number, since he does not distinguish between 'falling under a concept' and subordination. In his *Grundlagen*, Frege explicitly dismissed the usefulness of the concept of multiplicity for getting at number (*GA* §45, p. 58), and, furthermore, rejects Husserl's accounts of *kollektive Verbindung* and abstraction. Husserl's account of the process of abstraction, whereby we arrive at the concept of number from the contemplation of a multiplicity of objects, requires us to treat the constituent objects merely as things with no specific properties other than their being thought together in relation. This, as Frege sarcastically puts it, sounds as if things underwent 'a cleansing in a psychological wash-tub' (*Reinigung im psychologischen Waschkessel*), whereby their specific properties and differences are removed and they end up being treated as mere 'somethings' (*Rezension*, p. 181; 315). Frege himself confesses to being unable to form a concept of a totality in the manner suggested by Husserl; mathematicians simply do not have this magical ability.

Employing Husserl's example of three arbitrary objects – red, the moon and Napoleon – Frege states that he is unable to represent to himself different things as related in some way, without thinking of them as somehow unified in a certain way into a whole: e.g. the redness of a burning village, against which stands the figure of Napoleon illuminated by the moon (*Rezension*, pp. 185–6; 319). Frege holds, against Husserl, that the relationships between the entities to be counted are already given. In other words, we cannot think of undifferentiated things as merely related to each other without specifying the concepts under which we are going to relate them. Of course, Frege himself had difficulty explaining how the mind could have a non-sensuous 'grasp' (*Erfassen*) of numbers, and the 'context principle' is introduced in *Grundlagen* §§57–61 to justify the introduction of numbers without positing a non-sensuous, Platonic intuition of them.

Frege sees number as involved in bringing an object under a concept on the basis of a perceived relation. He says, following Aristotle, 'In a number-statement something is predicated of the concept', and again, 'in a number-statement there is contained an assertion about a concept' (*Rezension*, p. 185; 318, p. 186; 320). According to Husserl, when we count Berlin and Dresden and Munich, we treat them merely as a 'something' and a 'something', and a 'something', and reflection on this totality yields the number 3. But, for Frege, this is meaningless. We don't ask how many somethings there are; rather, we ask: how many *cities* are there? In other words, our inquiry seeks the 'extension' (*Umfang*) of a particular 'concept' (*Begriff*), which necessitates the employment of the concept, not getting away from it, as Husserl claims.[31] Thus, if we ask: 'How many moons has Mars?', the answer is a new piece of knowledge. For this reason also, Frege rejects Husserl's account of 0 and 1, as negative answers to the question: 'How many?' Frege retorts that the answer to the question: 'How many moons has the Earth?' is hardly a negative answer, as Husserl would have us believe (*Rezension*, pp. 189–90; 321–2).

Frege also criticizes Husserl for confusing the difference between a 'presentation' (*Vorstellung*), its meaning and its object, and of treating everything as a presentation – the act, the object of the act and the concept of the object (*Rezension*, p. 181; 315–16). In particular, Husserl seems to be confusing the numbers themselves with the presentations of number in consciousness. This might appear harmless in mathematics, but, as Frege says, it would be crazy to regard the Moon as generated by our act of thinking about it. Is not the Moon rather difficult to force into a mental act as a presentation? Sometimes, Frege complains, Husserl treats a multiplicity as a presentation, and sometimes as something objective; he is ignoring the distinction between the content and the object of the act, and the distinction between different kinds of acts. According to Frege, 'presentations' are to be understood as merely subjective, private mental episodes, which are individual, take place in time, cannot be shared, and may be coloured with emotion, whereas one and the same 'thought' (*Gedanke*) can be grasped by many people (*Rezension*, p. 182; 316), and so is objective and non-temporal. Frege criticizes Husserl on the grounds that 'everything is shunted off into the subjective', and as the boundaries between subjective and objective become blurred, everything becomes objective (*Rezension*, p. 182; 316). Crucially, for Frege, Husserl has confused the objectivity of numbers with the subjectivity of acts of counting, and thus is guilty of psychologism, the error of tracing the laws of logic to empirical psychological laws. Husserl has collapsed the logical nature of judgement into private psychological acts, has collapsed together 'truth' (*das Wahre*) and 'taking for true' (*wahr nehmen*), playing on the German word (*wahrnehmen*) for 'to perceive'.

## Husserl's Reaction to Frege

Due largely to the pioneering work of Dagfinn Føllesdal, Frege's review of Husserl has been widely interpreted as a demolition of the early Husserl and as *the* decisive influence forcing Husserl's change of direction away from psychologism in *LU*.[32] But, as we have seen, Frege has been somewhat unfair to Husserl, exaggerating his tendency towards psychologism. In fact, both philosophers agree on many essential points concerning numbers; for example, both agree that numbers as such are objective, ideal entities. As we have seen, Husserl was interested in explaining how our cognition of numerical entities comes about, not in addressing the metaphysical problem of the nature of numbers. Though, admittedly, his language is unclear as he wavers between talking about presentations of multiplicities and the multiplicities themselves, nevertheless Husserl never gives any hint that he thinks the numbers themselves are anything other than ideal objective entities, known in the Brentanian tradition as 'objectivities' (*Gegenständlichkeiten*). He even spoke of 'numbers in themselves' (*die Zahlen an sich*; 12: 260), as Frege noticed (*Rezension*, p. 191; 323).

Contrary to Frege's claim, Husserl was already aware of the distinction between a 'presentation' and its meaning 'content'; indeed, he had explicitly commented on that distinction in the 1887 dissertation, which is reprinted with minor changes in PA. Here, Husserl explicitly claims that a psychological phenomenon is to be distinguished from its 'meaning' or 'significance' (Bedeutung; 12: 31) or 'logical content'. As he says, 'the phenomenon is the basis for the Bedeutung but is not identical with it'. More than twenty years later, Husserl, in a footnote to his Ideen I (1913), explicitly invoked this passage as evidence that he had not fallen into psychologism in PA (Ideen I §124, p. 294; Hua 3/1: 256). In fact, he had criticized others for not attending to the difference between a word, its meaning content and its object: for instance, in his 1891 review of Ernst Schröder's Algebra der Logik (Algebra of Logic), where he criticizes Schröder for conflating the act of thinking with its ideal content.[33] Furthermore, an embryonic version of the distinction between meaning and object (paralleling Frege's Sinn and Bedeutung) appears in Husserl's 1890 article, 'Zur Logik der Zeichen' ('On the Logic of Signs'), where he distinguishes between what a sign 'means' or 'signifies' (bedeutet) and what it 'denotes' (bezeichnet).[34] In fact, in Ideen I, Husserl himself acknowledged that this distinction, popularized by Twardowski (as the content/object distinction), was 'well known' and had a long tradition in logic (in Bolzano, Kerry, Brentano and others).[35] Bolzano, for instance, distinguished between subjective and objective presentations or 'presentations-in-themselves' (Vorstellungen an sich; Wiss., pp. 20–1).

Indeed, though Husserl later acknowledged Frege's criticisms honestly, and, if we accept the evidence of Boyce-Gibson, took them to heart, there is considerable evidence that Husserl, in his writings after 1890, was already finding problems in his own psychological approach to the genesis of arithmetical concepts, when Frege's review was published.[36] Indeed, the main problem with PA is that its language is unclear, and that the kind of 'psychological clarification' being sought is not properly expressed. It is likely, in fact, that Husserl took Frege to be merely confirming his own position, or certainly the position towards which he was moving after PA was completed.[37]

## The Influence of Bolzano, Leibniz and Lotze

Husserl's own accounts of his intellectual development through the 1890s do not credit Frege for his recognition of ideal entities sharply distinct from the psychological operations in which these objects manifest themselves, but rather suggest that his thinking was motivated more generally by Leibniz's distinction between truths of reason (vérités de raison) and truths of fact (vérités de fait), Hume's distinction between 'relations of ideas' and 'matters of fact', and specifically by Bolzano's and Lotze's logics. Part of the legacy of Bolzano and Lotze that Husserl embraced was the 'Platonist' defence of the unique objectivity of ideal formations against the empiricist tradition (see *FTL* §56). He also endorsed Leibniz's conception of *mathesis universalis*, comprised not just of quantitative disciplines but also of the logical forms of arguments.

Husserl had heard about Bolzano's *Wissenschaftslehre* from Weierstrass in Berlin and Brentano in Vienna. He eventually found a copy of this rare work in a second-hand bookshop (*Chronik*, p. 463). He was drawn to, but perplexed by, its doctrine of 'propositions in themselves' (*Sätze an sich*) and the subset of these propositions, 'truths in themselves'. In *Wissenschaftslehre*, book 1, §19, Bolzano defined a *proposition in itself* as 'any assertion that something is or is not the case, regardless whether somebody has put it into words, and regardless even whether it has been thought'. A 'truth in itself' is a true proposition (*Wiss.*, bk 1, §25); it asserts what is the case irrespective of any reference to a thinker thinking or affirming that proposition. Thus examples of a proposition in itself would include 'there are no thinking beings' or 'there are truths which no one knows'. Bolzano sharply distinguished the subjective presentations in the mind which were parts of subjective propositions from the objective meaning-content of the proposition in itself:

> 'Idea' in this sense is a general name for any phenomenon in our mind . . . Thus, what I see if someone holds a rose before me is an idea, namely, the idea of a red colour. . . . In this sense, every idea requires a living being as a subject in which it occurs. For this reason I call them subjective or mental ideas. Hence subjective ideas are something real. They have real existence at the time when they are present in a subject, just as they have certain effects. The same does not hold for the objective idea or idea in itself that is associated with every subjective idea. By objective idea I mean the certain something which constitutes the immediate matter (*Stoff*) of a subjective idea, and which is not found in the realm of the real. An objective idea does not require a subject but subsists (*bestehen*), not indeed as something existing, but as a certain something even though no thinking being may have it; also it is not multiplied when it is thought by one, two, three, or more beings, unlike the corresponding subjective idea, which is present many times. Hence the name 'objective'. (*Wiss.*, Bk 2, Pt 1, §48, pp. 61–2)

Bolzano strongly influenced Husserl's recognition that the objects of logic, i.e. propositions and their parts and relations to one another, were ideal, timeless objective entities which do not have actual existence (in the sense of a location in space or time). Furthermore, in the 1891 exchange of letters between Frege and Husserl, it is clear that each had independently come to recognize the need to posit an intermediate meaning as a dependent part of the intending act between the individual psychological thought process and the object referred to, whether the object be real or ideal.

Husserl, then, did not get the distinction between presentation, ideal meaning and object from Frege, but rather arrived at it independently, from his own logical research. At most, Frege's review reinforced Husserl's recognition of the psychologistic dangers involved in confusing the domains of the psychologically real and the logically ideal, and in later writings he struggled to keep these domains apart. Of course, in his Draft Preface of 1913, Husserl also argued against making too much of Bolzano's influence on him, as some critics had alleged that he was simply repeating the earlier logician. Husserl's admiration for Bolzano was tempered with criticism, as when he later pointed out that Bolzano himself was not free from an 'extreme empirical' interpretation of the origin of mathematical and logical concepts (EV, p. 48; Fink, p. 326; 20/1: 308). On the other hand, Husserl's own lectures on formal logic in 1896 were very heavily influenced by Bolzano.

According to Husserl, it was Lotze's account of the independent validity of Platonic Ideas in his *Logik* that helped him to understand what Bolzano was getting at in talking of 'propositions in themselves'.[38] In his *Logic*, Book 3, chapter 2, §§313–21, Lotze attempts a clarification of the meaning of the Platonic 'world of Ideas' by arguing that they are the predicates of things in this world considered as general concepts bound together in a whole in such a way as to 'constitute an unchangeable system of thought' (§314) and which determine the limits of all possible experience (§315). Plato recognizes that in the Heraclitean world of change, black things become white, etc., but blackness does not change, even if a thing has only a momentary participation in it. Even when a momentarily appearing sound or colour is immediately replaced by another, different sound or colour, it is still the case that these two items stand in definite relations of contrast with one another. These relations, and indeed the intelligible contents of real things and events, may be said to have 'validity' (*Geltung*; §316). According to Lotze, the ascription to Plato of an absurd doctrine of the existence of Ideas alongside the existence of things is due to the fact that the Greek language did not have the capacity to express this validity, but referred to them only as being, *ousia*. They are ideal unities (*henades, monades*). Plato is not trying to hypostasize the Ideas by saying that they are not in space; rather, he simply wants to say that they are not anywhere at all (§318). Plato's Ideas have been misunderstood as having 'existence' (*Dasein*) separate from things, whereas, according to Lotze, in fact Plato intended only to ascribe 'validity' (*Geltung*) to them.

Inspired by this account, Husserl came to see that Bolzano's truths in themselves, which he had initially interpreted as 'metaphysical abstrusities' (*als metaphysiche Abstrusitäten*) or 'mythical entities, sus-pended between being and nonbeing', should rather be understood as the ideal correlatives of statements or, alternatively, as 'theorems' which are objectively true without necessarily being thought as exist-ing at all:

> I saw that under 'proposition in itself' is to be understood what is des-ignated in ordinary discourse, which always objectifies the Ideal, as the 'sense' (*Sinn*) of a statement. It is that which is explained as one and the same where, for example, different persons are said to have asserted the same thing. Or, again, it is what, in science, is simply called a theorem, e.g., the theorem about the sum of angles of a triangle, which no one would think of taking to be someone's lived experience of judging. (*EW*, p. 201; Hua 22: 156. See also *EV*, p. 37; Fink, p. 129; 20/1: 297–8)

In other words, Husserl claimed to have learned from Lotze how to distinguish the propositional content or sense of a statement from the state of affairs. Husserl also takes over from Lotze the notion that the *Sinn* is an *ideal species*, a trans-temporal identity, not an existent thing.[39] To use the language of the Second Logical Investigation, the ideal sense is a species that is instantiated in the particular 'sense-moment' (*Sin-nesmoment*). This distinction would bring Husserl to make major mod-ifications to Brentano's account of intentionality, and specifically to clarify what is meant by the 'content' of mental acts.

## The Road to the *Logical Investigations*

The outcome of Husserl's decade of logical reflections through the 1890s was the massive two-volume *LU* (1900/1), in which Husserl offers a strong defence of the nature of the ideal objectivities grasped in logic, and defends the direct intuition of universals and other higher, so-called categorial objectivities. His former mentor Brentano regarded Husserl's intuition of objectivities and universals as putting on the clothes that he himself had cast off. Brentano had earlier accepted *entia rationis* in the lectures that Husserl had attended, but in his later years had refused to recognize any existent things other than concrete indi-viduals (a position known as 'reism').[40]

The *Prolegomena* engages in an extensive refutation of psychologism. If numbers are constituted solely in acts of collecting and counting, then they could be misconstrued as simply products of the mind, and their truly objective status elided. Though Husserl had originally begun with the Brentanian assumption that psychology would ground all cognitive acts, he began to have doubts, as he said in the Foreword to the first edition of *LU*: 'I became more and more disquieted by doubts of principle, as to how to reconcile the objectivity of mathematics, and of all science in general, with a psychological foundation (*mit einer psychologischen Begründung*) for logic' (*LU*, Foreword, I 2; Hua 18: 6–7). Whereas Husserl's earlier researches had assumed that all scientific concepts could be clarified by tracking their psychological origins, he now came to the view that psychology was no help in explaining the objective nature and logical unity of the content of thought. He was pushed to reflect on the relationship between 'the subjectivity of knowing and the objectivity of the content known' (*LU*, Foreword, I 2; Hua 18: 7).

Partly in response to Frege's attack, but, more deeply and profoundly, because of his own recognition of the inadequacies of the Brentanian formulations he had employed in *PA*, Husserl began to see the limitations in his original analysis of number. Almost as soon as *PA* was published, Husserl began to recant his view that arithmetic was grounded in the positive whole numbers. He had particular difficulties explaining the nature of the imaginary numbers (which, as we have seen, for Husserl, included negative, irrational, complex, transfinite, infinite numbers – that is, any number which is not a natural number and does not correspond to a discrete quantity) by this means:

> Above all it was its [i.e. arithmetic's] purely symbolic procedural techniques, in which the genuine, originally insightful sense seemed to be interrupted and made absurd under the label of the transition through the 'imaginary', that directed my thoughts to the signitive and to the purely linguistic aspects of the thinking – and knowing – process and from that point on forced me to general 'investigations' which concerned universal clarification (*Klarlegung*) of the sense, the proper delimitation, and the unique accomplishment of formal logic. (EV, p. 33; Fink, pp. 125–6; 20/1: 294 n. 3)

The problem of imaginary numbers is to find out how they can be defined and what role they play in relation to the natural numbers. For instance, in what sense does the square root of minus one ($\sqrt{-1}$) give us an answer to the question: 'How many?'? This problem led to a broader concern. Husserl was worried about how our thinking employing pure signs and symbols is ever able to achieve insights into how things are. How is symbolic thinking possible? How does subjective thinking constitute objective validities? How can a deductive logic explain thinking unless it is accompanied by a proper theory of signs (*EW*, p. 436; Hua 22: 394)? These are the questions that Husserl will address in *LU* through his deepening appreciation of the Brentanian doctrine of the intentionality of mental acts.

Husserl took up the issues treated in *PA* again in his 1906–7 *ELE* (Hua 24), when he again entered into correspondence with Frege. In his letter to Husserl of 30 October/1 November 1906, Frege reiterates his view of psychologism and explains why psychological processes are never referred to in his *Begriffsschrift* (*Concept Notation*):

> Rightly does one find that the psychic processes are not truly represented through the *Begriffsschrift*; for that is not also its purpose. One even now always takes it to be the task of logic to study certain psychic processes. Logic has in reality as little to with this as with the movement of heavenly bodies. Logic, in no way, is a part of psychology. The Pythagorean theorem expresses the same thought for all men, while each person has his own representations, feelings, resolutions which are different from those of every other person. Thoughts are not psychic structures, and thinking is not an inner producing and forming, but an apprehension of thoughts which are already objectively given.[41]

Frege goes on to stress the danger of language misleading logic. For Frege: 'The main task of the logician consists in liberation from language and in simplification. Logic shall be the judge over languages. One should do away, in logic, with the subject and the predicate; or one should restrict these words to the relation of an object's falling under a concept (subsumption).'[42]

In *LU* Husserl too emphasizes the ideal independence of the Pythagorean theorem from all psychological thoughts about it, and also stresses the complete independence of logic from psychology. However, he develops a more complex relation between language and logic in the First Investigation.

I cannot here develop further the interesting connections between Frege's and Husserl's views of mathematics, logic and the role of language in both.[43] I will mention only that Husserl read Frege very carefully, heavily annotating his copies of Frege's writings. But Husserl was convinced that one could not do away with the subject–predicate structure of judgements, and was not willing to get involved in the development of the formal system for logic that Frege and others were developing. Husserl's interests were primarily philosophical, or 'epistemological'.

Before concluding, however, I should say a word about Husserl's views on mathematics and logic generally as they developed through his career.

## Husserl's Conception of Logic

Husserl saw himself as clarifying traditional ideas of logic, sharpening its concepts of the a priori, of form, of the nature of the analytic, and so on, in part through a detailed critique of existing logic textbooks. Following Bolzano and Brentano, for instance, he criticized Kant's account of analyticity as confused. But, he also saw himself as expanding logic in several dimensions.[44] He had a very interesting account of necessity and possibility and how these modal forms arise with relation to categorical judgements.[45] In the *Prolegomena*, and subsequently, he sided with the Bolzanian tradition, which characterized logic as *Wissenschaftslehre*, theory of science, and he never abandoned this conception, although he gave it a unique and original characterization as including in its highest form a 'theory of manifolds', or the 'theory of the forms of theory'. From his earliest days, he had recognized the deep theoretical connection between logic and mathematics and their common root. From the outset he saw the essential identity of formal logic and mathematics: as he put it in 1906–7, all formal calculation is essentially logical deduction (*ELE* §19; Hua 24: 84). He was in broad agreement with Frege and with Russell (somewhat later), who espoused the reduction of mathematics to formal logic. If anything, Husserl overestimated the possibilities of formal logic, in that he endorsed Hilbert's programme of complete formalization (with its axiom of the solvability of all mathematical problems; see Husserl's notes on Hilbert's 1901 lecture (Hua 12: 445–7)), and does not seem to have anticipated the problems posed by Gödel's Incompleteness Theorem (1931), which showed that no formalization of ordinary arithmetic is complete. Nevertheless, he was not a formalist as such, nor was he committed to symbolic logic. He identified flaws in the then current project of a purely extensional logic, and was aware of, and possibly even anticipated, Russell's – or Zermelo's – paradoxes regarding set theory. But at the time of writing *LU*, Husserl's main complaint was that those who advocated the reduction of arithmetic to logic had a mistaken conception of logic as a normative or practical discipline, and hence were vulnerable to psychologism (*ELE* §15; Hua 24: 56).

In the *Prolegomena* Husserl reveals a complex and very broad understanding of logic as having a threefold task. First, it was a doctrine of the primitive apophantic and formal ontological categories and the laws combining them. Second, it included the connection of categories in terms of the laws of consequence, understood so generally as to include both logic and arithmetic. Thirdly, it included a theory of the possible forms of theory and the corresponding formal ontological theory of manifolds. Logic requires formal grammar (the rules governing meaningfulness as such), *consequence logic* (logic of inference, *Konsequenzlogik*, bound only by the Principle of Non-Contradiction) and what he called 'logic of truth'.

In some respects his account of logic is quite traditional, being centred on the notion of judgement or assertion (Greek: *apophansis*), and hence, following Aristotle, characterized as 'apophantic logic' (see *LU* IV §14, II 72; Hua 19/1: 344; see also *ELE* §18; Hua 24: 71), although his detailed account of judgements goes far beyond Aristotle. Husserl always insisted on the judgement or proposition as the highest category in logic, and specifically the apophantic form 'S is P', the copulative judgement, as the absolutely fundamental form. Similarly, he took the Law of Non-Contradiction to be one of the absolutely basic ideal laws. One of his innovations is his view that formal logic in the sense of the science of the forms of implication needs to be complemented by a pure formal grammar specifying the rules for meaningfulness in the most general terms, offering an 'anatomy and morphology of propositions' strictly in regard to their sense (*ELE* §18; Hua 24: 71). Formal apophantics, which is concerned with truth and falsity as articulated in judgement, builds on this formal grammar. Before something is true or false, it must meet minimum conditions of coherence and meaningfulness as *a possible truth* – that is, as a possible *piece of knowledge*. Husserl always draws a distinction between the mere elaboration of consistent rules (rules of a game) and the specification of the possible forms of judgement understood as items of genuine knowledge (see *FTL* §33; *EU* §3). In *FTL* and elsewhere, Husserl refers to the unity of formal logic and mathematics as 'objective logic'. The counterpart of formal apophantics is what Husserl calls *formal ontology*, the theoretical account of all possible objects of whatever kind (see *EU* §1), the theory of something in general (*FTL* §54). Husserl recognized that formal ontology can in fact be pursued independently of logic. Formal ontology develops Brentano's, Twardowski's and Meinong's conception of *Gegenstandstheorie*, theory of objects, the account of what it is to be an object or a property or a relation, a unity, a plurality and so on. For Husserl, the objects of mathematics simply form one part of formal ontology, but there are other kinds of formal object that have nothing to do with numbers. Husserl recognized that mathematics itself was moving away from a fascination with objects, and was engaging in a reflection on its own methods. Thus geometry did not have to remain fixated on geometrical figures, but could express its results in terms of axioms and purely formal deductions (*ELE*; §19, Hua 24: 80). On the other hand, with his interest in genetic logic, Husserl wants to emphasize that the formal ontological concepts such as property, plurality and the like actually arise from 'nominalizations' of certain kinds of functions that are located in judgements, in formal apophantics. In his later years, Husserl became increasingly preoccupied with a genetic account of the emergence of forms of judgement. He was interested in giving an account of the emergence of logical forms from the life-world, from the domain of 'proto-logic', pre-predicative experience.

# 4

## Husserl's 'Breakthrough Work': Logical Investigations (1900/1901)

### The Meaning of Logic as Science of Science

Following a decade of 'isolated toilsome labour' (EV, p. 16; Fink, p. 109; Hua 20/1: 272) after *PA*, Husserl produced his 'breakthrough' work (EV, p. 32; Fink, p. 124; 20/1: 293), the vast two-volume *Logische Untersuchungen* (1900/1), running to almost 1,000 pages (in the original edition). This many-layered work is almost impossible to categorize. It includes, among other matters, an account of the nature of logic as 'the science of science', a lengthy refutation of psychologism, a broadly Platonist defence of ideal entities in logic and mathematics and cognition generally, a rejection of empiricist and nominalist accounts of abstraction, a defence of the direct apprehension of universals and 'categorial unities', a pure theory of wholes and parts (called in the second edition 'formal ontology'(Hua 19/1: 228)), a universal formal grammar specifying the ground rules for linguistic sense as opposed to nonsense, a 'descriptive psychology' or *phenomenology* of cognitive experiences (e.g. differentiating presentation from judgement), a defence of 'categorial' intuition (i.e. the intuition of non-sensory formations or objectivities such as 'X is Y'), and an analysis of the dynamic relations between intention and fulfilment in the process of knowledge, culminating in a revised account of truth as disclosure. In this chapter I cannot hope to cover all these topics in detail, but I plan to give an outline of the basic thrust of the work.

Husserl did not intend to publish *LU*, due to its 'imperfect form ... unevenness and fragmentary nature' (EV, p. 17; Fink, p. 110; 20/1: 273), but reasons of career advancement forced him to. It remains a work-in-progress, a 'patchwork' (*Stückwerk*) of different themes, charting Husserl's own path of discovery in regard to issues concerning the nature of logical and epistemic concepts. He describes his method as 'zigzag' (*im Zickzack*; *LU*, Intro. §6; 19/1: 22). Concepts are first employed, and only later clarified. That he does not use the phrase haphazardly is evident from its recurrence in later discussions (e.g. Hua 35: 94 and 391; *Krisis* §91), where he emphasizes the circularity of his interpretative efforts to clarify concepts:[1] 'Thus we find ourselves in a kind of circle. The understanding of the beginnings is to be gained fully only by starting with science as given in its present-day form, looking back at its development.... Thus we have no other choice than to proceed forward in a 'zigzag' pattern; the one must help the other in an interplay' (*Krisis* §91, p. 58; Hua 6: 59). This zigzag method sometimes gives a disorderly appearance to discussions. The effect is cumulative, and illumination comes slowly.

Husserl conceived *LU* primarily as a contribution to theory of knowledge or epistemology (*Theorie der Erkenntnis*). It focuses on logic as a 'theory of theories', because it provides the form of knowledge as such. The question of the nature of logic 'essentially coincides' with the cardinal question of epistemology: namely, the meaning of objectivity (*LU*, Prol. §3; Hua 18: 23), the question of 'the sense and object of cognition' (*Sinn und Gegenstand der Erkenntnis*, EV, p. 23; Fink, p. 116; 20/1: 280). Logic is not one science alongside others; in fact, it studies the formal a priori belonging to all the sciences as such. Logic is constitutive of the very idea of science (*ELE* §2; Hua 24: 5). A science is a science only to the extent that it exhibits a logical form.

Husserl's approach is broadly neo-Kantian: metaphysics requires the critique of knowledge; epistemology, not metaphysics, is *first philosophy*. He is, however, unhappy with the 'vague epistemology' of the neo-Kantian tradition, with its theoretical structures imposed from above; instead, he wants to begin 'from below' – a favourite slogan – with what is given in intuition. To preserve this metaphysical neutrality, he adopts a 'principle of presuppositionlessness' (*LU*, Intro. §7), putting all metaphysical speculation to one side. His aim, then, is an 'epistemologically "clarified" pure logic' (EV, p. 22; Fink, p. 115; 20/1: 279). This 'clarification' in turn requires *phenomenology*, and a vigilance to avoid reimporting speculative ('mythical') conceptions back into epistemology (see *IP*, p. 25; Hua 2: 32).

As we saw in the last chapter, *LU* 'revives old trends and theories' (EV, p. 16; Fink, p. 109; 20/1: 272). In particular, its conception of pure logic – as an a priori, formal science of ideal entities and the laws governing them – derives from Lotze and Bolzano, and ultimately from Leibniz's conception of a *mathesis universalis* (*LU*, Prol. §60), which Husserl has 'rediscovered'. In his Draft Preface to the second edition (1913), he also acknowledges that there are tensions due to his new insights. A major tension is the contrast between the 'formal ontology' of the *Prolegomena* and *LU* III and IV, and the properly phenomenological treatises (*LU* I, II, V and VI), which are concerned less with objects than with consciousness of meaning.

The *Prolegomena zur reinen Logik* (*Prolegomena to Pure Logic*; Hua 18) aims to sketch a new theory of science, largely by demolishing many prevailing misconceptions concerning logic, but specifically *psychologism*, the 'dominant' outlook in Germany (*Selbstandzeige* to *LU* volume 1; Hua 18: 261). The second volume (1901), however, primarily in the Introduction, advocates a new *method* called phenomenology. As Husserl says in the second edition of *LU*, 'psychologism can only be radically overcome by pure phenomenology' (*LU*, Intro. §2, I 169; Hua 19/1: 11–12). Husserl's subsequent researches aimed to clarify this 'breakthrough'. Central to his sense of phenomenology in *LU*, and to his critique of previous empiricism and rationalism, as we shall see, is that there are different kinds of givenness, and that it is important not to ignore any genuine form of givenness (EV, p. 27; Fink, pp. 119–20; 20/1: 283). Husserl saw himself as defending the multiplicity of forms of givenness of objects, and hence securing the true nature of objective knowledge: 'My so-called "Platonism" does not consist in some sort of metaphysical or epistemological substructures, hypotheses, or theories but rather in the simple reference to the type of original "givens" which usually, however, are falsely explained away.' (EV, p. 25, trans. modified; Fink, p. 118; 20/1: 282).

## Sense-Clarification of Epistemic Concepts through Intuition

According to the *Prolegomena*, science is 'grounded knowledge' (*Prol.* §64), concerned with the possession of truth, with knowing (*Erkennen*) or cognition (*Erkenntnis*) in a systematic, coherent sense, and to the highest degree possible, which means having grounds for one's knowing, possessing justified truths, judgements made with evidential insight (*LU, Prol.* §6, I 17; Hua 18: 30), as opposed to 'blind conviction' (18: 28) and 'baseless opinion' (18: 29). Science is the body of true propositions linked together in a systematic way (*LU, Prol.* §10). This 'system of truths' (*Zusammenhang der Wahrheiten*) expressed in propositions (*Prol.* §62) is a closed set. Each science ranges over a determinate set of objects: 'The field of a science is an objectively closed unity: we cannot arbitrarily delimit fields where and as we like' (*LU, Prol.* §2, I 12; Hua 18: 21). Each science is about a particular domain of entities (numbers, shapes, species of animals, etc.), understood as genuine objects with fixed essential properties (see also *Ideen* I §1). Moreover, scientific laws are not truths, because they are actually thought by minds; rather, laws such as Newton's laws of gravity are meant as universally true, holding even in the absence of any human minds (*LU*,

*Prol.* §35). Truths are truths even if unknown to anyone, Husserl maintains against neo-Kantians such as Sigwart, who maintained that truths were such only for a mind thinking them (Hua 18: 134). Not just objects, but meanings too, are ideal, Husserl maintains. 'Meanings in themselves' (*Bedeutungen an sich*) do not come into being and pass away when asserted, but have independent unity and validity. Furthermore, there are countless objective meanings which may never find human expression (*LU* I §35). Later, this Platonic realism concerning ideal entities was absorbed into his transcendental idealism, whereby the intrinsic being of these entities is treated as constituted.[2]

For Husserl in *LU*, phenomenology contributes to explicating the sense of both logic and knowledge, by clarifying their fundamental notions, e.g. 'expression', 'proposition', 'sense', 'content', 'object', 'state of affairs', 'consciousness', 'presentation', 'judgement' and 'truth', concepts that belong to the very form of systematic knowledge (*LU, Prol.* §67). Phenomenology brings these concepts to 'clarity and distinctness' by grasping their evidential character, which means tracing them back to their 'ultimate sources' (EV, p. 24; Fink, p. 116; 20/1: 280) – the intuitions that underlie them: 'Logical concepts, as valid thought-unities, must have their origin in intuition' (*LU*, Intro. §2, I 168; Hua 19/1: 10). Intuitions (*Anschauungen*), in his terminology, are concrete *experiences* in which what is intended is directly given. Cognitions and 'lived experiences' (*Erlebnisse*) become knowledge when confirmed or illuminated 'through a return to the adequate fulfilling intuition' (*LU*, Intro. §7, I 178, trans. modified; Hua 19/1: 27). Intuition is a kind of 'knowledge by acquaintance', to employ Bertrand Russell's phrase without, however, accepting the 'sensualist' account of exactly what we are acquainted with, or the manner of this acquaintance. To know something is to be able to verify it by tracing it back to some evident experiences that ground it fully. Husserl calls this illuminating experience *Evidenz*, 'evidence' or 'self-evidence'; and this involves the intuitive fulfilment of an empty intention (*LU* VI; Hua 19/2: 540), when the *meant* (*das Gemeinte*) comes into complete correspondence with the *given* (*das Gegebene*; *LU* VI; 19/2: 651). This can be immediate, but more usually is a gradual process, such as Husserl analyses in *LU* VI. As Husserl will clarify in *FTL* evidence is 'self-giving': 'Evidence . . . designates that *performance on the part of intentionality which consists in the giving of something-itself. . . . The primitive mode of the giving of something-itself is perception*' (*FTL* §59, pp. 157–8; Hua 17: 166). Knowledge in the most basic sense is a kind of (not necessarily sensuous) seeing, which is given with evidence and insight (*Einsicht*). Perception is the foundation for all other modes of knowing (24: 8). For Husserl, 'the most perfect "mark" of correctness is evidence' (*LU, Prol.* §6, I 17; Hua 18: 29). Evidence, moreover, is not any kind of psychological feeling, however intense (24: 78),[3] or a kind of mysterious, irrational hunch, but 'immediate becoming aware of truth itself' (*LU, Prol.* §6, I 17, trans. mod.; 18: 29) and one which is not verified by further acts, though of course these may act as subsequent confirmations of the original truth-grasping. Indeed, evidence is achieved only after long, hard endeavours.[4] Husserl insists, for instance, that there is no apodictic final evidence about empirical entities, due to their perspectival and serial mode of givenness.

As Husserl emphasizes, evidence should not be thought of as the preserve of the mathematical or logical domains, as in the statement 'A = A is evident or self-evident'. It is part of the novelty of *LU* that evidence is considered not just as encountered in rarefied disciplines such as mathematics and logic, but as an ongoing, everyday 'production' or 'achievement' (*Leistung*) in all cognitions where the object is given in a satisfactory form, with 'intuitive fullness' (*anschaüliche Fülle*), or as Husserl prefers to say, where the object gives itself. This is most obvious in normal perceptual acts, e.g. acts of seeing, which normally present the object with all the accompanying evidence necessary to warrant a judgement of the form 'I see x'. To get someone else to see the same thing requires drawing their attention to it, nothing more (*ELE* §3, Hua 24: 8). Evidence and givenness are coextensive, Husserl says in *IP* (Hua 2: 73); and in *FTL*: evidence is the 'intentional achievement of self-givenness' (*die intentionale Leistung der Selbstgebung*; *FTL* §59, p. 157; Hua 17: 166). It is not a one-off mystical or psychological experience attached to a single act of consciousness, but is the very functioning of intentionality itself, as it moves from intention to fulfilment. Evidence is a function of givenness (24: 154).

Items of scientific knowledge must be justified by relating them to the concrete intuitions wherein these 'meanings' are encountered as given. This is the meaning of his clarion cry, 'we must go back to the "things themselves"' (*Wir wollen auf die 'Sachen selbst' zurückgehen; LU*, Intro. §2, I 168; Hua 19/1: 10; repeated subsequently in his later works, e.g. *Ideen* I, the 1910/11 *Logos* article and *Krisis*). By going back to the things themselves, Husserl means that we cannot be satisfied with employing concepts whose evidential basis has not been properly clarified by being brought back to their original sources in intuition. Cognitions are to be related back to 'primal sources' (*Urquellen*) in 'giving intuitions' (*Ideen* I §1; 3/1: 7). The 'things themselves', then, are the immediately intuited essential elements of consciousness, viewed not as psychological processes but in terms of their essential natures as 'meaning-intentions' and their interconnected 'meaning-fulfilments', essential structures involved in all understanding (*LU*, Intro. §2, I 168; Hua 19/1: 11). Once these meanings are secured in pure intuition, it will be a straightforward, though undoubtedly difficult, task to 'fix' conceptually all the meanings required in logic, and then all the meanings required by scientific knowledge as such.[5] In one sense the commitment to intuition is a kind of empiricism, in so far as all thoughts must be anchored or 'founded' in concrete experiences (intuitions) that validate them (*Ideen* I §19). However, traditional empiricism has defined the experiential realm too narrowly, focusing solely on natural, physical things. As we shall see, in *LU* VI Husserl broadens the concept of intuition to include non-sensuous formal or 'categorial' intuitions. Immediate seeing, consists not only of sensuous seeing, but is to be understood as original, giving intuition of whatever kind appropriate to the level of cognition involved (*Ideen* I §19).

Husserl maintains that a phenomenological clarification of concepts means precisely gaining 'insight into the essence of the concepts involved' (*LU, Prol.* §67). He acknowledges that bringing concepts to 'ideational intuition' may seem a trivial task, an exercise in 'pettyfogging word-exercises' (*LU, Prol.* §67), but such painstaking clarification is precisely the work of the philosopher. His aim is to grasp *essences*, and hence he needs to defend the very possibility of eidetic intuition. As he puts it in *Ideen* I: 'The truth is that all human beings see "ideas," "essences," and see them, so to speak continuously; they operate with them in their thinking, they also make eidetic judgments – except that from their epistemological standpoint they interpret them away' (*Ideen* I §22, p. 41; Hua 3/1: 41). In order to justify knowledge, the grasp of essence has to be understood, in part by overcoming inherited epistemological prejudices.

## Husserl's Concept of Pure Logic

Rather than imposing his own view of logic at the outset, Husserl begins the *Prolegomena* by recognizing three current approaches – the formal, the metaphysical and the psychological – and endeavouring to see the rationale at work in each of these conceptions. While the psychological was the dominant outlook of the nineteenth century, earlier, Kant had sought to found a pure logic (*Prol.* §3), and, following Bolzano and Lotze, Husserl wants to revive this pure logic as 'theory of science' (*Wissenschaftslehre*), 'the science of the a priori of all sciences' (*APS*, p. 1; 17: 351), the 'pure idea of possible knowledge'.

Pure logic is an a priori analytic science (*Bedeutungslehre* §1, Hua 26: 4) consisting of 'truisms' or 'tautologies' (*Selbstverständlichkeiten*). It is concerned with purely formal concepts, as Husserl writes: 'for me the pure laws of logic are all the ideal laws which have their whole foundation in the "sense", the "essence" or the "content" of the concepts of Truth, Proposition, Object, Property, Relation, Combination, Law, Fact, etc.' (*LU, Prol.* §37, I 82; Hua 18: 129). Anything which violates these laws is simply absurd: 'A proof whose content quarrels with the principles whose truth lies in the sense of truth as such is self-cancelling'. (*LU, Prol.* §37, I 82; Hua 18: 129). Moreover, 'everything that is logical falls under the two correlated categories of meaning and object' (*LU* I §29). Logic is 'an ideal fabric (*Komplexion*) of meanings' (*LU* I §29); 'meanings in the sense of specific unities constitute (*bilden*) the domain of pure logic' (*LU* II, Intro., **I** 238; Hua 19/1: 112). Meanings here stand not for *hic et nunc* contents of experience, but for their timeless and ideal counterparts (*ELE*; 24: §13). Pure logic covers the whole domain of the formal a priori (as opposed to the material a priori domain explained in *LU* III), including mathematics, and may be more accurately described as 'formal ontology' (a phrase not used in the first edition; see EV, p. 28; Fink, p. 121; 20/1: 285).

Husserl sketches a threefold division of logic: logic is a theoretical science, but it is also a *normative science*, as well as being an art, or practical discipline, or 'technology' (*Kunstlehre*). A theoretical science studies pure theoretical truths as such. For example, if one says 'Of two contradictory propositions, one is false and the other is true', this is a purely ideal law. It simply states what holds as an ideal law, with no reference to how one *ought* to think. A *normative* science is concerned to lay down criteria or values to be followed, given that these ideal laws hold. Every pure theoretical law, therefore, has its normative transformation. So, on the basis of the ideal Law of Non-Contradiction, logic, construed as a normative science, will prescribe, for example, that one ought to recognize that of two contradictory propositions, only one can be true. As a normative science, logic holds up an 'Idea' of science that all other sciences should emulate (*LU, Prol.* §11). Logic as a practical discipline is concerned with concrete realization (see *ELE* §9; 24: 27–32). Schopenhauer, for instance, denied that one could be educated to be good, since all moral action depended on innate character. He therefore denied the possibility of morality as a technology, but maintained a view of morality as a normative discipline (*LU, Prol.* §15; see also *ELE* §9; 24: 28).

The prevailing nineteenth-century view (found, e.g., in Brentano) was that logic was a practical discipline, or 'art of reasoning'. Husserl accepts that logic has this practical dimension. Nevertheless, it is always his conviction that it is only with theory that genuine science emerges. His problematic is therefore 'a clarification of the essential aims of a pure logic'. Traditional logic developed haphazardly, and did not realize that the entire set of judgement forms and their interrelations can be set out formally and a priori, beginning with the primitive forms of judgement (apophantic forms) and progressing to the purely formal ontological categories and their laws. Husserl also wants to establish the logic of consequence, which examines the relations of deduction that hold between judgements purely with a view to avoiding non-contradiction, but not yet considering these judgements in terms of truth and falsity. Finally, he wants a logic of truth, which goes beyond what is simply meaningful, to address the conditions for the possibility of truth as such. According to views that Husserl had worked out before 1894, logic is broad enough to include the theory of the possible forms of theory and the corresponding theory of what mathematicians call 'manifolds' (*Mannigfaltigkeiten*; *LU, Prol.* §70). Logic in its highest form, for Husserl, is the a priori study of all possible forms of theory, and includes a pure science of propositions, understood as the meanings of senses of judgements or linguistic statements or sentences. Husserl never abandons this strong sense of logic.

## The Defence of Ideal Objectivities

The major theme of the *Prolegomena* is a strongly realist defence of the supra-temporal, ideal 'being in itself' (*Ansichsein*) of linguistic, semantic and logical entities, understood as unities (*Einheiten*) that can be grasped as identical in different acts of thinking directed to them. Besides 'real' or 'actual' existent things in the world, such as stones, horses and even conscious episodes (temporal slices of thinking), with their causal powers and interactions, there is another domain of objecthood, which contains such 'ideal' (later: 'irreal') objectivities as the 'Pythagorean theorem' or 'the number 4', which must be understood as abstract individuals (unities) of a peculiar kind: 'Anything and everything can be placed under the title "object": it can be an empirical thing, a physical thing or natural process; it can also be an ideal thing, such as the infinite number series, an elliptical function, or again a mathematical formula, a chemical concept, etc., even a meaning, as when we express sentences about sentences' (*ELE* §14; 24: 53, my trans.). Ideal objects, moreover, are *not* psychological entities or internal parts thereof.[6] Husserl credits Bolzano's truths in themselves and Lotze's 'brilliant interpretation of Plato's doctrine of Ideas' with making this intelligible to him (EV, p. 36; Fink, pp. 128–9; 20/1: 297). It amounts to a 'soft' Platonic approach to ideal objects, as stable unities having identity conditions but without existence in space or time. It is 'soft' because Husserl does not naively posit these ideal objects as existing in another realm. In fact, he dismisses Platonic realism regarding universals as a naive ontology that has already been refuted (*LU* II §7). Ideal entities do not dwell in a 'heavenly place' (*topos ouranios*; *LU* I §31); nor are they 'mythical entities suspended between being and non-being'. Science requires that there be such stable unities – the *number 3* must be identical in all sentences or formulae in which it occurs. Similarly, whole sentences form ideal unities, in terms of their ideal meanings and their corresponding ideal states of affairs. Even a false proposition has a supra-temporal ideality, Husserl emphasizes (24: 37). It has an ideal identical meaning-character and a truth-value. Moreover, two judgements may be considered to be the same if the exact same statements, and no others, can be made about or drawn from these judgements, and, in that sense, they have the same 'truth-value' (*Wahrheitswert*; *LU* V §21).

There are countless different kinds of ideal unities – not just mathematical entities, but also, for example, cultural entities. There is only *one* Kreutzer Sonata, despite its many reproductions (*APS*, p. 11; *Hua* 11: 358); there is only *one* word 'lion' in the English language, and so forth (Husserl discusses various levels of generality and types in *EU* §82ff). As he put it in his 1908 *Bedeutungslehre* (see also *Krisis*, p. 357; *Hua* 6: 368), the word *Löwe* occurs only once in the German language; it is a unified, ideal entity, no matter how many times it is repeated in print or is spoken in different accents, with different pitches, etc. (26: 31; see also *APS*, pp. 10–13; 17: 358ff). The domain of objects is, then, far broader than conceived by traditional empiricism: 'An object of knowledge may as readily be what is real (*ein Reales*) as what is ideal (*ein Ideales*), a thing or an event or a species of mathematical relation, a case of being (*ein Sein*) or what ought to be (*ein Seinsollen*)' (*LU*, *Prol.* §62, I 145; *Hua* 18: 231). There are many kinds of objects (or, Husserl's preferred term: 'objectivities'): 'In sober truth, the seven regular solids are, logically speaking, seven objects precisely as the seven sages are: the principle of the parallelogram of forces is as much a single object as the city of Paris' (*LU* I §31, I 231; *Hua* 19/1: 106). These ideal objects can be simple ('triangle', 'object') or complex unities (principle of the parallelogram of forces). A proposition such as 'Three angles of a triangle are equal to two right angles' is an ideal 'singularity', *eine Einzelheit*. As he commented in 1925: 'Such irreal, or as one also says, ideal objects are, in their numerically identical singularity, substrates of true or false judgements just as real things are; conversely "object" in the most universal logical sense means nothing else than anything at all concerning which statements can be made sensefully and in truth' (*Phän. Psych.* §3, p. 15; *Hua* 9: 22).

It is important to distinguish particular, existent things – not just physical things, but also occurrent psychological processes understood as temporal entities – from the sets of ideal meanings (species) which those acts instantiate and also from the objectivities to which those meanings refer. Thus, for example, this actual individual instance or token *red* is, in Husserl's terms, a 'red moment' (*Rotmoment*), which he analyses as a *dependent* (*unselbstständig*) part of the material (spatial) object, which would not exist unless the object did:

> A red object stands before us, but this red object is not the Species Red. Nor does this concrete object contain the Species as a 'psychological' or 'metaphysical' part. The part, the non-independent moment of red (*dies unselbständige Rotmoment*), is, like the concrete whole object, something individual, something here and now, something which arises and van-

ishes with the concrete whole object, and which is *like*, not identical, in different objects. (*LU, Prol.* §39, **I** 85; Hua 18: 135)

But this particular red moment itself founds the *colour* known as 'red', the species *red*, and indeed *colour* itself, the species *colour*. These *species* are *instantiated* in the particular red moment of the object. These *species* are, using the language of the Brentano school, 'objects of a higher order'. They differ from individual, temporal particulars in that they do not change over time; they have strict identity conditions, yet are multiply instantiable. Husserl writes:

> Redness, however, is an ideal unity (*eine ideale Einheit*), in regard to which it is absurd to speak of coming into being or passing away. The part (moment) red is not Redness, but an instance of Redness (*ein Einzelfall von Röte*). And, as universal objects differ from singular ones, so, too, do our acts of apprehending them. We do something wholly different if, looking at an intuited concretum, we refer to its sensed redness, the individual feature it has here and now, and if, on the other hand, we refer to the Species Redness, as when we say that Redness is a Colour. (*LU, Prol.* §39, **I** 86; Hua 18: 135)

Husserl is careful to distinguish between the individual (concrete or ideal), the species and the universal (see 24: §47); there is a difference between an ideal object A understood as a singularity and 'A in general'. Species too are ideal, and are grasped as Husserl put it at that time in an 'act of ideation based on intuition' (*LU, Prol.* §39), but they do not exist in a 'heavenly place' (*topos ouranios*) as Platonists hold; nor do they possess purely psychological or mental existence as the empiricists hold. They are supra-temporal unities and identities. Furthermore, here Husserl distinguishes between individual entities and their parts and moments, and these ideal species and the more complex ideal 'states of affairs' (*Sachverhalte*) and the 'situations' (*Sachlage*) which underlie them. That *the square on the hypotenuse is equal to the sum of the squares on the other two sides of a right-angled triangle* is said to 'obtain' (*bestehen*) as opposed to 'exist'.[7] We grasp these identities in acts of ideation quite distinct from sensory perception, and we are able to express meanings which correspond to those idealities.

Husserl distinguishes between ideal *objects* and ideal *meanings* (*LU* I) – both are ideal entities of different ontological strata. Meanings are universal species, but, at least according to the account in the first edition, they are instantiated in individual acts of meaning (*meinen, bedeuten*). But Husserl makes clear that linguistic unities are different in kind from other abstract objects: 'But the idealities of geometrical words, sentences, theories – considered purely as linguistic structures – are not the idealities that make up what is expressed and brought to validity as truth in geometry; the latter are ideal geometrical objects, states of affairs, etc.' (*Krisis*, p. 357; Hua 6: 368). Meanings are universal objects (*LU* I §32): 'But the meaning in which an object is thought and its object, the species itself, are not one and the same' (*LU* I §33). Meanings are modes of presentation of objects, and they are themselves kinds of objects.[8]

A true theory of science must be able to account for and handle correctly this enormous diversity of objects – something the prevailing nominalist empiricism had utterly failed to do, when it arbitrarily restricted the class of scientific objects to the observables. Husserl, then, is postulating different kinds of objects, not all of which are spatially or temporally located or sensibly graspable. He is attempting to clarify the different kinds of objectivities and their manner of relating to one another and being founded on one another.[9]

## The Denial of the Ideal in Empiricism and Psychologism

The *Prolegomena* mounts a defence of these ideal objects against 'psychologistic empiricism' ('*à la* Mill': 20/1: 286), which, for Husserl, betrays the very essence of science by explaining acts of knowledge in terms of naturally occurring temporal events in the world (*Prol.* §26). Such an empiricism is simply confused. Indeed, 'it is only inconsistency that keeps psychologism alive: to think it out to the end is already to have given it up' (*LU*, *Prol.* §25, I 56; Hua 18: 88). In opposition to psychologism, logic will be shown to be a pure a priori science of ideal meanings independent of psychology. Against psychologistic misreading of ideal entities, Husserl is even willing to allow his account to be termed an *idealism*, in that it recognizes ideal objects as belonging to the possibility of knowledge as such.

From the outset, the logical concern with meaning must be distinguished from the psychological approach:

> The pure logician is not primarily or properly interested in the psychological judgement, i.e., the concrete mental phenomenon, but in the logical judgement, i.e., the identical asserted meaning (*die identische Aussagebedeutung*), which is one over against manifold, descriptively very different judgement-experiences. (*LU*, Intro. §2, I 166, trans. modified; Hua 19/1: 8)

The entire psychological content of judgements in their varied occurrences has nothing to do with the ideal logical content: 'Multiplication of persons and acts does not multiply the propositional meaning (*Satzbedeutung*); the judgement in the ideal logical sense remains single' (*LU* I §31, I 229; Hua 19/1: 105). Logic studies the necessary laws governing the ideal *contents* of expressions, what gets expressed in acts of expressing – in other words, 'senses' (*Sinne*) or 'meanings' (*Bedeutungen*; *ELE* §11; Hua 24: 37), 'propositional contents' or 'thoughts' in Frege's sense. These contents are ideal and unchanging, even though they can be instantiated in diverse acts of thinking: 'There is a single truth, which corresponds to the multitude of individual acts of knowledge having the same content, which is just their ideally identical content' (*LU*, *Prol.* §66b I 151; Hua 19/1: 242).

## Knowing as Subjective Achievement

Although Husserl's discussions (especially in the Third Investigation) do point towards an a priori science of the possible forms of objects in general (*ELE* §16; Hua 24: 60), involving a clarification of pure 'empty' or formal concepts like 'object', 'property', 'relation' and so on, later characterized as *formal ontology* (*Ideen* I §10 and in the second edition of *LU*), nevertheless, in general in *LU*, he is not interested in specifying the multiple kinds of objects, real and possible (in *FTL* he acknowledges that this formal ontology can be carried out entirely separately from philosophical logic). This would require a foray into metaphysics, a topic he puts to one side here. Instead he focuses on another side of knowledge namely, the subjective acts of knowing (*das Erkennen*), cognitive activity or achievement understood in a specific non-psychological sense. Knowledge, as he always insists (not just after his transcendental turn), is an accomplishment of subjectivity; or, to put it another way, objectivity is an accomplishment of subjectivity. His unique insight is that science comprises not just a set of true propositions about a domain of objects; it is also a set of *achievements, accomplishments* or *performances* (*Leistungen*) of knowing subjects, 'a unity of acts of thinking, of thought-dispositions' (*LU*, *Prol.* §62). Every item of knowledge is gained, achieved and preserved in specific acts of judgement (*ELE* §11). Any theory of knowledge must recognize the fundamental contribution of subjectivity without 'psychologizing' it.

Of course, psychologism had in its own way recognized this deep interrelation between logical knowledge and the activity of the mind, but it had completely misconstrued it. As Husserl put it in his Draft Preface (1913):

> The reader of the *Prolegomena* is made a participant in a conflict between two motifs within the logical sphere which are contrasted in radical sharpness: the one is the psychological, the other the purely logical. The two do not come together by accident . . . Somehow they necessarily belong together. But they are to be distinguished, namely in this manner: everything 'purely' logical is an 'in itself,' is an 'ideal,' which includes in

this 'in itself' – in its proper essential content – nothing 'mental,' nothing of acts, of subjects, or even of empirical factual persons of actual reality. (EV, p. 20; Fink, p. 113; 20/1: 276)

Since the Investigations of the second volume do focus on subjectivity, critics could see here only a relapse into psychologism. Years later, however, he characterized the project of *LU* as that of defending the 'sense and legitimacy' (*Sinn und Recht*) of thematizing the subjective in logic (*FTL* §56), now understood as 'transcendental logic'. In fact, for Husserl, logic remains a science in *naïveté* if it does not tackle this subjective dimension, which above all, as he came to realize, is the problem of exploring the modes of experiencing (or evidencing, understood as the direct givenness of the object) in which objectivities are revealed (*FTL* §60). This exploration of the dimensions of givenness of objectivity to subjectivity he names *phenomenology*.

## The Psychologistic Threat

Psychologism is interpreted narrowly in *LU* as the denial of such ideal objectivities (for his broadening sense of psychologism, see *FTL* §65). In a 'psychologically obsessed age' (*Prol.* §28) the predominant tendency had been to explain science in terms of one particular positive science: namely, psychology. John Stuart Mill, for example, defined logic as 'the science of the operations of the understanding, which are subservient to the estimation of evidence'.[10] F. A. Lange, a neo-Kantian, could construe the Law of Non-Contradiction as a condition of possible experience of the human organism (see *Prol.* §28). Even the early Husserl, as he himself ruefully acknowledged in his Foreword to *LU*, had naively assumed that psychology – as the basic science of the mental – could ground logic; but he came to realize that it had no insight into the 'logical unity of the thought-content' (*die logische Einheit des Denkinhaltes*; *LU* I 2; Hua 18: 6). Psychologism is obviously a very seductive move for the logician. However, for Husserl, it leads to conceptual absurdities, to relativism (*Prol.* §38) and hence to scepticism.

In fact, for Husserl the idea of logic as a science cannot be formed inductively from existing scientific methods and practices; rather, its essence must be extrapolated from the goal or *telos* of science as such: logic must light the way for what he would later call the most profound 'self-knowledge of knowledge' (*APS*, p. 7; 17: 355). In its earliest beginnings in ancient Greek thought, logic had to assert the validity of knowledge over against sceptical and sophistic questioning (see *LU*, *Prol.* §13; and *APS*, p. 3; 17: 352). The great breakthrough of Greek rationality was first to consider seriously the challenge of *scepticism* and then to establish the ideal of scientific knowledge immune from such sceptical attack. As Husserl writes later in *Erste Philosophie* (1923–4): 'The first philosophy of the Greeks, which was naively directed at the exterior world, suffered a sudden arrest of its development under the influence of the scepticism of the Sophists. The ideas of reason in all its fundamental forms appeared to be devalued under the effect of the Sophistic arguments' (*EP* I; Hua 7: 8, my trans.). For Husserl, the Socratic–Platonic breakthrough was the recognition that the true concept of knowledge emerges only once scepticism has been overcome. Indeed, Husserl always credits Plato (rather than Aristotle) with inventing logic as a radical reflection on the essence of genuine knowledge. However, in the current age, psychologism – a literally absurd theory – has allowed scepticism to re-enter the edifice of knowledge and thereby endanger it.

The tradition stemming from Bolzano and Lotze, on the other hand, following on from scholasticism, had clearly distinguished between the thinking process and the thought or proposition expressed in that process. Lotze's student Frege, too, had repudiated psychologism in various works,[11] as a 'psychological falsification of logic'. Other German neo-Kantians, including Hermann Cohen, Windelband, Heinrich Rickert and Paul Natorp, also opposed psychologism, on the grounds that logic dealt with 'validity' (*Geltung, Gültigkeit*) rather than 'facticity' (*Faktizität*). Indeed, Natorp was a personal influence on Husserl in this respect. In Germany at that time, however, Husserl and Frege emerged as the strongest opponents of psychologism, and, since Frege's work was then largely in obscurity, it was Husserl's *Prolegomena* that produced the strongest counterblast.[12]

In making the case for pure logic, Husserl sharply distinguishes between *psychological* and *logical* laws. Psychology is a factual, empirical science of consciousness, and its so-called psychological laws (e.g. the 'law' of association of ideas) are merely inductions from experience (*LU*, *Prol.* §21; Hua 18: 72), limited by *ceteris paribus* clauses, expressible only as probabilities, at best mere approximations to the ideal laws. The laws of logic, on the other hand, are exact, universal and ideal. They are entirely independent of the causes that govern the processes of human thinking. Logic is an a priori science making no assumptions about the existence or nature of mental states; it knows nothing of actual presentations or judgements (*LU*, *Prol.* §23), or the 'facticities of mental life' (18: 81).

The most blatant confusion between psychology and logic relates to the interpretation of the Law of Non-Contradiction when it is formulated as a rule of reasoning, or even as a factual limitation on human conceptualizing: i.e. that we cannot posit a proposition and its negation as both true at the same time. Mill, for instance, interpreted this law as a generalization from human experience: we cannot enter-tain together a belief and its contradictory. Truly understood, the Law of Non-Contradiction states solely that a proposition and its negation cannot both be true, and makes no reference to what is actually, sub-jectively thinkable. Thus Husserl states the principle as: of two propo-sitions where one affirms what the other denies, the one is true and the other false (*ELE* §30; Hua 24: 145). This law is simply not about what humans or other consciousnesses (angels or gods) can entertain or affirm together. It refers to an a priori truth.

Husserl criticizes certain neo-Kantian interpretations of logic as having been seduced by a psychologizing tendency, in that they under-stand logic as a set of a priori psychological structures that every human possesses. Indeed, Husserl thinks that Kant himself was guilty of treating his transcendental psychology precisely as an account of structures factually possessed by the human species. Neo-Kantians, such as Friedrich A. Lange, tried to claim a kind of 'double status' for logical laws: on the one hand, they are *natural laws* determining actual reasoning; on the other hand, they are *normative laws* (*Prol.* §28). For Husserl, however, the laws governing the two domains are radically different in kind. Natural laws are generalizations, whereas logical laws are ideal and exact.

Husserl goes on to a general repudiation of psychologism, which, for him, turns out to be a kind of *relativism* and *subjectivism* (*LU, Prol.* §§34–8), and hence collapses into 'absurdity' (*Widersinn*). Psychologism can lead to a subjectivism that may be either individualist or specific in form. Protagorean relativism ('Man is the measure of all things') is one possible consequence of psychologism, whereby truth is relative to human nature, whether to each individual or to the species as a whole. Treating the logical laws as describing the thinking of human beings as such leads to a kind of 'species relativism' (*der spezifische Relativismus*) or what he calls 'anthropologism' (*Anthropologismus*; *LU, Prol.* §36), a kind of subjectivism that extends to the whole human species. Anthro-pologism maintains that truth is relative to the human species, and hence, without humans, there would be no truth. Kant's account of knowledge was anthropologistic in this sense, and Husserl accuses him of misunderstanding the subjective domain as if it were something natural, and hence of construing the a priori as if it were an essential part of the human species (*Prol.* §38). But Husserl maintains that this is a contradiction; 'there is no truth' would then be true. Truth as such does not depend on any facts, including facts of human nature. The Law of Non-Contradiction is not merely a law governing the species *Homo sapiens*. If there were no minds to think them, the logical laws would still hold, though as ideal possibilities unfulfilled in actuality (*Prol.* §39, p. 149; Hua 18: 135–6).

## The Six Investigations of *LU* Volume Two

Husserl first announces his methodology of phenomenology in the introduction to the second volume, although this account is far from systematic. Throughout the work, he adverts frequently to the 'phenomenological situation', 'phenomenological fact' (*LU* VI §8), 'phenomenological description' and 'phenomenological knowledge' (*LU* V §22), but he says little about how phenomenology is to be practised, other than that it involves (a) an avoidance of presuppositions, and (b) the tracing of concepts back to concrete intuitions that validate them. Phenomenology is to lead to a sphere of direct intuition (24: 219). Indeed, he says later that it was not until four years after *LU* that he arrived at 'an explicit but even then imperfect self-consciousness of its method' (*Krisis* §70, p. 243; Hua 6: 246), a method he describes as 'specifically philosophical' (*IP*, p. 19; Hua 2: 23). This consciousness of method coincides with his 'discovery' of the *epoché* and reduction around 1905, which set phenomenology off from descriptive psychology and moved it in an explicitly transcendental and anti-naturalist direction. In this version, phenomenology proceeds in pure 'immanence', with all existential and transcendent assumptions put to one side.

It strikes many readers (including early reviewers such as Natorp) – indeed Husserl was always somewhat defensive on this score – that the orientation of the second volume appears to be at odds with the *Prolegomena*. Whereas the *Prolegomena* offered an austere view of logic as a science of ideal, self-identical meanings independent of human minds, and refuted psychologism at considerable length, the second volume explored acts of meaning in a most dynamic sense, understood as subjective accomplishments that constituted or constructed meanings and objects, and seems then to be slipping back into psychologism (an accusation that Husserl tackles head on in his 1913 Draft Preface and elsewhere, e.g. *FTL* §67). Furthermore, although meanings in themselves are pure ideal entities with invariant structures and necessary relations to other meanings, there is also an undeniable and irreducibly subjective element involved in the attempt to express or understand meaning. Meanings emerge from acts of a signifying consciousness in a manner that needs to be clarified. Husserl sees this as doing justice to what he frequently calls the essential 'two-sidedness' of meaning and knowledge generally. As he put it in the Foreword to *LU*, he is interested in 'the relationship between the subjectivity of knowing and the objectivity of the content known' (*LU*, Foreword, I 2; Hua 18: 7). This particular way of uniting the subjective and the objective is the essence of phenomenology. Phenomenology is the science that explores the essential *correlation* between subject and object. To a limited extent,

Husserl already speaks of this 'correlation' in *LU* (see *Prol.* §62, e.g., where he speaks of the correlation between objectivity and truth), but he did not make it explicitly thematic until some years later: for example, in his 1906–7 lectures, where he speaks of the 'correlation between meaning and object' (24: 51), or in his Draft Preface (1913), where he speaks of the 'correlation between being and consciousness' (EV, p. 29; Fink, p. 122; see also 20/1: 255).

## The First Logical Investigation

Husserl is often portrayed as a philosopher uninterested in the manner in which language shapes thought. However, the First Investigation explicitly acknowledges that all theoretical knowledge comes to expression in linguistic statements (*Aussagen*). The study of scientific knowledge must begin, then, by examining the structure of such expressive statements (initially from the point of view of the speaker enunciating meaningful expressions). Taking his cue from J. S. Mill in particular, Husserl discriminates between the different functions of signs. Every sign (*Zeichen*) signifies something (*etwas*). Some signs operate purely as 'indications' or 'indices' (*Anzeichen*), and simply point beyond themselves to something else. Such pointing takes the form of establishing some link between two actually existing things: smoke indicating fire, or a fossil as a sign of a mammal, or a flag standing for a nation, a knot in a handkerchief serving as a reminder, where no intrinsic 'meaning' or 'content' links sign and signified, and the 'indicative relation' between sign and the signatum is causal or conventional, that is, external (*LU* I §2; see also Hua 26: §3) Indications as such do not *express* meanings; there is no mediation through the ideal.

Linguistic signs which function as 'expressions' (*Ausdrücke*) are more than indicators; they relate to an object *through* (*mittels*) a *meaning* (indifferently *Bedeutung* or *Sinn*): 'it is part of the notion of an expression to have a meaning' (*LU* I §15, I 201; 19/1: 59). *Expressions*, for Husserl, are primarily linguistic acts, thus excluding gestures and facial expressions that signify only by indicating. They *express* meanings, i.e. instantiate an ideal sense. A senseless, meaningless (*sinnlos, bedeutungslos*) expression is, strictly speaking, not an expression at all. A set of sounds (a chain of noises) becomes a communicable meaning only when endowed or 'animated' with an intention by the speaker (*LU* I §7). In that sense, a parrot cannot generate an expressive act even if it can articulate spoken sounds. As Husserl will later write: an expression intends a 'meaning' (*Meinung*), and 'in speaking we carry out an internal act of meaning (*Meinen*) that melds with the words, as it were, animating them' (*APS*, p. 14; 11: 360). Meaning depends on inner acts of intending-to-mean (*intendieren, meinen*).

With regard to expressions, Husserl distinguishes between the act of expressing or intending to mean, the psychological state of the person expressing, the ideal identical meaning expressed, and the object referred to. He also discusses the manner in which different instances of the same expression differ in physical nature (e.g. the same word spoken in different accents or at different pitches or tones) and the same expressed sense. While the single instances are multiple, the same identical meaning is expressed; hence that meaning must be an ideal unity entirely distinct from the physical sound pattern. This leads Husserl to discuss many different situations in which the same sense can be articulated in different expressions or in which different expressions refer to the same object using different senses – e.g. Napoleon can be referred to as 'the victor of Jena' or as 'the vanquished at Waterloo'. Husserl also considers the case of proper names (e.g. 'Socrates') and what he calls 'essentially occasional expressions' (indexicals such as 'here', 'there' 'now', 'this'), where the object referred to depends on the occasion on which the expression is used.

Expressions, of course, also serve as indications, in that they signal to someone that a meaning is being communicated; that is, they motivate the hearer to believe that the speaker is undergoing a mental process, entertaining a content, and seeking to communicate something (*LU* I §7). Husserl calls this the 'intimating function' (*die kundgebende Funktion*) of the sign: when someone is speaking, I listen to him as someone thinking, recounting, etc. The questioner signals his question in uttering the sentence. Husserl is here drawing on a fairly traditional account of the function of signs, as found in Mill. But these kinds of indication, which are often found 'interwoven' (*verflochten*) with expressive acts, differ sharply in essence from that of expression as such (see Hua 26: §3). Whereas logic is interested only in the expressed meanings and their formal interconnections (e.g. relations of inference), their essential kinds and differences (*LU* I §29), phenomenology focuses on the meaning-intending act.

Husserl rejects the traditional view of expressions that accounts for them solely in terms of the set of physical sounds or written marks, on the one hand, and a sequence of mental states joined associatively to the physical sounds, on the other. This account ignores the role of the ideal sense. Words spoken with intention incarnate sense or meaning. For Husserl, consciousness of sound and of meaning are interwoven into a complex unity, which serves as the basis for further modifications. In his 1908 reprise of this discussion, Husserl said that instead of the inadequate physical word/psychical event distinction, he had begun from Brentano's tripartite distinction between the word as communicating some information, expressing a meaning, and naming an object (Hua 26: §3). Normally, in seeing a word written on a page, we attend to and 'live in' what is signified, not the word itself, although this is clearly founded on seeing the word (26: §4). Our object of interest is not the physical or aural trace of the written word, but what it refers to (26: §4b). I listen to the content of what is being said, as opposed to, for instance, the person's accent. Awareness of the word has the specific function of conducting us to a consideration of the object.

In his 1908 *Bedeutungslehre* (Hua 26) Husserl is clear that consciousness of the word has itself the phenomenological feature both of *self-effacement* and of *conducting beyond* itself to its object. Normally we are not conscious of this 'pointing-away-from-itself' feature of our words. We rather live in what is meant (*APS* p. 15; Hua 11: 361). This holds true even in 'solitary mental life' (*im einsamen Seelenleben*; *LU* I §8), in one's private mental thinking to oneself. Here expressions continue to function as they do in public communication, without, Husserl believes, the intimating function being operative, as it is now unnecessary. One does not need to intimate to oneself.[13] The words (whether a phrase or a sentence) still perform the function of expressing meanings, but the thinker does not have to signal to himself or herself that he or she is having such a thought. Expression of meaning, then, is an essentially different act from 'communication' or 'intimation' (*Kundgabe*), though of course the different functions are usually found together in the one speech act. Moreover, we normally experience an expression as a set of words and meanings which are so unified that they cannot be separated. They have fused into a whole.

In this Investigation Husserl introduces two distinctions crucial for subsequent phenomenological analysis. First, he distinguishes between 'meaning-intentions' (*Bedeutungsintentionen*) and their 'fulfilments' (*LU* I §9). He will return to give a fuller account of these acts and their interrelation in the Sixth Investigation. Second, he distinguishes between an expression's meaning or sense and its objective correlate or 'objectivity' (*Gegenständlichkeit*). An expression '*means* something, and in so far as it means something, it relates to what is objective' (*LU* I §9, I 192, 19/1: 44). They say something *of* something; they *refer* (*bezieht sich auf*; *LU* I §12) to something. 'Meaning' (*Bedeutung*) is distinct from 'reference' (*Beziehung*). This relation between an expression and its meaning is itself an ideal relation, since meanings are ideal, self-identical unities (e.g. 'that the three perpendiculars of a triangle intersect in a point') which do not come into being or pass away, and which may be shared between speakers (*LU* I §11). Moreover, a point Husserl will constantly emphasize, a meaning is entirely different from the mental images that may accompany an act of thinking, and he derides the retarded state of descriptive psychology that has confused the two (*LU* I §17).

Furthermore, different expressions may pick out the same object through different *meanings*; thus 'the vanquished at Waterloo' and the 'victor at Jena' both designate the same entity, Napoleon (*LU* I §12).

Similarly, two expressions with the same meaning can actually refer to different objects: e.g. when I use the word 'horse' to refer to two different horses. Expressions not only refer to, or name, individual objects (like 'Napoleon' or 'a horse') but may also refer to more complex situations or states of affairs (e.g. 'the cat is on the mat'). At this point Husserl maintains that two different propositional senses ('a > b' and 'b < a') actually pick out the same state of affairs (*Sachlage, Sachverhalt; LU* I §12).[14] States of affairs are the objective correlates of complex intentional contents. They are ideal complex, non-linguistic unities, the ontological counterparts of propositional contents. States of affairs combine objects with objects or objects with predicates. Indeed, it is a structural feature of states of affairs that any things, including real spatio-temporal objects, can be a part of them. They are said to 'hold' (*bestehen*) or not to hold (24: 150); when they hold, the proposition expressing this state of affairs is said to be true. States of affairs, then, are what they are whether we assert their validity or not (*LU* I §11). In Husserl's terms, a state of affairs is a 'unity of validity' (*Geltungseinheit*). When I believe that it is raining, then I am intending the state of affairs *that it is raining*. Written in that format, states of affairs are often confused with the contents of judgements, or with the contents of sentences. But states of affairs are ontological entities, truth-makers, that which makes sentences true. It is part of their nature that they can be expressed as nominalizations, e.g. the *rose's redness*, the *being red of the rose*, and be the subject of further predications.

Husserl's account of sense and reference, although couched in a somewhat different technical language, is not dissimilar to Frege's, with which he had been familiar since the early 1890s. For both, reference is made *through* an ideal meaning (cf. *LU* I §13). Husserl of course, does not accept Frege's idiosyncratic terminological distinction between *Sinn* and *Bedeutung*, and uses the two interchangeably (*LU* I §15) (at times, as in *Ideen* I §124, he restricts *Bedeutung* to linguistic signification). Frege held the odd view that all true sentences have the same reference: namely, 'the true' (*das Wahre*), whereas for Husserl the references of sentences are states of affairs that they affirm as holding. For Husserl, expressions in so far as they have senses also have intended references, but these intended references may be quite vague and general until they are specified by context, and for some expressions (e.g. 'round square') the reference is incapable of being fulfilled. In general a meaning has a 'range of possible fulfilment' (*LU* I §13). Expressions like 'round square' do not lack meaning; they are not strictly speaking *meaningless*, rather they lack the possibility of referential *fulfilment*. They are absurd or counter-sensical rather than nonsensical. This allows Husserl to claim, in agreement with Meinong, that a *round square* is a different absurdity from a *triangular square*, since their *meanings* differ. 'The present King of France', likewise, is a meaningful expression, which at one time had a genuine object to which it referred.

It is not possible here to discuss Husserl's rich account of sense and reference in relation to earlier theories, such as those of Mill (who discussed *connotation* in his *System of logic*, vol. 1, Bk 1, ch. 2, §5), or indeed to more recent theories of signification. Suffice it to say that Husserl proposed a carefully differentiated account that can be seen as a challenging alternative to the Fregean account that has become current in contemporary philosophy. However, one part of Husserl's discussion deserves mention here. In the First Investigation, Husserl offers a treatment of expressions whose reference varies with the occasion of their use. He calls these 'essentially occasional expressions' (*wesentlich okkasionelle Ausdrücke*; *LU* I §26), and sees their meaning as tied to the circumstances of utterance, unlike mathematical expressions that mean the same thing in every context. These occasional expressions would now be termed 'indexicals' – e.g. personal pronouns, demonstratives, 'I', 'here', 'now', 'this', 'the president' and so on. Thus 'I' picks out whoever is currently saying it. His treatment of these occasional expressions (which he later admitted was still wholly inadequate) is quite general, and includes proper names in an account which runs directly counter to that developed by Mill and later by Russell.[15] Husserl rejects Mill's view that a proper name (e.g. 'Socrates') is merely an unmeaning mark that directly picks out the object it denotes without telling us anything about it (*LU* I §16). Mill has confused expression and indication. Proper names, for Husserl, are fully expressions, and have a *sense*. They are not, however, disguised descriptions. A proper name picks out a person or object, and has a meaning or represents some kind of content. Every time we use the name, we refer directly to the person, but we may also have different presentational contents.

## The Second Investigation

The Second Investigation – relatively self-contained and not revised significantly in the second edition – considers various aspects of the formal relations between individual instance and universal. Since 'universal' or 'general' meanings are essential to expression and to communication, *LU* II offers an account of the ideal unity of these species and other kinds of 'general objects' (*allgemeine Gegenstände*) required for logic and knowledge. Husserl is very precise, distinguishing, for instance, between an individual taken as an exemplar and a true universal. This Investigation includes a critique of the traditional empiricist accounts of universals, which see them as mere generalizations from particular instances arrived at through abstraction. The focus is on the ideal unity of the species and the nature of abstraction (as the act through which we *intend* or *mean* the species) developed through the critique of positions in the history of modern philosophy – e.g. Locke, Berkeley, Hume and others (further developed in *EP* I; Hua 7), to 'round off and complete' his own positive conception (*LU* II §6). Against this tradition, he defends an account of the grasping of the ideal through an abstraction (of the universal or species from the particular) against the improper account assumed by empiricist philosophers and psychologists, who have lost themselves in psychological analyses of the abstractive process in terms of its causes and effects (*LU* II §6). No psychological account of identifying likenesses, similarities or equalities in specific instances and then generalizing can account for the full universality of the species (*LU* II §4).[16] When we say 'all A's', we have a presentation of exhaustive universality (*LU* II §26). As Husserl makes clear, empiricist theories of abstraction essentially confuse genetic explanation with conceptual clarification (*LU* II §6).

For Husserl, it is phenomenologically evident that we have a direct awareness of universals, that we simply grasp ideal meanings. All attempts to explain this away are beside the point. The chief error of the psychologizing nominalists is that they simply ignore this perfectly valid act that brings the species into view. This specific act must be acknowledged, irrespective of all empirical accounts of human psychological processes (*LU* II §15):

> If we see that Red is a universal predicate, one associable with many possible subjects, our meaning (*die Meinung*) no longer relates to something whose existence is a real sense (*im realen Sinne*) governed by those natural laws which govern the coming and going of experiences in time. We are not talking of experiences at all, but of the single, self-identical predicate Red. (*LU* II §16, I 265; Hua 19/1: 153)

Universals are genuine objects in the sense that they are strictly self-identical and can be the subject of further predications (*LU* II §2): 'Object and predicable subject are equivalents' (EV, p. 26; Fink, p. 118; 20/1: 282). Meanings are *unities* – 'the principle of the parallelogram of forces is as much a single object as the city of Paris' (*LU* I §31). A meaning can serve as an identical subject of different predications ('the principle of the parallelogram of forces is a law'), or the identical term in different relations (*LU* II §2), and hence it must be an ideal unity.

Husserl rejects the nominalist view that universals are some kind of mental fictions or a *flatus vocis* (*LU* II, §8, I 249; Hua 19/1: 129). Locke's 'psychological hypostatization' of universals treats species or universals as merely having a reality in the human mind. He argues that Mill, who wanted to do away with species altogether in favour of relations between particulars, is forced to assume what he tries to deny, since his classification of relations into *types* reintroduces species on another level. On the other hand, he denied that universals are *in re* (24: 300). He denies that they *exist* in the temporal sense, and here he treats 'reality' or 'existence' as anything which exists in time or has a relation to time: 'for us temporality is a sufficient mark of reality' (*LU* II §8). Husserl's ideal objectivities do not belong to the temporal world; rather, they are trans-temporal or omnitemporal essences, universals, *ideal*. We must acknowledge, therefore, besides temporally located particulars, various levels of higher-order objects – individual and specific universals (e.g. 'the number 2' and 'number'; *LU* II §2), propositional meanings, numbers and so on.[17] For something to count as an object, it is not necessary that it exist in time. Ideal objects exist genuinely (*LU* II §8) and are not contents of the mind. If the predicate 'is an even number' attaches to 'the number 4', then *the number 4* is a genuine object, not a fiction or a *façon de parler*, Husserl says.

As Husserl had already stressed in the *Prolegomena*, the relation between an individual and a universal is the same as the relation between 'this red' and redness in general. 'This red' is an instance of (*ein Einzelfall von*) or moment of 'redness', but *not* an exemplification. *Instantiation* is, for Husserl, a primitive logical relation (*LU* II §1); species are 'tokened' in my individual occurrent acts of thinking. Husserl then focuses on the different ways in which we can intend the species. We can see an individual red object and attend to its *redness*, not to the object as such. The act of seeing the species is *founded* on the act of seeing the individual object. In the direct intuition of the universal – e.g. 'a triangle in general' – the sensuous element at the base of all intuitions is exactly the same as in the case of the intuition 'this triangle'; but the nature of the apprehending act has changed: 'the intuitive foundation being identical, the act character makes all the difference' (*LU* II §10). The act that grasps a species is essentially distinct from the act that grasps an individual (*LU* II §1, **I** 239; Hua 19/1: 113). The species act is a new categorial act of the kind Husserl will discuss in the Sixth Investigation (see *LU* II §1).

Husserl wants to replace the traditional Lockean and Berkeleian account of abstraction as a kind of 'selective attention' (*LU* II §13), whereby one attribute or property is separated off and attended to, with a phenomenologically informed theory of abstraction which acknowledges the identity of the species. For Husserl, the empiricist account presumes that an object is a collection of ideas. But the empiricist conception of an idea is ambiguous (*LU* II §10); it stands both for the representation and for the thing represented, and confuses the sensuous content of a presentation with its ideal meaning. Husserl makes pertinent criticisms of Locke's discussion of the idea of a universal triangle, which is 'neither equilateral, equicrucal or scalenon but all and none of these at once'.[18] Neither selective attention nor a kind of designation of the individual to stand for the universal will count as an adequate account of abstraction. Positively speaking, abstracting is not a separating at all; rather, it is a 'viewing', a 'beholding' of the species as something independently meant and referred to, if not independently existing.

Husserl insists that intending the species is essentially different in kind from intending the individual *qua* individual. In both acts, the same concrete object (*das Konkretum*) is given, with the same sense contents interpreted in exactly the same way (*LU* II §1), but we *mean* 'red' not 'red house', the species not the individual. In the act of individual reference, we intend this thing or property or part of the thing, whereas in the specific act we intend the species as such; that is, we intend not the thing or a property understood in the here and now, but rather the 'content' (*Inhalt*), the 'idea' (*die Idee*), that is 'red' as opposed to the individual 'red-moment' (*LU* II §1). As Husserl adds in the second edition (referring forward to *LU* VI), this specific act is a *founded* act, involving a new 'mode of apprehension' (*Auffassungsweise*), which sets the species before us as a general object. Grasping species is a higher-order act founded on the grasp of a sensuous particular, but different in categorial kind from that grasp of the individual (*LU* II §26). Species are grasped as the dependent contents of certain mental acts. However, in the second edition (1913), Husserl modifies the view that we grasp the species through abstraction, and instead claims that we have an act of *ideation*, an essential intuiting of the species themselves (see *EU* §88). In later writings he drops the term 'ideational abstraction' and prefers to talk simply of intuition: 'seeing an essence is also precisely intuition' (*Ideen* I §3). Husserl will say that he now prefers the term 'originary giving essential intuition' (*originärgebende Wesenserschauung*) to indicate that these essential intuitions are not given purely in acts of theoretical thinking. Individual intuitions can be transmuted into eidetic seeing (3/1: 10).

## The Third Investigation

Strictly speaking, the Third and Fourth Investigations are essays, respectively, in *formal ontology* and *formal grammar*, rather than phenomenology. The Third Investigation – the shortest, most underdeveloped ('small beginnings'; *LU* III §24) and, in Husserl's view, unjustly neglected – is an exercise in part–whole analysis, inherited from Brentano and Stumpf, but now extended beyond the domain of psychical acts and their contents to apply to any objects whatsoever,[19] amounting to a first sketch of 'a pure theory of wholes and parts', a logic of parts and wholes, closely related to both property theory and set theory. The aim is a 'formal ontology' (as Husserl terms it in the second edition; *LU* III, **II** 3; Hua 19/1: 227) of the object in general, in contrast to the various 'material ontologies' that deal with the essences of particular domains of objects (e.g. geometry is a material ontology of shapes; colour and sensation are other material domains; there is a general ontology of nature; and so on; *LU* III §11). This part–whole analysis underpins the analysis of the relations between parts of speech and whole sentences in the Fourth Investigation, and the relation between the meaning of an act and the act itself in the discussion of intentionality in the Fifth. Key contributions of *LU* III include strict definitions of the nature of the a priori and of the relation of *founding* (*Fundierung*; *LU* III §14), that plays a significant role in the description of phenomenological layers: 'If a law of essence means that an A as such cannot exist except in a more comprehensive unity which connects it with an M, we can say that an A *as such requires founding through an* M'. (*LU* III §14 **II** 25; 19/1: 267, trans. modified). In *PA*[20] and again in his 1894 essay, 'Psychological Studies in the Elements of Logic' (*EW*, pp. 139–70; Hua 22: 92–123) Husserl had discussed the formal relations holding between the parts of an object and the whole, a domain governed by 'fixed necessary connections, pure laws' (*LU* III §10) that are a priori and analytic (*LU* III §24). Brentano had spoken of the 'parts' of consciousness and distinguished between 'separable' (*ablösbar*) and 'non-separable' parts (*DP*, p. 15). Parts that can exist separately from one another and from the whole – e.g. the segments of an orange, the head of a horse, and so on – are said to be 'mutually separable' (*DP*, p. 83). Some kinds of parts are inseparable from the whole: for example, 'red' is inseparable from 'colour'; i.e. the concept of red 'contains' or implies the concept of colour, colour is inseparable from extension, and so on. These parts are in fact 'one-sidedly separable' as Brentano will say, because, although I cannot detach colour from extension, I can detach the concept of extension from that of colour. The concept of *extension* survives the removal of the concept of *colour*. Brentano refers to such non-separable parts as merely 'distinctional' (*distinktionelle*) parts (*DP*, p. 16). Brentano and Stumpf had applied this analysis of parts to the relations between sensory acts and their components (the seen colour, heard sound and so on) and to the relations between presentations and judgements. Husserl had some criticisms of Brentano's account of parts and wholes, especially his view that a species is a *part* of the individual – e.g. *colour* is a part of *red* – since he maintains that the species is an ideal entity, and not a real part of the individual.[21]

Stumpf employs the distinction between independent and dependent 'contents' (*Inhalte*) in his account of the relations of psychological acts.[22] According to him, the extension and colour of a surface are 'inseparable' (*unabtrennbar*) parts, since they seem to co-vary. If the extension grows smaller to a vanishing point, the colour seems to alter, also eventually disappearing. Stumpf thought of colour and extension as mutually dependent parts (*LU* III §5, **II** 9; Hua 19/1: 238). Similarly, when listening to two musical notes played together, there is a fusion of the tones. Again, Husserl adapts Stumpf's distinction between *dependent* and *independent* parts (*LU* III II 3; Hua 19/1: 227). For Husserl, a part is defined broadly as anything that can be distinguished in an object, everything which is 'real' in a physical object or which is a '*reell*' part of a psychic act: 'We interpret the word "part" (*Teil*) in the *widest* sense: we may call anything a "part" that can be distinguished "in" an object, or, objectively phrased, that is "present" (*vorhanden*) in it' (*LU* III §2, II 5; Hua 19/1: 231). Normally, one thinks only of separable 'pieces' (*Stücke*) as genuine parts, but Husserl also conceives of all *dependent* elements as parts. Thus, in his discussion of Stumpf's analysis of the relation between *colour* and *extension* (*LU* III §4), both colour and extension are parts of the same colour patch; but colour is founded on extension, whereas extension does not depend on colour. Husserl also distinguishes between *concrete* and *abstract* parts, and sees that abstract parts can be nearer to or farther away from the whole to which they belong. He conceives of concrete parts as 'moments': e.g. this individual red occurrence. A specific instance of a colour 'this red now' is a dependent, concrete part. Developing his discussion of species from the Second Investigation, the *species* Colour is an abstract dependent part of the act of seeing *red*. A dependent part can only be what it is in a larger whole bound up with other parts (*LU* III §10).

Husserl proposes six theorems which attempt to establish the 'laws of essence' or essential relations which govern wholes and parts (*LU* III §14). These laws include for example, the law that: if *a* is dependent part of a whole *W*, then it is also a dependent part of any other whole that has *W* as a part. This allows for parts to play the role of part in larger wholes that contain them. In later writings (e.g. *EU* and *FTL*), Husserl offers a somewhat different analysis, but part–whole analysis always remains a central methodology of his philosophy.

An important feature of this Investigation is its defence of synthetic a priori propositions, inspired by his study of Hume's relations of ideas, Leibniz's truths of reason, and Kant's analytic truths. Husserl distinguishes between formal ontology which studies 'empty', or what Husserl calls 'pure', categorial forms such as Unity, Object, Relation, Plurality, Whole, Part, Number and so on, and material ontologies which have concepts with genuine content (*LU* III §11), e.g. house, tree, sensation, space, etc. On this basis he distinguishes between formal and material a priori. As Husserl says: 'nature with all its thing-like contents certainly also has its *a priori*, whose systematic elaboration and development is still the unperformed task of an ontology of nature' (*LU* III §25, II 43; Hua 19/1: 297). That colour as such depends on extension involves necessity and universality, and hence the proposition expressing it is a priori. On the other hand, it is synthetic, not analytic. This leads Husserl to formulate a new account of analyticity (*LU* III

§12), which, he claims, purifies Kant's account of psychologistic and metaphysical distortions. Formal analytic statements are absolutely universal and contain only formal categories. They are without existential commitment; their truth is independent of their content. They are tautologies, where the terms of the proposition express correlatives (e.g. there cannot be a father without children; no whole without parts, etc.). Synthetic a priori statements, on the other hand, involve contents which are not correlative concepts (e.g. colour and extension). Every material specification of a necessary law is actually a priori synthetic, its necessity based on the essences involved.

## The Fourth Investigation

The Fourth Investigation is a first application of the general theory of wholes and parts, this time applied to the domain of linguistic meaning, in order to explore the possibility of an ideal, 'pure grammar' of meaning, which would lay the basis for logic, including the Law of Non-Contradiction.[23] Just as simple objects can be combined to produce complex objects, simple meanings combine to produce complex meanings. It must be possible to identify the rules of all such possible valid combinations a priori, combinations which produce well-formed expressions as opposed to nonsense. In such a priori syntactical rules, the role of what were traditionally termed *syncategorematic* words ('but', 'and', 'to', 'if' see, e.g., Mill, *A System of Logic*, vol. 1, Bk 1, ch. 2, §2) is crucial. Husserl here applies the terms in their original grammatical and logical senses. These syncategorematic expressions will be parts of the wholes, which are the well-formed expressions. Husserl's grammatical analysis here had an influence on formal grammarians, being acknowledged by Roman Jakobson (1896–1982) in his work on phonemes,[24] and indeed finds echoes in Noam Chomsky's project of universal grammar. In later writings, notably *FTL* and *EU*, Husserl maintained that 'formal grammar' provided the bedrock rules for meaningfulness that made logic possible.

## The Fifth Investigation: Intentional Experiences and their Contents

The Fifth Logical Investigation returns to descriptive psychology with its account of the 'constitution' (*Konstitution*) – in the second edition, the 'phenomenological structure (*Bau*)' – of intentional experiences (*LU* V §22), largely through a critique of ambiguities in Brentano's analysis of conscious acts, their contents and objects. Intentional experiences are treated as complex unities with both real (temporal) and abstract, ideal parts. They are isolable parts of the conscious flow that can *combine* with, be *founded* on, or *modify* other experiences: perceptions can be recalled in memory, judgements can be converted into questions, doubts become convictions, and so on. In the latter part of the Fifth Investigation he addresses what in his second edition he terms a 'cardinal problem of phenomenology': namely, the doctrine of judgement (*LU*, Foreword, **I** 7; Hua 18: 14), crucial for logic, and further treated in the Sixth Investigation as a building block in knowledge.

Husserl struggles to find an adequate way to express the phenomenological structure of experiences. In the first edition, he distinguishes between what he calls '*reelle* or phenomenological' contents and 'intentional' contents (*LU* V §16).[25] The 'phenomenological' contents of the act are all the parts, both concrete and abstract, that can really be identified in it: specifically, its quality and its sensational contents. Thus, to use his own example of a heard sound, the *reellen* parts are the component sound elements *as heard*, not the account of sound waves, ear bones, or indeed any ideal meaning that may be linked with the sound. Intentional experiences, too, have identifiable 'parts'. These internal or *reellen* parts do not include the object intended, which always *transcends* the act irrespective of whether the object intended belongs to the real world or is an ideal objectivity (*LU* V §20). It is important to note that a *reell* part does not necessarily mean actually existent in the usual sense. A fantasy object has *reellen* parts. A *reelles* moment refers to an identifiable element in the immanent temporality of the *Erlebnis*, in contrast to the *irreellen* moments such as the ideal meaning (*Sinn*) of the experience (see Hua 35: 89). The second edition offers a clearer picture (invoking the bracketing of everything empirical) of the difference between the immanent parts of an act and its transcendent object.

Husserl maintains that traditional psychological accounts have confused what he calls the 'intentional essence' (*das intentionale Wesen*) of the *Erlebnis* with various other attendant features. For instance, acts of imagining having the same intentional object imagined in the same way can be said to have the same intentional essence, even if they are presented more or less clearly, more or less vividly, with different accompanying visual imagery, and so on (*LU* V §21). For Husserl, the intentional essence does not exhaust the phenomenological (descriptive psychological) features of the act (*LU* V §21, **II** 123; Hua 19/1: 433), but does include what he calls the *quality* and the *matter* of the act and their specific way of combining. In particular, he will argue that presentation and judgement have different intentional essences, and he will strongly reject the Brentanian view that judgement is composed of a complete act of presentation plus a degree of assent.

Husserl begins this investigation by specifying briefly what he means by 'consciousness'. He finds his first concept of consciousness in psychologists such as Wilhelm Wundt, who understood

consciousness as the flow of real, individual, empirical conscious experiences or 'events' (*Ereignisse*) which interpenetrate and interweave in
the unity of a single consciousness (*LU* V §2). On this account, all acts,
their component parts, whether concrete or abstract, are counted as
part of the content of consciousness (whether or not they are accessed
by a special inner perception). In the second edition, he adds a paragraph (19/1: 357) acknowledging that this approach can be construed
in a purely phenomenological manner, if all reference to existence is
stripped away. In elaborating on this first conception, Husserl specifically discusses the important and often confused distinction between
different kinds of *appearances* (*Erscheinungen*): namely, apprehending
the object and apprehending the experience of some aspect of the object
(e.g. its colour). There must be a distinction between the manifest experience and the object that appears (*das erscheinende Objekt*) in it (*LU* V
§2 II 83; 19/1: 359). Clearly this first concept of consciousness can be
'phenomenologically purified' to yield the deeper notion Husserl
wants to work with. But he does not address this conception further in
the Fifth Investigation.

His second concept of consciousness relates to a more traditional
philosophical characterization, deriving from Descartes and found in
Brentano, of 'inner consciousness' and 'inner perception', which he
acknowledges is more primitive and has priority over the first sense
(*LU* V §6); but he recognizes that Brentano tended to merge these two
concepts together. There is an ambiguity between an adequate, self-
evident perception (one which yields the thing itself) and the more
philosophically problematic notion of an inner perception directed at
an inner conscious experience, and Husserl criticizes Brentano for
failing to distinguish between *adequate* perception and *inner* perception
(he will return to this discussion in the Appendix to the Sixth Investigation). Husserl does recognize that there is an important notion
embedded in the discussion of inner perception: namely, the kind of
self-givenness of *cogito* experiences; and this pushes him in the direction of the pure ego, but his remarks on this ego in the first edition are
confused. Already in the first edition he recognizes that the ego of the
*cogito* cannot be the empirical ego, but he adds in an 'additional note'
(*Zusatz*; 19/1: 376) that discussion of the ego is irrelevant here.

Husserl clearly had some difficulties in untangling the notions of
consciousness. In the second edition he excises a whole section (*LU* V
§7) that had been too Brentanian in tone in that it entertained the possibility of phenomenalism, that things may be no more than bundles
of phenomena. His third concept of consciousness is approached in
terms of intentional experiences, acts that bring objects to notice, and
it is with this concept that he remains for the rest of the Fifth Investigation. But it is not entirely clear how this third category is different
from the phenomenologically purified field of the first characterization

of consciousness. This third version emerges from consideration of the question of how being-an-object can itself be considered by us objectively (*LU* V §8). Husserl is focusing on what he tentatively calls (even in the first edition) the essential correlation between act and object. It is clear that he believes he still has some work to do on disentangling his own account of intentionality and adequate intuition from the traditional account of inner perception. He returns to these themes in the Appendix to the Sixth Investigation.

Husserl rejects the central tenets of Brentano's account, including the attempt to distinguish between 'psychical' and 'physical' phenomena. But he sees (and continues throughout his writings to credit Brentano in this respect) the discovery of intentionality as having independent value (*LU* V §9), although his former teacher's characterization of intentionality is misleading and inadequate, trapped inside the old Cartesian dualism of subject and object and with all the problems inherent in that representationalist account. Husserl carefully differentiates between the many senses of the term 'presentation', as used by Brentano, and offers instead his more general notion of an 'objectifying act'.

Reviving an old logical distinction, Husserl distinguishes between the *matter* and the *quality*, or 'general act-character', of intentional acts (*LU* V §20). Each is to be considered an abstract, one-sided, dependent part of the act. Acts of different quality (judgings, wishings, questionings) may have the same matter. To *ask* 'is there life of Mars?' is to operate on the same content as to *assert* 'there is life on Mars'. Husserl believes that the different grammatical constructions of such expressions offer a clue to their differing act-qualities (now often called 'propositional attitudes'). Moreover, every act-quality can be combined with every objective reference. Not all variation in the mode of reference to the object is attributable to the *act-quality*. Acts of the same quality and the same objective reference may vary by having a different 'intentional essence', which Husserl assigns to the *matter* side of the act. To judge about an *equiangular triangle* and an *equilateral triangle* is to judge about the same (ideal) object (*Gegenstand*) in the same way, but through a different essence or abstractly considered through a different meaning (*Sinn*). Not all our experiences are intentional in the sense of presenting something to our attention. According to Husserl, *sensations* in themselves are not intentional, they are not the object which we intend; rather, they accompany the intentional act and fill it out. Sensations belong to the 'matter' (and are grasped as such only in reflection), whereas the act-quality provides the form of the act.

With an eye to distinctions made by Brentano's followers, especially Kasimir Twardowski, Husserl goes on to develop the differences between the contents of experience and the properties of the mind-transcendent object. When I see an object, I only ever see it from one side, in a certain kind of light, from a certain angle and so on. As I walk around a box for example, I see different 'profiles' or 'adumbrations' (*Abschattungen*) or 'aspects' of the box; yet I know that I am getting glimpses of the same object in the different perceptual acts. The same object – the box itself – is presenting itself to me in different modes. Furthermore, as we shall discuss in the next chapter, it is an a priori law that physical objects are displayed in *Abschattungen*. Husserl's distinction (*LU* V §17) between the *object which is intended* and the particular mode under which it is intended forms the basis for his later distinction between *noesis* and *noema* in *Ideen* I (which I shall discuss in the next chapter). Husserl writes: 'We must distinguish, in relation to the intentional content taken as object of the act, between the object as it is intended (*der Gegenstand, so wie er intendiert ist*) and the object pure and simple, which is intended (*und schlechthin der Gegenstand, welcher intendiert ist*)' (*LU* V §17, **II** 113; Hua 19/1: 414, trans. modified). In other words, to intend the 'German Emperor' and the 'Emperor of Germany' is to intend the same person, but the *mode of intention* is different. Moreover, each intentional act has a *single*, if complex, object. Thus to *mean* the Emperor of Germany is to intend a specific *person*, despite the fact that the expression contains reference to a country (Germany) and a state office (Emperor). When we refer to the *knife on the table*, we refer to a single object: namely, the state of affairs, the *knife-being-on-the-table*, not separately to the knife or the table. Husserl insists on the *unity* of the object of intention, even when the elements or parts of that intention have their own partial acts of intentional reference (*LU* V §18). An intentional object is a unity.

Whereas Brentano recognized only three basic classes of psychical acts (viz. *presentations, judgements,* and what he called '*phenomena of love and hate*', Husserl recognizes myriad forms of intentional structure. Moreover, Brentano's basic a priori law of psychic experiences was that all psychic acts are either presentations or founded on presentations (*LU* V §23). Brentano treats presentations as integral parts of judgements, whereas, for Husserl, a judgement has a new intentional object, *what is judged,* and although this is in a sense 'presented', it is essentially different from what is available in a 'mere' presentation. Judgement is not a presentation *plus* a belief. In the course of *LU* V, Husserl completely reinterprets this 'supposed law' with its 'pretended self-evidence' (*LU* V §32). Taking up Bolzano, Husserl declares that judgements are different *in essence* from presentations. Judgements *assert* something to be the case (*LU* V §33). A judgement *articulates* in a 'many-rayed act' the parts of the situation that a presentation or nominalizing act presents in a 'single-rayed act'. The relation between presentation and judgement is not that of an assent supervening on a presentation in the Brentanian sense: 'Supervenient assent is not an act-quality supervening upon a prior act of mere presentation' (*LU* V §29).

There is a variety of different states between assenting to another's judgement, grasping what it means, pondering it, and actively performing the judgement oneself. These very different states are not all states about the same presentation unless we consider this 'presented' element as an abstract dependent moment of the act. Rather, what happens is presentation passing over into judgement through an act of fulfilment (*LU* V §29). Presentation and judgement are essentially different kinds of acts (*LU* V §37). In fact, *contra* Brentano, 'presentations' do not play a dominant role in knowledge (*LU* V §31); rather, the function of making present is an abstract dependent moment found in all acts. However, this 'presenting' is not a complete and separable act in itself. Husserl rejects an interpretation of 'presentation' as a wholly neutral act underlying other acts of judgement, but he does accept that we can understand that acts are founded on some kind of objectifying act. The role supposedly played by presentations is in fact played by non-independent abstract aspects of the intentional essences of acts (*LU* V §31).

Brentano had challenged the traditional Aristotelian account of judgement as a combining of subject and predicate and had interpreted a judgement, e.g. 'the cat is black', as an asserting or positing of a presentation, 'black cat'. Husserl denies that judgements can be treated as nominal acts, as simply *naming* complex states of affairs (*LU* V §17). We can, of course, transform a judgement into a nominal act by *nominalization*. This is, according to Husserl's eidetic analysis, an a priori essential possibility of judgements, just as geometrical forms have laws of transformation from one to the other (*LU* V §36). So, to the judgement 'the cat is black' corresponds the nominalization 'the cat's being black' which can then function as the basis for further judgements. But this internal relation between judging and nominalizing does not mean that they are essentially the same kind of act. Rather than operating with Brentano's simple and rather naive distinction between the presenting act and the presented content of an intention, or even using the broader notion of a 'nominal act', Husserl suggests that we ought to speak more generally of 'objectivating acts' (*LU* V §37) which include both the nominal and the judgemental act. Husserl thinks that the claim that all acts either are or are founded on objectifying acts is a more accurate reformulation of Brentano's basic law that all psychic acts are either presentations or founded on presentations. Husserl's clarification of the nature of presentation and judgement leads to his discussion of the manner in which these acts find intuitive fulfilment in the Sixth Investigation.

The Fifth Investigation is Husserl's first real contribution to the phenomenology of consciousness, including the beginnings of a phenomenology of perception and of judgement. I shall return to this theme in the next chapter.

# The Sixth Logical Investigation:
## Towards the Phenomenology of Knowledge

The long Sixth Investigation attempts to connect the previous analyses of the act of meaning to the notion of truth through a deeper exploration of the relations between the acts that intend meaning and the various levels of possible fulfilment in different kinds of conscious act: e.g. perceptions, imaginings and acts of what Husserl calls 'signitive intention' (*LU* VI §15), where meanings are handled in a purely symbolic way without intuitive fullness – e.g. when we mention something in its absence. Husserl gives the example of looking out on the street as opposed to describing it to someone who has not seen it. An empty signitive intention merely points to its object, rather than living in its presence (*LU* VI §21). Here Husserl revisits the distinction between meaning-intentions and fulfilments introduced in the First Investigation. He also rejects the 'antiquated' contrast between inner and outer perception (*LU* VI §46 and Appendix). His aim is to account for the nature of the 'consciousness of fulfilment' (*Erfüllungsbewusstsein*) that *is* knowledge. Knowledge simply is *fulfilled intention*, but there are degrees of fulfilment. As Husserl writes in his planned redraft of *LU* VI chapter 1: 'Thus talk of knowledge of an object and filling of a meaning-intention express from different standpoints the same situation' (20/1: 39, my trans.). The overall aim is a 'phenomenology of the varying degrees of knowledge' (*LU* VI Intro., **II** 184; Hua 19/2: 539), carefully discriminating between the many different senses in which something can be realized or fulfilled for us, in acts of perception, imagination, judgements of varying degrees of certainty, and so on. His goal is to clarify the state of certain knowledge and what is structurally implied in it, but he also needs to understand the various 'modalizations' of certainty, from surmise through varying degrees of belief. He wants to capture the whole register of cognitive states relating to knowing. His target is knowledge understood as fulfilment (*LU* VI §16) of an intention. In a sense this involves rethinking the Kantian oppositions of sensibility and understanding, intuition and concept (*LU* VI, **I** 184; Hua 19/2: 538–9).

This inquiry leads Husserl towards a reformulation of the classical definition of truth as *adequatio rei ad intellectus* to express more accurately the givenness of the object as it is meant in a fulfilling intuition.[26] The coincidence between signitive intention and fulfilling intuition *is* truth (*LU* VI §39), e.g. in sensuous perception where the object is experienced as self-given. The ideal of knowledge is complete coincidence (*Deckung*) between intention and fulfilment, but this precisely is an ideal. Intendings can be partial, or can be frustrated, subject to 'disappointment' or 'disillusion' (*Enttäuschung*), or lead to 'conflict'

(*Widerstreit; LU* VI §11). Husserl begins with the simplest cases of 'static' fulfilment (Husserl's own term), e.g. perception of a thing where it is given as it is 'in one blow', and moves to more complex cases of 'dynamic' fulfilment. In the static case we simply have 'being in co-incidence' (*In-Deckung-Sein*; 20/1: 40), consciousness of identity with the object. Mostly, however, we are dealing with partial fulfilment, and here there are many 'gradations' to be found (*LU* VI §24). Husserl always sees the paradigm case of a successful intentional act as an act where the meaning is fulfilled by full 'bodily presence' (*Leibhaftigkeit*) in intuition of the intended object: e.g. when I actually *see* something before my eyes, I have a *fulfilled* intuition (§16). Later, I can reactivate and relive this intuition as a memory, still oriented to the object, but not presented with the same presence or immediacy. In memory or in other forms of 'calling to mind' or 're-presenting' (*Vergegenwärtigung*), we may still have a full intuition of the object, but now no longer with the distinctive bodily presence that characterizes perception. Most forms of intending, however, are 'empty' (*Leermeinen*): e.g. when I merely think about something without having it in perceptual or cate-gorial intuitive grasp (*LU* VI §28). It is 'merely thought' (*bloss gedacht*; 20/1: 38). Empty or 'signitive' intendings, in fact, constitute the largest class of our conscious acts, and, from the beginning of his career, Husserl had been fascinated as to how these kinds of intentions can function as knowledge.

The Sixth Investigation challenges the Kantian assumption that human intuition is limited to sensuousness (*Sinnlichkeit*). Husserl inter-prets intuition and perception in a wider sense than is customary, 'beyond the bounds of sense' (19/2: 540; see *EU* §88). As he had defended in the *Prolegomena* and *LU* II, non-sensory objectivities (e.g. states of affairs) are correlated to a new class of intuitive acts, 'catego-rial intuitions' (*kategoriale Anschauungen*) founded on sensuous acts but with essentially new objects. According to Kant, our experience has two components: a receptive element of sensory intuition and an element of reflective conceptuality (which Kant called 'spontaneity'). Kant explicitly denied that humans had the capacity to *intuit* concepts. Husserl holds against Kant that we do have the capacity to intuit ideal 'categorial' entities, from the 'mixed category' of the concept of colour, to pure categories, at the highest level, logical categories such as unity, plurality and existence. Husserl had already spoken of such categori-ality in *PA* (p. 89; 12: 84). Categorial intuition is a kind of supersensu-ous perception, but it is genuine *perception*.

Husserl begins by examining the relation between concrete percep-tions and perceptual reports ('judgements of perception'). What gives meaning to a 'judgement of perception'? It cannot be the perception itself *tout court*, as I can utter different sentences with different senses or meanings based on the same act of perceiving (*LU* VI §4). Every alteration of my viewing standpoint yields a new percept, but I can express (verbally) the same sense: e.g. 'I see a blackbird'. Furthermore, a listener can *understand* the meaning of what I have just said, without herself enacting the act of perception or indeed re-enacting it in imagination. The listener can understand it as a *report* of my act of perceiving; she can think: 'he says that he sees a blackbird'. The sense of the expression 'I see a blackbird', then, is not carried by the perceptual act alone. There is an 'excess' here. Indeed, the *sense* of the statement can survive the elimination of the act of perception. Yet, at the same time, there must be an 'internal relation' between perception and expressed perceptual report (judgement of perception): 'It remains of course incontestable that, in "judgements of perception", the perception stands in an internal relation (*in einer inneren Beziehung*) to the sense of the statement' (*LU* VI §4, I 196; Hua 19/2: 551, trans. modified). The act of perception somehow anchors the meaning, but does not embody it completely. Husserl will speak of this relation as 'founding'; but, on the other hand, the perception is not 'the true carrier' of meaning. Another act has to be identified besides the act of perceiving and the expressing of the perceptual judgement. Husserl immediately recognizes that he must make a distinction between indefinite and definite expressions, and especially in relation to the stronger role the perception seems to play in indexical acts, e.g., 'this blackbird'. This leads him to revisit his earlier discussion of 'essentially occasional expressions' (*LU* VI §5), recognizing that meaning is not simply instantiated in an act, but that the act has its own specific form of intending wherein the meaning appears with its own mode of givenness which the instantiation model did not handle adequately. I say 'this', and the word has a certain general meaning ('something is being pointed out'). But I say 'this' and point to the piece of paper in front of me, and now 'this' definitely refers to the paper, but not simply by the percept providing the meaning. It is the act of pointing that specifies as it were what 'this' now means.

Having clarified perceptual expressions and indexical expressions, he then moves on to analyse the simplest acts in which concept and intuition come together, e.g. acts of *naming* (§6). I see an inkpot, and both object and word appear at once, albeit along different paths. The perceptual object appears, according to the earlier account, as a stream of sensations unified under a particular act of 'interpretation' (*Auffassung*, *Deutung*, or Interpretation) that gives it its objective sense. At the same time, the word is expressed in a manner in which the name appears to 'lay itself on' (*sich auflegen*) the perceived object. Here another act must be interpolated: namely, an act of *recognition* which bases itself on the perceptual act. Husserl then moves on to 'dynamic' cases in which we begin with an empty intention which is then progressively filled intuitively.

According to Husserl my intuition of a 'state of affairs' (*Sachverhalt*) – e.g. 'I see *that* the paper is white' – involves a complex intuition that something is the case. In a judgement of this kind I intuit *what is going on*, as it were. How is this 'being the case' intuited? Husserl agrees with Kant that being is not a predicate; that is, that the existing situation is not a property of the individual object (the white paper). Saying that something *is* does not give us an intuition of a new property in a manner similar to learning that something is red. But for Husserl this shows that assertion of the category of being does not involve grasping a property or the object itself. Nor does it emerge from reflecting on the act of consciousness, as some had thought; rather, the categorial structure belongs to the ideal structure of the object, to the objectivity as such. Categorial acts yield up the grasp of the pure categorial concepts, 'if . . . then', 'and', 'or' and so on, which have no correlates in the objects of the perceptual acts themselves. For Husserl, moreover, categorial acts are *founded* on, but do not *reduce*, to the sensory acts of perception. There is a 'relation of foundation' between a simple and a categorial intuition. For Husserl, categorial acts grasp states of affairs understood as 'new objects' that show up or are constituted in the very categorial acts themselves. Thus it is not the case that I grasp sensuously the components of the judgement and synthesize them using some kind of subjective rules of the understanding, as Kant suggests; rather, we apprehend the state of affairs of which the non-sensuous categorial elements are necessary constituents.

The Sixth Investigation caused Husserl the most difficulty, and he sought to revise it many times. He worked on revisions in 1913 and in subsequent years (see Hua 20/1). These revisions focus especially on the relation between various forms of signitive and empty intending and their corresponding modes of fulfilment. Husserl discusses the example of our consciousness of the objects in a room once the light has been switched off and we are in darkness. This is still a vague consciousness of the presence of the objects, although the sensuous filling is lacking. Somewhat different again is the conscious awareness of the non-presenting sides of various physical objects before us. This leads Husserl to conclude that 'Each perception is a complex of "full" and "empty" intentional components – the empty are darkly presenting, while the full are fully presenting (*voll präsentierende*)' (Hua 20/1: 242). It is clear that by the Sixth Investigation Husserl had come to think of our streams of experience as continuously confirming the presence and properties of an object. The stability of the object is a function of the harmony of the stream of experiences as it runs off into the indeterminate horizons of the future. In his subsequent work, Husserl turned to focus more specifically on the stream of conscious experiencing that is subjective life.

# 5

## *The Eidetic Phenomenology of Consciousness*

At this point in our narrative, it might be expected that we would proceed to discuss Husserl's next major publication, *Ideen* I (1913), and thence to his later works, e.g. *FTL* (1929), *CM* (1931) and *Krisis* (1936). But this is not what I propose to do. I shall now depart from the linear explication of Husserl's development in order to pursue a more systematic overview of his eidetic phenomenology. There are several reasons for this. First, while *Ideen* I is Husserl's most comprehensive exposition of his phenomenology as a method, it is also hastily written, poorly structured and, in places, quite sketchy. Moreover, in his mature work, Husserl was attempting a systematic exposition of phenomenology from several different points of view, and there is no canonical text offering a complete overview. Rather than concentrate on one text, therefore, I shall attempt a more synthetic account of Husserl's eidetic and transcendental phenomenology, ranging across texts from his later Göttingen and Freiburg years.

A major preoccupation of Husserl's was to develop an eidetic account of 'the wonderful constitution of consciousness' (23: 458), a 'science of pure consciousness' (10: 335), a project that involved the 'uncovering' (*Enthüllung*), 'illuminating' (*Erhellung, Aufhellung*) and 'clarifying' (*Aufklärung, Klarlegung*) of its essential 'forms' (*Gestalten*).[1] His interest in the 'multiplicities of manners of appearing and their intentional structures' (6: 175) began with the description of conscious experiences in *LU* V;[2] but, especially in his notes and lectures, he continued to pursue detailed characterizations of the essences of conscious states and acts – perception, memory, fantasy, the awareness of time, judgement[3] – throughout his career. These intentional descriptions form the backdrop to his later researches into the ego, the 'life-world', and the experience of *worldhood* as such. Here I shall focus on Husserl's account of *individual* conscious life, excluding the dimension of intersubjectivity, which will be discussed in chapter 7 below.

As we have seen, after 1905 Husserl believed that these eidetic structures only came properly into view following the *epoché* · and the phenomenological and transcendental reductions. In fact, however, the main features of his account of a priori pure consciousness did not change fundamentally through his career, although the account became increasingly elaborate and was inserted into new thematic contexts (e.g. the broader horizons of the natural life-world). While he believed that genuine phenomenology requires the *epoché* (understood in an increasingly enlarged sense) and the suspension of the natural attitude, he recognized that eidetic truths continue to hold (albeit in modified fashion) and are translatable 'sentence by sentence' in the new transcendental science of pure consciousness (see 34: 3–4). In other words, the account offered in this chapter of 'consciousness in its pure essentiality' is not one that will be reversed or contradicted by transcendental phenomenology. What distinguishes the *transcendental* from the *eidetic* approach is precisely that the eidetic still operates with 'belief in the world' (*Weltglaube*) and has not made the constitution of the world itself a problem, so is not yet a philosophy of 'ultimate foundations' which explicates just how the phenomenon of world is constituted.

Again, in his account of conscious states, Husserl focused primarily on specifically cognitive rather than emotional states such as anxiety or resentment, domains he left to other phenomenologists such as Scheler and Heidegger. Somewhat surprisingly, given that the will is a central component of consciousness and essential for knowledge, he does not analyse *willing* in detail (except in his lectures on ethics; Hua 28). In fact, he (following Descartes) takes a voluntarist position that treats all mental acts, especially judgings, as exercises of the will. Willing is a kind of *fiat* or 'let it be'.[4] Knowledge begins in a desire, a striving (*er-kennen*), and ends in recognition: 'Every step of cognition is guided by the active impulse of the will to hold onto the known as the same . . . Knowledge is an act of the ego, the goal of the will is the apprehension of the object in the identity of its determinations' (*EU* §47, p. 198; 232). But the will does not receive close attention in his main published works.

It must be borne in mind also that, in publications from *LU* to *CM*, Husserl's approach is predominantly individualist, or 'egological', describing conscious life primarily in the context of the individual self, for which he even invokes Max Stirner's title: 'the individual and his own' (*der Einzige und sein Eigentum*; 35: 94).[5] In *Ideen* I, for instance, he postpones discussion of the ego (*Ideen* I §34; Hua 3/1: 61). But he was always aware that this egological approach abstracts from the more complex domain of intersubjective, communal, social consciousness (the domain of 'social acts', 'we-intentions', etc.), and a comprehensive phenomenology must aim to describe subjective life in its wholeness, including rational, cultural and spiritual forms – an 'eidetics of the spirit' (4: 314). Here, however, I shall focus on the structure of individual conscious life.

## Consciousness as a Complex of *Erlebnisse*

After *LU*, Husserl emphasizes more and more that consciousness must be approached in its 'purity', in pure 'immanence', as a self-enclosed domain with everything contingent and all assumptions drawn from the actual, 'transcendent' world removed: 'consciousness considered in its *"purity"* must be held to be a *self-contained complex of being* (*Seinszusammenhang*), a complex of *absolute being* into which nothing can penetrate and out of which nothing can slip' (*Ideen* I §49, p. 112; Hua 3/1: 93). Consciousness is a unified 'complex' (*Zusammenhang, Komplex*), a seamless living stream involving a web of interrelated emotional and affective states, including desires, feelings, moods and so on. Acts and attitudes are founded on one another, interpenetrate and modify one another. It is not enough, therefore, to isolate the elements, the alphabet or 'ABC' of consciousness with its grammar and syntax. The interlocking interconnection of *Erlebnisse*, with its different layers, or 'strata', that 'interpenetrate or intersaturate' each other (*sie durchdringen sich oder durchtränken sich*; 16: 75), must also be mapped and understood. The 'connections of consciousness' (*Bewusstseins-verknüpfungen*; 7: 252) must be documented and clarified (and, ultimately, justified or validated). Intentional life takes many forms (35: 81), and these have to be identified, described, classified, with their myriad kinds of intentional reference, contents, objects, their 'modes of givenness' and 'modes of validation' (*Geltungsmodi*).

For Husserl, as for William James, consciousness is a constantly flowing stream. It appears as a seamless, streaming present, originating from a single source, and presenting itself as a kind of multiform yet unified whole, which yet can be divided into (abstractly) individual *Erlebnisse*, i.e. individual mental events or processes. An *Erlebnis* or *cogitatio* is to be understood in the widest sense to include any identifiable (distinguishable) but not necessarily independent part of the flow, i.e. an individual act (*Akt*), passive state (*Zustand*) or content (*Gehalt*) of consciousness that is immediately apprehended or 'appears' in conscious awareness, in contradistinction to its location in the spatio-temporal, psychophysical world (see *ELE*; 24: 216). Under the *epoché*, consciousness is considered independently of the existing, physical, causal world, in order to be grasped as an appearance in its own right: 'A *cogitatio*, a being conscious, is every kind of sensing, presenting, perceiving, remembering, expecting, judging, concluding, every kind of feeling, desiring, willing, etc.' (Hua 13: 150, my trans.). The *cogitatio* is chosen by Husserl because it is 'not infected with the problem of transcendence' (10: 346).

My psychic stream is immensely complex, with many nodes, even as it progresses seamlessly from moment to moment.[6] How distinct *Erlebnisse* or *cogitationes* are from one another is not entirely clear; Husserl speaks of them as 'waves' in the stream.[7] At times individual experiences can stand out from the flow, as when an explicit idea comes into my head. In general, however, no act is so self-sufficient that it stands entirely on its own. Conscious life also grows in the manner of a snowball, integrating experiences as it moves along. I can become musical, learn to ride a bike, forget all the poems I once knew. All these elements accrue to my life. My individual stream absorbs new acts and habits and collects them into unities in the context of a single 'streaming psychic life': 'However, the psyche is not just streaming life (*strömendes Leben*), but a life in which, inevitably, distinctive new unities, habitualities, are constituted, that is, passive and active abilities, abilities of perception, abilities of feeling, abilities of memory, intellectual abilities, etc.' (*Phän. Psych.*, p. 107; Hua 9: 140). Of course, Husserl maintains the metaphor of a 'stream' is misleading, if one assumes that conscious flow takes place in the objective time of nature. In fact, the temporal flow itself has to be constituted in this 'absolute' consciousness which cannot be objectified (since all objectification and constitution itself are themselves products of this absolute source; 10: 286).

## Intentional Consciousness and the Noetic–Noematic Correlation

Husserl's bedrock assumption, as we have seen, is that psychic states are essentially structured as intentional states. Intentionality – 'having something in mind' (*etwas 'im Sinne' zu haben; Ideen* I §90, p. 217, Hua 3/1: 185) – is 'the fundamental characteristic of all consciousness' (*Ideen* I §90): 'intentionality is the name of the problem encompassed by the whole of phenomenology' (*Ideen* I §146, p. 349; Hua 3/1: 303). Brentano, however, had failed to exploit the true potential of intentional analysis, and remained imprisoned in 'naturalistic prejudices' that prevented him from understanding the role of synthesis and constitution.[8] Intentionality, for Husserl, names the whole set of *correlations* between subjectivity and objectivity. In *Ideen* I §§87–96, in a fundamental rethinking of the components proper to the intentional process, Husserl introduces the correlation of noesis and noema. An enormous amount has been written on the noema, but in fact, aside from *Ideen* I, Husserl does not devote much space to specifying it; nor is it a major concept in his later writings (but see *Krisis* §48), where he prefers to talk quite loosely of the noetic–noematic 'correlation', or the 'noetic–noematic structure' (*Aufbau*; I *CM* §16, p. 40; Hua 1: 78).[9] Frequently, in his mature writings, he prefers to use the quasi-Cartesian language of *cogitatio* and *cogitatum* (*CM* §14; *Krisis* §50).

As we have seen, Husserl had been accused of Platonism for positing a realm of ideal entities including ideal meaning-unities, senses (*Sinne*) or meanings (*Bedeutungen*) entirely independent of the temporally located mental processes with their real components. He had become increasingly dissatisfied with his account of sense or meaning in *LU*, where the 'ideal self-same sense' is considered as the 'identity of a species' instantiated in the multiplicity of different acts (*LU* I §31). Around 1908 he dropped his claim that meanings are species. As he wrote years later to Roman Ingarden (5 April 1918), meanings are ideal objects independent of sentences, but that is not enough to make them species (see also *EU* §64d).[10] With the discovery of the transcendental reduction, he wants to suspend the whole discussion of these acts and their parts in terms of 'real' and 'ideal'. He continues to affirm their timeless identity and 'irreality', but he now thinks of meanings as always related to acts of intending-to-mean.

Husserl had already employed the term 'noetic' (*noetisch*) in the *Prolegomena* (*LU*, *Prol.* §65, I 149; Hua 18: 239n.) to distinguish purely ideal logical conditions of knowledge from psychological ones, and again to contrast the a priori conditions of knowledge from the purely logical conditions; but the term 'noema' does not seem to have emerged until the so-called pencil manuscript of *Ideen* I, dating from October 1912 (3/2: 567). In his 1906/7 lectures, he speaks of the perceived object as the object attended to in its immanence, with all existence positing excluded, so that its very manifestation as a phenomenon is made visible (*ELE* §38; 24: 230–2). The object understood in the 'non-riddle of immanence' (24: 407) is to be grasped as a *phenomenon*, an appearing correlated with an act of meaning-giving (*Sinngebung*). Thus, he writes in 1907, we have perceptual objects, fantasy objects, memory objects, *as they are intended* or *meant* (*so wie sie gemeint sind*; 24: 411). At that time he even considers the possibility of an 'ontic phenomenology' of these appearing objects, although he acknowledges this as problematic (24: 411–12). These peculiar 'ontic' entities stand in relation to appearing acts. These objects are concrete, and a final science of consciousness must be able to give an account of their constitution, including their peculiar form of temporality (24: 419).

In his 1908 *Lectures on the Theory of Meaning* (*Bedeutungslehre*, Hua 26), Husserl revisits the distinction made in *LU* between the object *that is intended* and the object *as it is intended*. He now speaks of the 'phansic' or 'phansiological' element of the act (26: 30; 10: 277n.), the side of the act which accounts for the appearing as such, as opposed to the object that appears understood as belonging to an 'ontic' phenomenological dimension. He now differentiates between the *object as such* and the *object as meant* (26: 36) and between an objectivity as such and a meant categorial objectivity (26: 38). He analyses the judgement of identity 'the victor of Jena is the vanquished at Waterloo'. This is a statement about Napoleon, and each phrase mediates Napoleon in a certain way. In one sense we are directed only to the object, but in reflection we grasp the different modes of presentation of the object. The meanings, the ways in which the object is presented, are different.

*Ideen* I introduces the noema and its noetic correlate. Every experience, no matter how varied, has a noetic side, understood as a 'direction of regard of the pure ego' (3/1: 181). It is responsible for 'sense-giving'. Correlated with this noetic content there is the 'noematic correlate', or 'noematic content', or *noema*. It is also called *Sinn* according to an extension of that concept, and Husserl frequently uses *Sinn* interchangeably with *noema* in this chapter, understood in the sense precisely of inhering intentionally in the *Erlebnis*. But this appearing sense is not what he calls the 'full noema'. In perception, the noema is the perceived as perceived; in remembering, the remembered as remembered (3/1: 182). The object as meant is an *immanent* content of the act (3/1: 182).[11] Furthermore, it is an individual, concrete unity, something that appears.

Husserl offers the example of a perception of a blossoming apple tree. Grasped in the natural attitude, the tree as a thing is something transcendent, out in nature. Under the *epoché* all relation to existence is bracketed, not just the tree but the actual relation holding between tree and the equally real *Erlebnis* is lost, and what is left is the 'pure immanence' of the perceiving as part of the stream of experiences. But even this phenomenologically reduced experience is still an experience of a blossoming apple tree, given *as* transcendent. Under this new transcendental attitude, we have before us the tree as perceived, the tree noema (3/1: 183). It is at this point that Husserl writes:

> The *tree simpliciter*, the physical thing belonging to Nature, is nothing less than this perceived tree as perceived which, as perceptual sense, inseparably belongs to the perception. The tree simpliciter can burn up, be resolved into its chemical elements, etc. But the sense – the sense *of this* perception, something belonging necessarily to its essence – cannot burn up; it has no chemical elements, no forces, no real properties. (*Ideen* I §89, p. 216; Hua 3/1: 184)

The 'sense' cannot burn up and cannot be destroyed (see also *Krisis* §70).[12] On the other hand, the noema, for Husserl, does not survive apart from the act; it is not self-sufficient. Yet it can be compared with other noemata, made the focus of reflective attention, and so on. It is an individual unity, not a universal (like a true sense or meaning).[13]

The question is: what is the nature of this *tree as perceived* or, more generally, of the 'appearing as appearing', as Husserl puts it? The matter is complicated by the fact that in *Ideen* I §89 he acknowledges that psychology too can make use of the noema, since 'the perceptual sense' also belongs to the phenomenologically unreduced perception. The perceived has to be considered as containing nothing more than what actually appears, and precisely in the 'mode of givenness' (*die Gegebenheitsweise*; 3/1: 184) in which it appears. Psychology and phenomenology can both make use of this 'perceived as perceived', but in different ways.[14] This is a very fine-grained concept of intentional sense.

Husserl uses a number of different, sometimes unfortunate, formulations to differentiate aspects of his account of the noema. He speaks of the 'noematic content', the 'noematic correlate', the 'pure noema' (§94), the 'noematic sense' (§90), the 'noematic nucleus', even the 'full noematic correlate' (§94), and 'full noema' (§94). He explicates the full noematic correlate as the sense in the widest extension of that term, and as 'the sense in the how of its mode of givenness' (§94). The 'full noema' is more than this appearance. The appearing sense is a kind of 'core-stratum', but there are more noematic moments (3/1: 185). There are noematic strata, and at times Husserl speaks of the *Sinn* as belonging to the noema. He had earlier referred to the distinction between really inhering components and intentional components. In *Ideen* I §97 he seems to be going against that account and emphasizing the *immanence* of the noema. As in *LU* the sense elements belong to the hyletic stratum or 'matter,' and these together with the 'sense-bestowals' and graspings which interpret these sensory elements also form a really inhering part of the *Erlebnis*.

In a series of influential studies, Dagfinn Føllesdal has argued that Husserl's noema is in fact a generalization of the Fregean notion of a sense (*Sinn*) to all acts of meaning-intending, including non-linguistic perceptual acts.[15] He relies heavily on Husserl's remark in *Ideen* III that 'the noema is nothing but the generalization of the idea of meaning (*Bedeutung*) to the field of all acts', to interpret the noema as an intensional entity, an abstract, ideal, timeless entity distinct from both act and object.[16] Føllesdal (and his followers) interpret the noema as the route which mediates between the act of the perceiving and the object perceived, the 'mode of presentation' of the object within the perceptual act. The noema, accordingly, is to be found in all conscious acts, not just linguistic acts, and hence represents a broadening of Frege's notion of *Sinn*. In order to explicate what is meant here, a brief detour into Frege's philosophy is necessary.

Arising out of worries about the logical status and epistemological significance of certain kinds of identity statements, where there appears to be something new that is learned, whereas identity statements should in fact be analytic and tautological, Frege proposed a now famous distinction between *Sinn* ('sense') and *Bedeutung* (which has been translated variously as 'reference' or 'significance' or 'meaning'). Frege had given an example to help clarify his meaning. He pointed out that one can think of or refer to the planet Venus by thinking of it either as 'the Morning Star' or as 'the Evening Star'. When one thinks of the Evening Star, one is referring to the planet, but under the *mode of presentation* of the star which appears in the evening. Thus it becomes clear that two people can be referring to the same thing without realizing it, because each is grasping it under his or her own *mode of presentation*. Now here the *mode of presentation* (Morning Star, Evening Star) should be taken as having the role of what Frege calls *Sinn* (sense, meaning, connotation), whereas what is being referred to, the planet Venus, is the *Bedeutung* (referent, denotation). Frege gives another example: looking at the moon through a telescope. The moon is the referent, but it is seen *through* the inverted image in the lens of the telescope, and this latter can be understood as the sense. Husserl discussed similar matters in the *LU* I and V, when he examined the situation of different intentional acts which pick out the same object under different descriptions or, as Husserl puts it, employing different 'meanings' (*Bedeutungen*): e.g. Napoleon as the 'victor of Jena' and the 'vanquished at Waterloo' (*LU* I §12). For Husserl, the object never coincides with the meaning: an act of meaning is the 'determinate manner in which we refer to an object' (LU I §13). For him, the noema is the *object as it is intended* in the act; it is the object, not a *Sinn* or 'sense', although it can be turned into a sense or can support a sense.[17] In *Ideen* I he distinguishes the noema and the *Sinn*: 'Each noema has its "content", that is to say, its "sense", and is related through it to its object' (*Ideen* I §129, p. 309; Hua 3/1: 267). Moreover, he also distinguishes the full noema from its various parts. Every noema has a noematic core that allows it to be a noema of the same object (although with a different mode of givenness). Within the core there is a necessary central element which Husserl calls the 'bearer' of noematic peculiarities specifically belonging to the core. This bearer is designated as an 'X', or the thought of an object in general. If the noema did not have this central 'hook', it would not be the thought of an object at all. Each noematic moment has its 'equal to X', but at the same time there must be a synthesis to connect all these together as noemas of the same object. This 'pure X in abstraction from all predicates' (*Ideen* I §131), 'the pure subject of predicating', is simply the idea of something determinable and as yet undetermined.

As in *LU*, Husserl is interested in the kinds of identity syntheses that are achieved in acts of perception. Something guarantees that other perceptual acts can return to what is now the object of my act and identify it as the same object. If I perceive a tree and later *remember* this perceiving of the tree, there must be something that functions to give the sense of the *same* object in both mental acts. For Husserl, this unity is achieved by the common 'noematic nucleus'. We should remember that Husserl is not thinking here of a separate ideal meaning 'tree', for example, but rather is recognizing one mental process somehow attaching itself to and modifying another. Mental processes can adhere to and transform each other a bit like the way Lego blocks fit together. But, of course, some blocks cannot be connected to other blocks (they have different connections, as it were). That which guarantees sameness of content in the act is the nucleus. On the other hand, when perceiving a tree and liking it, the tree is presented in slightly different formats, as it were, and this is the function of other aspects of the noema.

In a note to *Ideen* I §94, Husserl is trying to distinguish between the kind of noematic study which he had developed in *LU* – which he now thinks is too broad to be classified as phenomenological – and the particular kind of phenomenological study which is interested in the noema in its relationship to the conscious act attending to it. If it were, Husserl conjectures, then the mathematician Georg Cantor's work, or indeed the work of ancient geometers, would count as phenomenology in so far as they were interested in mathematical concepts and senses, whereas Husserl wants to make a pure science of the relationship between pure judgings and their judged contents. This is an entirely separate science, which studies the full noema. In other words, logic works with a generalized and purified conception of *Sinn*. For Husserl, the same *Sinn* can be present in noematically different experiences. The noema picks out an individual moment in an individual experience, but it can also be what is common to a number of similar experiences. In fact, in his late writings, Husserl tends to use the shorthand 'noetic–noematic' analysis to explicate the phenomenologist's task of describing what appears independently of the *Weltglaube* that dominates the natural attitude.

Having discussed the nature of the intentional correlation of consciousness with its object, I shall now review the main findings of Husserl's descriptive analysis of pure consciousness. The most important feature of consciousness is its temporal and synthetic, unifying character. As he had emphasized since *PA*, all conscious experiences take place in time, but they also have a consciousness *of* time. Time is the necessary condition for experiences to be grasped as combined and united. Time is part of the 'original material' (*Urmaterial*) of consciousness (24: 291; 10: 276). But, Husserl realized, time is also a sphere of extraordinarily difficult problems (3/1: 162). Brentano, Stumpf, William James, Bergson and the neo-Kantian philosophers had also all been fascinated by the essentially temporal character of conscious life, but Husserl's approach is the most detailed, and he devoted extensive analyses to temporality, which he recognized to be one with the appearing of the ego, and indeed the appearance of the world to the ego as a contingent fact. In fact, consciousness and temporality are so intimately related that Husserl can speak in 1906–7 of time as 'the form of consciousness' and the 'form of every possible objectivity' (24: 273; see also *EU* §38). He even speaks (prior to Heidegger) of the 'self-temporalizing' (*Selbstzeitigung*) of the ego. The deepest truth of consciousness is that its origins lie in an upsurge of temporality itself, raising the question of whether the source of this temporality has to be something non-temporal. Husserl describes it paradoxically as something 'absolute' and 'standing' in a kind of permanent present (*nunc stans*), yet as something flowing.[18] He also speaks of the infinite nature of the temporal horizons (3/1: 163), in that they run off without boundaries at every side.

## The Temporal Character of Consciousness

As we have seen, *LU*'s analysis of *Erlebnisse* is primarily static, albeit with some recognition of the perception of *processes* involving temporal duration (e.g. to see a bird *flying* is to have a perception that extends over a duration). From 1905 onwards, however, partly in reaction to Brentano's account of the 'origin' of time (10: 10ff), and partly because of his growing appreciation of the role of the ego as a unifying centre which is somehow always *present*, Husserl began to take great interest in the temporal character of acts and their objects, and in the temporal 'streaming' of the ego itself. Typically, Husserl distinguishes three layers of temporality. First of all, there is 'objective time', the time experienced in the world (variously referred to as clock time, the time of nature, cosmic time, worldly time; 3/1: 162). Under the reduction, of course, this objective time is bracketed (see 35: 88; 10: 339). Secondly, there is the immanent flow of appearing experiences with their mutually linked inner temporal structures (remembering, anticipating, experiencing as present), which he calls 'pre-empirical time' or 'phenomenological time' (*Ideen* I §81). These are constituted with their 'now phases and retentions' (10: 90). To speak of time-consciousness as such is confusing. Strictly speaking, for the early Husserl at least, time appears only in conjunction with an appearing object. We are not conscious of time as such, but rather of objects *in* time. We next have to distinguish temporal objects and their parts from the inner temporal structure of the *Erlebnisse* that present these objects (the phases of the musical tone have to be distinguished from the temporal phases of the hearing experience, although there is clearly a parallel between them). Husserl always insists that the experiences presenting time are to be distinguished from the objective properties of time, just as appearing space is different from the objective properties of space. Further, these experiences flow from an ego which itself constitutes time in a primordial way and so must be characterized as 'absolute' (10: 77). This third notion of *absolute time-consciousness* is absent from the earliest analyses of time, but it became apparent to Husserl that the ego must in a sense transcend time: 'subjective time becomes constituted in the absolute timeless consciousness, which is not an object' (10: 112). This 'primal consciousness' (*Urbewusstsein*; 10: 292) is the source of time, which in turn is 'the form of all individual objectivity' (10: 296).

*Erlebnisse* are temporal entities in a dual sense. Precisely as occurrences (distinct from their 'contents'), they belong to the natural world (as real as physical objects); they are temporal objects with a beginning, with phases, a duration, an end and so on: 'it belongs to the essence of the perception of a temporal object that it is a temporal object itself' (10: 232). It is a 'flux of becoming (3/1: 149). They also have *internal temporal relations*: 'Every *Erlebnis* has its internal temporality' (*Erlebniszeitlichkeit*; CM §18, p. 41; Hua 1: 79), its 'immanent' temporal structure (9: 310).[19] Furthermore, the unity of the appearing object and the unity of the experience are both features of the experience (10: 80); there is consciousness of both the transcendent unity of the object and the immanent unity of the experience (10: 91). The mental flow is not simple succession in the sense of one thing being replaced by another; there is a certain layering in experience, but it is synthesized into a unity:

> Perception is a process of streaming from phase to phase; in its own way each of the phases is a perception, but these phases are continuously harmonized in the unity of a synthesis, in the unity of a consciousness of one and the same perceptual object that is constituted here originally. In each phase we have primordial impression, retention and protention . . . it is a unity of continual concordance. (*APS* p. 107; 11: 66)

The 'now' turns into the 'just now', and then it is 'a moment ago' and so on.

If experience were purely a set of distinct and separate nows, it could never manifest the temporal phases of the intended object as parts of a unified succession. The apprehension of duration requires duration of the apprehension (10: 192). Consciousness has to 'reach out' beyond its now. It is not easy to articulate the sense of temporality belonging to the experience, as opposed to the temporal dimension of the object itself. None the less, they are as different as the sensation of red is from the red property of a seen object. Similarly, in turning the faces of a die, one can distinguish the temporality of the object phases (the different sides appearing) from the inner temporal duration and phases of the experience itself. As Husserl characterizes it, the object is experienced as a *unity* in the duration, whereas the experience itself is 'filled duration' (10: 273). For Husserl the idea of an empty 'now' or empty time is a nonsense; the flow of time is always filled (24: 271).

The appearing temporal object (to take the simplest case: a musical tone or sequence of tones) is understood as a cluster of sensuous contents apprehended in a certain way, what he calls 'primary impressions' (*Urimpressionen*). Consider a single note, middle C, played on a piano or a violin, held at the same intensity over a period of objective time: 'the tone endures, it is now and now again and again' (10: 275). Even this is an oversimplification; such a note in reality would have fluctuations (10: 86). But the tone can also be considered as an *immanent* object with everything transcendent excluded, as a 'unity in the flow of its time-phases' (10: 272, 275). These 'now' phases are, as it were, adumbrations of the immanent object. By concentrating on the manner of the tone's appearance, rather than the qualities of the tone, the 'wonder of time-consciousness discloses itself' (10: 280).

Husserl wants to see how the grasped sensations (sensuous contents) of the tone are regimented into a temporal experience with different phases. The 'now-moment' (*Jetztmoment*) gradually recedes and is replaced by another 'now-moment' with consciousness of the identical content. Every now has a just before as its limit (*Ideen* I §82). Each now has a 'fringe' of moments around it. The original now is modified into a past-now with the same sensuous content, except now indexed as 'having run off'. In listening to a transcendent temporal object such as a melody, we hear the present set of notes *as present*, but also hear them *as succeeding* an earlier set of notes, and *as about to be supplanted* by further notes or by silence. This 'now' presence is expansive and shared; it can include several items that are co-temporal. But the matter is complex: the present notes are stamped *as* present by having the character of coming after and coming before. There are 'retentions' and 'protentions' involved (10: 84). Moreover, the past notes are not just heard in some sense, but have the character of being *remembered* (10: 79), the character of *having taken place*, of having once been *now*; they also have the character of *leading up* to the present tone; they are continually being stamped with new characteristics. Husserl drew 'time diagrams' to illustrate how such a sensuous appearance endures in consciousness (see 2B §10, 10: 28; §43, 10: 93; and 10: 330–1). Each temporal phase or segment (*Querschnitt*, 'cross-section') seems to involve or is cross-referenced to other temporal phases. This 'retention', of course, is not an actual recurrence of the original now, but is something *intentionally* held in the current now phase: 'A continuity of elapsed tone-phases is intended in the same now' (10: 275). These continue to appear, but in a modified way. There is a reaching back from the present into the immediate past, and that past, Husserl says, is never empty.

For Husserl, retention (or, in earlier terminology, 'primary memory'; Hua 2: 67) is not yet memory in the strong sense ('secondary memory'), although it forms the basis or ground for both passive and active rememberings. Rememberings present objects as whole entities, whereas a retention is a part of a perceptual awareness; it is a 'just past' that is still there in a reduced or modified sense.[20] It still has a kind of 'impressionality'. Similarly, protention is not yet the fully-fledged conscious act of anticipation, but a structural component of any *Erlebnis*. The present 'now' is not a knife-edge, but has a certain thickness. Husserl criticizes Brentano's view that these retentions and protentions are actually 'represented' or 'imagined' experiences, not actually genuine parts of the perceptual process (10: 13). They belong to the class of what have been called 'representations', 'presentifications' or 'presentations' (*Vergegenwärtigungen*) rather than genuine perceptions that Husserl claims involve a making-present of the perceived object in fuller manner.

But what precisely in the sensory apprehension of a musical tone provides the element of 'now-consciousness' such that it is then retained? I hear a whistling sound and then I can become conscious of the now of the experience itself (10: 113). Do the object-sensations (whistling sounds) somehow also carry or add up to a *sensation* of time itself? These sensations or impressions cannot be simply elements appearing now, or they would simply have now-consciousness, rather than temporal becoming (10: 322). Initially, Husserl thought of the sensations or hyletic data as strictly speaking non-temporal, and attributed the temporal element to the apprehension (*Auffassung*) grasping these sensations. As we have seen, he does not want to posit an *act* of sensing, merely the sensory appearances themselves. In regard to temporal consciousness, the schema of apprehension/content (*Auffassung/ Auffassungsinhalt*) became problematic, and in later more speculative discussions Husserl talks of an *Urhyle* as if it itself was the source from which temporality flowed.[21] However, we cannot here enter further into these abstruse speculations. Let us continue our account of the fundamental structures of consciousness by addressing the issue of the distinction between the conscious and unconscious.

## The Unconscious, Drives and Instincts

In his early years Husserl focused primarily, although not exclusively, on *occurrent* conscious *episodes*, rather than what Gilbert Ryle called '*dispositional* states' such as believing oneself to be awake, or a Labour supporter, etc., states that are not always at the forefront of consciousness. He had little to say, at least in print, about emotional states, and even less about the unconscious (he made some references late in life to 'depth psychology', but generally avoided confrontation with Freud, Jung and psychoanalysis generally). In *Krisis* he does make reference to purely *unconscious* intentional acts as part of a discussion of the various modalities of perceptual acts and other acts that co-intend horizons which are more or less unconsciously in the background:

> Yet there are still, over and above these [horizonal intentionalities], 'unconscious' intentionalities, as can be shown by a more detailed analysis. This would be the place for those repressed emotions of love, of humiliation, of *ressentiments*, and the kinds of behaviour unconsciously motivated by them which have been disclosed by recent 'depth psychology' (although this does not mean that we identify ourselves with their theories). These too have their modalities of validity. (*Krisis* §69, p. 237; Hua 6: 240)

From the middle of his Göttingen period, he recognized the complex character of our feeling (*Gefühl*), emotional and affective states (areas explored by Max Scheler), acts of sympathy, love, fellow feeling and so on. These states are not fully acts of the ego; they do not belong to our spontaneity in the full sense (23: 459). He speaks of the 'living and striving' (*Leben und Streben*) of the conscious self, where the element of 'striving' refers to the drives and interests of consciousness. The primary drive of consciousness is towards living itself: 'my being is self-preservation' (15: 367). Especially in the Twenties (e.g. *APS* and *Phenomenological Psychology* lectures), he analysed the complex layerings of our pre-predicative life, our drives, our being affected, our being drawn towards certain things through a kind of 'attraction' or 'allure' (*Reiz*), our 'habits', 'convictions', 'attitudes' and other 'sedimentations'. But besides considering the unacknowledged horizons of *cogitationes* as belonging to the unconscious, Husserl focused more usually on the manner in which our conscious products settle down or sediment into 'convictions' which we hold but which we do not consciously have to frame (the domain usually referred to as 'pre-conscious'). Husserl did acknowledge the role of instinct, drives and what he broadly calls 'interests'.[22] He recognized that something has to awaken consciousness in the first place, that there belongs to it at a most primitive level a passively being affected, but also a kind of reaching out or desire, a focusing of interest, leading to something becoming a 'theme' (*Thema*) for consciousness. Conscious life as he says from *PA* onwards, is a 'life of interests' (*Interessenleben*), beginning with sensuousness and gradually extending outwards and rising to rational desires.

Husserl's starting point for the analysis of consciousness is the *waking* ego. Other forms of consciousness (sleep, dreaming, trance, coma, even death) must be seen as modifications of this primary wakefulness (*Wachheit*).[23] This is entirely consistent with his overall Cartesian approach to consciousness, although, in his mature writings, he did not consider all of consciousness to be as transparent as Cartesianism is supposed to claim (Descartes does think of the ego as, in a fundamental sense, always awake, and there are similar claims to be found in the late Husserl). On the other hand, Husserl has a Fichtean conception of consciousness running up against something 'other' or 'alien', something that does not belong to consciousness and that 'awakens' it. This 'other' can be characterized in different ways, but frequently he describes it simply as *hyle*, matter, stuff (*Stoff*). Consciousness functions only when it is directed towards something other than itself, and that other must be *given* in some way to consciousness. For instance, the senses seem to instinctively seek out their particular objects and are drawn towards them. Husserl recognizes that there are drives or strivings in the senses themselves, and acknowledges that Aristotle was right to say that the eye delights in seeing (MS C 16 IV, p. 306). Touching or reaching for something, or the desire to place something in the mouth or suck it, belong to primal instincts which are correlated with objects which are valued by those instincts.[24] At first instincts and their fulfilments are not fully differentiated, and their contents and objects are only vaguely apprehended. This object is something that is distinct from the feeling or drive towards it.

Husserl's main point is that the appearing world is always already a world appearing to a certain highly structured embodied set of sensuous perceivings. There is a certain 'affectedness' of the senses in a way that predisposes the object to appear in a certain way (see *APS* and *EU*, where the whole domain of 'pre-predicative' experience is explored). He also recognizes that these instinctive drives are layered over and appear in higher forms in more complex conscious acts. But, overall, in his work it is the structure of conscious life that is the primary focus of his attention.[25]

## Anonymous Living versus Phenomenological Reflection

First of all and most of the time, in waking life, conscious processes themselves are in the background of our conscious performances, lived 'anonymously'.[26] Normally, we unreflectively swim with the current of *Erlebnisse* and focus not on the current, but on the synthetically unified objects that appear in it. In Husserl's language: we *thematize* the object, whereas the manifold of flowing experiences is left *unthematic* (*APS*, 26; 11: 369). Of course, through a change of regard or reflection, I can also become aware of

> the complexes (*Komplexe*) of my manifoldly changing *spontaneities* of consciousness . . . complexes of investigative inspecting, of explicating and conceptualizing in descriptions, of comparing and distinguishing, of collecting and counting, of presupposing and inferring: in short, of

theorizing consciousness in its different forms at its different levels. Likewise the multiform acts and states of emotion and of willing: liking and
disliking, being glad and being sorry, desiring and shunning, hoping and
fearing, deciding and acting. All of them . . . are embraced by the one
Cartesian expression, *cogito*. (*Ideen* I §28, pp. 53–4; Hua 3/1: 50)

Husserl always stresses the experience of unconditioned freedom and
spontaneity at the heart of consciousness, evident in my ability to shift
or alter focus, attention or standpoint, the ability to make judgements,
be thus-and-so decided, and so on. I can switch from the straightforward perceptual report, 'I see this house', to the reflective consciousness, 'I am having an experience of seeing this house'. These
*cogitationes* themselves can be made the object or 'theme' of a specific
reflection: 'Every experiencing or other kind of directedness towards
the mental takes place in the mode of reflection' (*Trans. Phen.*, p. 217;
Hua 9: 306). While in the conscious state 'this object is red', I can also
say with a shift of regard, 'I am perceiving this object as red', thereby
embarking on a new *phenomenological* mode of perceiving (35: 69). In
other words, precisely to identify the domain of consciousness as such
is already to have adopted another stance, a reflective or phenomenological stance that brings with it a certain apodicticity, since I cannot
deny that I am undergoing this experience. This turning around of
attention also brings into view the fact that 'first of all and most of the
time' we live in what Husserl terms 'the natural attitude', a universal
attitude that informs us not only in our daily life but in our scientific
practice.

Consciousness is not always explicitly self-aware, but it always has
the ability to become *self-conscious*, to reflect on its own operative role
in experience, on the appearings (without necessarily reflecting on a
*self* or ego as such). However, even in the act of perceiving and object,
I am also aware pre-thematically, pre-reflectively, that I am in fact perceiving. This 'pre-reflective awareness' is an integral part of the original perception; indeed, as the Kantian tradition argued and as Husserl
also accepts, understood as 'apperception', it is a condition of the possibility of any perception (since perception is perspectival and must
recognize itself as such).[27] This pre-reflective awareness can be turned
into explicit reflection. Indeed, it is one of Husserl's eidetic laws that
every mental process is so structured that one can turn one's gaze on
it and identify its components (*Ideen* I §98, p. 241; Hua 3/1: 206). It is
a necessary structural feature of each mental act that it can become the
object – 'target' (*Ideen* I §98) – of another mental act: 'We see that
*the sort of being which belongs to the mental process is such that the
latter is essentially capable of being perceived in reflection*' (*Ideen* I §45,
p. 99; Hua 3/1: 84). The reflexive nature of conscious acts and the
manner in which an act can occupy the object-role in other acts are

important structural features, although normally we are preoccupied with the objects disclosed through the acts and not with the acts themselves.

Reflection has a complex structure. Conscious *Erlebnisse* can be iterated without limit: we can have memories of memories, and so on. Moreover, we not only experience these states passively, but we can freely and wilfully modify them, re-enact them, incorporate them into larger wholes, selectively highlight or isolate them, and otherwise interact with them in myriad ways. We can turn our attention to other parts of the perceptual field, to other parts of our conscious stream. I can initiate a memory, a fantasy and so on. Our acts present themselves to us, but also their objects *as remembered*, as doubted, as presumed. Furthermore, our very reflections on our acts give rise in turn to new kinds of acts with new objects and contents.

Complicating the distinction between pre-reflective and reflective awareness, Husserl operates with another distinction in his mature works between normal everyday reflection, 'mundane reflection', and the kind of special 'egological' transcendental reflection carried out by the phenomenologist (35: 72), based on the application of the *epoché* with its exclusion of all 'position-takings'. Similarly, from *LU* onward, he specifically rejects the Brentanian view that phenomenological reflection is a matter of 'inner perception' as opposed to 'outer perception' (*LU* VI Appendix; *Ideen* I §38). True phenomenological reflection leaves behind the whole naturalistic basis of that distinction, and enters into a reflection not bound by causal psychophysical assumptions. It grasps the manifold of 'subjective modes of appearing of the thing' (9: 147) in their synthetic unity, configurations, and so on, which natural reflection does not notice. For instance, in his 1910/11 lectures, Husserl gives the example of looking at a box of cigars and observing the grain of the box. But I can alter my attention and examine instead the series of phenomenological expectations or motivations: 'Now these phenomenological motivations have their determinate syntax, their form and rule, no matter how arbitrarily the wandering look glides over the object' (Hua 13: 166). To every appearance of the object belongs a 'determinate syntax' of possibilities on the subjective side. This is true not only of perception, but of all mental attitudes. There is a determinate range of possibilities that can be carried out through a priori transformation rules: judgements can turn into questions, expressions of doubt, and so on.

Phenomenological reflection grasps the immanent changing profiles and moments of the *Erlebnisse*, and these include the intended object and even the sense that that object transcends the perceiving act:

> In the case of a perception directed to something immanent, or briefly expressed, *an immanent perception* (so-called 'internal' perception), *perception and perceived* form *essentially an unmediated unity, that of a*

*single concrete cogitatio*. Here the perceiving includes its object in itself in such a manner that it can only be separated from it abstractively (*abstraktiv*), only as an *essentially dependent* [part of it]. (*Ideen* I §38, pp. 79–80, trans. modified; Hua 3/1: 68)

Phenomenological reflection is a reflection of what is 'immanent' in consciousness; yet within this sphere of immanence, transcendences are experienced. I am aware that the house I see does not belong to the stream of my acts of seeing; neither does the particular profile of the house that I am now viewing. The specific kind of 'transcendence in immanence' involved in perception is a matter of particular interest to Husserl from 1907 on. I have consciousness of seeing it from a side, but there are other possible perspectives and so on.

A crucial distinction is between the *inadequate* and essentially *corrigible* mode in which 'transcendent' objects present themselves in straightforward, externally directed consciousness and the *adequate* and *apodictic* mode in which conscious processes themselves appear. Objects are experienced as transcendent to the appearance itself: 'Now the *esse* (for transcendent objects) is in principle to be distinguished from the *percipi*' (*APS*, p. 55; 11: 18). On the other hand, *cogitationes* are as they appear; their *esse* is *percipi*.[28] They are given with 'adequate evidence'. Each *cogito* is grasped with its *cogitatum*, and so long as I remain in the *epoché* with its exclusion of worldly positing, then I am in the domain of apodictic evidence (although this means for Husserl only that every *cogitatio* carries with it absolute evidence of its being (10: 352), but not necessarily that I can legitimately make inferences beyond it, as Descartes himself erroneously was led to do). Every *cogitatio* has its appropriate mode of givenness; thus a memory must be approached according to the kind of givenness appropriate to it (it is not enough to simply 'doubt' the evidence of memory until the nature of that evidence is itself understood). This leads Husserl, on eidetic grounds, to distinguish completely between the domain of *cogitationes* and that of transcendent objects. An *Erlebnis* is not something spatial; the profile of an object is not a part of the object understood as a material thing. Although this may strike readers as a Cartesian presumption, Husserl believes he has reached it intuitively: 'The essence of the *cogitatio* and the essence of *extensio* have in principle, precisely as essences, nothing to do with one another. Naturally, we take *extensio* in the sense of the whole of thingly being' (Hua 13: 143). For instance, he draws the Cartesian conclusion that our own psychic acts are apodictically given, such that their very appearing guarantees their existence: 'Every perception of something immanent necessarily guarantees the existence of its object' (*Ideen* I §46). Similarly, a mental process never appears in profiles: 'a mental process is not adumbrated' (*Ideen* I §42). No *Erlebnis* sets itself out or 'presents itself' (*stellt sich nicht dar*; *Ideen* I §44).[29] As Husserl says many times, it is given as 'absolute'.

At times, especially in his later works (e.g. *CM*) Husserl does acknowledge that we cannot grasp an *Erlebnis* in a *completely* adequate way; but this is due to the fact that it is a temporal process with phases that can be grasped only in the 'now' of a reflection. The inadequacy of our grasp of an *Erlebnis* is completely different in texture from the inadequacy of our grasp of an object in transcendent perception, where adumbrations are essentially involved (*Ideen* I §44). Our self-aware grasp of an *Erlebnis* does not guarantee grasp of its *horizons*, any more than seeing one side of an object gives us in the same way the other sides, which instead appear in a kind of 'horizonal' consciousness. But Husserl never articulated clearly just what about the *cogitatio* and its 'phansiological' character, as he calls it, is given *absolutely* (10: 277n.).[30]

To every psychic being, no matter how inadequately its psychic stream is apprehended (with its past unremembered or whatever), there belongs the possibility of following through to the assertion of the *cogito*: 'I say unqualifiedly that I am, this life is, I am living: *cogito*' (*Ideen* I §46). Furthermore, this carries with it 'the guarantee of its absolute factual being'. In contrast, no experience of a transcendent being, i.e. an entity outside consciousness itself, carries with it an absolute guarantee of its factual existence; at some point some further experience may cancel it, whereas every reflection *eo ipso* guarantees its existence as a reflection. Husserl then accepts the consequences of the Cartesian *cogito ergo sum*. Even if my life is pure fantasy, a 'coherent dream', it is *my* experienced fantasy, and there is absolute evidence of its existence. On the other hand, as we shall see in the next chapter, Husserl believes that even Descartes did not fully appreciate the importance of this absolute evidence of the *cogito*.

Husserl denies that the difference of essence between material being and conscious being entails a metaphysical dualism (indeed, he explicitly rejects this dualism). He sees Descartes' metaphysical dualism as resulting from a certain mathematical-scientific approach to nature that splits off the psychic into a separate realm (*Krisis* §57). Husserl himself abstains from drawing metaphysical conclusions from his eidetic analysis of *cogitatio* and *extensio*. Their different essential character is due to their respective modes of appearance (immanent or transcendent) in consciousness. Even if the entire world were a fiction and did not exist at all, the stream of mental processes would appear entirely different from the world of things. Husserl is articulating a phenomenological dualism, entirely distinct from the actual make-up of both physical and indeed psychophysical being (see 35: 68). In fact, as we see in chapter 6, Husserl believed in precisely one world, and always emphasized the unity of body and consciousness in the one psychophysical being.

Although Husserl rejects metaphysical dualism, his eidetic contrast between material being and the being of consciousness leads him to state – notoriously – that consciousness is 'absolute' and alone is absolute being. By 'absolute' he here means 'non-relative': all other beings are related to consciousness, but consciousness stands on its own. Husserl elaborates: one can even conceive of a consciousness entirely isolated: 'No countersense is implicit in the possibility that every other consciousness, which I posit in empathic experience, is non-existent' (*Ideen* I §46, p. 101; Hua 3/1: 85). It is even speculated that consciousness can continue to exist even with the 'annihilation' of the whole world; i.e. its dissolution into incoherent experience! Husserl frequently reflects on the possible non-being of the whole world (see 35: 71). What he has in mind is the disintegration of the series of experiences which we currently have that give us the harmonious sense of a stable objective world. If our experiences disintegrate, we are left with a sense of collapse, but we still have a sense of the ego itself streaming on.

## Active Consciousness: Position-Taking (*Stellungnahme*), Founding, Modifying, Modalizing, Synthesizing

As we have seen, Husserl's entire account of consciousness rests on the intuition (given in direct experience) that consciousness has an inbuilt freedom to change its stance, *take positions (Stellungen), adopt attitudes,* acquire convictions (*Überzeugungen*), hold values, form habits, shift focus and 'modalize': that is, transform one attitude into another, e.g. move from certainty to doubt, from possibility to probability, from acceptance to questioning, and so on. It can perform higher-order actions such as altering the value of a judgement or even, in the 'transcendental attitude', suspending position-taking altogether. 'Attitude' (*Einstellung*) is one of Husserl's operative concepts; he seems to have thought that it did not need explication, possibly because it can also be found in Brentanian psychology and German empirical psychology of the period (and of course continues in current philosophy of mind).[31] To have an attitude in the broadest sense, for Husserl, is to be directed by or to activate an interest (e.g. as the botanist or chemist is), and thereby to highlight certain features of the world as a world of possible experience. An attitude opens up the world in a way, but also closes it down, operating somewhat like blinkers on a horse, Husserl says (34: 75). Husserl uses the term both for very general attitudes – e.g. the natural attitude, the personalistic attitude, the 'material' attitude (*die sachliche Einstellung*; 15: 646) that views things as material entities, the 'mathematical' attitude, the 'private' asocial attitude (15: 510), the 'abstractive attitude' (6: 242), the attitude of the disinterested spectator, even the 'absolute attitude' – and for specific 'position-takings', e.g. believing, doubting, surmising and so on. We partake of many attitudes, and indeed we are somewhat divided in our attitudes. Our entire life consists in such deliberate or passive-receptive position-takings: 'all life is taking position' (*Alles Leben ist Stellungnehmen*). Holding a value (*Wertnehmen*) is also a kind of position-taking. Furthermore, an attitude need not be rationally formulated or consciously chosen. Indeed, mostly we live in the undetected natural attitude.

The possibility of changing from one attitude to another is an essential characteristic of all acts (*Ideen* II §4, p. 10; Hua 4: 8). 'A change of attitude means nothing else but a thematic transition from one direction of apprehension to another, to which correspond, correlatively, different objectivities' (*Ideen* II §53, p. 221; Hua 4: 210). For Husserl, this represented a tremendous eidetic discovery. Much of the time this shift from one attitude to another is 'involuntary' and escapes notice (*Ideen* II §49, p. 190; Hua 4: 180). In order to bring any attitude into focus, a new special attitude is needed: the attitude which operates under the reduction. The attitude operating in the reduction is actually a purification of the *theoretical attitude*: the attitude of the detached, disinterested, uninvolved spectator, itself a historically late product of human cultural history, emerging with the Greek attitude of wonder, *thaumazein* (see Hua 6: 332). It is a crucial attitude, because it brings the other attitudes into view (whereas the natural attitude explicitly conceals the fact that it is an attitude, fuelling the dogmatism of the sciences that operate in that attitude). The natural attitude is self-concealing; the theoretical attitude, on the other hand, is self-involving and self-aware and ultimately universal, transforming all human *praxis* (6: 334).

Attitudes, like acts, are founded on one another. As Husserl makes clear in *LU* VI, a *judgement* of perception is founded on, but essentially different from, a *perceiving*. Acts can also *modify* other acts. A memory is a modification of an earlier perception. Conscious acts can be combined and connected. They can also be modified and modalized. Belief can turn into questioning, into doubt and so on. Foundation, modification and modalization are all structural features of our experiences, and their operations can produce new and more complex forms of consciousness. Modalized forms of consciousness are modifications of an unmodalized form, and, for Husserl, the basic unmodalized form of consciousness is normal perception, since it is accompanied by a kind of certainty that he characterizes as 'unmodalized' (*Ideen* I §104). Belief is normally fused with perception, and, as he repeatedly claims, etymologically '*Wahr-nehmung*' means 'truly grasping' (10: 273). Truth here is consciousness of the thing with evidence.

The inherent perceptual certainty – not yet articulated belief in the full, active, cognitive sense – can become modified into an uncertainty, a deeming likely, or questionable (*Ideen* I §103) and so on, but in its unmodified form, it has a privileged role as a *'primal belief* or *protodoxa'* (*Ideen* I §104, p. 252; Hua 3/1: 216), a kind of primitive certainty, a naive acceptance of the world: 'Original, normal perception has the primordial mode, "being valid *simpliciter*"; that is what we call straightforward naive certainty. The appearing object is there in uncontested and unbroken certainty' (*APS* p. 75; 11: 36). All other attitudes somehow modalize around this basic attitude. For example, affirmation and negation are considered as doxic modalities by Husserl.

Moreover, modalizations can themselves be combined and iterated; thus one can think of something as 'not impossible'. For every positional act, there is a modification which presents it as a non-positing fantasy act (23: 589). For every position-taking, there is a corresponding neutralization or nullification of position-taking. In *Ideen* I §109, besides these 'doxic modalities' (being possible, certain and so on), Husserl introduces what he regards as a very important but hitherto unrecognized modification: namely, the 'neutrality modification' (*die Neutralitätsmodifikation*), one that he claims is *universal* in that it can modify not just beliefs but all kinds of position-takings. Here he has moved beyond the cognitive states that are paralleled in psychological states (in our 'folk psychology'), positing a new universal form of position-taking. As he sees it, this neutralization is not negation, but a very different kind of annulment: 'It is included in every abstaining-from-producing something, putting-something-out-of-action, "parenthesising-" it, "leaving-something-undecided" and then having-an-"undecided"-something, being "immersed"-in-the-producing, or "merely conceiving" the something produced without "doing anything about it"' (*Ideen* I §109, p. 258; Hua 3/1: 222). Husserl claims that this genus of annulment modification has never before been made the subject of thematic study.[32] Moreover, he wants to consider these modifications independent of all notion of voluntary performing. They are acts in which the 'positing' element has become powerless. It is a *mere-thinking-of*, which has not got to the level of affirming; nor is it a kind of fantasizing, although the neutrality modification runs through both fantasy and the *epoché*. There is no way of having a reiteration of a neutralization, unlike a fantasy (*Ideen* I §112). The neutrality modification is the opposite of all positing, 'the counterpart of all producing', a 'shadowing' (*Schatten*), pointing to the 'radical separation' in consciousness (*eine radicale Scheidung; Ideen* I §114, p. 269; Hua 3/1: 232). For Husserl, the neutrality modification is a wholly unique yet universal structural feature of consciousness, and one that is tremendously important, in that its presence enables the very possibility of philosophical reflection on the life of consciousness. *Epoché*, idle fantasy, etc. are themselves all varieties of neutrality modification. The neutrality modification is a very deep part of consciousness, but, because it makes no claim on truth or validity, it is, according to Husserl, difficult to access.

Another key concept for articulating the nature of consciousness – one with a clear Kantian lineage that Husserl has been exploring since *PA* – is *synthesis* ('the obscure Kantian term'; 35: 86 see also *PA*, 12: 32–3). Following Kant, Husserl maintains that synthesis is 'a mode of combination exclusively peculiar to consciousness' (*CM* §17, p. 39; 1: 77). It is through synthesis that conscious experiences connect together into a *unity*, and that an identical object is grasped in the manifold of appearances. As Husserl writes in his *Introduction to Philosophy* lectures of 1922/3:

> Each individual perception and each phase in the continuity of an ongoing perception has, considered for itself and *in abstracto*, its intentional object. The whole continuity of manifold and changing perceptions is, however, a perception and has an intentional object. And if the perception changes over into a so-called fresh remembering or, better, retention, and then into a clear recollection that is related to the earlier temporal phases of the object, so there runs through all these modes of consciousness in their unity one and the same intentional object. (Hua 35: 87, my trans.)

This consciousness of unity and identity is effectively a higher form of consciousness. It is through synthesis that an ego is formed as a unity in the stream of experiences, and through synthesis that an object remains the same in the sequence of its appearances. Husserl calls this 'synthesis of identification' (*Ideen* I §41), but there are other kinds of syntheses: synthesis of unity, of harmony, of discordance, of determination otherwise, of contradiction (*Ideen* I §138), explicative synthesis, synthesis of 'overlapping' (*Überschiebung*; *EU* §24) and so on. *Identification* is the fundamental form of synthesis (*CM* §18), and the most basic form of this synthesis occurs in our internal consciousness of time. As we have seen, for Husserl, 'The *fundamental form* of this universal synthesis, the form that makes all other syntheses of consciousness possible, is the all-embracing *consciousness of internal time*' (*CM* §18, p. 32; 1: 81). The greatest synthesis and the most mysterious is how the *world* as such emerges in consciousness. This, for Husserl, is the 'greatest enigma' (6: 184).

## The Role of Sensation (*Empfindung*) and Interpretation (*Auffassung*)

Before going on to discuss perception as the most fundamental mental state, it is necessary to remind ourselves of Husserl's account of what is primarily given in experience. As we have seen, he rejects the representationalist view that what we see are our own sensations. He rejects all talk of *sense-data* (*Sinnesdaten*) or 'data of sensation' (*Empfindungsdaten*), a conception he regards as a false theoretical construct produced by the 'psychological attitude' (35: 82). In *LU*, as we have seen, he maintained that sensations and sensational complexes are not in themselves intentional; they are merely 'material' features of our intentional experience. They are really immanent, component parts of experiences, but they are not intentional objects as such (*LU* V §10; 19/1: 382–3; *Ideen* I §36): 'I see the box, not my own sensations' (*LU* V §14). Nor is there any 'act' of sensation; there is no positing. Sensations are simply 'given' as parts of the *Erlebnis*; they do not become perceptual objects in themselves: 'Any piece of a sensed visual field, full as it is of visual contents, is an experience containing many part-contents, which are neither referred to, nor intentionally objective, in the whole' (*LU* V §10, II 97; Hua 19/1: 383). Sensations are part of the experienced content of the mental act; they are 'lived-through' rather than perceived. When I undergo an *Erlebnis*, it simply presents itself as having a certain sensational colouring, its sensory 'filling' (*Fülle*).

Although sensations are not the objects of sense, they do play a vital role in perception. They provide a 'matter', which is *formed* by a certain kind of interpretative 'grasp' or 'interpretation' (*Auffassung*; *LU* VI §26; *Deutung, Interpretation*),[33] to yield an object with a particular sense or meaning. Sensations on their own, understood as raw givens, cannot by themselves play the role of constituting objectivities. But they are somehow 'bearers of interpretation'. This suggests that there are only acts that *take up* and *interpret* sensational complexes (*LU* VI, Appendix, II 358 n. 6; 19/2: 774n.). It is an 'animating apprehension' (*DR* §46, p. 136; 16: 160), enlivening 'dead matter' (*DR* §15, p. 39; 16: 46). In other words, meaning is not given by the sensations themselves, but by the *interpretative* act grasping them. In *APS* he warns that the 'interpretation' (*Deutung*) of sensory matter is not like reading a *meaning* off signs; there is some kind of point beyond experienced (11: 17). This is the reason why the same sensational cluster can underlie and ground different intentional experiences: I see a woman; I see a mannequin, based on the same sensations. Similarly, different acts on the basis of different sensations can perceive the same object, e.g. the tone of a violin heard nearer or further away (*LU* V §14).

Furthermore – and this will become important in his account of perception – there is always a *gap* between the sensed content and the more overweaning perception of the thing. This 'excess' (*Überschuss*) or *plus ultra* of perception is provided by the apprehension. In so far as these contents are apprehended so as to present the object, Husserl calls them 'presentational contents' (*darstellende Inhalte*; *DR* §15; see also *Ideen* I §36). Thus, in seeing a white paper, the presentational sensation of white is a 'bearer' of intentionality, of an interpretation, but not in itself consciousness of an object. Husserl recognizes a difference between *presenting* and *presented* sensations. The former sensations motivate our attribution of certain sensory features to a body. When I touch a smooth and cold surface, I have certain sensations in my fingers, but I attend through these sensations to the property of smoothness and coolness of the surface. It takes a reflective turn of regard to notice the sensations in my fingers. The sensations seem to be double-sided, as it were. They present themselves as belonging to the fingers, but also as 'presenting' or exhibiting (*darstellen*) properties of the object. Certain sensations are routinely attributed to external things, while others are located in us in a certain way. I may become aware that the *room* feels cold, or I may be aware that *I* feel cold in the room. There are feelings (like my sense of where parts of my body are) that seem to be constituted *internally*, so to speak, while others definitely come marked with transcendence. A person suffering from tinnitus may hear the irritating ringing noise as 'inside her head' and can separate it from persistent ringing noises that appear to be transcendent.

In *Ideen* I §85, Husserl introduces the Greek term *hyle* to refer to this sensible, temporally flowing matter of experience, in contrast to the intentional *morphé*, or form. This concept of a sensory base, or 'stuff', of experience is very complicated and is retained in Husserl's later writings. He characterizes it as a sensuous 'residuum'. The same sensory contents can be the basis for motivating different acts of apprehension; similarly, the same act of perceiving (I see John) can be based on different sensory clusters (I see his face; I see the back of his head). There is an even more complex relation involved in cases like memory, where my current perceptual *hyle* may not be implicated at all in the remembered presentation. Husserl developed a very complex account of the sensational component in perceptual experience, but his main theme is that sensation is not perception. His later works stresses the highly ordered and regulated nature of the streams of sensations; there is a continuous harmony, a constancy of experience (11: 108, 263). In fact, Husserl always experienced a certain problem about the nature of the given, in the sense of the 'primordial matter' (*Urhyle*), the 'primordially given' (*das Urgebene*), the ultimate residuum in experience. His researches into time-consciousness seem to have convinced him that his matter/apprehension account of sensations cannot be correct; otherwise he would have to posit some kind of time sensations for our sensory experience of entities in temporal situations.[34] But in late works the *Urhyle* stands for whatever is given to the ego such that the ego itself awakes to itself in the midst of this givenness. Let us turn now from sensation to perception.

## The Foundation of Consciousness: Perception as Originary Evidence

In all his writings, published and unpublished (from *LU*, through *DR* (1907) and *Ideen* I, on to *APS*, *Phän. Psych.*, *Krisis* and *EU*), Husserl develops a remarkably consistent account of the phenomenology of perception (*Wahrnehmung*). Perception, of course, is not his final goal, which is the nature of judgement: 'The interest in perception . . . is only the forestage (*Vorstufe*) of the interest in cognition in the proper sense' (*EU* §47, pp. 197–8; 232). Nevertheless, perception is the important first step on the road to cognition. Perception is the most 'original experience' (*Urerlebnis*; 3/1: 149), where 'the originary' is first encountered.

He gives extensive, detailed descriptions of just *what* we see and *how* we see it (involving the nature of the act of perception, the nature of the perceived object, the role of temporal awareness in the structure of perceiving, the dynamic nature of perceptual content, the nature of the indeterminate accompanying horizons, and so on). What changes, as we have seen, is his account of the role of sensations, his appreciation of the 'excess' involved in perception over and above what is actually given, and his increasing concern with the complex background assumptions involved in perceiving the horizoning 'world of things' (*Dingwelt*; 13: 27 n. 1) or 'thing environment' (*Dingumgebung*; *DR*; 16: 80).

In his 1907 *Ding and Raum* (*Thing and Space*) lectures (Hua 16), and subsequently in *Ideen* II, Husserl gives some of his most detailed analyses of the perception of a physical, spatial object, peeling away the various layers of constitution involved in the grasp of independent physical objects. In part, his aim is to show that the kind of sense object discussed by classic empiricism is actually self-contradictory, i.e. involves a 'counter-sense' (*Widersinn*). He begins with the most elementary kind of seeing – monocular vision (*DR* §48). He describes the presented visual field as a 'two-dimensional manifold which is in itself congruent, continuous, utterly coherent, finite, and indeed, bounded; it has a margin beyond which there is nothing' (*DR*, p. 140; 16: 165–6). It is not yet a surface in objective space.

Husserl likes to speak of a thing just as it is seen as a 'visual thing', a 'sight-thing' (*Sehding*; see also *Ideen* I §42). In this lecture course, and later in *Ideen* II, he introduces the notion of the 'phantom': that is, the sensible schema of the thing, the thing merely as it is grasped in outline by the senses, as opposed to the 'full' thing of normal consciousness (see *DR* §23, p. 65; 16: 78), where some kind of supposition of existence, some position-taking, is involved. The phantom is the object as encountered in a single sensory experience, e.g. just what is seen or touched, abstracted from the causal nexus. Thus, when we see a rainbow in the sky, we do not experience its causal power, but if we see a rock drop on the ground and make an indentation in the soft earth, we do experience its causal power. Thus the functional properties are also stripped away in the phantom; e.g. strictly speaking, a child does not see a *hammer* in the sense of identifying its function.[35] The various constitutional layers have both their specific attitudes and their specific objects.

In general, Husserl begins with direct, immediate perceptual experience, which for him, as for Aristotle and for modern empiricism, forms the basis of all consciousness and offers a paradigm of the kind of consciousness in which intention finds immediate fulfilment, in which the activity of perceiving receives constant confirmation and collaboration, and hence is a paradigm of the evidence, the 'primordial form' (*Urmodus*) of intuitiveness (*APS* p. 10; 11: 68).[36] Perception is, according to *Ideen* I, the 'ultimate source which feeds the general positing (*Generalthesis*) of the world effected by me in the natural attitude, the source which therefore makes it possible that I consciously find a factually existing world of physical things confronting me and that I ascribe to myself a body in that world'. It is 'a primal experience (*Urerfahrung*) from which all other experiencing acts derive a major part of their grounding force' (*Ideen* I §39, pp. 82–3; Hua 3/1: 70). As he writes in 1918: 'This originality of giving is fulfilled in perception' (*Diese Ursprünglichkeit des Gebens vollsieht sich in der Wahrnehmung*; 23: 500). What is given is the 'bodily original actuality' (*leibhaftige Urwirklichkeit*) that is called presence (23: 500).

According to Husserl, perceptual consciousness gives us our first sense of objectivity, physicality and the experience of 'world':

> [Perception] is what originally makes us conscious of the realities existing for us and "the" world as actually existing. To cancel out all such perception, actual and possible, means, for our total life of consciousness, to cancel out the world as objective sense and as reality accepted by us; it means to remove from all thought about the world (in every signification of this word) the original basis of sense and legitimacy. (*EP* I; Hua 7: 251; my trans.)

As Husserl already made clear in the Sixth Investigation, an act of perceiving (*Wahrnehmung*) has the sense that an object is given immediately in a straightforward, direct way. Perception involves an immediate fulfilment through the 'synthesis of thingly identity' (*Synthesis der sachlichen Identität*; *LU* VI §14). In perception, the object is given as really there in the now. Moreover, the perceptual object is given as transcending the perception itself: 'With an absolutely unconditional universality and necessity it is the case that a physical thing cannot be given in any possible perception, in any possible consciousness, as something inherently immanent' (*Ideen* I §42, p. 89; Hua 3/1: 76). Perception has the promise of offering us the thing itself as it actually is, 'it itself' (*es selbst*). It belongs to the very sense of a perceptual act to be the self-appearance of the object (*LU* VI §14; 19/2: 589; *ELE*, 24: 310). The object is given 'itself' (*selbst*), 'there' (*da*), 'in the flesh', 'bodily' (*leibhaftig*), *in propria persona*, in the actual temporal present, in its own being and 'being so' (*Sosein*; 7: 251): 'the object stands in perception as there in the flesh, it stands, to speak still more precisely, as actually present, as self-given there in the current now' (*DR* §4, p. 12; 16: 14). 'Presence in the flesh' is, then, a necessary structural feature of any perception whatsoever (*DR* §5), at least while it is actually happening, in the 'now' phase of the experience.[37] Clearly, presence here has both a spatial and temporal meaning. This undeniable emphasis on the temporal now of perception does not rule out that certain aspects of the perceived are seen as building on the past and running on into the future. There are elements of conservation and constancy and also of anticipation.

Husserl defines perception thus:

> Perception in itself (*Wahrnehmung in sich*) is perception of a perceived (*eines Wahrgenommenen*); its essence is to bring some object to appearance (*Gegenständliches zur Erscheinung*) and to posit what appears as something believed (*glaubensmässig*): as an existing actuality. (*DR* §40, p. 118; 16: 141)

As he puts it in *CM*, 'External perception too (though not apodictic) is an experiencing of something itself, the physical thing itself: "it itself is there"' (*CM* I §9, p. 23; 1: 62). Three main traits of perceiving emerge here:

1  Perception presents an object directly, immediately and currently.
2  The act of perceiving involves unquestioned acceptance, belief.
3  Perception is always adumbrated.

On the noetic side, the perceiving is straightforward and has the character of certainty; on the noematic or object side, the object perceived has the character of existing actuality (*CM* II §15). Perception is characterized by a primitive kind of *certainty*, which does not get 'thematized', does not come specifically to awareness, unless there is some possibility of conflict or challenge built into the perceptual act. In this sense, perception is a kind of *passive* and *receptive* state (*APS* p. 105; 11: 64). The belief involved in perception is passive *doxa*. It is not yet a positional act of ego. Nevertheless, Husserl insists: 'One speaks of a believing inherent in perceiving' (*APS*, p. 66; 11: 28); 'every normal perception is a consciousness of validity' (*APS*, p. 71; Hua 11: 33); 'the primordial mode is certainty but in the form of the most straightforward certainty' (*APS* p. 76; 11: 37).

Furthermore, perception is essentially 'simple' or 'straightforward' (*schlicht*; *LU* VI §46) for Husserl; this means that there is no reasoning or inference or 'articulation' involved: 'What this means is this: that the object is also an *immediately given object* in the sense that, as *this object*

*perceived with this definite objective content,* it is not *constituted* in relational, connective, or otherwise articulated acts, acts founded on other
acts which bring other acts to perception' (*LU* VI §46, **II** 282; Hua 19/2:
674). We receive the object 'in one blow' (*in einem Schlage*), as he puts
it. It delivers the object at once, in the modes of actuality and certainty.
But, of course, it does not mean that we see only a single object at a
time. We can have simple straightforward perception of complex
objects, e.g. a pile of books. Husserl believes that we see individual
'things' (*Dinge*), but also their 'characteristics' (*Markmale*), 'properties'
(*Eigenschaften*), 'determinations' (*Bestimmtheiten*), their independent
parts and dependent moments (*Momente*) in Husserl's language. We
also see things in 'process' (*Vorgang*): the falling (*das Fallen*) of leaves,
the crashing of a car, and so on (see 3/1: 71). We see static things and
relations, dynamic events and processes:

> 'I see' means in every case: I see something, specifically either a thing
> (*ein Ding*), or a property (*ein Eigenschaft*) of a thing, or a thingly process
> (*Vorgang*). I see a house, I see the flying up (*das Auffliegen*) of a bird, I see
> the falling down (*das Fallen*) of the leaves. I also see the color of the house,
> the structure (*die Gestalt*) and size of the leaf, the form of its motion, and
> so on. (*DR* §2, p. 8; 16: 9–10)

He conclude: 'Seeing and hearing relate in the first instance . . . to what
is bodily' (16: 10).

As we saw in the last chapter, Husserl, however, expands the term
'perceive' to apply beyond the sensory domain: 'In the widest sense
even universal states of affairs can be said to be perceived ("seen",
"beheld with evidence"). In the narrower sense, perception terminates
upon individual, and so upon temporal being' (*LU* VI §45, **II**, 281; 19/2:
673). Indeed, he is insistent that we use the term 'seeing' for our immediate supersensuous cognition of ideal and categorial objectivities also
(e.g. *EU* §88).

It is important to recognize that this experience of the object as there
before us should not be construed as meaning that we have the sense
of the object *causing* the experience. We do not perceive the object
*causing* the perceptual act. But perception does communicate the essential 'otherness' (*Anderssein*) of the object, its non-immanence in consciousness: that is, its *transcendence*. It belongs to the very nature of our
perception of physical objects that they are grasped as other than the
way in which they appear and as existing 'in themselves' independent
of their appearance (13: 113). Moreover, in perception of external
objects, we know that the sides, etc., can actually be visited in further
perceptions, which give us confirmations of the original experience.
Perceptual adumbrations have their own kind of fulfilment (*Erfüllung*)
or confirmation, and in this process genuine knowledge is acquired

(*APS*, p. 44; 11: 8), in which aspects perceived at one moment are retained in the following moments. Moreover, it confirms for us the sense of transcendence whereby an abiding world is on view, at our disposal (*APS*, p. 47; 11: 10), present-at-hand (*vorhanden*).

In *Ideen* I §41 Husserl speaks of the experience of perceiving a table while walking around it. I can shut my eyes and open them again and still have a perception of the table, albeit from a different side or angle. In this sense sight is *discontinuous*, whereas touch or bodily sensuous feeling is continuous, and belongs very basically to my own corporeality, without which perception would be impossible. But even in perceiving the uniform colour of a table, this colour is given through a series of perceived shadings or adumbrations. For Husserl, as we have seen, there is of essential necessity a difference to be made between the shifting experience of colour shadings and the 'transcendent' colour of the object: 'The color of the seen physical thing is, of essential necessity, not a really inherent moment (*kein reelles Moment*) of the consciousness of color' (*Ideen* I §41, p. 87; Hua 3/1: 74). We experience the colour as a transcendent property of the object; on the other hand, the adumbratings are mental acts, and it would be wrong to treat them as somehow extended entities. Thus the adumbrated shading of a colour is not itself a spatial entity, although the colour is. Similarly, the perspectival appearing of a triangle is not a spatial thing. Similarly, a side is unthinkable by itself (*DR* §16, p. 43; 16: 51).

As Husserl makes clear elsewhere, even if it is the case that the perception is only of one side under one aspect, nevertheless, it is clear that *the whole object* is intended and 'meant' in the act of perceiving:

> Let us begin by noting that the aspect, the perspectival adumbration through which every spatial object invariably appears, only manifests the spatial object from one side. No matter how completely we may perceive a thing, it is never given in perception with the characteristics that qualify it and make it up as a sensible thing from all sides at once. (*APS* §1, p. 39; 11: 3)

Indeed, it takes a reflective shift of attention to realize that what one has in view is precisely a *profile* of the object. Husserl further maintains that what we think of as peculiarities particular to us are actually eidetic insights that belong to the 'Idea' of a physical thing as such. A material thing unveils itself in endless spatial profiles or 'adumbrations' (*Abschattungen* – Husserl also speaks of 'aspects', *Aspekte*). No act of perceiving a physical object can give me all sides at once, or all perspectives. Even God can grasp a physical thing only in profiles (*Ideen* I §149, p. 362; Hua 3/1: 315). Similarly, a material thing also reveals itself in perception in a series of temporal moments. Unrolling in spatial and temporal profiles pertains to the essence of a material thing (*DR*,

16: 66). Husserl frequently calls this a priori law an eidetic law: 'even the most intuitively vivid and rich presentation of a real thing must be in principle one-sided and incomplete' (*LU* IV §3, II S3; 19/1: 307). This in fact becomes one of Husserl's most cited 'eidetic laws', laws that govern the very manner in which any physical object can be accessible to any consciousness whatsoever. Not even God can alter this eidetic truth (*DR* §19, p. 55; 16: 65). According to Husserl, it is neither an accident nor purely a feature of human constitution that a spatial thing can appear only in profiles (*Ideen* I §42). On the other hand – and this becomes something of a Cartesian dogma for Husserl – a mental process does not adumbrate itself, does not appear in profiles (*ein Erlebnis schattet sich nich ab*; *Ideen* I §42, p. 90; Hua 3/1: 77; its *esse* is *percipi*).

Husserl is not entirely clear about the status of the profile or adumbration: is it a real or intentional part of the object, or is it a real or intentional part of the experiencing act, the *Erlebnis*? It seems that the adumbrations are a complicated fusion of both sensations and interpreting grasp. They are interpreted sensations that are projected outside on to the object, as when I have a sensation in my fingers and interpret the surface *as* smooth. The 'smooth' profile is that through which I grasp the thing, but I also grasp it as more than this smoothness, as having other profiles (e.g. I could tap it with my finger and experience 'solidity' instead of smoothness).[38]

Nevertheless, what I perceive is the 'full thing' (*das Vollding*: *APS*, p. 40; 11: 4) and not just its profile. Perception always promises more than it actually supplies: 'External perception is a constant pretension to accomplish something that, by its very nature, it is not in a position to accomplish. Thus, it harbors an essential contradiction, as it were' (*APS*, p. 38; 11: 3). This is precisely the 'excess' or 'transcendence' which is always a structural feature of external perception, as we have seen. In relation to the fact that one profile does duty for the whole object, he speaks of the essential 'inadequacy' (*Inadäquatheit*; EPII; 8: 44) and 'a radical incompleteness' (*DR* §16, p. 44; 16: 51) of perception. We have the sense of a 'more' attaching to the object. Elsewhere he speaks of a *plus ultra* given in the empty horizon: 'Every appearance implies a *plus ultra* in the empty horizons' (*APS*, p. 48; 11: 11), that are determinable by future experience *in infinitum* (24: 341).

As in other forms of cognition, in thing perception, one side is given *genuinely* (*eigentlich*) or *originarily* (*originär*), and we are 'co-conscious' of other sides in an inauthentic, non-originary manner, in a mode of emptiness, which is not complete nullity. Husserl also distinguishes between the whole or 'full thing' (*Vollding*, the object itself) and what is specifically sensed in the integration of the senses – the 'sense thing' (*Sinnending*) or 'phantom' (*Phantom*; *Ideen* II §18, p. 77; Hua 4: 72), the thing specifically as it appears (e.g. the image in the microscope; 4: 36).

We build up our sense of the object itself, the object as part of nature, from the experience of the object as sensed; the sense object is itself constituted by us.

We perceive an object through its profile. But, at the same time, we *apperceive* the absent sides that are somehow prefigured according to the sense or noema of the object perceived (4: 35). Husserl is emphatic that these absent sides are not *inferred* or reached by some cognitive calculation; rather, they are immediately and even sensibly grasped, although in a reduced, even 'empty' mode. The front side carries a *sense* of the whole object that includes 'indications' of these other sides. Husserl distinguishes between what is 'properly' or 'genuinely' (*eigentlich*) or narrowly given in perception (sometimes, e.g. *DR* §5, referring to the proper element as a *Perzeption*) and what is improperly co-intended. We see the front side of a house, but we grasp it as an object having other sides. There can be no 'proper' intuition of an object from all sides (*DR* §16; 16: 52–3). When we see the front side 'properly', we also see the object as having other sides. 'Noetically speaking, perception is a mixture of an actual exhibiting that presents in an intuitive manner what is originally exhibited, and of an empty indicating that refers to possible new perceptions' (*APS*, p. 41; 11: 5). Husserl is aware that the 'presenting sensations' that are grasped in a synthesizing awareness present not just the front side, but somehow also the rear sides. However, he sees a difficulty in saying that the front side is presented by the sensations directly, while the other sides are given 'indirectly (*indirekt*), not by resemblance but by contiguity, not intuitively but symbolically' (*symbolisch*; *DR* §17; 16: 55). This had been his approach in *LU*. He now thinks this is wrong, because nothing in the sensations gives them a presentative function (*DR* §17, 16: 55). He now prefers to talk of something being given 'emptily', or in varying modes of 'obscurity' or 'darkness'. There is a difference, for instance, between the way the back of an object is emptily intended and the manner in which, when a blade is seen, its sharpness is also seen (but not with what Husserl calls 'clarity'). These issues preoccupied him in his attempt to revise the Sixth Logical Investigation. In these draft revisions (Hua 22/1) Husserl goes into the nature of empty intention and the 'emptiness modification' in great detail. I close my eyes, and the objects in the room are still present, but now in the mode of darkness, a mode different from the sense of absence or complete emptiness.

In perceiving a physical object, the 'components of the apprehension' (*Auffassungskomponenten*) of the front side refer beyond themselves, the front 'refers' (*weist auf hin*) to the backside (*DR*, §18; 16: 56). But what precisely does 'refer' mean here? What precisely is the mode of givenness of the hidden side? Is it a kind of indicating (*Aufweisung*) in the manner in which smoke indicates fire? It is not that there is already a kind of symbolic or 'signitive' function occurring in perception. It is not like reading the meaning of marks on paper. In *APS* Husserl speaks of an 'appearance core' (*APS*, p. 41; 11: 5), 'a constant X', 'a constant substrate' (*APS*, p. 42; 11: 5) upon which are built a system of 'referential implications' (*Verweisen*). The thing 'calls out' to us that there are still more sides to see (*APS*, p. 41; 11: 5). These indications are also 'tendencies' which push us in a certain direction: 'They are however not single indications, but entire indicative systems, indications functioning as systems of rays that point toward corresponding manifold systems of appearance' (*APS*, p. 42; 11: 5–6). This suggests that the organization of sensations themselves is somehow responsible for leading the subject beyond what is presented. This leads Husserl to his analysis of association, the passively experienced coherence at the very heart of sensuous experience itself.

Husserl sees the process of perceiving an object as a dynamic procedure involving sequential fillings and emptyings: 'In order to gain a deeper understanding we must pay attention to how fullness and emptiness stand in relation to one another at each moment, how emptiness adopts fullness in the flow of perception, and how fullness becomes emptiness again' (*APS*, p. 44; 11: 7). Husserl speaks of these anticipations or prefigurations as 'protentions' (*APS*, p. 44; 11: 7): 'Thus even what is already seen is laden with anticipatory intention. . . . There is a constant process of anticipation, of pre-understanding' (*APS*, p. 43; 11: 7). What enable anticipation and prefiguration of this kind are various kinds of motivation based on association. Husserl distinguishes between 'open' possibilities and so-called enticements to believe (*APS*, p. 83; 11: 43): 'Something entices me as a possibility, something speaks in favor of it; but there are other opposing possibilities' (*APS*, p. 85; 11: 45). I can see a ball as uniformly coloured, and hence as the same colour extending around the back. If not the same colour (it may be a black and white ball, each colour occupying a hemisphere), then we may still experience it as 'coloured', as shaded in some way, etc. If we see a spherical ball with a certain pattern running around the side facing us, we will more than likely assume that the pattern and surface smoothness continue around the part we cannot at present see. Of course, we may be surprised if the other side of the sphere is actually indented or of a different colour, but the original perception *intends* the object as having a back of similar content to the front side. Some kind of determinateness is presumed, something Husserl calls 'indeterminate generality'; e.g. we assume that the rear surface will be coloured in some way (*APS*, p. 80; 11: 40).

> The indeterminateness is an immanent character of the apprehension, and we must note well that it is not at all identical everywhere and, as it were, of a monochromatic character but instead has many tints and grades. Indeterminacy is never absolute or complete. Complete indeter-

minateness is nonsense; the indeterminateness is always delimited in this or that way. (*DR* §18, p. 49: 16: 58–9)

For instance, the back of the house is still a body and must have a certain colour, although I don't know *what* colour, a certain roughness, or smoothness, and so on. Furthermore as Husserl says, 'determinability (*Bestimmtbarkeit*) pertains to the essence of this indeterminateness, and indeed this is determinability within a strictly delimited general domain, such as spatial figure, coloration, and the like' (*DR* §18, p. 50; 16: 59). There is a 'unity of coincidence' (*Deckungseinheit*) between determinability and determinacy.

In actual perception of an object, the front side is given fully in the mode of certainty, but the other possible adumbrations (the anticipations of future perceptions of the rear side) are given in the mode of neither uncertainty nor certainty. In other words, I simply cannot be sure of the colour of the rear of the ball. The rear of the ball is prefigured only 'ambiguously' (*APS*, p. 82; 11: 42). There may very well be a predeliction to assume that one side will be the same as the other, in which case both possibilities are not presented equally. There is, Husserl says, a certain 'enticement to believe' it is one way rather than another way, as opposed to pure 'open possibility'. But this 'enticement to believe' (which is experienced passively) does not necessarily pass over into a decision or a conviction. The possibilities may just be kept in play. Normally, Husserl believes that in perception the unfilled non-present other sides are given according to a certain delimited set of possibilities, with a degree of 'leeway' or 'play room' (*Spielraum*; *APS*, p. 87; 11: 47).

In seeking to make the indeterminate determinate, imagination may intrude; I can run through and apply various imagined possibilities (I imagine the colour on the rear side). But it is important to stress that Husserl differentiates sharply between perceiving and imagining; imagining is not an intrinsic component in perception. Imagining, of course, can play a variable role in filling out a perception, but imagining itself is not part of the 'sense' perception (see *LU* V §21). I don't know if the colour on the front of the house continues around the back. Perhaps I can imagine that it does. But simply intuiting in a kind of 'empty' way (*Leermeinen*) the rear side of the house is not a kind of imagining; it is precisely an empty component of perception, and hence a kind of intuition rather than reasoning. His reasoning here is simple, but persuasive. If we do think of the empty intending of the rear as a kind of imagining, then what is our analysis of an act of imagining the same act of perceiving; e.g. I *imagine* the back of the object I now am looking at. If I imagine seeing the front of the house, then I am still, in the act of imagining, intending the rear side emptily. Now if this is an act of imagining, then the act of imagining contains an act of imagining and so on, *ad infinitum* (*DR* §18, p. 47; 16: 56). Perceiving, then, does not necessarily include imagining, and similarly, the empty envisaging of the hidden aspects of an object is not the same as the kind of signitive giving involved in sign consciousness. It is in these subtle and intricate analyses that Husserl's genius comes to the fore.

## Horizons of Experience

According to Husserl, every actual mental process bears within it a set of unique essential possibilities that go to make up what he calls the 'horizon' of the experience. These are not just empty possibilities, but are 'intentionally predelineated in respect of content' (*CM* §19, p. 44; Hua 1: 82), predelineated potentialities (I: 82). There is a 'horizon of references' built into the experience itself: 'everything that genuinely appears is an appearing thing only by virtue of being intertwined and permeated with an intentional empty horizon, that is, by virtue of being surrounded by a halo of emptiness with respect to appearance. It is an emptiness that is not a nothingness, but an emptiness to be filled out; it is a determinable indeterminacy' (*APS*, p. 42; 11: 5–6). Husserl also recognizes that we do not perceive objects in isolation but against a *background* (*Hintergrund*) and in the midst of a 'surrounding world' (*Umwelt*) of other objects and also of other living bodies which are other persons, animals and so on (*Ideen* II §51).[39] The 'horizon of all horizons' is the world (*Ideen* I §27), which has the sense of being infinite and unbounded in every direction. How the same object is experienced as the same by multiple co-subjects is precisely the problematic of how a 'world' comes into being (4: 80).

The side of the object that appears in a series of adumbrations always promises more; there are pointers to other sides, an inside. But the horizons do not stop there. There are not just the other sides of the object, but also the possibility that the perception itself could have been conducted in a different way (from a different angle, distance, etc.). Thus, for example, I know that if I approach the wooden table more closely, certain features of the grain will stand out more clearly. These lead to a certain indeterminacy within the experience of the object, yet also a certain determinateness and a certain set of further determinables. The object is a 'pole of identity' (*ein Identitätspol*; *CM* §19) for a set of experiences, 'a constant X, a constant substrate' (*APS*, p. 42; 11: 5).

*Inner horizons* consist of the set of anticipations and prefigurations that I have already in mind as I approach the object (*APS*, p. 43; 11: 7; see also *CM*). Husserl sees the process of perceiving an object as a dynamic procedure involving progressive fillings and emptyings. Certain prefigurations get filled in intuitively, while new expectations are opened up. But in *APS* Husserl specifies more clearly the role of retention in this process. What becomes invisible is not lost, as it is retained when the new side of the object is seen (*APS*, p. 45; 11: 9). Thus every perception invokes a whole series or system of perceptions. There is no final perception that can exhaust the thing completely. Indeed, to be a physical thing is precisely to be essentially inexhaustible.

This leads Husserl to say in *Ideen* I §143 and elsewhere (see *FTL* §16c) that every transcendent thing is really a Kantian idea: 'An idea that lies at infinity belongs to every external perception' (*APS*, p. 58; 11: 21). 'The thing is a rule of possible appearances' (*Ideen* II §18g, p. 91; Hua 4: 86). No finite consciousness can run through all the courses of possible experience belonging to any transcendent object, any physical thing in nature. However, this does not rule out that what we see is an actual, sensible, material thing. The sensible present appearance is a component in the larger non-sensory aspect of perception:

> We always have the external object in the flesh (we see, grasp, seize it), and yet it is always at an infinite distance mentally. What we grasp of it pretends to be its essence, and it is it too, but it remains so only in the incomplete approximation, an approximation that grasps something of it, but in doing so, it constantly grasps an emptiness that cries out for fulfillment. (*APS*, pp. 58–9; 11: 21)

Nevertheless, as each line of experience is explored, a series of ordered and harmonious results is achieved. The thing is determined ever more closely with this particular attribute, and so on. In this sense, Husserl believes, we are experiencing the object more deeply; it is not that we do not experience the object at all and grasp only its partial determinations.

## Normality and Optimality

Husserl is fascinated by the fact that we *constitute* a physical body (e.g. a table) as the same even as we see it under different light conditions, with different shadings, varying reflectivity and so on. It belongs to the very essence of a physical thing that its appearance keeps changing according to the available light, yet we think of it as having the same colour throughout, as being the *same identical* thing. Moreover, were we to become blind, we would not think that there is now only blackness, but rather that things still retain their colours and we simply cannot see them. There is a certain condition of the object given as the *normal* perception, under *normal* conditions, and these normal conditions are considered optimal. There is a normal, healthy condition of the body and the sense organs (4: 306). Thus a car has a certain colour as seen in daylight, in the air, without mediation of coloured glass, and so on. Moreover, the car is assumed to be this colour even if we see it appear as a different colour in a sunset. These so-called normal appearances Husserl terms 'orthoaesthetic' (*Ideen* II §18, p. 71; Hua 4: 66). The thing as normally experienced is counted as the thing pure and simple, the thing as it really is (4: 306–7).

There is, for Husserl, *only one normally constituted world*, and it is because of this that certain experiences can be classed as semblances or illusions. This 'normal' world is not only constituted by a healthy organism interacting with a normal environment; it assumes a certain mood or emotion (and later he will recognize that it requires certain cultural expectations, etc.). It is on the basis of such normal encounter with the object considered as stable that we are able to think of the thing as an identical substrate with varying properties.

Although Husserl's description of perception focuses primarily on seeing, it is not his sole focus. He makes interesting claims (later elaborated by Merleau-Ponty) concerning the intermingling of different sensations, e.g. visual and tactile. From the time of Aristotle, there had been a debate about what sensations are 'proper' to a particular sense organ and which can be said to be 'common'; i.e. perceived by two or more senses. Colour, for example, can be apprehended only by an eye; smoothness can be both seen and touched. The question is: is it the *same* sense quality that is both seen and touched? Against Berkeley, Husserl maintains that it is the *very same* smoothness that is both seen and felt. He does not want to give priority either to sight or to touch, but is here emphasizing the unity of the body which is seen and touched. If I wear glasses that sharpen my vision, then my vision will attain priority in the grasp of the spatial field which might previously have been occupied by touch.[40] But there is much more to be said about the forms of sensory consciousness, and *DR* is probably Husserl's most extensive investigation in this area.

## Representation, Memory and Other Forms of 'Calling to Mind' or 'Presentification' (*Vergegenwärtigung*)

Perception, as we have seen, is foundational for consciousness; it provides the *Urdoxa* upon which other modalities of belief are based. All other forms of conscious experience are in one way or another *founded* on perceptual, sensory consciousness. In general terms, Husserl contrasts the *self-givenness* of perception (e.g. *FTL* §86) with that of a very large class of forms of consciousness that are 'representational' (*vergegenwärtig*) or work through a modification of presencing, which Husserl terms *Vergegenwärtigung*, 'presentification', 'presentation' or 'calling to mind' (not just in memory, but in fantasy, wishing, etc.). When we remember, imagine or fantasize about an object, we do not have precisely the same sense of the immediate, actual, bodily and temporal presence of the object. Indeed, in memory and in expectation, we are sure that the object is not presently there, but there is still some kind of reference to its being; it is still being posited (as future or past) in a specific way. Memory, for instance, posits the real 'having-been' of something. Imagination entails no such positing of the real existence of its object in any temporal mode (Hua 23: 16ff). Memory, moreover, is not the same as picture-consciousness (10: 316). It is a *thetic* or positing act, but the object is presented as 'being-past', 'having been' (13: 164) and as 'having-been-perceived-by-me' (7: 252), and having been experienced originally *in a mode other than memory*. In other words, in an act of remembering, the experience remembered is presented as one originally experienced by me, but now with a *temporal distance* separating it from my current experience. This temporal distantiation is characteristic of memory: 'Recollection is not simply the being-conscious once again of the object; rather, just as the perception of a temporal object carries with it its temporal horizon, so too the recollection repeats the consciousness of this horizon' (ZB, p. 113; 10: 108). Husserl puts enormous stress on the structural importance of remembering, for a number of reasons. It is in remembering that consciousness first comes to meet itself as an object. Lipps had already noticed this. There is already a split or chasm between the self that is remembering and the experience of the self that is being remembered. For instance, if I have a memory of myself as a child swinging on a particular swing, I perceive myself through a different consciousness from that of the child on the swing. There is a doubling of consciousness and a peculiar experience of both difference and identity. My empathic grasp of the cognitive life of the other also falls under the general category of 'presentification' (*Vergegenwärtigung*) for Husserl.

Other differences emerge concerning the status of the object represented or 'presentified'. The issue of the putative existence of the object becomes irrelevant in acts of fantasy and imagination, where existence is simply left to one side. What is fantasized is not necessarily past, present or future, but is presented 'as-if' (*DR* §4), and is not an actual perception. This is a structural feature of fantasy itself: it has the character of 'depicting', not presenting (23: 16). In fantasy, then, we make no effort at positing the object:

> In phantasy, the object does not stand there as in the flesh, actual, currently present. It indeed does stand before our eyes, but not as something currently given now; it may be possible to be thought of as now, or as simultaneous with the current now, but this now is a thought one, and is not that now which pertains to presence in the flesh, perceptual

presence. The phantasized is merely 'represented' (*vorgestellt*), it merely places before us (*stellt vor*) or presents (*stellt dar*), but it 'does not give itself' as itself, actual and now. (*DR* §4, p. 12; 16: 14–15)

Imagination neutralizes or suspends the thetic function.[41] One is indifferent to the existence of the imagined object; it does not stand in the middle of our perceptual field (23: 49).

Moreover, the object seen in fantasy is not located in the same space as a perception. It 'hovers', or floats, before us; it is not continuous with the objects or the space around it. Secondly, there is no temporal distance or gap experienced as there is in the case of memory. The fantasized image is apprehended in the present tense, although that present is not itself experienced as perceptual present tense. On the other hand, the fantasized image can reappear and be recovered in memory, so it has a certain kind of identity transcending the act of fantasy. Thirdly, the imagined object (in earlier works Husserl speaks of a 'representation', *Vorstellung*; 23: 18) does not have the same identity conditions or 'selfhood' (*Selbstheit*) as the perceptual object. It is characterized by a certain confusion. Imaginative presentations (*Phantasievorstellungen*) are mediated through a 'presentation' (*Vorstellung*; 23: 24) that is lacking in the case of perception. There is a kind of 'non presence' (23: 58–9) associated with the imagined object.

## Image- or Picture-Consciousness (*Bildbewusstsein*)

Besides memory and fantasy, there are other forms of presentification or 'presentation'. As we have seen, from the outset Husserl was particularly interested in the 'signitive' or 'symbolic' consciousness that accounts for mathematical consciousness (which relies on symbols). As a mathematician and logician, he was particularly interested in those kinds of conscious acts wherein we attend to and manipulate symbols. His first major contribution is his careful distinction between perceiving, imagining, 'picture-consciousness' (*Bildbewusstsein*) and sign consciousness or 'signitive consciousness' (*LU* V §14), worked out in *LU* and elaborated in his lectures in Göttingen (Hua 23). Imaginative consciousness is a certain way of orientating ourselves towards something wherein we do not assert that thing as existing. Picture-consciousness (or 'depicting consciousness', *Bildbewusstsein*) is a new kind of representative consciousness, but a very complex one. One of Husserl's most significant achievements is to show that picture-consciousness is a specific modality of consciousness. The error of modern philosophy had been to misconstrue perception and imagination as picture-consciousness, as if we saw a picture or image of the thing. In fact, they

are entirely different constitutional processes (3/1: 186). To say that perception involves depiction is to begin an infinite regress (of the kind
we discussed earlier in relation to supposed imaginative elements
inserted into perception).

According to Husserl, when we see, for example, a photograph or a
postcard with the picture of a bridge on it, then we see both a physical object and a picture with its 'theme'. There is a blend of perceiving
and imaging. The photograph is a genuine object that is perceived (23:
19). It is a kind of paper, can be felt, tasted, etc. But it is a special kind
of thing, a 'picture-thing' (*Bildding*; 23: 489). The actual image in the
photograph – the bridge – floats somewhat free of the physical object
and is an appearance. In his lectures of 1904/5 Husserl calls the image
itself the 'representing object' (*das repräsentierende Objekt*) or the 'picture
object' (*Bildobjekt*; 23: 19). It is distinct from the actual object presented
(the real bridge which the photograph shows), which Husserl often
calls the 'subject' (*Sujet*, 23: 39) of the picturing (*Bildsujet*; 23: 489). The
picture object is an apparent thing (*Scheinding*; 23: 19), belonging to the
'world of appearance' (*Scheinwelt*), yet it appears as vividly as a perceptual object. Husserl says that it is not a real part of the physical
object. The colours, lines, etc. are real parts of the photograph, but the
picture object is not a real part of it. Husserl sees the image as a kind
of 'nullity' (*Nichtigkeit*; see 11: 351), repeating his view of the fantasy
image. Picture-consciousness differs from fantasy, in that fantasy needs
no physical substrate or support (*Bildding*). The fantasy is not based on
a physical object, and indeed belongs within consciousness itself. Moreover, the image does not survive the end of the act of imagining or fantasizing, whereas a picture based on a physical object does survive.[42]
The picturing thing is in a different time and space from the physical
object (23: 537). It is an ideal object.

A picture-consciousness is different from the consciousness of an
illusion (23: 486). A statue is not an illusion; it is a real object grasped
in perception, but there is also picture-consciousness operating, which
sees it as a statue of Napoleon. When I look at a wax figure in a wax
museum, knowing what I am experiencing, then I see it as *representing*
a woman. But I can even be mistaken and perceive it simply as a
woman (cf. *LU* V; also Hua 11: 350–2; 23: 487). In that case it is an
instance of straight perception, but it is illusory. Only after the assumed
object has collapsed or 'exploded' and I see it as a wax figure on which
is superimposed the figure of a woman do I have a more complex situation, part perception and part picturing consciousness.[43] There is a
shift from pure perception to picture-consciousness, both acts being
constructed on the same sensational complexes which are *experienced*
but not directly *perceived*: 'Sensations, and the acts "interpreting" them
or "apperceiving" them, are alike experienced (*erlebt*), but *they do not
appear as objects*: they are not seen, heard or *perceived* by any sense.

Objects on the other hand appear and are perceived, but they are not experienced' (*LU* V §14, **I** 105; Hua 19/1: 399). Furthermore, fantasy comes into a certain conflict with actual perception – I am conscious of the fact that my fantasized object is not actually there. Image-consciousness offers a different kind of conflict. When I see that the visitor to the Panopticum museum is really a wax figure, the wax thing simply is, while the image of the woman is still somehow floating there as an unreality, a 'nullity' (11: 351). The two 'perceptions' are somehow entwined, yet in conflict, and one is founded on the other. Strictly speaking, only one event is a perception in the proper sense. There is also a third stage where we are somehow between the two, when we are doubtful, our mental act has the character of 'doubtfulness' (*Zweifel-haftigkeit*) and 'questionableness' (*Fraglichkeit*). These orientations are also modifications of the perception of 'being', which is foundational (Hua 11: 352).

As early as his 1894 essay, 'Psychological Studies in the Elements of Logic', Husserl gives as an example the difference between looking at a certain arabesque which has affected us aesthetically (we are attracted to the beautiful pattern) and then recognizing that it is made up of letters (*EW*, p. 161; Hua 22: 115; repeated in *LU* V §14, **II** 105; Hua 19/1: 398). What is the surplus element involved in the recognition that it is a letter? The same sensory material would be present in both circumstances, but in the act of perceiving a letter *as* a letter, a transformation of consciousness has been effected. I am now looking at an essentially new phenomenon. This led Husserl to believe that the role of sensory contents had been radically misunderstood in traditional philosophy, and even in Brentano. When I see the object in the picture, I do not see the paint and brush strokes as such. I am directed to the 'subject' or theme. Husserl is nothing if not systematic, and indeed he attempts an exhaustive classification of the different forms of representing: actors in a theatre playing roles, novels, photographs, sculptures all have different relations between the physical objects, the picturings and the depicted objects. He even discusses the case of mirrors (23: 495), where what is 'in' the mirror is precisely nothing (as distinct from a painting or photograph, there are no actual marks on the mirror surface).

Husserl's original, rich discussions of the cognitive forms of pre-sentification are offered as steps in his account of the layers of conscious life. But his target is always the life of the mind, cognition and rationality in the fullest sense. In this respect, nothing gave him more trouble than the effort to analyse higher forms of signitive consciousness where objects are grasped in their absence and through the mediation of symbols (e.g. writing, formulae), which forms the basis of more abstract thought in extremely powerful sciences such as mathematics, logic and the formal sciences generally.

## Perception and Judgement

Judgement is crucially important for knowledge and for human beings as rational subjects. Our life is a striving for cognition, and that means a striving for judgements. Husserl speaks of our 'judicative life'. Judgement is linked to truths and with establishing something as valid (*APS*, p. 97; 11: 56). He approaches judgement as a higher-order activity that builds on the more basic acts of perceiving, imagining, remembering, etc. He makes many attempts to develop a phenomenology of judgement (e.g. in *LU* VI, *APS*, *FTL* and finally *EU*). Already in *LU*, he had been concerned to distinguish perception from judgement as acts with essentially different structures. Although perceptions may very well motivate judgements, they are not judgements. They are different forms of intentionality (*APS*, p. 94; 11: 54), although clearly there are, for Husserl as for Kant, perceptual judgements, judgements of perception, as a distinct and important class. Previous philosophers have not made much progress in the theory of judgement precisely because they misconstrue the subjective dimension of judging (*FTL* §85). The act of judging has been confused with the judged proposition. While Husserl has much to say about the structure of the judged, the 'proposition', especially in earlier years, in phenomenological terms, he is specifically interested in judgement as a performance, as an egoic act of position-taking, as a categorial activity, an act of *kategorein*, accusation (*EU* §47, p. 198; 233). Judgements are voluntary acts of the will, and when I retain a judgement, I *will* it continuously (*EU* §48). He also employs Kantian terms: whereas perception belongs to receptivity, judging is a higher-order activity of 'predicative spontaneity' (*EU* §49). Judging is essentially involved with conceptualization and generalization. When I judge that S is red, a relation to redness is already involved, and an essential generality (*EU* §49), although this generality ('redness') is not explicitly thematized.

Husserl begins from the simplest cases of judgement: namely, the perceptual judgement, which he takes to be a categorial formation of the form S is P, where a certain objective unity S is focused on and enriched by having a predicate P asserted of it. In *APS* and *EU* he discusses how continuous perception where there is a sharpening of focus on a property of the object is the intuitional basis for this kind of perceptual judgement, e.g. looking at a copper bowl, we let our glance run over it, and we can tarry over distinctive features and examine them singly, but we remain conscious of the abiding unity of the object itself: 'In all this we are continually oriented toward the entire object; we have apprehended it and hold fast to it as a thematic substrate' (*EU* §24, p. 117; 130). From such perceptual chains the concept 'subject' emerges, as does the concept 'predicate'. Indeed, Husserl maintains that all the conceptual categories involved in judgement have their foundation in 'pre-predicative experience': 'It is true, we can only begin to speak of logical categories in the proper sense in the sphere of predicative judgment . . . But all categories and categorial forms which appear there are erected on the prepredicative syntheses and have their origin in them' (*EU* §24, p. 115; 127). This is the basis for his 'genealogy' (his term) of the forms of judgement in *FTL* and *EU*.

Husserl criticizes Brentano's view of judgement as the approval (*Anerkennung*) of, or 'saying-yes' to – or denial of, or 'saying-no' to – a presentation. Judgement cannot be construed as a certain attitude of belief supervening on the presentation of an object.[44] For a start, while judgement has an act–object intentional structure, the object of a judgement is a 'state of affairs' or 'fact that something is the case', and not a simple object or cluster of objects as in a perception (*LU* V §28). But in *LU* Husserl is mainly concerned to articulate the object of a judgement (a state of affairs) and its content (what is judged, the 'proposition') as something ideal. Against Frege and Brentano, Husserl revives the Aristotelian account of judgement as a relation between subject and predicate. More clearly than Aristotle, he emphasizes that judgement is a *positing*, not just an entertaining, of a proposition. It is a thetic act. Judgement is involved in positing or 'constituting' higher-order categorical objectivities ('that the cat is on the mat'), but, as we saw with the noema, in a fine-grained way. In *FTL* Husserl speaks of these constituted objects of judgement as irreal: 'in judging, something irreal becomes intentionally constituted' (*FTL* §63).

In his later discussions, Husserl focuses a great deal on the different levels of conviction which a judgement can articulate with respect to the situation judged. Judgement in the true 'predicative' sense is founded on modalities present in perception and the 'sense certainty' of perception: 'What one so hotly debated under the rubric of the theory of judgment in the newer logical movement since Mill, Brentano and Sigwart is at its core nothing other than the phenomenological clarification of the essence of the logical function of the certainty of being and the modalities of being' (*APS*, p. 66; 11: 28). Judgement emerges from perception only when there is a 'splitting' of the perception so that a certain part of its content is offered ambiguously and calls for a decision. The 'concordant' perception 'harbours' a decision (*APS*, p. 104; 11: 63). But perceptions themselves do not harbour judgements. The empty intuitive grasp of the non-presented side of an object is not a matter of inference. Husserl does not accept the view that all seeing is propositional 'seeing-that', e.g. seeing *that the ball is uniformly spherical and green*. Seeing is a living experience of being in the presence of the object. It is not yet the yea-saying affirmation of the object, but it provides the foundation for such an affirmation: 'When it [the ego] simply perceives, when it is merely aware, apprehending what is there and what, of itself, is presented in experience by itself, there is no motive for taking a position provided that nothing else is present' (*APS*, p. 93; 11: 53). In part, Husserl thinks that the difference between perceiving and judging has to do with the role of the ego. Judging is an activity of the ego (*FTL* §63; *EU* §47). It is a specific act of position-taking that requires a certain amount of uncertainty, of opposing motives being in play. Judging can arise 'in the primordial sphere of a motivating perception', but that is only when a conflict has been apprehended. In ordinary 'smooth' perceptions, where no conflicts present themselves, there is no role for the ego. Judging, on the other hand, requires active appropriation on the side of the ego. When I judge something to be valid, it becomes an abiding part of my convictions, it is accepted by me as settled. Perceptions are not incorporated in the same way, but have to be continually renewed. There is a different temporal reference in perception by comparison with judgement (if I break off a perception, I still have perceived the object; if I break off in the middle of judging, the judgement is not actualized). Judgings have different levels of clarity and distinctness. A judgement can be completely vague (*FTL* §16), and it can progress or be articulated into clarity.

In this chapter, I have tried to give a general exposition of the central features of Husserl's painstakingly detailed phenomenological descriptions of conscious acts, their contents, modes of givenness, and modes of validation. Obviously, I have just skimmed the surface of these extraordinarily complex analyses, particularly in the modalities other than perception. Needless to say, there is much that can be challenged, but I believe it is important to try to present the outlines of the system to show that Husserl founds his overall philosophy on what he takes to be eidetic truths about consciousness and cognition. In the next chapter, I shall characterize the transcendental phenomenology that completely preoccupied Husserl's mature years (1907–38), and absorbed this eidetic ABC of consciousness into a new transcendental – and indeed idealist – framework that recognized all consciousness as part of the mysterious transcendental life of the subject in an intersubjective community of co-subjects.

# 6

# Transcendental Phenomenology:
## An Infinite Project

## From Eidetic Phenomenology to
## Transcendental Idealism

Following on from the *eidetic* description of the a priori forms of consciousness in the last chapter, I shall now focus on Husserl's development of what he envisaged as a 'radical and genuine' *transcendental* phenomenology and transcendental philosophy.[1] During a sustained period of intensive research (and few publications) from around 1905 until his death in 1938, he devoted an enormous amount of energy to explicating various possible approaches to transcendental philosophy, which, from as early as 1906, he explicitly construed as an *idealism*, with a growing sense that he was recovering and revitalizing the true sense of past German idealisms (especially those of Kant and Fichte). In his 1906–7 *ELE* lectures, for instance, he claims that 'all objectivity has its source in phenomenological ideality' (24: 340). Husserl sees this commitment to idealism as arising out of the phenomenological *epoché* and reduction: 'Taken fundamentally, there lies indicated already *in advance in the phenomenological reduction*, correctly understood, *the route into transcendental idealism*, as the *whole of phenomenology* is nothing other than the first, *strictly scientific form of this idealism*' (*EP* II, 8: 181, my trans.). Transcendental philosophy sets a task for the whole of humanity (7: 236), the task of becoming universal, self-conscious, rational beings in a community and world that is recognized as humanity's own accomplishment.

Husserl often introduced transcendental phenomenology in terms of the *evolution of modern philosophy* (cf. London Lectures; *EP* I; *Krisis*). For him, 'genuine' transcendental philosophy recuperates the true sense of both the Cartesian and the Kantian projects; it correctly articulates the true sense of the necessary correlation between subjectivity and objectivity, gives a true grounding to objectivity and to 'empirical' realism, is the first true science of the subjective, and so on. Husserl's Fichte Lectures (1917/18),[2] given in Freiburg in the final year of the Great War, are a particularly fervent endorsement of his commitment to German Idealism. Here he criticized Kant for still retaining this mythical view of transcendent things in themselves affecting our sensibility, as if subjectivity needed a stimulus to waken it from its original passivity, whereas, for Husserl, as for Fichte, consciousness has, or is, an original *activity*. Elsewhere, however, as in his address to Freiburg University on 1 May 1924,[3] in celebration of the bicentennial of Kant's birth, he stressed the 'inexorable necessity' that led him to transcendental philosophy, and his 'obvious essential relationship' with Kant (7: 230). As he put it in *Krisis*, transcendental philosophy must attempt a radicalization of the truth hidden in Kant (§32).

The first published announcement of this idealism (without using the word) came in *Ideen* I (1913).[4] However, this idealist turn was widely repudiated by Husserl's Munich and Göttingen followers,[5] and he later conceded that this 'scandal' affected the reception of *Ideen* I (see Hua 5: 150). Nevertheless, in the Twenties, beginning with his *Introduction to Philosophy* lectures and his London Lectures (both 1922), he continued to plan a 'system' of transcendental philosophy (see 35: 49).[6] Although he sometimes rejected the description of his phenomenological philosophy as a 'system' (as in his 1933 letter to Parl Welch[7]), he continued to characterize his philosophy as idealism in all his late publications, e.g. *FTL* (see §99), *CM* (see §41), *Krisis* (§§26ff) and in his Author's Preface (1930) to the English translation of *Ideen* I.

Transcendental philosophy, as it came to be understood with Kant, is concerned not so much with elaborating a metaphysical account of the objective world as with a justification of our sense of that world as objective. It is a formal inquiry into the conditions for the possibility of knowledge. As Kant writes in the *Critique of Pure Reason*: 'I call all cognition transcendental that is occupied not so much with objects but rather with our a priori concepts of objects in general' (*CPR*, A11–12). Husserl, too, is interested in the *how* of knowledge. But he envisages transcendental phenomenology as the science that grasps in a fundamental way the meaning of the whole *accomplishment of spiritual life*: that is, what makes rational, communal and societal life possible, what gives it objectivity. He is seeking self-critical, self-justifying knowledge, 'a science based on ultimate self-responsibility' (5: 139), capable of justifying even its own essential possibility and validity. In this sense, his vision of transcendental philosophy goes well beyond Kant's 'naive' version that keeps open 'at least as a limiting concept, the possibility of a world of things in themselves' (CM §41, p. 86; Hua 1: 118). Husserl will deny the meaningfulness of speaking of things in themselves that transcend our cognition; all being must be understood as essentially correlated with consciousness. Husserl's specific targets become (a) *transcendental realism*, the view that 'things in themselves' – the 'world as such' – exist entirely independently of subjectivity; and (b) *psychological idealism* (*CM* §41), the view that the world depends on, or is enclosed in, psychological subjectivity (5: 154). As he put it in *Krisis*, he is against any 'absolutization' of the world which would treat it as a thing 'in itself' independent of our consciousness and knowledge of it.

In *Krisis*, Husserl interprets 'transcendental' as signifying 'the motif of inquiring back into the ultimate source of all the formations of knowledge, the motif of the knower's reflecting on himself and his knowing life in which all the scientific structures that are valid for him occur purposefully, are stored up as acquisitions . . . This source bears the title *I-myself* (*Krisis* §26, pp. 97–8; 6: 100–1). Transcendental philosophy, for Husserl, finds all sense as issuing from transcendental subjectivity. In this sense it is science of the ego, *egology*; but Husserl also insists on its essentially intersubjective character. He wants to explore the transcendental character of *intersubjectivity* – the transcendental 'we-community' (5: 153) of spirit (*Geist*) – in the full, concrete, living sense of all of humanity, with its cultural institutions and historical development, understood as in teleological process towards absolute rationality. How transcendental science is both egology and a plural 'monadology' (borrowing Leibniz's term) is itself part of the set of transcendental problems for Husserl. He seems to regard the plurality of co-subjects as somehow 'within' transcendental subjectivity (5: 153). In the next chapter, I shall discuss Husserl's explication of the transcendental ego. Here I shall concentrate on the meaning of transcendental philosophy.

Husserl optimistically envisages his phenomenology as the 'final form of transcendental philosophy' (*Krisis* §14) – even the essence of *all* genuine philosophy – taking up and completing all previous tasks of philosophy, reinstating the original idea of philosophy as inaugurated by Plato (5: 139), embracing and redeeming the entire philosophical tradition (*EP* I; 7: 256; 5: 141). He finds the first seed of genuine transcendentalism in classical Platonic idealism (which treated all reality as mere appearance and elevated the soul to genuine being, and in that sense offers an advance over materialism; 35: 276). Now, with the breakthrough to phenomenology, the project of philosophy as a rigorous science reaches its final form; final justification becomes transcendental justification, i.e. justification in terms of the sense-giving (*Sinngebung*) of the transcendental ego (the ultimate source of all justification and validation). In contrast with transcendental philosophy, all other sciences, even a priori ones such as logic and mathematics, in Husserl's view, remain 'positive sciences', proceeding in 'transcendental *naïveté*', and suffering periodic *crises of foundation* until they are transcendentally justified by phenomenology in its role as 'first philosophy'.[8] Furthermore, transcendental philosophy is not a 'theory', not a product of argument (*CM* §41); rather, it simply executes itself as a 'universal idealism': 'It demonstrates this idealism by means of its own sense as transcendental science in each of its separate constitutive domains' (Postscript to *Ideen I*; Hua 5: 152). It is carried out by 'sense-explication' (1: 119). For Husserl, there can be only one method for transcendental philosophy: 'one must study cognising life (*das erkennende Leben*) itself in its own essence achievements (*Wesenleistungen*)', (*EP* I; Hua 7: 248).

Transcendental phenomenology even expresses the inner essence of religion (*Krisis* §53; Hua 6: 184), and provides him, as a deeply religious if unconventional Christian, with the only philosophically justified basis for comprehending God, given the 'absurdity' of thinking of him as an item in the factual world (see *Ideen* I §51, p. 116; Hua 311: 96). As he put it in *FTL*: 'Even God is for me what he is, in consequence of my own productivity of consciousness' (*FTL* §99, p. 251; 17: 258), although he goes on to insist that this does not mean that consciousness 'makes' or 'invents' God. He considers the breakthrough into transcendental philosophy and to the 'transcendental attitude' as producing a permanent reorientation of human culture towards higher, more rational and more self-aware goals, even to the extent of producing a new universal humanity. Consciousness assumes self-responsibility (5: 162) through a 'self-explication' (*Selbstauslegung*) of its own accomplishment of 'mundane objectivity' (*Krisis* §58). This self-explication, which, for Husserl, is permanently ongoing, belongs to our 'endless transcendental life' (8: 126). Indeed, transcendental philosophy does not just offer a critique of naive life, it seeks a *critique* of transcendental life too (*CM* V §63).

## Intimations of Idealism in *LU*

Although lacking the concepts of *epoché* and reduction, and of course all discussion of the transcendental ego, the first edition of *LU* nevertheless contains some hints of Husserl's later idealism. Indeed, he always maintained (see, e.g., 5: 154) that the roots of the transcendental turn were already present in the first edition. Here he defended a kind of 'Platonic' objectivism concerning ideal and categorial entities that challenged empiricism and 'critical realism'. On the one hand, it was seen as a return to realism, as his student Edith Stein recalled: '[*LU*] caused a sensation primarily because it appeared to be a radical departure from critical realism which had a Kantian and a neo-Kantian stamp. It was considered a "new scholasticism" because it turned attention away from the "subject" and toward "things" themselves.'[9] Yet Husserl himself characterized this defence of the objectivity of categorial unities and universals as 'idealism'. Thus he writes – *nota bene* in the first edition of *LU* (1901) – that the defence of the objectivity of ideal objects 'is the point on which relativistic, empiricistic psychologism differs from idealism, *which alone represents the possibility of a self-consistent theory of knowledge*' (19/1: 112, my emphasis). He clarified this comment in the second edition: 'To talk of "idealism" is of course not to talk of a metaphysical doctrine but of a theory of knowledge which recognizes the "ideal" as a condition for the possibility of objective knowledge in general, and does not interpret it away in psychologistic fashion' (*LU* II, Intro., II 238; 19/1: 112).

In one sense, *LU* had prepared the ground for his full-blooded idealist turn, with its extensive critique of all forms of indirect or representational realism, which claimed the immediate objects of cognition to be mental representations, that he found in modern philosophy (not just in the empiricists but also in Kant, and indeed in Brentano and Stumpf).[10] Representationalism led inexorably to a *subjective idealism* by making impossible direct access to the genuine object of knowledge. Indeed, this is the 'chief error' of modern philosophy: 'The holders of this view are misled by thinking that the transcendence belonging to the spatial physical thing is the transcendence belonging to *something depicted* or *represented by a sign*' (*Ideen* I §43, p. 92; Hua 3/1: 78). Husserl shrewdly diagnosed that Kant's account of knowledge also retained some representationalist elements, not to speak of his commitment to a 'mythical' thing-in-itself. Husserl's own transcendental idealism must be a direct 'empirical' realism that also entirely repudiates the idea of a transcendent 'world in itself', which somehow comes into contact with consciousness, as sheer nonsense (*FTL* §99).

## Consciousness as Absolute Being

Husserl's transcendental idealism asserts not just the necessary correlation between objectivity and subjectivity, but also the ontological priority of subjectivity as that which constitutes the object in its sense and essence. The whole 'being and sense' (*Sein und Sinn*) or 'being sense' (*Seinssinn*) and 'validity' (*Geltung*) of the world itself, not just all actual being but all possible being, and even the 'sense' of actuality and possibility, is to be construed as a cognitive accomplishment, production or achievement (*Erkenntnisleistung*) of transcendental subjectivity (*EP* I; 7: 248). This subjectivity must, however, be characterized more precisely – whether it be actual or possible, embodied, individual or plural, intersubjectively shared subjectivity.

In *Ideen* I Husserl's commitment to idealism emerges in his Cartesian-style reflection on the self-evidence of immanent perception or of one's conscious processes. He starts by accepting that the *cogito* demonstrates that every conscious experience contains the essential possibility of its being reflected on in such a way that it confirms its actual occurrence in an irrefragable manner. As he puts it: 'To each stream of mental processes and to each Ego, as Ego, there belongs the essential possibility of acquiring this evidence; each bears in itself, as an essential possibility, the guarantee of its absolute existence (*seines absolutes Dasein*)' (*Ideen* I §46, p. 101; Hua 3/1: 85, trans. modified). Any conscious process is 'originarily and absolutely given', not only in respect of its essence but also with the certainty of its existence. Of course, Husserl emphasizes how limited is the evidence which is given by such 'immanent' seizing of one's own processes. One cannot, for example, infer from the existence of the processes themselves that they are components of a real human being (as Husserl himself noted in a marginal entry). In *EP* II he further acknowledges the difference between recognizing the irremovability of the self and its experience from any thought of the world, and, on the other hand, the kind of transcendental self-awareness which results precisely from the critique of this mundane self-experience and which is entirely incapable of being thought away (*EP* II; Hua 8: 70). This requires moving beyond the 'human-I' (*das Menschen-Ich*; *EP* II; Hua 8: 71) to discover myself as subject *for* the world rather than subject *in* the world. Even if I were to try to think away the existence of the world and of my mundane human self, I would still discover myself as existing: 'I would be and would remain someone whose being is not touched by any nothingness affecting the world (*Weltnichtigkeit*), someone who can never be annihilated in a so-called epistemological annihilation (*erkenntniskritische Vernichtung*) of my body and of all the world' (*EP* II; Hua 8: 73, my trans.). Husserl even says, allowing himself the use of religious language (inadmissible at this stage in strict science), that one could think of this as a kind of survival like that of an angel or a pure soul. There is a sharp differentiation to be made between my mundane and my transcendental self-experience.

In contrast to this apodictic self-givenness of immanent experiences, Husserl claims that it is an eidetic law that physical existence is never required as necessary by the givenness to consciousness of anything physical. The transcendent physical is by its essential nature always contingent (*Ideen* I §46, p. 102; Hua 3/1: 86). The existence of the world in phenomenological terms is simply the presumption that my experiences continue to be harmoniously filled in the appropriate ways (5: 153). But there is never any absolute guarantee that this harmonizing will continue indefinitely. The self-givenness of immanent conscious processes, on the other hand, is entirely different, and is absolutely given. It belongs, Husserl says, to 'a sphere of absolute positing' (*eine Sphäre absoluter Position; Ideen* I §46, p. 102; Hua 3/1: 86). In contrast to this contingent posited world, the positing ego is *necessary* and *absolute*.

There is what Husserl calls an 'essential detachability' (*prinzipielle Ablösbarkeit*) of the whole natural world from consciousness (*Ideen* I §46, p. 104; Hua 3/1: 87). He presents the 'detachability' or one-sided separability of the world from consciousness as the discovery implicit in the Cartesian *cogito*. The essence of the transcendent world is such that it has meaning only in essential interconnection with consciousness – and not just possible consciousness but *actual* consciousness.

Husserl's idealism, then, is primarily concerned with the inability to conceive of an object independent of a subject. One must rather think of the object as constituted out of activities and structures of consciousness, according to predetermined essential laws. Husserl's first published version of this argument is in *Ideen* I §§49–50. There is absolutely no sense to the notion of 'thing in itself'. What we think of as this first reality is in fact always second: 'The being which is first for us is second in itself; i.e., it is what it is only in "relation" to the first' (*Ideen* I §50, p. 112; Hua 3/1: 93). He constantly refers to pure consciousness as 'absolute being' (§76), 'the primal category of all being', 'the primal region', and so on. Consciousness simply cannot be thought away.

Husserl's formulations concerning the one-sided detachability of the world from consciousness in *Ideen* I shocked and alienated his realist followers. One of his most notorious claims in *Ideen* I is that we can perform a thought experiment envisaging the very *annihilation of the world* (*Weltvernichtung*) without thereby being able to think of the disappearance of consciousness. This claim is repeated in *Ideen* II:

> If we think of monadic subjects and their streams of consciousness, or rather, if we think the thinkable minimum of self-consciousness, then a monadic consciousness, one that would have no 'world' at all given to it, could indeed be thought, – thus a monadic consciousness without regularities in the course of sensations, without motivated possibilities in the apprehensions of things. (*Ideen* II §63, p. 303; Hua 4: 290)

It is even conceivable that there might be no empirical consciousness at all, no world, but that absolute consciousness would still be what it is (*Ideen* II §63, p. 308 n. 1; Hua 4: 294 n. 1). Of course, by 'annihilation' Husserl means the dissolution, distintegration or coming apart of the streams of experience. It is possible that our experience would no longer harmonize in ways we could make sense of. It is not the claim that the stream would stop. I have no sense that my stream will dry up, as it were. Rather, what dries up is my commitment to the real existence of the world. I must continue to exist. I cannot think myself away. My consciousness has *necessary* not contingent existence. Husserl embraces the Cartesian claim that, even if God were to create an entirely 'illusory world' (*Scheinwelt*), I would still be a true subject of this illusory world (*EP* II; Hua 8: 73). Later he admitted that the formulation of this bold claim in *Ideen* I was 'incomplete' and 'suffered from imperfections' (5: 150), but he never withdrew it; instead, he embedded it more and more in a broader framework of the necessity of the transcendental ego.

## From Absolute Consciousness to Transcendental Life

Husserl interprets transcendental philosophy as leading to the discovery of a 'new sphere of being' (*eine neue Seinssphäre*; EP I, 7: 270), a sphere of life, of 'pure subjective living' (*rein subjektives Leben*; 7: 272), including the sphere of transcendental *experience* (*transzendentale Erfahrung*; EP II, 8: 166)[11] – a conception that would have been anathema to Kant. As Husserl writes in his draft *Encyclopedia Britannica* article: 'The transcendental reduction opens up, in fact, a completely new kind of experience that can be systematically pursued: transcendental experience. Through the transcendental reduction, *absolute* subjectivity, which functions everywhere in hiddenness, is brought to light along with its whole transcendental life' (*Trans. Phen.*, p. 98; Hua 9: 250). Husserl always stresses that the transcendental domain is an autonomous domain of living experience (5: 141). The reason why Husserl thinks of the transcendental domain as a domain of *living* subjectivity is that he recognizes that reflection on the conditions for the possibility of knowledge is reflection that is carried out by an ego, and that ego is ineliminably *living through* the reflection. Its individuation conditions, including its temporality, are different from those of the ego being reflected on. What is discovered thereby is not just a set of formal conditions (in Kantian manner), but a living ego that can reflect on its own accomplishment and also interrogate the very standpoint from which this transcendental reflection itself arises (what Husserl will see as the standpoint of *theoria*, which, for him, has its *Urstiftung*, or 'primal foundation', in ancient Greek philosophy). In his later works, from the 1920s on, he speaks about gaining the attitude of the 'detached', 'non-participating' spectator (*unbeteiligter Zuschauer*; Hua 34: 9), or 'disinterested' spectator (*uninteressierter Zuschauer*; 34: 11), which, however, raises questions about the ontological status of this transcendental viewer.

## Hegelian Echoes

In his mature writings (including *Ideen* II), Husserl often talks more explicitly about 'spiritual life' and the domain of 'spirit' (*Geist*), even 'absolute spirit', presumably influenced by the German Idealist tradition from Fichte and Hegel to Dilthey, emphasizing in particular its teleological life.[12] In the Vienna Lecture, he writes:

> It is my conviction that intentional phenomenology has made of the spirit *qua* spirit for the first time a field of systematic experience and science and has thus brought about the total reorientation (*Umstellung*) of the task of knowledge. The universality of the absolute spirit surrounds everything that exists with an absolute historicity, to which nature is subordinated as a spiritual structure. Intentional phenomenology, and specifically transcendental phenomenology, was first to see the light through its point of departure and its methods. Only through it do we understand, and from the most profound reasons, what naturalistic objectivism (*der naturalistische Objektivismus*) is and understand in particular that psychology, because of its naturalism, has to miss entirely the accomplishment, the radical and genuine problem of the life of the spirit. (*Krisis*, pp. 298–9; Hua 6: 346–7)

In his later discussion of the communalization of egos and of spiritual life, he stresses the rootedness of spirit in embodied human subjectivity. All possible forms of spirit (e.g. animals, angels, God) are thinkable only from the perspective of, and as variations of, human subjectivity. Indeed, human subjectivity in a way enfolds all other possible forms of subjectivity.[13] But he never accepts Hegelian philosophy. For instance, in *Krisis* §57, he criticizes the overly 'constructive' (i.e. speculative) nature of post-Kantian idealist systems, which, while 'engrossing', are unscientific and not grounded in evident intuitions (6: 203). In the end, Husserl claims (in Hegelian manner but without explicitly invoking Hegel), spirit is absolute and self-sufficient: '*The spirit, and indeed only the spirit, exists in itself and for itself, is self-sufficient (eigenständig); and in its self-sufficiency, and only in this way, it can be treated truly rationally, truly and from the ground up scientifically*' (*Krisis*, p. 297; Hua 6: 345; italics in original). By understanding the very meaning of the human teleological quest, transcendental phenomenology establishes itself as the genuine 'first philosophy'.

## Ways into Transcendental Philosophy

Initially (e.g. *Ideen* I) Husserl did not distinguish clearly between 'pure' and 'transcendental' consciousness. When we draw back from our normal, everyday lives as conscious subjects 'busy' with the world, and reflect on our consciousness itself in all its forms and interconnections, actual and possible, we have in a sense already opened up the domain of *pure* consciousness. This is strictly speaking not yet the transcendental, which only becomes visible through performing the transcendental *epoché* and reduction (*EP* I; 7: 254). Pure consciousness can be considered in terms of its eidetic forms, without attention being paid to the overall unity and activity of the ego, whereas transcendental inquiry must face up to pure consciousness 'as the *absolutely self-contained realm of purely subjective being* ... with its purely immanent interconnections, abilities, sense-structures' (*EP* I; 7: 254; my trans.).

Transcendental subjectivity is discovered and made visible only under a special kind of attitude and a specific kind of reflection (that inaugurated by Descartes). Transcendental subjectivity must be distinguished from all psychological – or what in his later years he called 'mundane' (*mundane, weltlich*) – subjectivity. In the Twenties, transcendental phenomenology was systematically explicated in relation to a 'critical history of ideas' (*kritische Ideengeschichte*; *EP* I; Hua 7). The search for a 'consistent transcendental philosophy' (*FTL* §96b) involves a scrutiny of the 'unity of motivation' (7: 142) discoverable in the progress (or decline) in modern philosophy, from the transcendental breakthrough of Descartes (who unfortunately misunderstood the transcendental ego as a 'bit of the world'; *FTL* §93), through the psychologizing naturalism of Locke, to a failed form of the transcendental in Hume and Kant (who did not grasp the true nature of the a priori and the ideal; *FTL* §100). Other ways to enter into the transcendental attitude come from a reconsideration of the nature of psychology as the most developed science of the subjective. But let us first examine Husserl's historical approach to transcendental philosophy.

## How is Knowledge Possible?
## The Kantian Transcendental

As we have seen, Husserl often expressed his approach in terms of a radical rethinking of Kant, however much he later complained of being misinterpreted as 'retreating to Kant'.[14] Of course, he had been reading – and even lecturing on – Kant more or less from the beginning of his career; e.g. in *PA* he had criticized Kant's account of number. Initially, he had absorbed the Brentanian portrayal of Kant as the beginning of the demise of scientific philosophy, whose 'mythic constructions' opened the way to scepticism, subjectivism and ultimate irrationality. However, through the influence of Natorp – himself following Hermann Cohen[15] – he found a way to interpret the Kantian a priori stripped of subjectivism and 'anthropologism'. In the *LU Prolegomena* he presents himself as broadening Kant's transcendental inquiry into the conditions which make objective knowledge possible: 'We are plainly concerned with a quite necessary generalization of the question as to the "conditions of the possibility of experience" (*Bedingungen der Möglichkeit einer Erfahrung*)' (*LU, Prol.* §65, I 149; Hua 18: 239). However, Husserl believes the ideal conditions of experience must be given a far stricter determination than Kant had done. He is interested in *ideal* conditions, which again he divides into two kinds: the *noetic* and the *logical*. Noetic conditions concern the subjective elements that must be in place for any kind of 'thinking being': truths must be grasped as truths, and as consequences of other truths and so on. These are different from the logically objective conditions that concern the laws governing the truths themselves, which hold independently of our grasping them. But Husserl also wants a stricter determination of the meaning of possibility and of the kind of apriority involved. Possibility, for Husserl, refers to 'essentiality' (*Wesenhaftigkeit*; *LU*, *Prol.* §66). The a priori refers to essence, *eidos*. In *Ideen* I Husserl announced that he was avoiding the term 'a priori' and instead introducing the term *eidos*, and in *FTL* he claimed that the only sense that the term 'a priori' has in his writings is that of *eidos* (*FTL* §97, p. 248 n. 1; Hua 17: 255 n. 1).

In the Twenties, Kant's critical project moved centre stage in his self-reflection on phenomenology, e.g. his Freiburg address of 1924, 'Kant and the Idea of Modern Philosophy' (*EP* I; Hua 7: 230–87). He came to see that Kant offered an entirely new vision and new approach in philosophy. Kant had set a task that remains 'the most exuberant of all scientific tasks for mankind' (*EP* I; Hua 7: 236), 'the greatest of all theoretical tasks that could be given to modern humanity' (*EP* I; Hua 7: 242). This critical but appreciative engagement with Kant continues through the Thirties (e.g. *Krisis*).

Husserl also had a long and intense interaction with neo-Kantianism in Göttingen with Natorp, and later, as is evident from his correspondence with Rickert, Cassirer and others, in Freiburg, then a renowned centre of neo-Kantianism. In a letter of 3 April 1925, for instance, Husserl told Ernst Cassirer that he was learning greatly from Kant and the Kantians. On the other hand, from the *LU Prolegomena* onwards, he was also a sharp critic of neo-Kantianism.[16] While agreeing with its critique of psychologism and naturalism, he thought the neo-Kantian conception of epistemology was not as radical or fundamental as it itself maintained; in fact, it was naive, in that it continued to presume the very givenness of the world (34: 19–20) and the 'fact' of the sciences as sciences of the world. Transcendental argument according to the Kantian paradigm accepts the *fact* of knowledge, and then inquires into the conditions of possibility. Husserl's transcendental philosophy, on the other hand, must put even *the world* and the nature of its *facticity* in question. How is something like *world* possible? How is the unlimited expanse of world with its infinite horizons given to consciousness so that consciousness discovers itself both *in* the world and *for* the world? How does the world gain its 'thereness' (*Vorhandensein*) for us? In order to answer this question, one must engage not only in Kantian-style transcendental thinking, but also in a Cartesian-inspired bracketing of the world, radicalizing the meaning of Descartes' 'putting into question' of the external world. In short, neo-Kantianism had failed to carry out the transcendental *epoché*.

In his early years Husserl frequently posed his central question in epistemological terms: how is objectivity possible? In *IP* (1907), he acknowledges the affinity between his own problematic and that laid out by Kant in his *Prolegomena to Any Future Metaphysics*: namely, how objectivity comes into play in the difference between *judgements of perception* and *judgements of experience*. As in the *Prolegomena* to *LU*, however, Husserl is at pains to distinguish his approach from that of Kant, who, he believes, could not free himself from the grip of 'psychologism and anthropologism':

> Kant did not arrive at the ultimate intent of the distinction that must be made here. For us it is not a matter of merely subjectively valid judgements, the validity of which is limited to the empirical subject, and objectively valid judgements in the sense of being valid for every subject in general. For we have excluded the empirical subject: and transcendental apperception, consciousness as such, will soon acquire for us a wholly different sense, one that is not mysterious at all. (*IP*, pp. 36–7; Hua 2: 48)

Similarly, in *DR* (1907), he argues for the impossibility of solving the problem of the constitution of objectivity if it is posed in terms of Kant's question (in his famous Letter to Markus Herz of 1772): how subjective representations reach outside themselves to gain knowledge of the object.[17] As Husserl says, such questions are 'perversely posed' (16: 140), already surrendering to representationalism and thus reimporting the possibility of scepticism. Husserl finds this surrender to scepticism not only in Hume, but also in neo-Kantians such as Vaihinger and all those who reduce the world to appearance:

> The genuine transcendental philosophy . . . is not like the Humean and neither overtly nor covertly a sceptical decomposition of the world cognition and of the world itself into fictions, that is to say, in modern terms, a 'philosophy of As-If.' Least of all is it a 'dissolution' (*Auflösung*) of the world into 'merely subjective appearances,' which in some still senseful sense would have something to do with illusion. It does not occur to transcendental philosophy to dispute the world of experience in the least (*EP* I, p. 22; Hua 7: 246–7)

In his 1906–7 lectures, Husserl expressed dissatisfaction at the way in which the neo-Kantian practitioners of transcendental philosophy had criticized his phenomenology as psychologistic. He laments that 'the Kantians are blind to what is phenomenological; the empiricists to that which relates to the theory of knowledge' (*ELE* §35; 24: 202). Kant had quite a restricted conception of experience in the First Critique, whereby it is limited to sensuous intuition. Our reflection on that structured intuition can reveal its transcendental structure, but Kant denied that we could directly *experience* that transcendental world.[18] Husserl, on the other hand, has broadened the concept of experience and the attendant concept of intuition in *LU* VI so as to include supersensuous categorial *intuition* (as well as conceptualization). By not arbitrarily – and for purely metaphysical reasons – limiting the range of experience in advance, Husserl believes he is being more loyal to Kant's project that Kant himself had been. Of course, he agrees with Kant that we cannot *sensuously* intuit categorial unities and formations. But neither should we take our intellectual constructions to be signs standing for hidden realities that could be sensuously intuited, had we, as it were, the right equipment. Husserl explicitly dismisses this possibility in *Ideen* I: 'Not even a divine physics can make simply intuited determinations out of those categorial determinations of realities which are produced by thinking, anymore than a divine omnipotence can bring it to pass that someone paints elliptical functions or plays them on the violin' (*Ideen* I §52, p. 123; Hua 3/1: 102).

For Husserl, Kant was only the 'preshaper of scientific transcendental philosophy', who left it half submerged in mythical concepts. He has no time for Kant's 'metaphysical' thing-in-itself, the doctrine of *intellectus archetypus*, the mythology of transcendental apperception, and so on (*EP* I; Hua 7: 235). Kant did have a genuinely profound sense of the fundamental nature of *synthesis*, and was carrying out genuine intentional analyses (*EP* I; Hua 7: 237). Indeed, Brentano's failure was precisely his inability to connect intentionality with synthesis (see *CM* §17). Phenomenology must take up and purify Kant's efforts (24: 340). For instance, Kant had too readily assumed that the form of the world (i.e. the framework of space and time) was more or less as given in Newtonian physics, whereas Husserl himself recognized the need to question even these scientific constructions, and ultimately to trace the origin of these idealizations back to the life-world. Kant lacked a rigorous method, had an unclarified sense of the a priori, assumed a too rigid separation between sensibility and understanding, and in fact had lost the impetus towards a genuinely radical philosophy (6: 430). Nevertheless, phenomenology can only be truly scientific when it is at the same time transcendental and attempts to bring transcendental subjectivity to intuition (6: 431).

## The Transcendental *Epoché*

While Husserl gradually radicalized the Kantian question of the objectivity of knowledge from *LU* on, his explicit transcendental turn began with his 'discovery' of the *epoché* and reduction, treated in manuscripts around 1905, where the *epoché* and reduction are introduced as a methodological manoeuvre for excluding naive positings and judgements about transcendent entities, with the intention of bringing the genuinely epistemological domain into focus and distinguishing it from psychology. He speaks of an 'epistemological reduction' (24: 214; 2: 43) and the 'law of the *epoché*' (2: 44) aimed at excluding judgements of transcendence. The context is an argument against the view that all conscious experiences must be treated as belonging to inner perception. Husserl argues that conscious processes are events in the world, in objective time, and hence are as transcendent as other kinds of objects. But in order to get at their sense, it is important to exclude issues connected with facticity and existence, and treat them on their own, in what he calls 'pure immanence' or 'absolute givenness' (2: 44). With this reduction to immanence, Husserl is already going in a transcendental direction. The concept 'transcendental', for Husserl, expresses a relation, between what is immanent and what is transcendent.[19]

Husserl's radicalization of transcendental philosophy is based on the recognition of sense-giving (*Sinngebung*) and constitution everywhere at work, and this recognition is possible only through rigorous and vigilant application of the *epoché*. In his Göttingen years, in his analyses of time-consciousness and of perception of material objects in space, Husserl uncovered deeper and deeper layers of constitution. In our perceptual experience, for example, certain qualities of an object are understood or intuited as constant (a uniform colour of a sphere, for example), although in fact the given patches of the sphere are subject to different degrees of mottling, changes in the light, shadowing and so on. The uniformity of the object is *constituted* for us and according to certain a priori fixed laws of essence.

In private manuscripts in 1905, and first publicly discussed in his 1906–7 lectures (*ELE*; Hua 24: 211ff) and in *IP* (1907) (Hua 2: 18), where he characterizes it as the move to the *philosophical* attitude,[20] Husserl introduced the new set of procedures known collectively as *epoché* and 'reduction', aiming to overcome pervasive naturalism and grasp the essence of experiential consciousness without distortion. Initially, Husserl characterizes the exclusion of presupposition as an essentially *epistemological* move, whereby the true nature of epistemic structures and the laws governing them is sharply distinguished from psychological accounts of the knowing process. Thus, in 1906–7 he speaks of the 'epistemological reduction' (24: 214), but it was a short step to consider consciousness in an entirely new light, no longer as a 'component part' (*Bestandstück*) of nature, but as a set of pure noetic acts (ultimately rooted in an ego) with their own distinct essences and correlated objectivities. The transcendental *epoché* suspends not just particular beliefs and theories about the world, but the very basis of all 'thetic' positing, 'world-belief' (*Weltglaube*) itself. The *epoché* aims to make transparent how consciousness constitutes within itself all worldly transcendences; how world as such is constituted. In a sense, this is a radicalization of Kant's insight that the objective world is the outcome of syntheses and constitution on the part of subjectivity. As Husserl says: 'there is phenomenological correlation-research, which explores the possible world and its ontic structures (as a world of possible experience) with regard to the possible bestowal of sense and the establishment of being, without which that world equally could not be thought' (*Trans. Phen.*, p. 99; Hua 9: 251).

Of course this procedure of *epoché* (a term Husserl uses with increasing breadth to stand for the whole set of operations that exclude the naive, natural, objective attitude to the world) is modelled on Cartesian doubt, which puts the existence of the world in question in a radical way. Husserl refers to Descartes' 'quasi-sceptical *epoché*', but he is clear that his phenomenological *epoché* is different from Cartesian doubt (*Ideen* I §32), in that he interprets the actual, historical Cartesian doubt as a kind of dogmatic scepticism, involving the dogmatic denial of the existence of the world, rather than as the more Pyrrhonian scepticism, which keeps existential judgements in suspense and remains uncommitted (see *ELE* §33). Thus Husserl interpreted Descartes as attempting a universal world negation, whereas he himself sought not negation but rather *neutralization* of commitments to the world. The positing of our natural attitude remains what it is, yet it is effectively corralled or put in brackets. The *epoché* puts the natural attitude 'out of action' by suspending it or parenthesizing it. This achieves '*a certain annulment of positing*' (Hua 3/1: 54): 'the positing undergoes a modification: while it in itself remains what it is, we, so to speak, "put it out of action," we "exclude it," we "parenthesise it"' (*Ideen* I §31, p. 59; Hua 3/1: 54). *Epoché*, then, is a double action; it excludes and at the same time preserves the thetic function, but in brackets (in a 'change of value', as in mathematics). In *Ideen* I Husserl is clear that what is excluded is the whole of nature and all positings involving the transcendent, so that what is left is our 'pure consciousness in its absolute being' (*Ideen* I §50). He speaks not of loss but of 'gain' – we have gained insight into constituting consciousness as it posits transcendences (Hua 3/1: 94). Phenomenology, then, is concerned not with the *existence* of the perceived, but with clarifying the *essence* of perception or cognition and the *essence* of the perceived thing or the cognized thing as such. As he will later say in *Krisis*: 'The point is not to secure objectivity but to understand it' (§55, p. 189; 6: 193).

It is in *Ideen* I that Husserl first characterizes in print the phenomenological reduction as *transcendental*:

> The characterization of the phenomenological reduction and, likewise, of the pure sphere of mental processes as 'transcendental' rests precisely on

the fact that we discover in this reduction an absolute sphere of stuffs and noetic forms (*eine absolute Sphäre von Stoffen und noetischen Formen*) whose determinately structured combinations possess, according to immanent eidetic necessity, the marvellous consciousness of something determinate and determinable, given thus and so, which is something over and against consciousness itself, something fundamentally other, non-really inherent (*Irreelles*), transcendent; ⟨the characterization of mental processes as 'transcendental' further rests on the fact⟩ that this is the primal source (*die Urquelle*) in which is found the only conceivable solution of those deepest problems of cognition concerning the essence and possibility of an objectively valid knowledge of something transcendent. (*Ideen* I §97, p. 239; Hua 3/1: 204).

In order to be able to bring the epistemological attitude into focus, to bring it to self-understanding, a fundamental change of attitude (*Einstellungwechsel*) or shift of regard (*Blickänderung*) must take place. Husserl speaks of this as a 'transformation'; 'revolution', 'reversal' (*Umwendung*; *EP* I; Hua 7: 271), 'inversion' (*Umkehrung*; 6: 204), 'conversion' or 'overthrow' (*Umsturz*) of the existing attitude. The disruption of the natural attitude brings a new attitude into play, and there can never again be a complete return to the *naïveté* of the natural attitude; nevertheless the natural attitude is not abandoned either. It somehow runs in the background, but its value is altered.

In later works (e.g. *EP* II; Hua 8), Husserl attempts a 'theory' or justification of the phenomenological reduction itself. He acknowledges that talk of 'excluding' the world is misleading, in that it suggests that only subjectivity is left as a 'residuum'. In fact, he wants the objective world now for the first time to become a theme of properly phenomenological or transcendental inquiry (*EP* II; Hua 8: 432). Here he tends to merge various stages of the *epoché* and indeed talks about the 'Cartesian way' and the 'way from psychology' as essentially achieving the same goal. He also wants a certain 'broadening' (*Erweiterung*; 8: 129) of the concept of the *epoché* so that it is now a 'transcendental' and 'universal' (8: 129), disclosing me to myself as 'transcendental I' and also disclosing foreign subjectivity and transcendental intersubjectivity, and the 'transcendental I-universe' (*das transzendentale Ichall*). As such, the universal *epoché* puts the world before me for the first time as a self-accomplishment of the ego. Everything worldly is an index of a multitude of accomplishments. The *epoché* functions to bring about an essential alteration in my relation to myself (34: 10); it enables a kind of 'splitting of the ego' (*eine Ichspaltung*), where I stand as a 'disinterested spectator' on my own, accomplishing life and the kind of objectivity belonging to it (8: 420–1). My interests have altered, and in a sense my life of interest has even been suspended. I have gained a new theoretical *habitus* (8: 419). I do not stand on 'natural ground' (8: 429). I can no longer speak of myself as a worldly being, as a human among other humans, or even as an 'I' in any usual sense:

> The *epoché* creates a unique sort of philosophical solitude which is the fundamental methodological requirement for a truly radical philosophy. . . . I am not *an* ego who still has his *you*, his *we*, his total community of co-subjects in natural validity. All of mankind, and the whole distinction and ordering of the personal pronouns, has become phenomenon within my *epoché*. (*Krisis* §54, p. 184; 6: 188).

All my convictions about real being, about actuality, my theoretical convictions as a scientist, my aesthetic and ethical convictions and values, are all inhibited (8: 422). According to these later accounts (see esp. Hua 34), the *epoché* is more and more related to the suspension of the natural attitude of worldly life. The phenomenological attitude takes over the natural attitude in its totality, with all its natural position-takings and its givennesses, and transforms them into *themes* (*EP* II; Hua 8: 431) of a science of pure subjectivity.

Husserl gives many characterizations of the *epoché* and reduction. These ways of approaching the *epoché* may be considered as different ways of bringing the transcendental into view, ways of gaining the transcendental 'attitude' (*Einstellung*) of the 'distinterested spectator'. Husserl sees the 'Cartesian way' as the most basic; but he also sees a way into transcendental philosophy through the rejection of naturalistic science (especially naturalized psychology), but later through a scrutiny of the emergence of the mathematically exact sciences from the pre-scientific, pre-given *Lebenswelt* (both approaches are discussed in *Krisis*, part III).[21] In a sense, the way into the transcendental domain through a critique of psychology is essentially the same as that developed through a critique of the modern natural-scientific tradition. Both ways focus on overcoming distortions of the subjective domain through a naturalism and false objectivism. In the Amsterdam Lectures and *Krisis*, Husserl is particularly concerned with the move from phenomenological psychology to transcendental phenomenology. It is, however, simply a 'means' (*Mittel*; 34: 9) to bring the realm of 'transcendental selfhood' into view. Once we have arrived there, we no longer need to retain phenomenological psychology, although we thereby have a safeguard against falling back into *naïveté* and 'transcendental psychologism' that assumes the results of transcendental investigation of consciousness to be *psychological* results (*EP* I; 7: 255). Husserl always emphasizes the difficulty of sustaining the transcendental attitude: 'The complete inversion (*Umkehrung*) of the natural stance of life, thus into an "unnatural" one, places the greatest conceivable demands upon philosophical resolve and consistency' (*Krisis* §57, p. 200; 6: 204). From 1910/11 onward, Husserl was aware that the reduction needed to apply not only to the ego, but to intersubjective life and its forms. This was necessary to avoid a solipsistic interpretation of the reduction as a return to my private subjectivity (8: 434–6). In some texts he even speaks of an 'intersubjective reduction'.

One of Husserl's chief concerns is to distinguish phenomenology carried out as a kind of *pure* or 'rational psychology' from properly transcendental phenomenology.[22] The same insights occur in both sciences, but their meaning changes in transcendental phenomenology. But no psychology – not even a pure psychology – can found transcendental philosophy as such. Nevertheless, in *Ideen* I §76, Husserl acknowledges that every discovery of transcendental phenomenology can be reinterpreted as an eidetic-psychological finding, and Husserl continued to claim a strict *parallelism* between the natural and the transcendental, and an 'indissoluble inner alliance' (6: 210) between psychology and transcendental philosophy. Nevertheless, confusing the two domains is a gross error, one that leads to what he calls *transcendental psychologism*, seeking to ground reality in psychological subjectivity (5: 148). Psychology remained imprisoned in a psychophysical dualism and in an incorrect account of inner experience (*Krisis* §60).

The Cartesian regress to the *cogito* brings both the empirical ego and the transcendental ego into view, but the transcendental ego requires an additional change of attitude, one which puts in suspension the world. Husserl repeatedly emphasizes (see *CM* II §15) that phenomenological or transcendental reflection is to be distinguished from the natural reflection we perform all the time. As natural reflecting beings, we discover our empirical subjectivity, as a human among humans. This reflection can yield ourselves as subjects, but it does so in the context of an unquestioned, dogmatic commitment to the world, that does not reveal the functioning of the ego in all its constitution. *Transcendental* reflection, on the other hand, neutralizes this world-belief (9: 313). Moreover, transcendental reflection is a practice that must be sustained against all temptations to relapse into the natural attitude.

## Recognition of the Natural Attitude *as* an Attitude and its Alteration

The exploration of this 'transcendental' domain of pure consciousness, centred in an ego related to other egos, and rising to the realm of reason and freedom, demands, as we have seen, an alteration of attitude. The nature of this new attitude and how it is to be adopted and sustained became central concerns of Husserl's thought in the Twenties and Thirties. The phenomenological reduction is nothing other than an alteration of attitude (8: 436), the suspension of the natural attitude. Husserl pays enormous attention to the natural attitude (*die natürliche*

*Einstellung*), the sphere of *doxa*, the 'natural theoretical attitude' (3/1: 94), the 'natural-naive attitude' (5: 148) which is correlated with 'world' (*die Welt*) or with nature, initially understood as 'my natural surrounding world' (*meine natürliche Umwelt*; *Ideen* I §28), the world in which I find myself all the time and which supplies the necessary background for all intentional acts, and for all other worlds which it is possible to inhabit (e.g. the world of science, the world of mathematics, the world of religious belief, and so on). The world is the 'horizon of horizons', the permanently present yet always receding background for all consciousness. In our natural experience, we live naively in this world, swimming with the flow of its givens, that have the character of being 'on hand' (*vorhanden*) and 'actual' (*wirklich*; *Ideen* I §50). The natural world has the character of actuality and presence. It is simply there.

The natural attitude appears in his 1910/11 *GPP* lectures (Hua 13) and, in his influential *PSW* (1910/11), where it is linked with naturalism as its accompanying outlook. All activities of consciousness, including all scientific activity, indeed all knowledge, initially take place within the natural attitude (Hua 13: 112). Natural cognition 'begins with experience (*Erfahrung*) and remains within experience' (*Ideen* I §1, p. 5; Hua 3/1: 7): 'The natural attitude is the form in which the total life of humanity is realized in running its natural, practical course. It was the only form from millennium to millennium, until out of science and philosophy there developed unique motivations for a revolution' (*EP* I, p. 20; Hua 7: 244).

The 'correlate' of the natural attitude is the *world* (*Ideen* I §50), the horizon of possible investigations, 'the horizon of horizons'. All sciences are sciences of the world. According to Husserl, the 'world' as here understood is an ideal, a limit idea, an 'idea lying at infinity' (*EP* I; Hua 7: 274). It is the idea of a correlate of the sense-bestowing functions of conscious life. In this sense, Husserl believes that the world *as phenomenon* emerges along with the *cogito* from Descartes' radical move in the *Meditations*. Everything experienced is originally experienced as part of this encompassing 'natural' *world*. It is first and foremost revealed as a 'world of things' (*Dingwelt*), but it is also a world of other human subjects, their cultural products, even scientific constructions. In this sense the world of mathematical entities is no more or less puzzling than the world of physical things. Both are products of constitution.

Husserl first gives a detailed description of the natural world in *Ideen* I, but he remained fascinated by the manner in which there is one, common, shared, communalized world for us, a world which includes natural things, living things, animals, humans, communities and cultural establishments of every kind (*EP* I; Hua 7: 243). The 'pre-scientific' world in this sense is always 'pre-given'; it always unfolds before us in our waking life; it is the 'totality of realities' (*die Allheit der*

*Realitäten; EP* I; Hua 7: 244) given to us in a harmonious, albeit always incomplete and one-sided manner. It is so intimately present that we cannot speak of it as a presupposition so much as the form of all convictions which lie concretely at the heart of every natural conscious experience (*EP* I, p. 22n.; Hua 7: 246 n. 1).

The natural attitude itself, while it pervades our consciousness, is not articulated; it is 'unthematic, unthought, unpredicated'. It is always 'on hand', and yet in a sense indeterminate. It is blind to the fact that it is an *attitude*, that it itself is an *achievement* (*Krisis* §58), and that it is correlated with a specific kind of objectivity. Reflecting on the manner in which all natural activity operates with a general stance, Husserl becomes aware of the phenomenon of the 'connectedness' (*Zusammenhang*) of all experience, the 'pre-given' experience of a 'world' (Hua 13: 124). Traditional philosophy and the sciences have offered a description of this world, but to that extent they have remained philosophies and sciences of the natural attitude. It is precisely a 'world-belief' (*Weltglaube*) that pervades naturalness. This belief can be unplugged, and the world as meant can come into view (*CM* II §15). The aim of the *epoché* is to overcome the natural attitude with its 'general thesis' of the world; all positing (*Setzung*) becomes the 'phenomenon of positing' (Hua 24: 212).

## The 'Cartesian Way' and the Historical Discovery of Transcendental Philosophy

Transcendental subjectivity is the very source of the world, at the same time, for Husserl, that the transcendental attitude and self-aware transcendental subjectivity emerge in particular 'primal institutings' (*Urstiftungen*) in human history and culture. The transcendental domain had in fact to be *discovered* (8: 78–9) in history, through an original 'breakthrough'. The historical discovery of the transcendental is exhibited through original and bold readings, not only of Descartes, the 'epoch-making awakener of the transcendental problematic' (9: 248), but also of Leibniz, Berkeley and Hume. Transcendental philosophy is the inner essence and inevitable outcome of the modern philosophical tradition as it came to grips with the Cartesian project. In his Paris Lectures he speaks of his work as 'almost' a 'new Cartesianism' (Hua 1: 3), one which aims to show that the supposed results of the Cartesian foundation of objective knowledge burst apart at the seams (as he said in *Krisis* §16). As Husserl would proclaim in 1924 in his Kant lecture, *Ideen* I achieves a new Cartesianism (see also 3/1: 87):

[With the *Ideen*] the deepest sense of the Cartesian turn of modern philosophy is, I dare to say, revealed, and the necessity of an absolutely self-enclosed eidetic science of pure consciousness in general is cogently demonstrated – that is, however, in relation to all correlations grounded in the essence of consciousness, to its possible really immanent moments and to its noemata and objectivities intentionally-ideally determined therein. (*EP* I, p. 12; Hua 7: 234)

Strictly speaking, however, Descartes is only 'a precursor of transcendental philosophy' (*EP* I; 7: 240), in whom is found the 'seed' (*Keim*; 8: 4; 6: 202) of transcendental philosophy. Like Moses, he *saw* the Promised Land, but did not set foot there. Descartes' founding insights must be rethought to recover their true meaning, a meaning to which he himself had been blind. Specifically, it was Descartes' *Meditations* and his method of doubt (9: 330) that first made visible transcendental subjectivity by showing up the doubtfulness or possible non-being of the world and at the same time the indubitability of the *cogito* (8: 80).

Descartes operated with the principle that whatever was immune from doubt had the character of certainty. However, he was blind to the need to discover the level of certainty within the ego. Husserl distinguishes between natural certainty and apodictic certainty. No empirical truth can completely ensure against the possible non-being of the world altogether. Transcendental reflection, for Husserl, must go beyond empirical certainty to *apodictic* certainty. He speaks of the 'reduction to the apodictic' (35: 98). In this regard, his *epoché* aims to achieve an improvement over Descartes' methodic doubt. He regards Descartes as having been misled about the apodicticity of the ego as discovered through the doubt. Husserl himself thinks that only the ego in its now moment is in fact given apodictically. But of course, strictly speaking, this is also the Cartesian position, when Descartes insists that the '*I am, I exist* is true whenever it is put forward by me and conceived by my mind'.[23] Descartes, of course, illegitimately moved from the certainty of the 'I think' to the givenness of the ego as thinking *substance*. Husserl, on the other hand, wants to remain within the givenness of I, and recognizes that its horizons of past and future are not given apodictically. Indeed, it belongs to transcendental philosophy to offer a critique of the modes of apodicticity (*CM* §63). The regress is to the transcendental ego, which is not a substance or a 'thing' understood as a 'real object within the world' (5: 146), although quite misleadingly Husserl dubs it as 'absolute'. It is 'subject for the world': 'the Ego (and I am this Ego) that bestows ontological validity on the being of the world . . . the Ego that exists in itself and that in itself experiences the world, verifies it, etc.' (Postscript to *Ideen* I; Hua 5: 149).

Post-Cartesian modern philosophy showed a 'steady direction of development towards transcendental philosophy' (35: 313), but, until Husserl, still had not achieved pure self-consciousness as to its nature and purpose (*APS*, p. 6; 11: 355). The *transcendental turn* initiated by

Descartes was, according to Husserl, dissipated in the *naturalism* and *psychologism* of Locke.[24] Locke, the 'patriarch of modern psychologism' (*ELE*; Hua 24: 206–7), legitimately founded modern psychology, but remained blind to intentionality.[25] Locke recognized the possibility of a purely immanent theory, and made the first systematic attempt to provide a theory of the constitution of the world by the human knower (*EP* I; Hua 7: 150), but completely misinterpreted the quest for origins, and thus lost all possibility of transcendental viewing. He sensed nothing of the true nature of the Cartesian *epoché* and of the problem of self-transcending consciousness (see *Krisis* §22).

In his 1906–7 *ELE* lectures, Husserl expands on Descartes' sceptical method, and, while recognizing the similarity between Descartes' global doubts and his own method of putting everything into suspension, he also stresses the difference of intention between them (Hua 24: 189). Descartes wanted to identify a first principle upon which to build a demonstrative science *more geometrico*, whereas in the performance of Husserl's *epoché* the existing sciences are neither augmented nor diminished, but merely achieve clarification (*Aufklärung*) of sense. Indeed, Husserl sees it as the fundamental error of rationalism that it took mathematics as the model for philosophy. Husserl distinguishes the scientific spirit from the spirit of philosophical critique (*ELE* §33; Hua 24: 192). For Husserl, the originally Platonic ideal of philosophical science, and the ideal of all genuine philosophy, is first put into action by Descartes. True philosophy can never remain within what Husserl calls 'naive' standpoints (what Plato called *doxa*), and is inevitably committed to becoming true knowledge (*epistēmē*), an insight requiring the *transcendental* turn.

First of all, Husserl accepts Descartes' claim that the way of doubt or suspension of belief is entered into in a purely voluntarist manner, according to which one can voluntarily direct one's doubt at any belief whatsoever. Undoubtedly such a reading of Descartes is supported by certain texts, although Descartes also often emphasizes that one needs *reasons* for doubting (and indeed he supplies reasons for doubting in the First Meditation, for example).[26] In the *Meditations*, Descartes' 'hyperbolic doubt' in the form of the worry about the *malin génie* puts in question the very existence of the world, and even the existence of the inquirer in the most radical way. It is entirely possible to imagine that the world itself is an illusion and does not exist. Husserl himself endorses this proposal in *Ideen* I, using it to argue (in parallel with Descartes) that one cannot imagine away oneself as doubter or inquirer. The domain of individual self is the 'phenomenological residuum' (*Ideen* I §33) which is left over. For Husserl, then, the world is not the final fact, but is always correlated with a more original, founding ego.

Descartes' key insight was that all sciences gain their validity with reference to self-knowledge and the experience of the *'ego cogito, ego sum'*. But, in his later years at least, Husserl interprets the specific sense of this insight (as he puts it in the *Amsterdam Lectures*) as:

> Every real thing, and ultimately the whole world as it exists for us in such and such a way, only exists as an actual or possible *cogitatum* of our own *cogitatio*, as a possible experiential content of our own experience … Thus, for us, true being is a name for products of actual and possible cognitive operations, an accomplishment of cognition (*Erkenntnisleistung*). (*Trans. Phen.*, p. 236; Hua 9: 329)

In *Krisis*, he concedes that the 'Cartesian way' to transcendental subjectivity was too abrupt, in that it brought one into the transcendental realm too quickly, revealed it as 'apparently empty of content', and passed over the whole complex layers of the 'life-world' (*Krisis* §43, p. 155; 6: 158).

## The Proof of Transcendental Idealism

As we have seen, transcendental phenomenology as such was first systematically explicated in print in *Ideen* I (1913), where a 'proof' is offered on the basis of a thought experiment concerning the possibility of thinking the annihilation of the world itself. In unpublished manuscripts of this same period, Husserl speaks explicitly of *transcendental idealism* and even of a 'proof' (*Beweis*; 36: 130, 132ff) of this idealism.[27] An argument for transcendental idealism appears, for instance, in his reworking of *LU* VI (see 20/1: 269–71), where he argues that actual entities depend on the existence of an actual consciousness. Roman Ingarden has claimed that Husserl initially formulated his idealism at Göttingen in a tentative manner, sensitive to opposing arguments; but by 1927 he had become absolutely committed to it.[28] The newly published texts of Hua 36, however, indicate a long-standing commitment to idealism from as early as 1908; but it can be detected even earlier in his 1906–7 *ELE*.

For Husserl, the central claim of transcendental phenomenology is that all experience is related to a subject, that there is, in his words, a 'noetic–noematic correlation' operative in all knowledge. As Roman Ingarden has written: 'Thus the fundamental thesis of "transcendental idealism" is obtained: what is real is nothing but a constituted noematic unity (individual) of a specific kind of sense which in its being and quality (*Sosein*) results from a set of experiences of a special kind and is quite impossible without them.'[29] Being is unthinkable without a subject with which it is correlated. However, what kind of subject is at issue here? Several recently published texts (in Hua 36 and 20/1: text no. 4) provide the answer Husserl worked out between 1913 and 1920, and appears never subsequently to have abandoned.[30] Here he maintains that 'real being' (*reales Sein*), the actual existence of the world as a whole, is unthinkable without an actual, coexisting subject (20/1: 269), and indeed, further, that this subjectivity must also be *embodied* in the world (36: 132). Every factual existing thing of whatever kind demands the necessary coexistence of a knowing subject: 'every thing lies a priori in the environment (*Umgebung*) of an actual I' (36: 114). That is, even if it is not currently being thought, every object is thinkable by an I and lies in its horizon. The notion of horizon here does crucial work. Moreover, a *world* can only be thought to be possible if it is in fact actual, since world means the totality of horizons. There is no such thing as a world as a whole that is merely 'logically possible'.

Corresponding to the two modes of existence, of 'thingly' entities and ideal, 'irreal' entities, such as mathematical entities, are two kinds of possibility: *real* possibility (*reale Möglichkeit*) and *ideal* possibility (*ideale Möglichkeit*). For ideal entities, e.g. essences, to exist means simply to be logically or 'ideally' possible, which means to be possibly knowable (36: 140). To such entities, according to Husserl after *LU*, there is correlated only a *possible* subject. Our being is irrelevant in the case of an ideal entity, and we can even exclude every *actual* consciousness from it: the ideal possibility of a truth is equivalent to its actual validity (20/1: 266). On the other hand, 'a merely logically possible subject is no substrate for *real* possibilities' (36: 139, my emphasis). Really possible entities require correlation with an *actual* existing subject (36: 113ff). In a text from 1914–15 Husserl goes further: a material world is thinkable only as a psychophysical world, containing something like human modes of being in it (36: 138). Indeed, transcendental idealism requires that the world of real being be known not just by a subject as such, but by an *embodied* subjectivity (*eine leibliche Subjektivität*; 36: 132). Furthermore, all worlds must relate to this world. There cannot a priori be separated individuals in their own world; all worlds are variants of this world; all subjects belong to the one community of subjects.

These are very strong metaphysical claims, and Husserl is aware of the difficulties they pose. Every existent 'real' thing (including everything past) must be related to an actually existing knower. But does every temporal phase of the world require relation to an existing consciousness in the same temporal period as that phase? The past world of dinosaurs or the early cosmos after the Big Bang are thinkable only from the standpoint of ourselves or from subjects existing at some stage, but not necessarily minds existing at the same time as the dinosaurs. Husserl's answer is: 'A world without subjects who actually experience it (who have spatial-temporal-causal intuition) is only thinkable as the past of a world with such subjects' (36: 144 n. 2, my trans.). In other words, to think of a world of objects without subjects is thinkable only as a 'past' (or presumably a 'future') of the world that now exists for us subjects. Furthermore, subjects are born and die, and Husserl wants to argue not just that transcendental idealism requires the embodiedness of the subject, but that it also requires a priori that subjects be born and die (36: 142)! Similar pronouncements are to be found in his Fichte Lectures. In one passage (marked for exclusion, so it is not clear if he fully endorses it) he writes:

> There is no meaning in saying: A world exists in itself and consciousness is an incidental event in it. Rather the world is nothing else but a lawful structure of appearances of consciousness encompassing all conscious subjects; it is a lawful structure of appearings which constitute themselves in the course of consciousness, some of which are conscious as actual experiences, some are reliable appearings in accord with solid experiential laws; and over above this they have no meaningful existence.[31]

But what kind of self or consciousness is meant here? Husserl has rejected as absurd the naturalistic interpretation that the world could depend on psychological subjectivity. The world *as* world depends on transcendental subjectivity. But here the issue of the temporality and individuality of the transcendental ego comes into question. If transcendental subjectivity is embodied subjectivity, then it is individuated. How can an individuated consciousness or 'communally bound' set of such subjects constitute a world stretching infinitely into the past and into the future? (see 36: 145).

Husserl continued to develop his idealism (now with more attention to the history of philosophy) in his 1922 lectures (Hua 35), and it is most strongly asserted in *CM*, where he states: 'phenomenology is *eo ipso* "transcendental idealism", though in a fundamentally and essentially new sense' (*CM* §41, p. 86; 1: 118). As he writes: '*The proof of this idealism is therefore phenomenology itself.* Only someone who misunderstands either the deepest sense of intentional method, or that of transcendental reduction, or perhaps both, can attempt to separate phenomenology from transcendental idealism' (*CM* §41, p. 86; 1: 119). Husserl's idealism, his assertion of the primacy of consciousness over objective being, is emphasized even in works not normally considered to have this orientation: e.g. *Ideen* II claims that nature is always relative to absolute spirit (§64, p. 311; Hua 4: 297). From very early on, Husserl emphasizes that the knowledge of the world depends essentially on its relation to consciousness. As Roman Ingarden formulates Husserl's position:

> The existence of what is perceived (the perceived as such) is nothing 'in itself' but only something 'for somebody,' for the experiencing ego. '*Streichen wir das reine Bewusstsein, so streichen wir die Welt*' ('If we exclude

pure consciousness then we exclude the world') is the famous thesis of Husserlian transcendental idealism which he was already constantly repeating in lectures during his Göttingen period.[32]

# The Notion of World and the Mundanization of the Ego

For Husserl, there is a world essentially connected with every possible act of consciousness (*Ideen* I §47). Furthermore, any actual experience points beyond itself to other possible experiences, which in turn point to other experiences, and so on (*Ideen* I §47). Similarly, the natural world too has unlimited temporal and spatial horizons stretching in all directions. Despite the plurality of individual worlds (thing-world, life-world, cultural world and so on), Husserl always insists that all such worlds must be conceived as part of a single world. There is and can be, for him, only *one* world.

The actual existence of this world, moreover, is an irrational, *contingent* fact (*EP* II §33; Hua 8: 44–50). There is no necessity governing the fact that the world is the way it is and not some other way. All facts including the fact of the world, are contingent facts (8: 50). They can be otherwise or not be at all (8: 50). Transcendental phenomenology has to recognize the contingency of the world, and indeed my contingency as actually existing *cogito*. Husserl meditates frequently on the possibility of the non-existence of the world. He is emphatic that the reduction does not in any way operate on the hypothesis of the non-existence of the world; rather, it excludes all reference to existence. Furthermore, although the ego is the source of all meaning in its absolute nature, it is also an eidetic necessity that the ego be individualized as this or that person, and that it be included in a factual world – 'mundanized' in Husserl's terminology. Gradually Husserl realized that our focus on this 'naturally pre-given' world actually limits our transcendental inquiry, and we need to reach further to inquire into the possible forms of world as such in the universe of a priori possible consciousnesses whatsoever. Questions arise as to how consciousness is able to effect its singularization, and also how it achieves its intersubjective and communicative aspects. Even the inquiry into the possibility of a purely solipsistic consciousness outside all community is itself one of the transcendental problems (*EP* I; Hua 7: 257–8).

From early in his Göttingen years, and expressed in *Ideen* I §53, for instance, Husserl recognizes that the world contains other conscious organisms, the domain of *psychophysical nature*, as he terms it. Who can deny that other animals and humans have conscious streams like us? The question is: how are such streams constituted? How can there be such streams as events within the world, yet the domain of consciousness be a self-enclosed region? How can purely immanent consciousness relinquish its immanence and take on transcendence? Consciousness must first be inserted into the world through a concrete body. Only thus can it apprehend or understand other consciousnesses through their bodies.

As we have seen, Husserl, who was both familiar with and deeply impressed by Berkeley (as we know from the Second Logical Investigation), always denied that he was advocating a subjective or Berkeleian idealism (see *Ideen* I §55), since such idealism involves an 'absolutizing' of the world that actually turns the sense of world into a 'counter-sense' (*Widersinn*). Similarly, he denied that he was advocating the 'dissolution' (*Auflösung*) of the world to a stream of appearances (*EP* I; Hua 7: 246) or treating the world as a 'fiction'. There really is a 'being in itself' (*An-sich-sein*) of the world and indeed of all objectivities. The point is to grasp *how* this being in itself arises; how does it get its sense (5: 152)? Husserl believes he has determined *the correct sense* of world: the world only has the sense of something that has received its 'sense bestowal' (*Sinngebung*) from consciousness.

First reality is absolute consciousness. But there is no question of the world being 'swallowed up' (*verschlingt*; *Krisis* §53, p. 180; Hua 6: 183) in the subject. The next step is to grasp how the subject can both constitute itself and the world and also be a contingently occurring object within the world, among a plurality of other objectivations of transcendental egos. This transcendental intersubjectivity, for Husserl, is the deepest problem of transcendental philosophy. Transcendental philosophy becomes the systematic 'self-development' (*Selbstentfaltung*) and 'self-theorizing' (*Selbsttheoretisierung*) of transcendental subjectivity (*EP* II §52; Hua 8: 167).

## The Critique of Transcendental Experience

Husserl was fully aware that he was deepening and widening the domain of the transcendental beyond anything previously found in German Idealism. Moreover, once the realm of transcendental self-experience had been opened up, he saw a great many new sciences springing up or old sciences getting a renewed vigour and orientation. One such science would be the purely descriptive exploration and cataloguing of the domain of transcendental subjectivity. He even wanted to go further to provide a *critique of transcendental experience* (CM II §13), even an 'apodictic critique of transcendental experience' (8: 169). He even wanted to develop a final science of the teleology of the course of transcendental subjectivity and intersubjectivity, one that took history

– the 'great fact of absolute being' (8: 506) – into account and gave it meaning.

In his late years, Husserl developed increasingly complicated – or, one might say, refined – conceptions of the transcendental, speaking not only of transcendental subjectivity and transcendental intersubjectivity, not just transcendental experience but transcendental *life*, of transcendental *facts*, of a transcendental *past* and *future*, transcendental *rationality* and even transcendental *irrationality*, and so on. There is a transcendental account of persons, of children, adults, even insane people and others outside the bounds of 'normality'. In so doing, he was fully aware of extending the concept of the transcendental beyond anything envisaged in previous philosophy; but he insisted he was merely charting its authentic essence. Whatever is constituted demands a transcendental account of its constituting. There is a science of the transcendental life of animals, and indeed, though Husserl discusses this more rarely, of other entities constituted as living, e.g. plants. Husserl sees all kinds of beings, including all living things, as having a transcendental sense that must be understood by analogy with the human self (*Krisis* §55) and of course, 'The meaning of this analogy will then itself represent a transcendental problem' (*Krisis* §55, p. 187; 6: 191).

According to Husserl, the discovery of the transcendental brings with it a responsibility to live life on a new level. One remains a 'child of the world' (*Weltkind*; 8: 123; 34: 12), but one is also a disinterested spectator grasping this natural life as the unfolding work of the transcendental ego. The meditator must live thereafter in the very splitting of consciousness brought about by the *epoché*. There is no going back from the *epoché*, no healing of the split in consciousness. Genuine transcendental idealism requires living *both* in the natural attitude and in the transcendental philosophical attitude, and somehow achieving a 'synthesis' of these two attitudes (Hua 34: 16–17). For Husserl, the adoption of the transcendental attitude is like a person born blind who recovers his sight as a result of an operation (8: 122). The newly disclosed world looks completely new, and one cannot rely on any of one's previous habits and convictions with regard to this entirely new landscape. We have left behind the childhood of naive natural existence and have entered, to invoke Husserl's own frequent religious imagery, 'the kingdom of pure spirit' (*Reich des reinen Geistes*; *EP* II; 8: 123).

# 7

## The Ego, Embodiment, Otherness, Intersubjectivity and the 'Community of Monads'

The mature Husserl of the Freiburg years presented the science of transcendental subjectivity as the sphere of 'absolute phenomenology' (*CM* §35), the ultimate science (*FTL* §103). He maintained that the most basic or original concept (*Urbegriff*; 35: 261) of phenomenology was the 'transcendental ego' (*das transzendentale Ego*), or 'multiformed *cogito*' (4: 99). Thus, in 1927 he could write: 'The clarification of the idea of my pure ego and my pure life – of my psyche in its pure specific essentiality and individual uniqueness is the basis (*das Fundament*) for the clarification of all psychological and phenomenological ideas' (Hua 14: 438, my trans.). His analysis of the ego widened after 1905 to include a range of related issues: the unity of consciousness, the nature of self, subjectivity and personhood, the 'communalization' of the self (*Vergemeinschaftung*; 1: 149) with the 'open plurality of other egos' (*FTL* §104), amounting to the whole 'intersubjective cognitive community' (*FTL* §96), or what Husserl in his 'reconstruction' of Leibniz (15: 609) calls *monadology*. He further maintains that only phenomenology has correctly understood the transcendental ego as 'communicating subjectivity' and delineated its 'true autonomy' (8: 506).

For Husserl, the ego is a dynamic entity, constantly gathering its experiences together into an abiding unity through the performance of various complex syntheses. It is an identity, a unity. Furthermore, it is always active, even when passively experiencing: *functioning, synthesizing, uniting, constituting*. From *Ideen* I onwards, he characterizes it as an 'I-pole' (*Ichpol*) or 'I-centre' (*Ich-Zentrum*), 'the centre of all affections and actions' (4: 105). It is a 'centre' from which 'radiations' (*Ausstrahlungen*) or 'rays of regard' stream out or *towards* which rays of attention are directed. It is the centre of a 'field of interests' (*Interessenfeld*), the 'substrate of habitualities' (*CM* §34, p. 69; 1: 103), 'the substrate of the totality of capacities' (*Substrat der Allheit der Vermögen*; 34: 200).

This I 'governs', it is an 'I holding sway' (*das waltende Ich*; 14: 457) in conscious life (4: 108), yet it is also 'passively affected'. In its full concretion' (14: 26), it is a *self* with convictions, values, an outlook, a history, a style and so on: 'The ego constitutes itself *for itself* in, so to speak, the unity of a history' (*CM* IV §37, p. 75; 1: 109). It is present in all conscious experience and cannot be struck out (*undurchsteichbar*). It is more than a formal principle of unity (in the sense of Kant's unity of apperception). Similarly, it is grossly misunderstood if it is treated as a 'piece of the world'; it is not a 'thing' or *res* at all; rather, it functions both as the *anonymous* source of all meaningfulness and as a growing, developing self, with a history and a future, in relation to other selves, possessing *life* in the fullest sense of the word. It may be viewed naturally or trans-cendentally, and indeed it is not always clear when Husserl is referring to the self in the natural sense and when he is talking about the transcendental ego.

Since the transcendental ego covers 'the universe of the possible forms of lived experience' (*CM* §36), it is extremely difficult to give a precise and definitive account of it, its 'self-experience' (*Selbsterfahrung*) and 'other-experience' (*Fremderfahrung*), i.e. its encounter with the other in general, including other egos.[1] This unity of the self can be considered 'statically' in its current constitution (*CM* §37), or 'genetically', according to its formation across time, leading Husserl from around 1917 to speak of a distinction between static and genetic phenomenology. Thus in *CM* he declares: 'With the doctrine of the ego as pole of his acts and substrate of habitualities, we have already touched on the problems of phenomenological genesis . . . the level of genetic phenomenology' (*CM* §34, p. 69; 1: 103). The peculiar nature of the ego, then, calls for both constitutive and genetic phenomenology.

Furthermore, Husserl's account of the transcendental ego constantly evolved. He usually begins (even in *LU*) with the *embodied* human psychophysical subject understood both as a transcendent object in the world and also as somehow providing the unity of conscious experience. He then progressively traces the layers of constitution of the self, correlated as they are with different attitudes. The ego is more than an empty 'pole' that sends and receives conscious 'rays'; it is a living self, an individual, with its unique history (4: 300) and finite temporal duration, a person. It lives and dies. There are diverse modalities of the ego: sleeping, awakened, dead and alive, clear or dull. A true science of the subject must understand how these different modalities are given and how they cohere in the unity of an 'ego-life' (*Ichleben*), e.g. the sleeping ego has no temporal awareness and apparently no being 'for itself', yet it has the capacity to be awakened (14: 156) and to return to unity with itself. There are periods of 'dullness' and 'alertness' (*Ideen* II §26). The ego has drives and instincts (4: 255), seeks its self-preservation, and so on. It can also overcome or inhibit drives and tendencies and develop habits, forming itself in the process. While living in time, the ego is also somehow the source of time itself; it has its own 'temporalizing' (*Zeitigung*), yet it also unifies with a communal temporalizing (15: 576–7).

Focused on objects in our 'natural-normal world experience' (15: 81), we are not normally aware of the ego. One experiences conscious episodes rather than the ego itself. Under the reduction, however, it is discovered as the 'performer of all validities' (6: 174), involved in the *constitution* and indeed '*creation*' (*Schöpfung*; 16: 179) of the whole world. All sense formations; all being, meaning and validity flow from it. It is even involved, paradoxically, in its own 'self-constitution'. This notion of a founding level to the ego leads Husserl sometimes to talk of a 'pre-egoic' level, and leads to a debate as to whether he was positing a domain prior to the ego.

Husserl sees the 'self-explication' (*Selbstauslegung*; 34: 228) of the transcendental ego as a set of 'great tasks' (*CM* §29), but it is beset by paradoxes such as: How can the ego be that which constitutes the world and also that which is concretized, mundanized and corporealized in the world? How can the transcendental ego, the source of all meaning and being, inquire into itself as a meaning- and being-constituting entity? Part of the complexity stems from the very self-referentiality of the ego's self-knowledge. How can I inquire into what founds me as a self? When I as investigator turn to examine the ego, I am in fact *doubling* back on myself, inquiring into what constitutes me *as* functioning self. This necessarily involves a 'splitting of the ego' (*Ichspaltung*), and is extraordinarily difficult to carry out without lapsing into various forms of transcendental illusion. Indeed, Husserl acknowledges that even to say that the I who reflects is 'I' involves a certain equivocation (6: 188). There is both identity and difference in this I. The reflecting ego is in a different attitude and different temporal dimension from the ego reflected on, yet there is a consciousness of the unity or 'coincidence' (*Deckung*) of the two.

As we saw in chapter 6, Husserl's concept of the transcendental has both Cartesian and Kantian dimensions, and so has his concept of the ego. Thus he speaks of a 'critical reinterpretation and correction of the Cartesian concept of the ego' (*Krisis* §54b, p. 184; 6: 188), referring to *ego*, *cogito* and *sum* (separately or together). But he also invokes the Kantian formula that the 'I think' can accompany all my experiences (3/1: 109) and the Kantian conception of the I as the performer of syntheses. Combination is, for Kant, an 'act of the self-activity of the subject' (*CPR*, B130). However, Husserl gives the ego far more content than it has in Kant's more formal concept. The pure I – the I of transcendental apperception – is, for Husserl, not a 'dead pole of identity' (9: 208); it is a living self, a stream that is constantly 'appearing for itself' (*als Für-sich-selbst-erscheinens*; 8: 89). It is sometimes described, in Hegelian language, as simply 'for itself' (*für sich*).

Husserl's terminology is wide-ranging. He speaks of 'empirical ego', 'personal ego', 'human-I' (*Ich-mensch*), 'ego-body' (*Ichleib*), 'I-pole' (*Ichpol*), 'I-life' (*Ichleben*), 'animate body' (*Leib*), 'living body' (*Leibkörper, Körperleib*, depending on the emphasis), 'pure ego', 'phenomenological ego', 'transcendental ego', 'soul' (*Seele*), 'psychic life' (*Seelenleben*), my 'psychic' or 'soulful' being (*mein seelishes Sein*; 1: 129), the 'egoic' (*das Ichliche*), the 'sphere of ownness' (*Eigenheitssphäre*), my 'self-ownness' (*Selbsteigenheit*; 1: 125), the 'primal I' (*Ur-Ich*; 6: 188) of the *epoché*, and so on. He also frequently employs traditional terms such as 'person', 'personal subject', 'life', 'subjectivity' and so on, often endowing these terms with a new meaning. He talks of 'self-consciousness', the 'splitting of the ego' (*Ichspaltung*; 8: 86; 1: 16) – a concept taken over from Konstantin Oesterreich,[2] and invokes the Leibnizian concept of the *monad* to indicate the whole united course of a concrete personal life, or the term 'innerness' (*Innerlichkeit*), which has its source in the German mystic tradition, e.g. Eckhart. Husserl draws on all these locutions in trying to articulate his sense of the meaning of subjective life in its first-person, individual consciousness with its many layerings (including those that might properly be described as 'pre-ego' (*Vor-Ich*) and 'pre-personal'), as well as in its connection with other selves and in its moral, social and rational nature, amounting to its communalized 'life of spirit' (*Geistesleben*). In fact, subjectivity understood as 'primordial, concrete subjectivity' 'includes the forms of consciousness, in which is valid nature, spirit in every sense, human and animal spirit, objective spirit as culture, spiritual being understood as family, union, state, people, humanity'. (15: 559, my trans.)

Moreover, Husserl never treats the transcendental ego in purely solipsistic fashion, although undoubtedly he always begins with the *solus ipse* in his meditations. He clearly recognizes that every ego is individualized (*Ideen* II §64), with its special 'thisness' (*haecceitas*). But it also belongs to a 'type' (15: 632). Each ego must recognize each other ego as an *alter ego*, a 'counter-pole' (14: 276) to it. Husserl is fully aware that the true concrete ego is always a socialized ego that finds itself and functions fully in community with others (such that a true Robinson Crusoe is a priori impossible). Some of his most potent phenomenological insights concern the experience of other selves, the experience of otherness or alterity, of what is 'foreign to the self', 'alien-to-the-I' (*ich-fremd*). His analyses of the foundation of the experience of others in one's own self-experience and his original discussion of the 'I–you' relation (*Ich-Du-Beziehung*; 14: 166; *CM* V §58), independently of Martin Buber, have strongly influenced Alfred Schütz, Merleau-Ponty, Emmanuel Levinas and others. Following Fichte, Husserl maintains

that every I has its You. But again, Husserl is paradoxical, insisting both
on the genuineness of the experience of the other *as* other, and at the
same time trying to locate all discussion methodologically in what he
controversially calls the 'sphere of ownness' (*Eigenheitssphäre*), 'sphere
of originality', or 'primordial sphere' of myself, leading to the charge
of solipsism.

## The Emergence of the Concept of Ego in *LU*

As Husserl himself acknowledges (see *Krisis* §54), the ego as a theme
emerged rather slowly. Initially, emulating Hume and Brentano, he
deliberately bracketed it in order to focus exclusively on *acts*, although
he did acknowledge its 'unity-function' (*Einheitsfunktion*) as underlying and unifying the stream of experiences. Brentano's descriptive psychology had no place for the 'soul', but did allow for a functional unity
of human intentional activities, and Husserl explicitly adopted this
conception in the first edition of *LU*, with its Humean 'bundle' account
of the self.[3] Husserl's focus is on the internal structure of the atomic
elements of the 'Heraclitean flux' of consciousness, not specifically
on its source in an ego or *sum* (*LU* V §6).[4] He side-steps *metaphysical*
claims about the mental or the physical. The ego is, at best, a 'unity
of change' (*Einheit der Veränderung*, *LU* V §6, **II** 88; Hua 19/1: 369).
In ordinary speech, the 'I' is simply understood as an individual,
empirical object, a thing, like a tree (*LU* V §4). The self is embodied,
an 'animate I-body' (*Ich-Leib*; *LU* V §4) in the world, and hence
already an object; but phenomenology treats it as an interconnected
unity or 'experiential complex' (*Erlebniskomplexion*; *LU* V §4, **II** 86;
19/1: 363).

In the first edition of *LU*, Husserl invokes the neo-Kantian distinction between the empirical and 'pure ego' (*das reine Ich*; *LU* V §8), but
he is suspicious of the metaphysical import of this distinction, and
specifically criticizes the neo-Kantian conception, referring specifically
to Paul Natorp's 1888 *Introduction to Psychology According to a Critical
Method*[5] (19/1: 372), with its neologism *Bewusstheit* ('conscious-ity'),
used to refer to consciousness as a 'primitive centre of relations' (19/1:
372), which is always an 'appeared to' but can never itself appear as
object, since it is pure subject. Husserl rejects Natorp's approach,
arguing that if the ego is really unexperienceable, then it cannot be
described.[6] Husserl is equally suspicious of certain philosophical
claims about the empirical ego, since these fall strictly within the
domain of empirical psychology. On the other hand, he is interested in
intentional relations and their interconnection, without needing to pos-
tulate a 'pure ego' or 'I-principle' (*Ich-prinzips*; *LU* V §4) behind them

(see also his discussion of the relation of the ego to its experiences in his 1905 lectures, Hua 23: 7–8).

## New Views on the Ego and the Reduction

The ego emerged as a topic due to the need to address issues in the experience of time. Between 1901 and 1913, Husserl – on the basis of Cartesian and Kantian arguments – had become convinced of the need to acknowledge a persistent self-identity behind the stream of *Erlebnisse*, although this unity is not itself experienced as part of the stream. Nevertheless, the temporal stream of experience forms a unity and has continuity through time; temporalizing belongs to the ego as such. Already in the first edition of *LU* he refers to a 'stream of consciousness' (*Bewusstseinsfluss*) and to the subjective experience of time that accompanies and forms part of that stream (a conception already discussed in *PA*, Hua 12: 31–2). The second edition at this point (*LU* V §6) is somewhat more specific about the nature of this temporal flow, and Husserl now says that the empirical ego is constituted in the phenomenological ego, now understood in a rich sense as not only participating in the flow of time-consciousness but as having not only time experiences but a sense of a whole time horizon. In this densely written paragraph added to the second edition, Husserl is emphatic that as part of the whole there must be an individual part which guarantees identity, and that 'this part is played by the presentative form (*die Darstellungsform*) of *time* which is immanent in the stream of consciousness' (*LU* V §6, **II** 88; Hua 19/1: 369).

In his 1913 revision of *LU*, however, Husserl admits that his earlier account of the ego is problematic.[7] He now recognizes that the ego can be understood 'in a purely phenomenological manner' (*LU* V §2, **II** 82; Hua 19/1: 357) without reference to its actual existence. Understood as a unified stream of psychical experiences, it becomes what Husserl calls the 'phenomenologically reduced ego' (*LU* V §4; Hua 19/1: 363). Nevertheless, he continues to maintain, in the revised edition of *LU*, that discussion of the ego is essentially irrelevant to the kind of monadic analyses being carried out.

By *Ideen* I, Husserl had come to see the empirical ego as constituted from some kind of 'pure ego', which he then begins to characterize as 'pre-personal' and 'anonymous'. The empirical ego is now treated as a kind of transcendent object, akin to the intentional object that also transcends the *Erlebnis*.[8] In the 1913 revision of *LU*, he states that 'the empirical ego is as much a case of transcendence as the physical thing' (19/1: 368). In his 1910/11 *GPP* lectures, he clearly distinguishes between the 'empirical ego', as a natural, worldly, individual being in the world, and the 'pure ego' of phenomenology (e.g. 13: 155), and in

his 1912 *Ideen* II manuscript, he devotes considerable time to an elucidation of the pure ego (§§22ff) as that which directs the rays of regard
of consciousness. Husserl tends to use the terms 'pure' and 'transcendental' interchangeably (e.g. *Ideen* I §33). The pure or transcendental
ego lies behind the empirical ego as its source.

After 1905, the ego's relation to other egos – i.e. the problem of *Einfühlung* or empathy – receives special attention as Husserl begins to
address the problem of the intersubjective constitution of objectivity.
However, his published work from the same period – *Ideen* I – avoids
a major discussion of the ego, although its tentative account does lay
the basis for his mature position. *Ideen* I begins from the natural attitude, where one encounters the empirical, embodied, 'worldly' ego, the
self with its sensuous and psychic life. Normally, this 'I' is lived anonymously, since the focus of interest is on objects and the world; the ego
is busy with its mental activities (*Ideen* I §80). It is possible, however,
to focus just on the psychic side of this life (*Ideen* II §22); even when
attending to objects, sometimes I myself come into view, as when I love
somebody and then find myself yielding or resisting that desire. 'Ego-
rays' go towards the object; 'counter rays' go back towards myself
(4: 98). This is not yet reflection, but a kind of pre-reflective self-
awareness. In *Ideen* I, the ego is said to present a transcendency of a
very peculiar kind, 'a transcendency within immanency' (*eine Trans-
zendenz in der Immanenz*), one which in a certain sense is not constituted
(3/1: 110). However, the *epoché* and reduction exclude this 'human
being' (Hua 3/1: 160) along with the world, but I am still left with the
irreducible 'pure I' which cannot be investigated much further, Husserl
says, since it has no 'explicatable content', it is 'pure ego and nothing
more' (ibid.).

Gradually, however, Husserl came to recognize more and more
levels of self-awareness and self-reflection, which themselves can
be targeted in complicated ways. He explicitly rejects his earlier
'bundle' view, his 'complex of experiences' view, even his 'constructed
self' view:

> The ego is not a box containing egoless lived-experiences or a slate of
> consciousness upon which they light up and disappear again, or a bundle
> of lived-experiences, a flow of consciousness or something assembled
> in it; rather the ego that is at issue here can be manifest in each lived-
> experience of wakefulness or lived-experiential act as pole, as ego-center,
> . . . it can be manifest in them as their outward radiating or inward radi-
> ating point, and yet not in them as a part or piece. (*APS*, p. 17; 17: 363)

In his *Nachwort* to *Ideen* I written many years later, he acknowledged
that 'what specifically characterised the ego' had not yet been broached
in *Ideen* I (5: 159). Let us now look more closely at the concept of the
ego in *Ideen* I.

## The Ego as Centre of Radiation
## (*Ausstrahlungszentrum*) in *Ideen* I

Husserl's later thoughts on the ego were strongly influenced by his growing appreciation of Descartes' discovery of *cogito ergo sum* through the application of the *epoché* and reduction (the ego is introduced immediately after the *epoché* in *Ideen* I §§32–3). He was also undoubtedly influenced by the Kantian (and neo-Kantian) conceptions of the transcendental ego and of the self as person and as autonomous, rational agent. In the war years, too, Fichte emerges as important, as Husserl recognizes that positing the ego implies at the same time positing the 'non-egoic' or 'non-I'. The 'pure' ego as it appears in *Ideen* I is characterized as a non-real source of all meaning and reality. It is a 'residuum' left over in phenomenological reduction that excludes all factual being (although, as we saw in the last chapter, this residuum is not the private subject, but precisely the subject correlated with its worldly experience). While it cannot be excluded, all theories about it must be suspended (*Ideen* I §57). He speaks in *Ideen* I §81 of a certain 'two-sidedness' (*Zweiseitigkeit*) in the analysis of a mental act: it is both directed towards an object and issuing from a subject. Both need to be investigated; but *Ideen* I focuses on the 'objective' or noematic side of the correlation, whereas, in *LU*, he had focused on the noetic side.[9]

In *Ideen* I Husserl reaffirms the view of *LU* that the ego is neither a mental process itself nor any real part of one: 'it cannot in any sense be a really inherent part or moment of the mental processes themselves' (*Ideen* I §57, p. 132; Hua 3/1: 109). Rather, it appears to be 'there continually, indeed necessarily . . . the Ego belongs to each coming and going mental process; its "regard" is "directed" through each actual cogito to the objective something' (*Ideen* I §57). Husserl's analyses of judgements, especially in his draft revisions of the Sixth Investigation (written in 1913; Hua 20/1), emphasize judgement as an action of the ego, as active synthesis. Judgements specifically bring the ego into play. In the reduction it must be counted a phenomenological datum, albeit of a peculiar kind, a 'residuum', and also a sphere of 'individual being' (Hua 3/1: 58).

This pure ego is 'necessary' (*Ideen* I §57). In all its processes it is actually present (*aktuell dabei*; *Ideen* I §80); it is something identical through all changes of consciousness. *Erlebnisse* are experienced as having a certain 'mineness'. When I reflect on my ego in ordinary life, I grasp myself as a human being, a human experiencer. However, once I perform the reduction, I exclude everything human: 'what remains behind is the pure act-process with its own essence' (*Ideen* I §80, p. 190; Hua 3/1: 160). The phenomenologically reduced self is anonymous, a kind of 'no one'. It is empty of 'essence components'; it is 'pure ego and nothing more' (ibid.). In *Ideen* I, as we have seen, Husserl speak in print for the first time about the absolute being of this consciousness or ego (the terms are reasonably interchangeable). Already in his *Ding und Raum* lectures of 1907, Husserl had stated that things are constituted by consciousness, whereas consciousness itself 'is absolute being and for that precise reason not thingly being' (*DR*, p. 34; Hua 16: 40). But the pure thinking investigated by phenomenology belongs to 'no one' (*niemand*), and in exploring absolute consciousness, one is not dealing with a transcendent ego at all.

In *Ideen* I, Husserl emphasizes the 'free spontaneity' of the ego (*Ideen* I §122, p. 291; Hua 3/1: 253), in a manner reminiscent of Descartes, who also thinks of the *cogito* as free to engage with whatever set of mental acts it sees fit and to turn its attention or 'ray of regard' whatever way it wants. It is the source of all 'position-takings' (*Stellungnahmen*), and hence of all positing. Husserl now characterizes the pure ego as an 'I-pole' (*Ichpol*) and a 'centre of actions and affections' (see 4: 310), something that has abiding properties and actions, that can be thus-and-so decided, in such and such a mood, and so on. There is a strong emphasis on the enduring unity of the ego through change and also an emphasis on the ego as constituting itself among a wide field of possibilities. Each act of the ego is surrounded by a whole field of possible acts. The ego seizes on a specific path and actualizes it, insofar as it is what Husserl calls a 'vigilant ego' (*Ideen* I §35). The conception of the ego developed in *Ideen* I lays the basis for the mature conception which Husserl elaborates up to his death, but there is still a degree of unclarity about its nature, an unclarity also evident in the 1913 second edition of *LU*.

## The Ego and its Body (*Ideen* II)

Husserl had been thinking radically about the embodiment and corporeality of the subject from around 1907, first and foremost with regard to perception. In fact, his 1907 *DR* lectures, his 1910/11 *GPP* lectures (esp. 13: 113–20), and *Ideen* II all explore the sense in which I encounter myself as an embodied self (*Ich-Leib*),[10] and this continues to be a major theme in his researches in the Twenties and Thirties (e.g. in Hua 13–15), where the issue of the complex encounter with another *Leib* is also examined.[11] *Ideen* II focuses on the experience of the self as embodied, as *Ich-Leib*. Strictly speaking, the inquiry into the constitution of the animate body, and the various strata of constitution from physical body up to moral and social *person*, can be carried out without involving the reduction. The experienced body belongs to our 'natural conception of the world'. Husserl simply describes in phenomenological terms the manner of the givenness of the living, animate body (*Leib*), which is first constituted in the stream of experiences (13: 5). The body is sensitive, reactive, responsive, but it also has freely willed movement, and spontaneity, the basis for the autonomy that enables it to operate as a rational subject. I am both a living organism (*Leib*) and a physical corporeal thing (*Körper*), an 'external body' (*Aussenkörper*), a natural body, a spatio-temporal, material object (14: 456), that conforms to the laws of nature (gravity and so on; see Hua 16: 373ff).

There is a special kind of corporeality, embodiment or 'lived-bodiliness' (*Leiblichkeit*) belonging to the ego. It has its own kind of objectivity, its own peculiar mode of givenness. Through my body I am an actor in the world. My living body is the 'organ of worldly life' (*Organ für das Weltleben*; 14: 456), and the world is the theatre where I display myself through my *Leib*. My body is primarily experienced as an instrument of my will, a 'field of free will' (4: 310); it is the centre of a series of 'I can's', of my 'being able to' (*Können*), of 'powers' or 'capacities' (*Vermögen*). I can move my eyes, head, limbs, alter my gaze, position, direction of attention. I can jump, swim, run, wiggle my finger, raise my eyebrow, and so on. I can 'tune out' noises around me, focus on the feeling of my feet in my new shoes. I can even put my body in a position to invite sleep.

The body is experienced as unified with a psychic stratum (4: 25); it is a 'psychophysical unity'. The psychic or conscious stratum supervenes on the living body and is 'interwoven' with it such that they interpenetrate (4: 94). The psychic, as Husserl understands it, is not an independent domain, but one dependent on or 'founded on' the physical (4: 310). This interpenetration of psychic with physical is personally experienced – I decide to raise my arm, my indigestion affects my mood, and so on. There is a sense of 'I' pervading the whole body; I *animate* my body from within. The sense of *physical body* is arrived at only by abstracting from this animation (9: 131). Moreover, peculiarly, I can experience myself both from the point of view of the purely physical (my body is subject to gravity, I fall down the stairs; it can twitch under an electric shock, impulses that are other than self, '*ichfremd*'; 14: 89). I can move myself, I can leap out of the window. The 'body' in the sense of a Cartesian physical object is an abstraction that focuses on certain properties and ignores 'practical predicates' (4: 25); rather, I experience my own 'innerness' (*Innerlichkeit*), my 'inner flesh' (*Innenleib*), my alertness, relaxedness and so on. Only when we abstract from the essential 'two-sidedness' of the animate body, do we experience the purely physical body (Hua 9: 131). Husserl always stresses the bodily sensations and experiences that are 'I-related', connected in some way with my will or that awaken my interest. But not every bodily movement involves an explicit act or *fiat* of the will (14: 447ff). I may move my hand 'involuntarily' because its position was uncomfortable (4: 260); I involuntarily reach for a cigar (4: 258). When I play the piano, I don't *wilfully* move my fingers, but they do move voluntarily (14: 89). There are zones between the willed and the truly involuntary (e.g. a twitch), and these layers need to be carefully documented. Action and affection can be functionally interwoven (4: 338–9).

Through different 'rays of regard', I can freely attend to various parts of my experience: e.g. the taste in my mouth, the sensation of contact of my shoes on the floor, a certain experience of warmth, of tiredness, a certain memory possessing me, and so on. Normally, I do not draw a line between body and consciousness (is my tiredness a matter of mind or body right now?). On the other hand, I can feel restricted by my body in many instances; it becomes an impediment to my intentions. It weighs me down. My hand can fall 'asleep' so that I cannot move it (4: 259). But either way, the body is an intimate expression of myself. It is not a fixed thing given once and for all. Rather, Husserl thinks of the constitution of the body as something ongoing; it is a 'remarkably incompletely constituted thing' (*ein merkwürdig unvollkommen konstituiertes Ding*; 4: 159).[12] Whereas, at least in principle, I can fill out perceptions of currently hidden sides of a transcendent object, I am not able to fill out certain perceptions of my own body – for instance, of the back of my head (except through using a mirror, which is a distinctive kind of image-consciousness in its own right, not direct perception). I experience my living body as an external body with 'gaps' (*Lücken*). I cannot see the reverse side, for example, no matter what position I take. On the other hand, I cannot even imagine away the body. It is, as Merleau-Ponty also emphasizes, never absent from our perceptual field (*Krisis* §28, p. 106; Hua 6: 108). It is always in the background, and in some sense is 'co-experienced' in acts of perceiving other objects. Even in a dream, I am dream-seeing *from some bodily perspective*; there is a sense of seeing through eyes, of having my body moving 'below' me, and so on. Husserl makes the claim (later inspiring Merleau-Ponty[13]) that the *lived-body* (*Leib*) is always present in all perception, 'constantly there' as the very 'organ of perception' (*APS*, p. 50; Hua 11: 13), the 'medium of perception': 'The body is, in the first place, the *medium of all perception*; it is the *organ of perception* and is *necessarily* involved in all perception' (*Ideen* II §18, p. 61; Hua 4: 56).

The *Abschattungen* of perceptual experience are in part a product of the object itself and in part a product of the orientation and motor capacities, etc., of my body. Although in normal perceiving we attend only to the object and are oblivious to our own presence in the experience, nevertheless, all perceiving is bodily activated in the most real sense. It is, of course, the medium and instrument through which we explore other things. In this sense it is a perceiving and 'self-moving' body (Hua 11: 14). The body or the I-body moves itself. It is characterized phenomenologically as a subjectively free system; I can embark on this or that course of movements (of eyes, hands, head, etc.) yielding new streams of appearances. I am conscious of my possible movements in an empty horizon 'which is the horizon of freedom' (*APS*, p. 52; Hua 11: 15).

The body, for Husserl, not only has an orientation in space, it also orients space around it. It is the 'bearer of the zero point (*Nullpunkt*) of orientation, the bearer of the here and now' (*Ideen* II §18, p. 61; Hua 4: 56; see also 16: 308). Every space is experienced from the inescapable 'here' of my body: right and left, up and down, near and far. All orientation involves a body, and all distances are marked off taking the body as the point of departure. Even if one is imagining a centaur, one imagines seeing it from a particular bodily perspective, facing towards or away from one; I can look over the body of the centaur and grasp its orientation, and so on. Spatiality itself is 'created' (*DR* §44) or 'constituted' by the movement of my body and of the thing. Moreover, this null-point moves with me in space, and indeed is the condition for such movement (Hua 16: 308). Spatiality is also constituted both through vision and through touch. Visual space and tactile space also must be brought together into a fused identity.

Furthermore, the human body is not a closed, determinate set of possibilities like a natural thing, but is, in an extraordinary way, capable of *constituting itself*. One need only think of the manner in which an anorexic person relates to and attempts to constitute her own body.

## Bodily 'Kinaesthetic' Sensations as Motivations to Experience

Perception is not just the passive reception of sensory features of an object (its colour, etc.); it also involves (as early empiricists such as Berkeley also emphasized in his 1709 *New Theory of Vision*) the activities of the sense organs themselves. In order to see, the eyes move, and the head turns; the fingers must stretch out to touch, and so on. This is a kind of *spontaneity* built into bodily perceiving: turning my head, hands reaching out and so on.

Following German psychology, Husserl, somewhat misleadingly, calls these 'kinaesthetic' sensations, by which he seems to mean that they are sensations of movement (*kinesis*) that can be freely undertaken (although they are not fully modes of will; 15: 330). In *EU* he writes: 'We call these movements, which belong to the essence of perception and serve to bring the object of perception to givenness from all sides in so far as possible, *kinaestheses*' (§19, p. 84; 89). They are ordered into systems: 'In this way, from the ordered system of sensations in eye movement, in head movement freely moved, etc., there unfold such and such series in vision. . . . An apprehension of a thing as situated at such a distance . . . is unthinkable, as can be seen, without these sorts of relations of motivation' (*Ideen* II §18, p. 63; Hua 4: 58). Husserl repeatedly emphasizes that these kinaestheses form a *system*, and can be freely ordered in different ways (14: 520, 553). These 'kinaesthetic' bodily sensations of moving one's limbs, head or eyes *motivate* us to expect to receive sensory information about the object of a certain harmonious kind (see *APS*, p. 50; 11: 13). These motivating sensations situate the thing in a context, give it its orientation, and so forth. These are given in the form of 'if-then' sequences: if I move my head in this direction, then I will see the object in such and such a way. These movements manifest themselves in regulated series; they have their own horizons of possibility: I can turn the eyes in my head left and right, up and down; I can also turn my head itself, or I can turn the body with the head; I can move my body while turning my head, and so on. All these movements or kinaestheses yield different series of appearances of the object: 'The coming-into-view of the images is "in my power"; I can also cause the series to break off, e.g. I can close my eyes. But what is not in my power, *if* I allow the kinaestheses to run their course, is having another image come into view' (*EU* §19, p. 84; 89). What Husserl is articulating here is the complex relation between activity (active turning of regard or attention) and passivity (simply undergoing the experience) that characterizes perception.

Husserl makes an important distinction between the *sensations* (*Empfindungen*) that are properly speaking *of* sensory properties of the physical object perceived (colour, shape, texture, smoothness) and those *sensings* (*Empfindnisse*) that motivate us to see the object as spatial, but which are primarily experienced as modifications of my sensory organs (4: 146). I can touch the table and feel its coldness and smoothness, or I can, with a change of regard, advert to the sensings in the tips of my fingers (these sensings often linger after the fingers have withdrawn from the object; Hua 16: 162). I can perceive an object and apperceive the kinaesthetic system that accompanies the perception (I realize that I am cocking my head to one side to follow the movement of the object, etc.). Husserl is emphatic that we combine both the motivating series of sensations and those that yield the properties of the body into one unitary act of perceiving. I do not have space here to further develop Husserl's views on the sensory experience of embodiment. I can only say that it is extremely complex; we can have fingers touching fingers, sensations touching and being touched, and so on. Here touch is distinct from sight, where the eye does not itself appear in the act of seeing. This 'field' of bodily experience is also experienced under conditions of normality or abnormality, sickness, health and so on. As we saw in our discussion of perception, there is an optimal setting for experiencing – in terms of the quality of my eyes, my health, etc. (14: 235). But, above all, Husserl is emphasizing the 'intertwining' between our lived-body and our experience of physical objects (Hua 16: 162).

It is clear that there is, for Husserl, a new science of the experience of the living body in the natural world. In fact, he is one of the first philosophers in the Western tradition to pay detailed attention to embodiment, and his descriptive analysis of this corporeality or 'incarnation' of the ego is ground-breaking. It recognizes the ambiguity and double-sidedness of embodiment itself, giving a full description that avoids reducing it to a purely 'medical' or physiological account of the body. Husserl calls this new science 'somatology' (5: §2) – and elsewhere refers to 'the somatological' (4: 77, 90, 462). Somatology would specify the conditions for the possibility of embodiment as such, as a kind of underlying science for individual body sciences.[14] This clearly opens a new field of inquiry. However, in this chapter we are concerned with embodiment solely as it relates to the ego since *Leib* is the 'original field of its holding sway' (4: 90).

## The Ego as Person in *Ideen* II

We are not just experiencing and embodied subjects, we are also social and autonomous moral persons living in a communal world. Beginning in *Ideen* II and continuing in his later writings (including the Kaizo essays), Husserl builds up from the experience of natural object to a rich and distinctive philosophy of the person and the interpersonal world (which Husserl, following Dilthey and Hegel, calls 'spirit', *Geist*). The person is precisely the subject as social and relational, whose acts are judged from the standpoint of reason (4: 257) and reflection (14: 48).[15] We encounter each other primarily as persons within the spiritual or cultural world:

> That which is given to us, as human subject, one with the human Body, in immediate experiential apprehension, is the human person, who has his spiritual individuality, his intellectual and practical abilities and skills, his character, his sensibility. This Ego is certainly apprehended as dependent on its Body and thereby on the rest of physical nature, and likewise it is apprehended as dependent on its past. (*Ideen* II §34, p. 147; Hua 4: 139–40)

'The development of a person is determined by the influence of others' (4: 268). But my person is not a different entity from my lived-body; they are 'two sides of the undivided unity of experience' (14: 458). I am a physical body under the physicalistic attitude, an ego under the psychological attitude, an embodied self in the psychophysical attitude, and a person under the personalistic attitude. First and foremost, the person is a genuinely objective thing, constituted in objective time and belonging to the spatio-temporal world (9: 418). On the other hand, its essence is quite distinct from that of 'thingly realities' (*Ding-Realitäten*; 8: 493).

Persons only come into view in the 'personalistic attitude' (*die personalistische Einstellung*), but this is not to deny that persons are real entities of a unique kind. The specifically personalistic attitude is 'the attitude we are always in when we live with one another, talk to one another, shake hands with another in greeting, or are related to another in love and aversion, in disposition and action, in discourse and discussion' (*Ideen* II §49, p. 192; Hua 4: 183). It is a 'pre-theoretical' attitude. In *Ideen* I, the 'natural attitude' includes our normal relations to others as persons and in their social roles. He speaks of the 'interlocking' (*ineinandergreifen*) between natural and personalistic attitudes (*Ideen* II §62), but he explicitly differentiates the personalistic attitude from the natural, and indeed maintains that the natural attitude is 'subordinated' to the personalistic (*Ideen* II §49). The natural attitude is actually reached through a self-forgetting or abstraction of the self or ego of the personalistic attitude, through an abstraction from the personal which presents the world in some kind of absolutized way, as the world of nature (9: 419).

Husserl thinks that while it may be necessary to view the human body as a physical body in order to highlight certain kinds of property (e.g. the body as a physical object in causal interconnection with other physical objects), it is a gross distortion to the human being if it is treated solely in this naturalized way: 'He who sees everywhere only nature, nature in the sense of, as it were, through the eyes of, natural science, is precisely blind to the spiritual sphere, the special domain of the human sciences' (*Ideen* II §51, p. 201; Hua 4: 191). The person is primarily an individual with an identity through changing states (infancy, childhood, maturity). Nevertheless, I grasp myself as person through apprehending others as persons within the wider enabling context of the personal world of 'co-humanity' (*Mitmenschheit*). We actually live in personal relations with one another, in community with others whom we understand as 'companions, not as opposed subjects but as counter subjects who live "with" one another' (4: 194). As he writes in 1925:

> I direct my interest purely toward the personal, that means, purely toward how persons behave as persons and behave toward one another, how they define themselves and others, how they form friendships, marriages, unions, etc. . . . If I do this, nature as nature is never my theme in all that, neither the physical nor the psychophysical. (*Phän. Psych.*, p. 168; 9: 220)

Moreover, social life is constituted by specifically social, communicative acts (Husserl has a great deal to say about 'social acts' and about we-subjectivity and I–we relations; 14: 166ff). The personal arises out of the social (14: 175).

In later writings, Husserl uses the term 'person' broadly to include higher psychic formations such as those of animals (which he thinks are constituted as 'abnormal' versions of humans, *CM* §55; 1: 154). In his *Phenomenological Psychology* lectures (1925) he regrets that there is no broad term to refer to all these kinds of psyches, which have more than mere passive life and have activities pertaining to an I (9: 130). Indeed, for Husserl all high forms of psychic organization are built on the basis of the 'somatologically psychic' (9: 132). The 'psychic' finds its foothold in the physical through animation, Husserl says: 'The psychic comes into the spatial world only through a species of annexation; it is not extensional in itself, but acquires secondary participation in extensionality and locality only by a physical body' (*Phän. Psych.*, p. 103; Hua 9: 135). There are also communal selves, 'personalities of a higher order' (14: 192). We belong in an open-ended, many-layered 'communicative sociality' (*Kommunicationsgemeinschaft*; 14: 194), where consciousnesses 'coincide' with other consciousnesses in a unity. 'Communication creates unity' (14: 199). For instance, in the community of philosophers, I can range across time. Plato and I can be one, can agree, disagree and so on.

Husserl always emphasizes that the person is integrated into an environment; indeed, the person is the centre of that world (*Ideen* II §50). Moreover, there are levels to that environment correlated to the levels of self and personhood. The attitude of the professional botanist recognizes not only the environment of plants and vegetation, but this outlook tints his or her overall outlook. Attitudes are diverse from each other, and so are the objects correlated with them; on the other hand, they run together into a unity. Husserl stresses the social and cultural predicates of that world and of the subjects who are encountered there. Later on, in *Krisis*, both personalistic and natural attitudes are seen as co-implicated in the constitution of the life-world. This world around the self is not the world of physical things as such, the world of the 'in itself, but the world of intentionalities and themes' (§55), the world that is 'for me' and also 'for everyone'. If one knows nothing about physics, then physics is not part of one's *Umwelt* (§50).

An essential trait of our personal lives is that they belong to a special world of *motivational* causality (*CM* §37). For Husserl, the world of truly personal human life (and the world of transcendental subjectivity) is a world of *motivated* rationality, as opposed to a purely causal world. Human sciences operate with motivation or *motivational causation* (*Ideen* II §55), as opposed to physical causation that operates between bodies in the natural world and also between bodies and minds, as in what Husserl calls 'psychophysical causation'. The spirit is precisely something that takes a position and is motivated (§64): 'motivation is the lawfulness of the life of the spirit' (§56). Thus the stale air in the room *motivates* me to open the window; this is different from mechanical causation. The direction of the arrow for motivation points backwards, whereas causation moves in a forward direction. Motivation may even be carried through unconsciously (and can be brought to light by psychoanalysis; §56). Motivation is founded on what Husserl calls 'association': that is, relations established between earlier and later moments of consciousness. There is a kind of passive motivation whereby one thought leads to another, and there is a distinct kind of motivation by reason.

## The Ego and its Temporality

Complex issues relating to time-consciousness and intersubjectivity led Husserl to reflect in more depth on the nature of the transcendental ego. How can this unity sustain itself across time? How does it develop and grow? How can we begin to grasp the *self-constitution* of the ego (*CM* §31)? What are its layers, beginning with the 'pre-egoic' out of which it emerges (statically and genetically), the drives and interests that motivate it to turn towards the world, and so on. Husserl has a great deal to say about the hierarchical layerings (*Stufenbau*) of the ego in his lectures of the Twenties. In his 1922/3 *Introduction to Philosophy* lectures, he speaks of the counterpart of the objective contents or intentional objects of individual *Erlebnisse* as the 'egoic' (*das Ichliche*) and the manner of its being affected (35: 91), although he admits that it is extremely difficult to characterize in words. The 'I' is still a kind of 'centralizing or polarizing' (*Zentralisierung oder Polarisierung*) of *cogitationes* (35: 92), with the form of being acted on and acting. There is, to use Kantian language, 'self-affection' of the ego. But in *APS* and elsewhere he pays more attention to the bottom of the hierarchy of experience – the primitive being affected or 'streaming-in' (*Einstrahlen*). Much of this 'genetic' phenomenology of the ego is necessarily speculative and 'reconstructive'. How can one speak of the deepest experiences that form the ego and 'awaken' it towards the world?

The key to conscious experiences is that they are essentially temporal; time is the form of 'transcendental genesis' (*transzendentale Genesis*; *CM* §32, p. 66; 1: 100). All experience comes to be in a temporal manner, through a kind of 'temporalizing' (*Zeitigung*), and the primary mode of temporal experience is a kind of self-experience whereby consciousness is made present to itself in a kind of 'self-presencing' (*Selbstgegenwärtigung*). Furthermore, different egos have their different streams of temporalization, and it is a complex issue how a 'common form of time' (1: 156) is constituted. Ultimately, the absolute itself is 'nothing other than absolute temporalization' (15: 670).

There is a 'now-moment', an unchanging centre, at the heart of our self-experience. Gradually, Husserl shifts to articulating this in terms of his mysterious notion of the 'living present' (*lebendige Gegenwart*), the 'standing, streaming' living present. Clearly, in its earlier formulations, this notion of a living present of consciousness has much traditional philosophy behind it – from Augustine to William James.[16] Husserl, like James, recognizes that the ego has a kind of presence that overlaps in past and future. There is a certain passivity about the experience of this stream; it simply presents itself to us. There is, in Husserl's terms, a 'primary association', whereby one experience melds or comes into concordance with the next. One experience also motivates the next. Out of this original streaming, somehow, comes the unified ego. As Husserl will claim, the problem of the self-constitution of this ego in fact covers all phenomenology. This problem, for Husserl, is identical with the full reach of phenomenological problems (*CM* §33).

The ego, even when grasped in its ownness with everything foreign excluded in a thought experiment, still has inner horizons not only of the past but also of the possible, of what 'could have been' (*CM* V §46), 'still could be', and so on. The present ego has a relation to its past ego and is in dialogue with it (*Krisis* §50) such that it becomes an 'enduring ego' constituting itself in temporal modalities:

> Let us here point out only what is the most important, the most general aspect of the ego's form, namely, the peculiar temporalization by which it becomes an enduring ego, constituting itself in its time-modalities: the same ego, now actually present, is in a sense, in every past that belongs to it, another, – i.e., as that which was and thus is not now – and yet, in the continuity of its time it is one and the same, which is and was and has a future before it. (*Krisis* §50, p. 172; Hua 6: 175)

Paradoxically, reflecting on the inner reaches of the ego leads Husserl inexorably to reflect on the kind of transcendences already, as it were, built into the ego. We cannot think of the ego as a subject without an object. As he repeatedly stresses, the ego and what is foreign to it, the 'not-I' (*das Ichfremde, das Nicht-Ich*) cannot be separated, e.g.: 'The I is not something for itself (*für sich*) and the not-I (*das Ichfremde*) something separated from the I such that between both there is no room for any referring. Rather I and its not-I are inseparable (*untrennbar*).'[17] This, in fact, for Husserl, is a consequence of his theory of intentionality, as he elsewhere writes that 'the I is not thinkable without a not-I to which it intentionally relates' (*Das Ich ist nicht denkbar ohne ein Nicht-Ich, auf das es sich intentional bezieht*; Hua 14: 245). Indeed, to each I there belongs a kernel of *hyle* that is not-I, and without this 'pre-given' stuff, the I is not possible (14: 379). This recognition of the not-I seems to delimit considerably Husserl's claims for the 'absolute', *through-itself* (*per se*, echoing Spinoza; 14: 292ff) being of the ego. This non-egoic *Urhyle* is thought of in terms of the streaming of temporality. The ego experiences the upsurge of experiences other than itself, but it is extremely difficult to be more precise about what Husserl is getting in these late texts.

## Home World and Alien World

Husserl's later discussions of the ego emphasize its 'worldliness'. To every 'I am' is correlated an 'it is' or 'the world is'. The overall natural or worldly life is a life of acceptance; it is also a life of belonging, of 'feeling at home', leading to Husserl's development especially in manuscripts written in the early 1930s (now Hua 15) of the concepts of 'normality' (*Normalität*; 1: 154) and 'abnormality' (*Anomalität*), 'home-world' (*Heimwelt*; 15: 196) and 'other world' (*Fremdwelt*) as substructures to his overall theme of world.[18] The home world is the familiar world, our circle of friends, our home environment, our street, etc. Of course, it begins even closer in: I feel at home in myself, in my body.[19] There are enlarging circles where we belong – my home, my workplace, my colleagues, my neighbours, my culture, my nation and so on, but there are also circles of strangeness matching each of these familiar circles. Husserl speaks at different times of different conceptions of world without carefully and consistently distinguishing between them – there is the 'surrounding world' (*Umwelt*), the 'everyday world' (*Alltagswelt*), the 'near world' (*Nahwelt*), the 'professional world'. Ultimately, all are contained in the overarching horizon of the 'life-world' (*Lebenswelt*), which is the ground (*Boden*; *Krisis* §37) and horizon of all our living and action. All possible worlds point back to the life-world (*Krisis* §37). It is 'always already there' (*immer schon da*; 6: 145) and is essentially the spatio-temporal world of things as experienced by us 'pre-scientifically' (*vorwissenschaftlich*), prior to scientific objectification, the world we live in *intuitively* (*anschaulich*; 6: 159). In that sense, it can never be willed away by us, and all our experience takes place within its horizon. It is essentially correlated with the natural attitude, and as such is invisible, but it becomes visible in transcendental reflection. This world flows along with an extraordinary layering of horizons. There are the horizons of my perceptual field, and my encounter there of things which have their own horizons; furthermore, my own experience is 'communalized' with others, and so on (*Krisis* §47). When, as mostly they do, my experiences gel with those of others, then there is an experience of 'normality' (*Krisis* §47, p. 163; 6: 164). But I can also experience contexts as foreign or alien (*Krisis* §36). Husserl's point is that my normal encounter with others is one of familiarity; it is not the situation of the war of all against all so beloved of Hobbesian-style thinkers. My experience of others is as 'co-subjects' (*Mitsubjekte; Krisis* §47, p. 164; 6: 167). For Husserl, individual experience cannot be understood apart from its harmonizations and conflicts with other co-experiencing subjects, apart from the 'intersubjective constitution of the world' (*Krisis* §49, p. 168; 6: 171). He recognizes that if we emphasize what is common in what different groups of 'normal' people (Chinese, Indian, African, European, etc.) experience, then we are on our way towards science, towards the concept of universal objects; but even without this abstraction, there is a stable structure to the life-world, although its stable physical bodies are not the body as understood by exact science, and so on (6: 142). We can turn towards this natural life in the world, and recognize that it is an experiencing of the world with other persons in it: 'But in *living with one another* (*Miteinanderleben*) each can take part in the life of others. Thus in general the world exists not only for isolated humans but for the human community; and this is due to the communalisation (*Vergemeinschaftung*) of even what is straightforwardly perceived' (*Krisis* §47, p. 163; 6: 166, trans. modified).

## The Experience of Others (*Fremderfahrung*) and Otherness

A major theme of Husserl's mature years is the constitution of the 'foreign' (*das Fremde*) or other (*das Andere*), the other material object, other individual person, animal, plant, etc. The best-known and most influential treatment occurs in the Fifth Cartesian Meditation, but interesting discussions abound in the Intersubjectivity volumes (Hua 13–15) and in *Krisis*. As a phenomenologist carrying out systematic reflection, Husserl usually begins from the Cartesian position that I experience my own lived experiences in a uniquely given, immediate, 'originary' (*originär, primär*) manner ('experience is original consciousness'; 1: 139), which is not the case with our experience of that of others. As early as *LU*, he describes how we encounter objects and other people as *transcendent* to our own experiences, but he does not there discuss the manner of our experience of other people, except briefly in the First Investigation, in dealing with expression, where he does recognize that we communicate not just senses to others, but also (this is the intimating function, *kundgebende Funktion*) that we are undergoing mental experiences. As we have seen, in *Ideen* II, Husserl recognizes that, in the natural-personalistic attitude, we do not experience others merely as transcendent objects; rather, we grasp them naturally and primarily as *persons*, as other *subjects*, even if we do not have unmediated insight into their states of mind. In *CM* V §43, he speaks of grasping the other not merely as a physical natural object, but as a subject 'holding sway' in its own living animate body. I experience others not only as in the world, but as 'subjects for this world' (1: 123), and not just as hypothetical constructions, but as actual other living presences. The phenomenologist interested in subjectivity must be able to give an account of the constitution of this 'foreign subjectivity' (*Fremdsubjektivität*). How do I constitute someone else as an *alter ego*, as another ego (*Ich*), with its own 'centre' and 'pole' of psychic experiences, affections and performances? How do I constitute 'other subjects' (*Fremdsubjekten*; *CM* §44) as true *subjects* and not just as objects?

Husserl's chief tool for investigating the subjectivity of the other is his concept of *Einfühlung* (usually translated as 'empathy' or 'intropathy'; e.g. 1: 124), a topic that had received considerable treatment in German psychology, especially in the writings of the Munich philosopher and psychologist Theodor Lipps, with whom Husserl was in close correspondence.[20] Husserl's earliest use of the term *Einfühlung* occurs first in his lectures on judgement (*c*.1905).[21] He was unhappy with this expression, and employs many others, such as *Miterleben* ('co-experiencing'), *Nacherleben* ('reliving'), *Einempfindung* ('sensing-in'), *Hineinversetzen* ('projection', 'introjection'), *sich hineinphantasieren* ('imaginative self-insertion'), *sich hineindenken* ('thinking oneself into'), to describe generally one's ability to grasp (*erfassen*), comprehend (*verstehen*), gain knowledge of (*wissen*), and, in a special way, experience (*erfahren*) the conscious life of another person. Empathy is about 'apperceiving' not just another's emotional states, but all his or her cognitive states. But it is a kind of 'apperception', a making 'co-present' (1: 139), and apperception always presupposes a 'core of presentation', of genuine perception (1: 150).

Husserl at times speaks of a 'second reduction' whereby I separate my own ego from that of the 'alter ego': e.g. *GPP* (1910/11). It is further developed in *CM* as a 'new kind' of 'abstractive *epoché*' (1: 126). The basic idea is that, having performed the reduction to return to the life of consciousness, one has to perform a second reduction to remove all foreign elements associated with others. Husserl acknowledges how difficult this is – it is not just a thought experiment wherein I cancel out factual others as if they had all died during a plague (*CM* V §44), because that would still leave the world with the sense 'there-for-everyone'. I need to go behind this sense and enter my own reduced sphere, the sphere of 'ownness' (*Eigenheitlichkeit*), my monadic self-ownness (*meine monadische Selbsteigenheit*; 1: 125), which is precisely experienced as 'non-alien' (*CM* V §46). Of course, it is a feature of my own intentionality that it is 'other directed'. There is a routing to the other (in the widest sense of that term) already built into me. My abstractive reduction, according to Husserl, leads me to the founding stratum of my own *Leib*, in which I immediately 'hold sway' (1: 128). Further reflection led Husserl to recognize that part of this self already intends transcendences other than itself (*CM* V §48). But the truly 'first' form of otherness is in fact another ego (1: 137) – in fact, another *Leib* (1: 153). It is only through others that the 'identity-sense' of an intersubjective object world becomes established. However, in *CM* and elsewhere, Husserl agonizes about how to move effectively from the sphere of ownness to the recognition of the other, how to make this 'first step' (*CM* V §50).

Others are now experienced in this primary domain precisely as non-primary, and Husserl always emphasizes the perceptive/apperceptive duality of all experience. As in perception of objects, more is perceived to be given than what is actually given in full. In *Ideen* I §1 Husserl had already made a distinction between what is experienced in an originary manner – namely, external transcendent things in immediate perception, experience of our own states of consciousness – and what is given in some derivative or founded way. He already says at this point that we do not have originary experience (*originäre Erfahrung*) of others in empathy (*Ideen* I §1, p. 6; Hua 3/1: 8). Empathy is mentioned right at the beginning of *Ideen* I, already with the parallel with non-originary experiences such as the object given in memory or expectation. My experience of the other is mediate and non-originary, but it is still genuine experience (8: 176). A fuller account of how this empathic recognition is achieved is given in *APS*:

> Empathy necessarily arises in its original form in connection with transcendent perception. It is based (*sie stuft sich auf*) on the perception of the alien lived-corporeality (*fremder Leiblichkeit*) as a physical thing-like body (*als physischer Dinglichkeit*), by this thing being apprehended through its similarity (*Ähnlichkeit*) to my own lived-body as lived body (*als Leib*). In a manner similar to the way in which I become co-conscious (*mitbewusst*) of the non-visible aspects of a thing through the empty intentions of perception, through 'empathy' I become co-conscious of the alien psychic life, an alien psychic life that is inaccessible to direct perception as such, and for the most part in an empty manner. Thus empathy means here a level of founded presentation that is connected to the perception of the lived-body-thing, a presentation which, when brought to intuition has its own mode of bringing to intuition (*Veranschaulichung*) and its own mode of fulfillment. It is an empty making co-present (*eine Leere Mitgegenwärtigung*), a presentification of consciousness that is made co-present and that belongs to the lived-body, a consciousness, however, whose process of bringing to intuition certainly has to embark upon quite different paths than those peculiar to the non-visible aspects of the thing-like body. (*APS*, pp. 373–4; 11: 240)

There is more 'otherness' than what I grasp as other, more to the other's lived-body, and so on. I see the other person in this world through seeing her lived-body, and by a peculiar kind of analogy, or transfer, I perceive it too as a site of sensation, of sensitivity, and of psychic acts similar to mine. I 'apperceive' the other person according to Husserl, which means I perceive that other consciousness in a way I can never bring to personal experience. We assume that others with similar lived-bodies (which we directly perceive) have sensations like ours, because of a certain kind of similarity relations which we extend to them through 'pairing' and 'association'. There is 'apperceptive transfer', or 'carrying over' (*Übertragung*; 1: 140), but not in any deliberate or even passive inferential way. Husserl argues that empathy is not feeling; nor is it based on any kind of self-inspection. I do not reason or infer from my own states to those of the other. As he put it in 1907–8: 'inference is a sophism' (*Also ist der Schluss ein Sophisma*; 13: 38). Rather, I directly apprehend or intuit the other as *Leib*, with an individual 'inner' psychic life, through an 'intuitive, presentive act' (*ein anschauender, gebender Akt*), but not one which presents *originär*. I grasp the psychic life (*Seelenleben*) of another as really present before me, but not in an originary or 'first-person' way. It belongs to the class of acts known as 'presentifications'.

In *CM* §50 Husserl speaks of the apperception of the other as based on a primal instituting (*Urstiftung*), a first moment of individual recognition (as when a child grasps a pair of scissors as scissors, and thereafter can grasp other models with different shapes and forms also as scissors; 1: 141). Here there is no 'explicit reproducing, comparing and inferring' (1: 141). Rather, there is some kind of 'pairing' based on association, which is a form of what Husserl calls 'passive synthesis', a paradoxical form of synthesis to which he gave considerable attention (e.g. *APS*).

There are considerable problems with Husserl's account of the apperception of the other in *CM* V, and he himself was aware of these problems: notably, how is it that we do not in the end just reproduce or project our own subjectivity on to the other? How can there be genuine grasp of the other which at the same time falls within the concept of *constitution*? How is genuine otherness something constituted by me? Husserl wants to maintain both that the other person is genuinely empirically real and that his or her *Leib* as *Leib* is constituted by me, according to ordered series of possible appearances and confirmations. My constituting the other means elucidating his or her proper sense (8: 180).

## Intersubjectivity and the Surrounding Life-World

Husserl does not consider the 'Cartesian way' (elaborated in the 1920s from the London Lectures to *CM*), which begins from primordial self-experience, to be the last word on the establishment of the other as other, but at the same time there is no denying its prominence in the mature Husserl. While he usually begins with self-experience and moves outwards to a transcendent sense of the objective world (Hua 14), he is also explicit that one does not actually establish oneself and the world first solipsistically and then intersubjectively:

> I do not first constitute my things and my world solipsistically, then grasp by empathy the other 'I', which too grasps itself solipsistically as constituting its world, and then and only then, the constituted unity of both are to be identified; my sense unity (*Sinneinheit*) exists because of the fact that the foreign multiplicity indicated is not different from mine, it is *eo ipso* the same as his one given [to me] by empathy. (Hua 14: 10, my trans.)

In fact, the solipsistic way of approaching onself is a one-sided abstraction. The self is never experienced without the other. Moreover, the presence of other persons is a necessary condition of the experience of objectivity. The first other experienced is in fact the other living body; e.g. the mother. The recognition of *Leib* as *Leib* is the first step towards objectivation (14: 110), as we have seen.

The objective world depends upon some kind of a priori harmony between myself and other subjectivities. Without the mediation of foreign subjectivity, the 'transcendent' object of my experience would remain merely 'transcendent for me', with the possibility that it remained something merely intended, as opposed to absolutely transcendent. But this point is difficult. A pain, for example, that I apprehend is also an objective fact about the world. But the experiencing subject does not derive confirmation of the experience from anyone else. Rather, he experiences it himself. There is a consistent and harmonious course of experience and of possibilities that belong to this pain experience. Moreover, Husserl thought that it was possible to bracket all cultural predicates, etc., coming from others. I experience on my own in my ownness. Yet, for a genuine sense of objectivity, it must be possible for this experience to be experienceable by anyone in the same situation (e.g. my aching muscles after a run are akin to your aching muscles). It cannot be the case that to experience a pain as pain requires the mediation of the other (this point is entirely distinct from arguments about the language of pain). Nevertheless, it is part of Husserl's transcendental idealism to claim that the objectivity of the transcendent real world outside us is an achievement of 'transcendental intersubjectivity'. This is already articulated in his 1910/11 lectures (e.g. Hua 13: 184), and it is constantly reiterated in later works, e.g. the 1928 Amsterdam Lectures:

> Transcendental intersubjectivity is the absolute and only self-sufficient ontological foundation (*Seinsboden*). Out of it are created the meaning and validity of everything objective, the totality of objectively real existent entities, but also every ideal world as well. An objectively existent

thing is from first to last an existent thing only in a peculiar, relative and incomplete sense. It is an existent thing, so to speak, only on the basis of a cover-up of its transcendental constitution that goes unnoticed in the natural focus. (*Trans. Phen.*, p. 249; Hua 9: 344)

Everything we experience as transcendent has the 'value' written on it 'valid for all', *für Jedermann* (*CM* §43). Everything I experience outwardly is in principle what someone else could experience. This is the very meaning of objectivity (note that Husserl reconstrues the assertions of ideality of *LU* in the language of intersubjective constitution in later works).

## Transcendental Ego: Singular or Plural?

Despite his return to this problem over and over again, Husserl's oscillation between the sphere of ownness and the intersubjective 'communalized' sphere is never resolved satisfactorily. How is the ego related to other egos? In what sense is the transcendental ego singular or plural, for Husserl? Procedurally, as we have seen, Husserl's approach is usually egological: that is, the meditating self brackets everything external and foreign to itself (including whatever is gained by empathy) and focuses on its own self-experience, its 'primordial ownness' (*CM* §61; 1: 169), thus bringing the constituting function of the transcendental ego into focus. The beginning meditator has no choice but to commence from his or her own position (1: 110). I try to identify what is purely *mine* in experience. The problem is: what kind of identity or singularity belongs to this transcendental ego as thus uncovered? In what sense, when I reflect most deeply on myself, do I encounter myself as 'one' in the sense of being singular or 'declinable', as Husserl says? Although Husserl proceeds through a kind of solipsistic method in *CM* and elsewhere, and indeed recognizes that each self has its own 'solipsistic world' (14: 110), nevertheless, he always denies that solipsism is an end-point or conclusion of his phenomenology (8: 181). Indeed, solipsism is a kind of transcendental illusion (*FTL* §96), one that has bedevilled all attempts at a consistent transcendental philosophy. He recognizes that all meaning-giving, including my constitution of the other, has its source in *me* (15: 209). As transcendental I, I reflect on myself and my ownness (15: 109). Yet 'I' in this sense am something of an *abstraction*, since to be me is also to be involved with others in a deep and necessary way (see 15: 117ff). The solipsistic ego is an abstraction in the same sense that my animate body by abstraction can be considered purely as a physical body. Further, more concrete levels of analysis of the ego would restore this intersubjectivity. Husserl speaks of 'widening' out egological phenomenology to take account of the experience of the other (15: 109).

For instance, each meditating self will encounter other similar zones of selfhood. There is a plurality of selves, and hence a plurality of spectator-selves. At times, Husserl speaks of an individual transcendental ego matching or corresponding to (even identical with) each empirical ego, e.g.:

> To each empirical I there corresponds a transcendental I. The world is the totality of constituted being and demands a transcendental interpretation, through which it can be known as constituted. Not all being is nature, is psychic being, is personal, is spiritual being, but every objective being of this kind is what it is as a 'product' of self-developing and transcendentally self-forming absolute subjectivity, which, furthermore, must not be understood in a personal sense. (*EP* II; Hua 8: 496, my trans.)

According to this view, a solipsism of the transcendental ego on its own would be unthinkable, a nonsense (*Unsinn*; 8: 496). Each ego discovers itself as 'open' to others. It also recognizes that there are other subjects with their own validities and their own centres of meaning-giving, over which I hold no sway. Transcendental subjectivity is, *contra* Kant, irredeemably plural (29: 120), or, as he sometimes puts it in Cartesian terms: 'we think' (*nos cogitamus*; 8: 316). We have a 'we-past' and a 'we-future' (15: 66). Moreover, to grasp another person as a person as a 'functioning subject' (*als fungierendes Subjekt*; 8: 493) is at the same time to apperceive them *as* another transcendental subject. I experience transcendental subjectivities other than my own, and I validate them as such.

Yet, at other times, Husserl speaks confusingly of the absolute uniqueness and singularity of the ego; it is the 'only one' (*das Einzige*), the 'one absolute existent' (*FTL* §103), 'the universal, absolute transcendental ego' (1: 130), something that seemingly cannot be plural.[22] Husserl often speaks of anchoring intersubjectivity in the 'primal I', with its 'personal indeclinability' (*persönliche Undeklinierbarkeit*; *Krisis* §54). This unique ego would be, in Alfred Schütz's words, *singulare tantum*. Thus *Krisis* (6: 188) speaks of an *Ur-Ich* that constitutes both intersubjectivity and itself among subjects.[23] Husserl is always explicit that other egos get their sense and validity from my ego (*FTL* §96), and this is an 'enigma'. How can I be the meaning-source of everything (if it were not for my consciousness, nothing at all would appear) yet encounter within myself an experience of genuine otherness, not just other objects but other subjects? But in his main late texts (e.g. *FTL*, *Krisis*) Husserl prefers to argue that there is only an apparent contradiction in finding others at the heart of my own self-analysis (*Krisis* §54). In a text closely paralleling *Krisis* §54b, Husserl maintains that the 'absolute I' contains in itself not just my being but the being of others, and to such an absolute I the concept of an *alter ego* makes no sense (Hua 15: 586).

Eugen Fink believes that the late Husserl traces the transcendental ego back to a non-personal or pre-personal ground which might be thought to be neither singular nor plural.[24] Dan Zahavi suggests that Fink is wrong to interpret Husserl's remarks about the pre-egoic pre-individual strand of 'original life' (*Urleben*) as if it were somehow a layer of absolute being prior to the ego. Rather, Zahavi believes, this layer ought to be interpreted as the ego in its stages of passive affect-edness: 'When Husserl speaks of "egoless streaming," the expression "egoless" does not refer to the lack of an I, but rather to the primal passivity of the streaming, which is beyond egoic influence'.[25] There is not a single ego-less transcendental life behind the plurality of transcendental egos; rather, there is just a plurality of egos coming together to produce the one world. It has to be said, however, that Husserl does not clearly articulate how transcendental egos relate (he also at times speaks of a 'primal we'). Certainly the plurality of I's live 'through one another' (15: 371). But they have a harmony, one that is established through communication. At times, Husserl distinguishes between 'monadic transcendental subjectivity' and the transcendental ego as such (15: 74).

Part of the problem is how far we can legitimately found meta-physical claims on phenomenological descriptions of experience. Clearly, Husserl recognizes the crucial importance for transcendental philosophy of the inner relations between the observing I and the I that is observed. This leads him to recognize an absolute I (subjectivity without an I-centre is unthinkable for Husserl). But, phenomenologi-cally, I can grasp that subjectivity only as I. In other words, I cannot personally grasp its inherent plurality (perhaps this is why Husserl for so long considered the pure I to be 'anonymous'). On the other hand, the stable objectivity of the accomplished product – the world with its genuine objects *and* other subjects – suggests that there are plural streams intentionally corresponding and agreeing, and hence that there is a plurality of transcendental functioning. To state whether the func-tioning ego of another is the same as my I is in a sense to transgress the boundaries of phenomenology. It is to make an ungrounded meta-physical identity claim.

## Subjectivity and Mundanization

There is another paradox associated with the transcendental ego: how it can both be 'for the world' and 'in the world', as Husserl put it in *Krisis* §53. The transcendental ego is not only world-constituting; at the same time, again paradoxically, it is actualized as a concrete being in the world. There is 'mundanization of the ego' (*die Verweltlichung des Ego*; CM §36). In fact, it appears *necessary*, according to Husserl, that the ego is mundanized as a human being. The ego is also incarnated in a body and has a fundamental situatedness and locatedness in geographical space, time, its generation, tradition, culture and history. The ego undergoes mundanization, corporealization, individualization, reproduction from generation to generation and so on; it must encounter birth, death and other such existential phenomena (Hua 15: 211). This led to an essentially unresolved tension in Husserl's later work. Part of the enigma of subjectivity is that the transcendental ego is always individualized, 'embodied' and 'enworlded'. The empirical worldly ego, the embodied self, of course, will die. The transcendental ego, on the other hand, at least in some of Husserl's formulations, never dies (see *APS*, p. 467; Hua 11: 378). It makes no sense to think of it living or perishing: 'We would have the absurdity that the absolutely existing ego, in the duration of its being, would encounter itself as not being' (*Ideen* II §23, p. 110; 4: 103). It is without beginning or end. In part, this is because the transcendental ego is that which makes manifestation possible. Without the ego there is no phenomenality, no givenness and hence no world. In this sense the ego is the *primary phenomenon* of phenomenology.

The great challenge of phenomenology is to grasp the deepest meaning of the transcendental subject *as* interwoven with transcendental intersubjectivity (see *Krisis* §73), or what Husserl calls 'transcendental all-subjectivity' (*transzendentale Allsubjektivität*; Hua 8: 482). He speaks of transcendental egos that are not only 'for themselves' constituting the world, but also 'for each other' (*füreinander*; 8: 505; 15: 191). I experience others not just as in the world but as subjects *for* the world (*CM* V §43). Most often in his later works, Husserl articulates this intersubjectivity in terms of monads and a monadology.

## Monads and Monadology

From roughly the middle of his Göttingen years,[26] Husserl employs the term 'monad' (see also 4: 108; 14: 42), borrowed from Leibniz, to refer to the person or concrete ego. It is difficult to judge how seriously to take Husserl's invocation of monads. He denies that the term is to be understood in a metaphysical or speculative manner (*CM* §49); monads are not hypothetical entities or inventions; rather, they express individual *concrete* lives understood as temporal wholes. A monad is an individual, living, whole *concrete* unity (1: 157; *eine lebendige Einheit*; 14: 34), established over time (*CM* §33) as a life, with its own temporal field (*Zeitfeld*; 14: 43), and capacity for self-development (25: 322). It is a 'unity of becoming' (*Werdenseinheit*; 14: 34); it includes not just the person at present, but how he or she has evolved or become – that is, including the various intentional layers that have sedimented (14: 35).

The monad also includes those parts of a concrete life where the ego is not awake or appears absent or 'dull', e.g. in sleep (14: 46). As there is no consciousness without hyletic data (14: 52), a unique set of hyletic data belong to it. The monad is a 'substratum of habitualities' (Hua 14: 43) and acquires a personal style or character over time. The monad is a self that includes his or her history. Monads also seem to contain within themselves the possibilities of what they may become.

Monads are unique, 'absolutely separate' individuals (1: 157); nevertheless, they are 'communalized' in a community of monads (*EP* II; Hua 8: 190), a 'harmony of monads' (1: 138). There is a transcendental 'universe of monads' (*Allheit der Monaden, Monadenall*; 15: 609) that is complete and unalterable. Part of Husserl's puzzle is how a monad grasps itself both as an absolute being for itself and as 'a' monad, one that leaves open the possibility of a plurality of such monads (Hua 15: 341). Monads have being not only 'for themselves' but also 'for one another' ( *für-einander-Sein*; 1: 157; 15: 194) in genuine community. The self has not just an 'I-sense' but a 'we-sense'. These others have reciprocal communal relations with each other, leading to the notion of an open community of monads, i.e. 'transcendental intersubjectivity' (1: 158). Monads have an exact 'accord' and 'parallelism' with other monads (13: 7). They have indefinitely many windows (Hua 13: 473; 14: 295; 14: 260), and intuitively grasp other beings as persons or subjects. Individual monads die or become 'sleeping', but the universe of monads goes on; indeed, its process is the 'self-realization of the Godhead' (15: 610). Husserl even speculates about the kind of 'sleeping' life of monads in the world prior to the evolution of conscious entities. For Husserl as a transcendental idealist, all being is correlative to consciousness, but one cannot make the pre-human past of the world into a construction of *present* consciousness. There must in Husserl be a kind of absolute consciousness (possibly construed as a set of sleeping or dull monads; 15: 609), even in the earliest stages of evolution of the cosmos.

Generally speaking, Husserl allows considerable room for facticity ('monadic possibilities are existence-relative'; 14: 158), but he also tends to stress that an individual can become only what his or her essence allows her to become. Monads that actually exist are in community with other actual monads (1: 157), belonging to the same 'real' time (1: 166). Indeed, Husserl thinks it a priori impossible that two communities of monads could exist in worlds closed off from one another. There cannot be such absolutely unrelated intersubjectivities; there is only the single community of all existing monads (*CM* V §60). Moreover, it is only phenomenology that can do full justice to the concrete becoming of transcendental subjectivity and the community of subjects in history; for 'history is the great fact of absolute being', and the 'ultimate question' concerns the 'absolute meaning' of this history (8: 506).

## Husserl's Metaphysics of the Ego

As we have seen, Husserl moves gradually from an early bracketing of the ego to the view that the ego and its self-constitution are more or less the whole of phenomenology. Husserl uncovers deeper and deeper layers of selfhood and self-experience, correlated with different attitudes. The ego is the source of all experience, and hence is source of the world itself. Each ego has its private sphere, its own world, yet it also shares the one world with other subjects. Especially in his late work Husserl offers complex, paradoxical and deeply ambiguous claims about the transcendental ego and its relationship to other egos. Besides his exploration of the paradoxes of absolute and mundanized ego, singular and plural, he also engages in Hegelian-style talk of an absolute to which all egos belong. He brings all egos together in some kind of Absolute or All, sometimes spoken of as 'absolute subjectivity' in a unique sense, more often as the ongoing community of egos. Whereas individuals are born and die, there is a kind of permanent, 'ever newly constituting universal wakefulness' that runs on (15: 618). There is an 'all-personality' that is permanently becoming (15: 618), and which seems to run through the periods of sleeping and waking of individual monads. Husserl tried to develop a systematic account of the universe as a whole as something with *teleological* and even *theological* meaning. The world of spirit coheres into a unity, for Husserl. It is a goal-oriented, rational, communicative world, a 'community of monads' (*Monadgemeinschaft*), a 'world of development' (*eine Welt der Entwicklung*), a world of reason, where, according to one lecture, as in Aristotelian and Platonic philosophy, everything takes place for the sake of the Good.[27]

I believe that Husserl's inescapably metaphysical language and his ambiguous statements suggest that he did take seriously the claim to have found an absolute source of the world. The transcendental ego is the 'bearer of the world' (Hua 8: 505). 'Absolute' here means that this ego is not relativized against anything, that it has existence *per se* (sometimes Husserl even speaks of *causa sui*). Husserl prefers to say that the empirical ego is the 'self-objectification' (*Selbstobjektivation*; 6: 190) of the transcendental ego. But there seems also to be a split within the transcendental ego, between, specifically, the absolute source that is not born and cannot die, and the conception of the transcendental ego having temporalization across an individual life. In the end, Husserl does not want us to think (naturalistically) of the transcendental ego as a moment in the life of the natural worldly ego. It is precisely the other way round for him: the natural world in which we live and move and have our being is the outcome of an attitude, the natural attitude, which itself is just one aspect of the transcendental life of spirit.

Once we enter the true transcendental life, we see the natural world, its transcendences, temporal order, etc., as only one way of looking at a much richer living transcendental life. Or, at least, that was Husserl's claim.

# Conclusion: Husserl's Contribution to Philosophy

It is time to reflect on Husserl's achievements. He took over an existing form of descriptive psychology, extracted it from its naturalistic setting and radicalized it, first as eidetic, then as transcendental phenomenology. In his earlier work, especially, he identified key problems in the standard approaches of his day (empiricist, positivist, rationalist, neo-Kantian) to the epistemological assumptions concerning the nature of objectivity and the role of the subject in attaining that objectivity. He showed convincingly how psychologism, naturalism and scientism all misunderstood the true nature of objectivity in its relation to subjectivity. In *LU* he produced a devastating critique of psychologism, and in *ELE*, PSW and elsewhere also repudiated the project for the 'naturalization of consciousness' that he correctly identified as the emerging dominant model both in the sciences and in much contemporary philosophy. His own project for a description of the a priori, essential forms of consciousness, his 'ABC of consciousness', is a sharp counterpoint to this naturalism. His detailed analyses of perception, memory, imagination and judgement are full of original, enduring insights for cognitive science and philosophy of mind. His original account of the role of embodiment in conscious experience (his proposed 'somatology') is also of tremendous philosophical importance, providing a corrective to centuries of neglect of this topic, and laying the basis for the discussions of sensuous signification in Merleau-Ponty and others. Phenomenology, moreover, studies not just the individual knower, but also how that knower develops 'sociality' (*Sozialität*) and undergoes 'communalization' (*Vergemeinschaftung*; CM V §55), and enters into a common objective world, 'communal spirit' (*Gemeinsgeist*) and into history.

Husserl also had a very demanding conception of the practice of philosophy. He saw his phenomenology as gathering up, completing –

and, in his view, radicalizing – previous forms of philosophy. He identified with the traditional Greek and Roman definition of philosophy
as the knowledge of all things: it is 'nothing other than the intention
towards absolute knowledge' (Hua 13: 150). He was a defender of the
idea of *philosophia perennis*, and had a strong sense of the mission of
philosophy to provide an overarching theory of rationality, a *mathesis
universalis* as prefigured by Leibniz. Only a completely rational science
is science at all, he claimed (see *APS*, p. 7; Hua 11: 355). Both Descartes
and Kant had struggled to renew philosophy and make it scientific.
Husserl too wanted to reawaken the spirit of 'philosophical self-
responsibility' (*CM*, Intro. §2). Philosophy must become more scientific.
In the same way, Husserl believed, the sciences themselves must
become more self-reflective and philosophical. His aim, therefore, was
to make a beginning in setting philosophy on the path of science by
clarifying the essential elements in the achievement of knowledge. Philosophy must abandon all mystification and obfuscation, as well as illusory forms of satisfaction. Such was his radical honesty that he did not
even claim to be a philosopher, but simply to be laying the foundations
for a first beginning in philosophy.

The ancient Greeks set the agenda with their *telos* of 'humanity that
seeks to exist, and is only possible, through philosophical reason'
(*Krisis* §6). Philosophy, Husserl wrote in the 1920s, has provided the
most self-aware and rationally justified conception of 'genuine humanity' (*echte Humanität*). His struggle for philosophical clarification
amounted to nothing less than an appeal to live a truly rational life,
which, for him, was not just an individual life but a communalized,
social and, indeed, 'spiritual life' (*Geistesleben*) – that is, the life of
culture and civilization and world history.

Adopting Brentano's slogan, Husserl considered philosophy to have
only one form; it could exist only as a rigorous science. In part, this was
also an attempt to *reunify* science and philosophy, which had been sun-
dered since the birth of modernity. As he put it in his written address
(never delivered) to the Eighth International Congress of Philosophy
in Prague in 1934: 'where genuine science actively lives, there lives philosophy, and where philosophy is, there also is science: an inseparable
interlacing' (*ein untrennbares Ineinander*; Hua 27: 185, my trans.). The
objectivity of the sciences would be suitably clarified and qualified; the
domain of the subjective would also for the first time receive scientific
clarification and articulation. Furthermore, the splitting of philosophy
into specialized sub-disciplines with no attention to their unity and
common ground also endangered the possibility of science. But even
more, as he said in his London Lectures of 1922, it led to a frustration
and anti-scientific reaction in the younger generation and to their
seeking refuge in 'mysticism' (*LV*; 35: 312). But Husserl was also always
extremely clear that science itself cannot substitute for philosophy. The

methods and procedures of natural science can never be those of philosophy: 'Philosophy, however, lies in a wholly new dimension. It requires a *wholly new point of departure* and a wholly new method, a method that distinguishes it in principle from every "positive" science' (*IP*, p. 20; Hua 2: 24). Whereas positive sciences apply a strict method and then advance 'naïvely', the philosophical sciences are born from reflection and the effort to acquire clarity of sense. Husserl saw himself as engaging in fundamental investigations of meaning or 'sense investigations' (*Besinnungen*) of a most radical kind; he was struggling at the very base of the structures of meaning, but the structures which gave rise to meaningful acts of cognition and those structures which belonged to the essence of meaning itself in all its forms. In this respect, i.e. in the area of sense-clarification, even the most rigorous mathematical science is not better placed than common experience (*IP*, p. 21; Hua 2: 25). Philosophical reflection is a new kind of reflection. It is not meant to complete the task of the sciences but to enter into radical thinking of an entirely different kind.

Nevertheless, he took over many tendencies from previous philosophy and gave them his own peculiar stamp. He rejected metaphysical speculation and construction, and drew on the older British Empiricist tradition of Berkeley and Hume, and its revived form in Mill and Brentano, as well as the positivism of the French thinker Auguste Comte (1798–1858). He always admired the rationalists, especially Leibniz, but also saw deficiencies in their approach. He was a lifelong critic of all forms of philosophical irrationalism and anti-scientism. To that extent he was a natural ally of empiricism and logical positivism, whose basic positions he sought to reformulate in a coherent way. In *Ideen* I, he even calls himself a 'positivist': 'If "*positivism*" is tantamount to an absolutely unprejudiced grounding of all sciences on the "positive," that is to say, on what can be seized upon originaliter, then *we* are the genuine positivists' (*Ideen* I, §20, p. 39; Hua 3/1: 38). On the other hand, he regarded positivism, in particular, as a rather narrow sham or 'dummy' philosophy that completely misunderstood the nature of the given.[1] He criticized it for ignoring the subjective dimension, and for denying the obvious fact that we do intuit essences (*Ideen* I §25) and entities beyond the sensory. In its refusal to see beyond facts, positivism 'decapitates' philosophy (*Krisis* §3, p. 9; Hua 6: 7). He similarly rejected empiricist accounts of abstraction and the cognition of the universal. Empiricism, in particular, offered a distorted and indeed abstract ('one-sided') account of experience. Husserl is a particularly brilliant critic of the shortcomings and 'naïveté' of representationalism and sense-data theories common in empiricist accounts of knowledge, and offers his own elaborate analysis of the complexities of image-consciousness as a corrective to this crude naïveté.

Husserl sees phenomenology not just as a radicalized form of empiricism, but also as completing the rationalist project: 'Thus philosophy is nothing other than rationalism through and through . . . it is *ratio* in the constant movement of self-elucidation (*Selbsterhellung*),' (*Krisis* §73, p. 338, 6: 273). Or again: 'Phenomenology is the most extreme completion of rationalism, it is also to be reckoned just as much as the most extreme completion of empiricism' (Hua 35: 288). His main claim is that previous philosophies – be they positivist, empiricist or rationalist – have underestimated the complexity and diversity of thought forms. Instead of imposing views 'from above', they need to attend to the nature of the scientific disciplines themselves; e.g. one must enter into mathematical activity from the inside to determine its meaning (*Ideen* I §25). Phenomenology, on the other hand, proceeds 'from below' and thereby offers a more inclusive way of attending to the diversity of experience – the diversity of givenness, as he would say. Indeed, as his thought developed, he came to see phenomenology as expressing the inner essence of all genuine philosophy. In this sense, phenomenology, as he wrote in 1922/3, is the 'original method (*Urmethode*) of all philosophical methods' (Hua 35: 51).

Besides his critique of empiricism and positivism and his rethinking of rationalism, Husserl made other important contributions to philosophy, including a powerful defence of the ideality of meanings, universals and abstract objects generally, a novel account of indexicals and of reference, and a defence of categorial intuition. *LU* offers an exciting and original approach to issues of semiotics, semantics, reference, the theory of parts and wholes, and formal ontology. For instance, his analysis of the sign attracted the interest of linguists such as Roman Jakobson as well as critics such as Jacques Derrida.[2] Indeed, some critics think that Husserl's work never again reached the heights of *LU*. But I believe that there are many new ideas and rich analyses in the later work also. Husserl continued to document the complex achievements and syntheses of consciousness, identifying the passive syntheses of the pre-predicative life as well as the active syntheses of judgement and of the specifically egoic activity. His mature conception of objectivity as an intersubjective achievement and his analysis of the kind of abstract formalization at work in the mathematical sciences, as opposed to the experience of things in the life-world, are also enduring contributions. His late phenomenological reflections on the nature of natural wordly life, worldhood, cultural formation and interculturality provided a strong stimulus to the development of social and interpersonal phenomenology, and have had a strong influence on social philosophy (e.g. Alfred Schütz).

Husserl's characterizations of the 'natural attitude' – the normal attitude in which we live and move and have our being – and of the 'life-world', in which humans live in their pre-reflective, pre-scientific, practical lives, are enduring insights that allow philosophy to gain a special insight into the attitudes that disrupt the natural life of humans in the world, especially the new technological calculative attitude that has come to dominate world culture. Husserl's account of the natural attitude is highly nuanced. He recognizes that the 'naturalization of spirit' is part of the nature of human being in the world, although it can become distorted in the naturalistic outlook:

> Everything mundane participates in nature. The naturalization of spirit (*Die Naturalisierung des Geistes*) is not an invention of philosophers – it is a fundamental error if falsely interpreted and misused, but only under these conditions. In fact it has its ground and justification in this, that mediately or immediately, all that is worldly has its place in the spatiotemporal sphere. Everything is here or there, and its place is determinable, in the same way that everything spatiotemporal is determinable, i.e., temporally determinable by means of physical instruments, whether hourglasses, pendulum clocks, or any sort of chronometer. In this way, everything nonsensible (*alles Unsinnliche*) partakes of the sensible; it is an existent *from* the world, existing in the one spatiotemporal horizon. (*EU* §8, p. 34; 29)

Husserl's whole philosophy is, in a sense, driven by the recognition of different *attitudes* (natural, personalistic, aesthetic, scientific) correlated with different forms of objectivity, some of which are given detailed description, others of which are simply assumed. Husserl is particularly interested in identifying the strata of attitudes. At the base of his account, Husserl assumes a free spontaneity of the ego that can adopt or discard attitudes, which can accept them as habitualities or can reject them as alien. The whole of consciousness seems to depend on a free ego that belongs to the life of spirit, which can be individualized, spatialized and temporalized. Husserl does not give a detailed philosophical account of what it is to be an attitude; rather, he focuses in particular on descriptions of the natural attitude and the scientific attitude and on their interrelation.

Husserl documents in convincing fashion (in a manner that no doubt strongly influenced Heidegger) how the modern scientific attitude, coupled with all-prevailing technologization of culture, now completely dominates the age. While he defends the universalization of the truly scientific attitude, he is also conscious that this universal scientific attitude must come to know itself for what it is, and not ignore the ever-functioning natural attitude on which it builds and depends and to which it must return. Indeed, the self-forgetting of the scientific attitude is at the heart of many of the problems of technology and the universalization of the scientific world-view. To employ an image, the space station Mir is still in orbit around the Earth. To live within it is to live entirely within the products of the scientific world. But the space station is dependent on the Earth and is precisely a satellite of it; and the satellite dweller is still an embodied human being with the particular capacities and limitations that this demands. The scientific attitude must make thematic its relation to the natural attitude, and this includes making a scientific study of the natural attitude itself.

Husserl has a strong insight that the 'natural' thing, the thing as experienced in natural, worldly life, cannot be replaced by the scientific formal model of the thing; rather, the aim of science is precisely to explain the experienced, perceived thing: 'The physical thing which he [the scientist] observes, with which he experiments, which he continually sees, takes in his hand, puts on the scale or in the melting furnace: that physical thing, and no other, is also the subject of the predicates ascribed in physics, such as weight, temperature, electrical resistance, and so forth' (*Ideen* I §52, pp. 120–1; Hua 3/1: 100). Of course, Husserl has a particularly interesting conception of a physical thing as the bearer of, or belonging to a context of, endless series of horizons. Every finite thing has an indefinite and indeed infinite series of horizons. Husserl's concept of 'horizon' is a particularly fruitful concept, which received some development in Aron Gurwitsch (drawing on Gestalt psychology) and Hans-Geong Gadamer (hermeneutic understanding is achieved through 'overlapping horizons') but which still has not been fully explored.[3] Every conscious act has its horizons; these enable further acts to develop latent elements. For Husserl, horizons overlap, point beyond themselves to other horizons, and are bounded by the horizon of the world, a horizon that also seeps or reaches into the particular horizons. Husserl, then, has a very rich sense of the world as constituted of objects related to subjects in contexts that can be elaborated indefinitely. His later metaphysical speculations on the nature of monads and their interrelation tries to articulate further this vision of an intersubjectively constituted objective world.

## Problems in Husserl

Let us now turn to what is problematic. All his life Husserl struggled for clarity; yet in some of the most basic aspects of his philosophical account he is entirely unclear. His central notion of *intuition*, whatever is yielded by our direct perceptual experiential engagement with the world, needs careful handling in the contemporary philosophical context. There is a considerable suspicion of the reliability of first-person witness accounts and especially those that concern so-called introspective experience of one's own conscious states. Clearly, Husserl saw his work as proceeding by reflection rather than introspection. His results had to be checked with others, philosophizing with others. However, Husserl is not always clear as to how the science of objective subjectivity is to be carried out. For instance, his entire philosophy of intentionality is based on a contrast between intuitions where the object itself is given direct and those where it is merely meant but not directly seen or grasped. There is a basic contrast in Husserl between presence and absence: some things are given *originär*, in the flesh, as they are (in perceptions, for instance), but there is a huge variety of other forms of givenness (these include memories, fantasies, experiences of others in empathy (Hua 13: 60–1), and so on) which do not have full presence and indeed shade off into complete absence, 'emptiness' or 'darkness', all impressionistic terms he employs to express the non-originarily given. Husserl has a rather limited technical language to cover all these kinds of 'absent' intuition: he calls them 'apperceptions' (*Apperzeptionen*) or 'presentiations/presentifications' (*Vergegenwärtigungen*). As he says in *CM*: 'There are different levels of apperception corresponding to different layers of objective sense' (*CM* §50, p. 111; 1: 141). But he is never precisely clear as to how presence is to be recognized in contrast to absence, and appeal to evidence and intuition here is somewhat beside the point. He seems not to be able to give us a proper philosophical analysis of the kind of 'fullness' and 'presence' that belong to the complete intuition of the object in its presence. Concepts such as 'empty' and 'full' intuition come dangerously close to the subjective and psychological. Indeed, his terminology seems to appeal largely to psychological considerations, although clearly this is the opposite of his intent.

To give an example, how does Husserl explicate the relationship between presence and absence with respect to perception? Despite his many careful analyses, he never unambiguously states how it is that we recognize that a box (whose front side we are now looking at) also has a reverse side which we cannot now see, but whose profiles accompany the actual perception as dependent moments of it. Sketches of an answer can be found, but are not worked out rigorously. He thinks that we *intuit* (in some sense of a direct but 'empty' apprehension, even categorial intuition) not only *that the box has other sides*, but also in some sense how these other sides are presented in their absence. The front side carries a *sense* of the whole object that includes *indications* of these other sides. The other sides are 'apperceived'. He speaks here of an empty presentification (*Vergegenwärtigung*) founded on an actual presentation. For Husserl we *apperceive* the absent sides at the same time as perceiving the present side. He is emphatic that the absent sides are not *inferred*, but immediately and even sensibly (rather than intellectually) grasped. Of course, we can explicitly *judge* the proposition *that the box has other sides*, but our actual perception as such does not include this judgement. Rather we have a 'thick' intuitive experience that somehow has the *sense* of the whole box with dimensions other than the presented side. On the basis of this pre-predicative experience, judgements can be founded. But the perceiving itself seems to have this double aspect of both presence of the whole box through its presented side and an experienced 'moreness', which nevertheless shades off into emptiness. This is startling stuff, but it needs far more articulation if it is to be attractive to philosophers of perception.

There is another problem with regard to his claim that perception yields the object itself: is this claim true for all sensory modalities? While it may be said to be true of sight – I *see* an object from one side and am at the same time co-conscious or apperceptive of other sides (in an empty or partially filled way based on association and analogy and 'prefigurations') – it is not necessarily true for the other senses. It is not entirely clear that the sense of *smell* yields 'profiles', although there may be different smells in different parts of the sensory field. A smell can appear to be getting stronger or weaker or waft in a particular direction, and so on. If I smell gas in the kitchen and then smell it in the garage, do I think I am perceiving the same object through different profiles? It is not immediately clear that the notion of profile attaches in the same way to an object of this sense. The situation is even more complicated for taste. It is not always clear either that we are, in the case of touch, touching the same object, and, to be fair, Husserl does acknowledge the differences between the senses especially in *DR* (Hua 16). I can hold an object between forefinger and thumb and sense the two sides as belonging to the same object. But I can also use the same fingers in the same spread to bridge a gap between two objects. It is not clear that the sense of touch on its own yields a sense of *profile* at all. Perhaps his account is sufficiently robust to withstand these probing questions, but I believe his whole analysis of the physical object in terms of appearing profiles needs to be revisited.

Similarly, Husserl's philosophy depends on intuitions being given with *Evidenz*. But what is this evidence? How do we recognize it and more explicitly distinguish its cognitive component? How do we tell it from *seeming* or *misleading* evidence, from a false trail? Husserl's notions of evidence, givenness, intuition, and the 'it itself there' of the self-given are all interwoven notions central to phenomenology, yet Husserl never adequately characterizes them. This has led critics such as Jacques Derrida to find an unacknowledged and uninterrogated adherence to a classic 'metaphysics of presence' at the heart of Husserl's philosophy, with a continuation of the metaphysical concept of form and the domination of the 'look' that presents the thing itself.[4] Similarly, in *Being and Time* and elsewhere, Heidegger implicitly challenges Husserl's commitment to an outdated 'Cartesian' metaphysics that assumes the extantness of things rather than emphasizing the ex-static, temporally dispersed nature of human experience. There is no doubt that Husserl bases all his analyses on the experience of present-ness of the object in actual current perception. In such cases, as Husserl says, we have the object before us in person; we seize it by the hair with both hands, as he says in *APS*. The object has a presence such that it is *other* than us; it has its own density, its own withdrawal from us (to use Heidegger's image). All of this is metaphorical. Indeed, Sartre has probably described the alienness of objects in the most dramatic terms (in his 1938 novel *La Nausée*, for example). But Husserl's analysis of this presentness usually focuses on the fact that it has endurance and self-identity through successive apprehensions, and that the 'now' is never pure now but always has phases reaching backwards and projecting forwards. There are many remarks concerning the 'standing living present', which do seem to indicate his commitment to some kind of stable, permanent 'absolute'.

Continuing the criticism of a latent metaphysics at the heart of Husserl, both Ingarden and Heidegger independently have observed that there is a residual Cartesianism in Husserl's philosophy. This is not a product of his self-conscious adoption and radicalization of the Cartesian method of universal doubt; rather, it is based on his 'formal ontological' account of the difference between the essences of physical things and the essence of consciousness. Physical things are characterized as *res extensa* and as essentially relational to consciousness, while being transcendent to the experiences that view them, whereas the essence of consciousness is to be absolute, self-enclosed and immanent. A principle, for instance, that Husserl sets out in *Ideen* I §38 is that consciousness can form a whole only with other conscious experiences and specifically excludes from itself as parts all material things. Husserl makes it clear that a mental process is possible only as a mental process, not as something spatial (*Ideen* I §41, p. 88; Hua 3/1: 75). Husserl regards it as a matter of eidetic necessity (even grasped from within the natural attitude) that conscious experiences are of an essentially different kind from material beings. As Husserl put it, the regional essence 'mental process' can be perceived only in immanent perception, and the regional essence 'spatial physical thing' can be perceived as transcendent only to the act of perception (*Ideen* I §42). Immanent perception is characterized by *esse est percipi*, while the opposite situation characterizes external or transcendent perception. According to Husserl, immanent objects are constituted 'in their absoluteness' by inner perception (*APS*, p. 59; Hua 11: 21).

Similarly, in *Ideen* II §64, he sees the individuality of natural things as being dependent on the individuality of the consciousness that grasps them: 'Objective thinghood (*Objektive Dinglichkeit*) is determined physicalistically (*physikalisch*) but is determined as a this (*als Dies*) only in relation to consciousness and the conscious subject. All determination refers back to a here and now and consequently to some subject or nexus of subjects (*Subjektzusammenhänge*)' (*Ideen* II §64, p. 315; Hua 4: 301). It is not at all clear (as some commentators have suggested) that Husserl modified or abandoned this position in his later works. His dualist essentialism is evident in *Ideen* II and in *Krisis*. The emphasis on embodiment does not mitigate this dualism any more than it does in Descartes. Husserl never seems to have felt the need to question the Cartesian determinations of extension and thinking as essential attributes of physicality and consciousness.

Many phenomenologists after Husserl (including Merleau-Ponty and Heidegger) identified deep problems in his account of the reduction. For instance, Husserl maintains that the beginning of the reduction involves the suspension of normal 'belief in the world' (*Weltglaube*). Yet, in his eidetic characterization of perception, for instance, he recognizes that one essential component of the act of perceiving is its accompanying conviction of the existence of its object. There is a primal certainty in perceiving, a primal belief, an *Urdoxa*. Now, if one is to apply the reduction to the analysis of the perception, surely one has at least to 'uncouple' or 'bracket' this very world-affirming confident character of perception. Perception, then, as presented in the reduced form, is something distorted or incomplete. This is unconvincing, especially as the account Husserl gives of the essence of perception *after* the reduction turns out to be exactly the same as that achieved by normal reflection *before* any reduction. There are more and more obscurities in the later Husserl. He attests, for instance, to the strict 'parallellism' between the findings of transcendental phenomenology and those of phenomenological psychology; but, despite the amount of space devoted to it in the later writings, the contrast between these disciplines – indeed, the nature of the distinction itself – is deeply unclear.

There are immensely complex and vexing issues regarding Husserl interpretation, especially the nature of his commitment to metaphysics in general and transcendental idealism in particular. For instance, he begins by abjuring metaphysical claims, yet in his mature philosophy he does speak about the 'Absolute', and at the end of *CM* and elsewhere he looks forward to a purified and genuine metaphysics. It is not clear how a purely descriptive science can ever be the fundamental science of the absolute. In *Ideen* I consciousness is deemed 'absolute', since it is not relative to the world, whereas the world is relative to consciousness. In later works Husserl speaks of a primal absolute 'fact'. This absolute appears to be an 'original temporalizing' that constitutes even the primary streaming of the ego itself. Thus Husserl writes:

> The Absolute is nothing other than absolute temporalization; and even its interpretation as the absolute which I directly encounter as my stationary streaming primordiality is a temporalization, a temporalization of this into something primally existing. Therefore, the absolute totality of monads – i.e. the primordiality of all the monads – only exists by virtue of its temporalization. (Hua 15: 670).[5]

Husserl appears to be placing some kind of temporalizing process at the very source of being, prior even to the transcendental ego. This process is itself considered to be a non-temporal present by Husserl: 'The absolute itself is this universal, primordial present. Within it lie all time, and world in every sense' (Hua 15: 668). The primal present is not a modality of time; it is a kind of 'supertemporal' *nunc stans*. This is puzzling. But there are further paradoxes. At times, however – indeed, even in the same manuscript – Husserl insists that everything including time has its source in the I understood as the 'sole one' (*das Einzige*; 15: 667). The most original ego has a kind of presentness, but this too is not in time, according to Husserl.

There are similar puzzles concerning the relationship between my ego and other egos. Clearly, the world has 'being and sense' for me only because I am alive and a 'living streaming' consciousnesses in the present. But there are also other living consciousnesses, other monads, indeed an entire 'community of monads'. What is the relationship between myself as absolute source and these monads which are absolute sources of their own world-experiences? In one sense, Husserl believes that every conceivable transcendental ego must be constructed on the ground of my actual ego (15: 383 n. 1). Yet he also argues for a coincidence (*Deckung*; 15: 668) among egos and of their 'being for one another' (15: 334). How egos or monads (entire streams of life) relate to one another is a difficult problem that Husserl is not able to answer. At best he can give detailed description of the structure and nature of this interrelation and communication.

This raises the question of whether the transcendental ego lives perpetually or whether it can be born and die. Husserl seems to subscribe to both views at the same time, whereas Heidegger, who rejects the transcendental ego, puts strong emphasis on death as belonging to the constitutional structure of human existence (*Dasein*). Husserl both affirms the non-temporal presentness of the ego, which can never be cancelled or thought away, and insists on the contingency of the 'fact' that I exist at all. That 'I exist' is a contingent fact, but the transcendental I must exist. But how can a contingent fact which has as its counterpart a transcendental ego be the source not only of the being of the world but also of all essentiality and truth? While there is an attempt in the late Husserl to see the transcendental ego as simply the natural ego viewed from the transcendental perspective, there is another aspect of Husserl that says we must leave behind everything from worldly life if we really want to understand transcendental life on its own terms. Husserl contrasts worldly life and transcendental life, but his descriptions of transcendental life bring back in all those elements of thought that belonged solely to worldly life – historicity, temporality, finitude and so on. Perhaps this is what Merleau-Ponty meant by the impossibility of a complete reduction. The transcendental does more than mirror the worldly; it is both responsible for it and also an actor in it. Husserl, to my mind, never succeeded in disentangling these strands, despite all his later analyses of the life of the 'world-child' *Weltkind*, versus transcendental life (on its way to being the 'divine life'). But, as Derrida comments, it is clear that we are not dealing with an ontological duplication, even if there is a doubling of the *sense* of ego when we distinguish between natural and transcendental ego.[6]

Of course, it is obvious that, at first glance, many aspects of Husserl's thought seem uncongenial to the contemporary mood in philosophy. It is often said that Husserl is not a philosopher who has undertaken the linguistic turn, and his constant return to Descartes seems to emphasize his connection with earlier pre-linguistic modern philosophy. One problem that phenomenology had from the beginning was to convince philosophers that it had something significant to say, as opposed to stating the obvious or the trivial. Of course, philosophy is the discovery of difficulties in trivialities, for Husserl. There was perhaps too much emphasis on the laying on of hands, of being 'trained' in phenomenological viewing almost by a kind of apprenticeship with the master, reminiscent of Plato's account of the imparting of philosophical wisdom. Thus Hans-Georg Gadamer complains that there was a certain 'craft-secret' approach to passing on the method of phenomenology.[7] Husserl also made many claims about the supposed apodicticity and incorrigibility of the results of phenomenological seeing. But frequently, he denied that this freedom from error was to be understood as meaning that phenomenologists could not make errors in their work.

## Husserl's Influence

Finally, let me say a few words about Husserl's influence. Largely through the impact of his 'ground-breaking' work, Edmund Husserl inspired several generations of gifted students in Germany, from his days at Göttingen to his final days at Freiburg. Originally, these students sought to carry on the rigorous programme outlined in *LU*, and developed realistic phenomenology. These students included philosophers such as Adolf Reinach (1883–1916), Alexander Pfänder (1870–1941), Johannes Daubert (1877–1947), Moritz Geiger (1880–1937), Theodor Conrad (1881–1969) and Hedwig Conrad-Martius (1888–1966). Other students attracted to Husserl included Max Scheler (1874–1928), Edith Stein (1891–1942) and Roman Ingarden (1893–1970), all of whom went on to develop original philosophical positions informed by phenomenology. These distinguished students formed what became known generally (and by Husserl himself) as the 'phenomenological movement' (*die phänomenologische Bewegung*), although he ultimately disowned most of them as they failed to follow him into the 'Promised Land' of transcendental philosophy.[8] Husserl had an early influence outside Germany too, with Ingarden actively promoting phenomenology in Poland. *LU* was translated into Russian in 1909, and had an influence on Gustav Šhpet (1879–1937) and later on Roman Jakobson's development of linguistics.

When Husserl began publishing a yearbook, *Jahrbuch für Philosophie and phänomenologische Forschung*, other leading phenomenologists immediately began publishing their works there, including Scheler, Stein and Geiger. Most famously, Martin Heidegger's *Sein und Zeit* (*Being and Time*, 1927) originally appeared in *Jahrbuch* volume 8. By the time Husserl took over Heinrich Rickert's chair in Freiburg in 1916, he had become the foremost philosopher in Germany, and had embarked on a serious rethinking of neo-Kantianism. After the First World War, students flocked to hear him expounding a systematic approach to phenomenology as the true 'first philosophy' and also exploring the themes of moral and spiritual 'renewal' (*Erneuerung*). From 1919 until his retirement in 1928, his lectures were attended by the emerging generation of brilliant German philosophers: Hans-Georg Gadamer (1900–2002), Hannah Arendt (1906–75), Herbert Marcuse (1898–1979), Oskar Becker (1889–1964), Hans Jonas (1903–1993) and others.

Husserl also had considerable influence on other philosophical currents of the time. Some members of the nascent Vienna Circle (such as Moritz Schlick (1882–1936) and Rudolf Carnap (1891–1970) recognized his significance, even if they fundamentally disagreed with his approach. Schlick attacked Husserl's intuitionism and his 'intuition of essences' in his *General Theory of Knowledge* (1918),[9] while Carnap spent a year (1924–5) living near Freiburg and attending Husserl's seminars, while working on his own *Logische Aufbau der Welt*. (Translated as *The Logical Structure of the World*, London: Routledge & Kegan Paul, 1967). Even alternative currents of thought such as the Frankfurt School felt it necessary to engage with phenomenology, as is evident from the writings of Max Horkheimer and Theodor Adorno, who devoted several detailed studies to Husserl. Jürgen Habermas later credited Husserl for his notion of the life-world (*Lebenswelt*): that is, the world as it is lived and experienced in the 'naïve' natural attitude prior to transcendental reflection.

Husserl had followers in France more or less from the beginning. French philosophers also studied with Husserl: first, Jean Héring (1890–1966), and in 1928 the Lithuanian-born French national Emmanuel Levinas (1906–1995) spent two semesters in Freiburg. Levinas's first book on Husserl, together with his translation of Husserl's Paris Lectures of 1929, had an extraordinary effect on French philosophy, converting a whole generation that included Sartre, Merleau-Ponty and de Beauvoir, to the study of phenomenology. He even influenced the French anthropologist Lucien Lévy-Bruhl (*Briefwechsel*, 6: 161–4). Husserlian phenomenology was further developed in France by Paul Ricoeur and Jacques Derrida.[10]

Husserl also had an early impact on philosophy elsewhere in Europe and in North America. He had followers in Russia (Gustav Šhpet and later Roman Jakobson (1896–1982)), in Poland (Ingarden), in Czechoslovakia (Thomas Masaryk and Jan Patočka). From the days of the *Logical Investigations*, Husserl had attracted American students, including William Ernest Hocking (1873–1966) and later Marvin Farber, Dorion Cairns and Fritz Kaufmann. Early in the century, phenomenology spread to Japan, and after the Second World War it enjoyed a major renaissance in the USA through the influence of Schütz, Gurwitsch and others.

In his later years Husserl felt himself increasingly isolated intellectually, convinced that his work was being undermined and his discoveries credited to other philosophers. Husserl's early hope, Adolf Reinach, had fallen in the Great War; Pfänder and the Munich phenomenologists did not accept Husserl's reduction and idealism. After 1928, Heidegger, too, was a bitter personal disappointment to him. Husserl spent his last years attempting to rescue the true meaning of the science of phenomenology from Heidegger, who had turned it into anthropology, just as earlier Scheler had weakened it into a form of life philosophy. Indeed, Husserl even remarked in a letter to his friend Gustav Albrecht in 1931 that he felt so isolated and separated from his students that he now counted himself as the greatest enemy of the famous 'Husserlian Phenomenological Movement' (*Briefwechsel*, 9: 79). Husserl's sense of betrayal was deepened by the rise of the National Socialist movement in Germany. An indication of his isolation was that he felt compelled to write to Landgrebe at one point, asking him if he was a member of the Nazi Party. Husserl was acutely aware that he had no genuine successor (expressed in letters to Ingarden and Pfänder) – he referred to himself as an 'appointed leader without followers' (*als beruferer Führer ohne Gefolge; Briefwechsel*, 2: 182), and that the scientific conception of phenomenology which he had promoted had now dissipated into many separate styles of inquiry in many diverse areas.

Of course, phenomenology continued to expand and develop far beyond – and indeed often in explicit opposition to – the vision of Husserl, but still there is no escaping his own foundational efforts. Indeed, it is always surprising the extent to which, in his own manuscripts, Husserl himself anticipated many of the later developments of phenomenology. However, the later Heidegger's anti-humanism, structuralism's theme of the 'end of man', and postmodernism's deconstruction of the subject, presence and identity, all combined to ensure that Husserlian phenomenology appeared to slip from view in

European philosophy in the second half of the twentieth century. Meanwhile, the rise of behaviourism and linguistic analysis in Anglophone philosophy also occluded interest in the phenomenology of consciousness. All this has changed in recent years, and there is once again a keen interest in the cognitive life of the subject. Husserl's influence continues to be felt in philosophy of mind, cognitive science and philosophy of science. Undoubtedly, his vision of the phenomenology of consciousness and his radical account of transcendental philosophy will continue to set challenges for philosophy in the twenty-first century.

# *Notes*

## Introduction

1 Edmund Husserl in conversation with Adelgundis Jaegerschmid in 1935; see A. Jaegerschmid, OSB, 'Conversation with Edmund Husserl, 1931–1938', trans. Marcus Brainard, *The New Yearbook for Phenomenology and Phenomenological Philosophy*, 1 (2001), p. 339.

2 Jean-Luc Marion, *Reduction and Givenness: Investigations of Husserl, Heidegger and Phenomenology*, trans. Thomas A. Carlson (Evanston, Ill.: Northwestern University Press, 1998), p. 1.

3 Analytic interpreters of Husserl include Dagfinn Føllesdal, David Bell, Kevin Mulligan, Barry Smith and David Woodruff Smith.

4 Husserl also calls it the 'stream of experience' (*Erlebnisstrom*).

5 See e.g. the essays collected in *Naturalizing Phenomenology: Issues in Contemporary Phenomenology and Cognitive Science*, ed. J. Petitot, F. J. Varela, B. Pachoud and J.-M. Roy (Stanford, Calif.: Stanford University Press, 1999).

6 L. Binswanger, 'Dank an Edmund Husserl', in H. L. Van Breda and J. Taminiaux, eds, *Edmund Husserl 1859–1959: Recueil commémorative publié à l'occasion du centenaire de la naissance du philosophe* (The Hague: Nijhoff, 1959), p. 65.

7 This concept is also found in the work of Wilhelm Dilthey.

8 It is important to note that Husserl disparaged existing metaphysics as unscientific and ungrounded speculation, but he did not reject the possibility of metaphysics as such; indeed, he included it as an indispensable part of philosophy, and paid more and more attention to it in his later writings (see *CM*; Hua 1: 182).

9 While Husserl is deeply indebted to Brentano's account of intentionality, he does not accept that everything mental – i.e. every psychological *phenomenon* – is characterized by intentionality. In a footnote in *LU* V (§10, **II** 353 n. 5; Hua 19/1: 382 n.) he states that he is untroubled by questions of whether *all* mental phenomena are characterized by intentionality, since the question can be asked whether these phenomena are mental at all. Husserl takes

it that intentionality gets to the essences of mental experiences as such, even if not all components (sensations, e.g.) of conscious acts are intentional. Since there are no *acts* of sensation for Husserl, sensations as such are not intentional; they are simply *experienced*, and objects and their properties are the focus of intentions.

10 See Aristotle, *Metaphysics*, Book Z ch. 7, 1032b1–2: 'By *eidos* I mean the essence (*to ti en einai*) of each thing and its primary substance (*protē ousia*).'

11 The term 'attitude', as used in current analytic philosophy (e.g. 'propositional attitude') to refer to cognitive stances towards objects and mental contents, was employed by Bertrand Russell and others to translate the term *Einstellung* then current in German psychology.

12 See the entry '*epoché*,' in *A Greek–English Lexicon*, compiled by Henry George Liddell and Robert Scott, 9th rev. edn (Oxford: Clarendon Press, 1990), p. 677. The term *epoché* is usually attributed to Arcesilaus, although Pyrrho is said to have been the first to use it in reference to attitudes of mind. See also Chrysippus, *Stoicorum Veterum Fragmenta*, ed. H. Arnim (Leipzig: Teubner, 1903), bk. 2, p. 39.

13 See Sebastian Luft, 'Husserl's Theory of the Phenomenological Reduction: Between Life-World and Cartesianism', *Research in Phenomenology*, 34 (2004), pp. 198–234.

14 The first two parts of this work were published in 1936 in Belgrade in the journal, *Philosophia*. Husserl had completed a typescript of Part III when he became ill in 1937. The first critical edition appeared in 1954.

15 Husserl appears to have invented the term *Lebenswelt* and to have introduced it first in the draft manuscript of *Ideen* II §64, supplement (Hua 4: 375), but he had already been talking about the human environment or 'surrounding world' (*Umwelt*) and of the everyday experienced world from as early as 1906–7 (see also *Ideen* II, 'communal environing world'; 4: 288). In *Ideen* I Husserl does refer to our ordinary natural experience of the world and the perceptual world (3/1: 72). *Ideen* I (3/1: 102) makes reference to the *Lebewelten* of the palaeontologist. This may be a misprint for *Lebewesen* (living beings). The term may have been inspired by Richard Avinarius' discussion of the 'natural concept of the world' in his *Der menschliche Weltbegriff* (Leipzig, 1891), with which Husserl was familiar. See David Carr, 'Husserl's Problematic Concept of the Life-World', in F. A. Elliston and P. McCormick, eds, *Husserl: Expositions and Appraisals* (Notre Dame, Ind.: University of Notre Dame Press, 1977), pp. 202–12; Fred Kersten, 'The Lifeworld Revisited', *Research in Phenomenology*, 1 (1971), pp. 33–62; and Toru Tani, 'Life and the Life-World', *Husserl Studies*, 3 (1986), pp. 57–78.

16 See K. Held, 'Heimwelt, Fremdwelt, die eine Welt', *Phänomenologische Forschungen*, 24/5 (1991), pp. 305–37.

17 See e.g. the classical studies of Robert Sokolowski, *The Formation of Husserl's Concept of Consitution* (The Hague: Nijhoff, 1964); *idem, Husserlian Meditations: How Words Present Things* (Evanston, Ill.: Northwestern University Press, 1974); John J. Drummond, *Husserlian Intentionality and Non-Foundational Realism: Noema and Object* (Dordrecht: Kluwer, 1990); Rudolf Bernet, Iso Kern and Eduard Marbach, *An Introduction to Husserlian Phenomenology* (Evanston, Ill.: Northwestern University Press, 1993); Anthony J. Steinbock, *Home and Beyond: Generative Phenomenology after Husserl*

(Evanston, Ill.: Northwestern University Press, 1995); Donn Welton, *The Other Husserl* (Bloomington, Ind.: Indiana University Press, 2001); and Dan Zahavi, *Husserl's Phenomenology* (Stanford, Calif.: Stanford University Press, 2003).

18  For Husserl's influence on the European phenomenological tradition, see my *Introduction to Phenomenology* (London and New York: Routledge, 2000).

19  R. Ingarden, 'Edith Stein on her Activity as an Assistant of Edmund Husserl', *Philosophy and Phenomenological Research*, 23, 2 (Dec. 1962), p. 158.

20  E. Husserl, *Briefwechsel*, ed. Karl Schuhmann in collaboration with Elizabeth Schuhmann, Husserliana Dokumente, 10 vols (Dordrecht: Kluwer, 1994).

21  While these lectures are important, there has been a tendency recently to exaggerate their novelty. In preparing the posthumously published *Erfahrung und Urteil: Untersuchungen zur Genealogie der Logik* (Prague: Academia-Verlag, 1938; now Hambung: Meiner, 1999), trans. J. S. Churchill and K. Ameriks as *Experience and Judgment: Investigations in a Genealogy of Logic* (London: Routledge & Kegan Paul, 1973), Ludwig Landgrebe drew heavily on the then unpublished *APS* (see his Foreword to the 1948 edn, *EU*, p. 5; xxiv) and indeed faithfully articulates Husserl's accounts, e.g., of the transitions within perception between the original moment of fullness and a later, closer inspection and determination of various attributes (compare *APS*, p. 45; Hua 11: 8 and *EU* §24).

22  A new translation is scheduled to appear as E. Husserl, *Phantasy, Image-Consciousness, Memory*, trans. J. Brough, in *Collected Works*, vol. 11 (Dordrecht: Springer, 2005).

23  These collected texts are, however, somewhat problematic, in that they include many notes and excerpts where Husserl ruminates on a topic without appearing to come to a conclusion or make up his mind. Also, some entries (on empathy) are straightforward excerpts from the Munich philosopher Theodor Lipps, with only bare hints from Husserl about his own position in so far as it supplements or departs from that of Lipps. These are very tentative explorations, not meant for publication, and thus difficult to incorporate into Husserl's overall philosophical outlook without due qualification.

## Chapter 1  Edmund Husserl (1859–1938): Life and Writings

1  Gerda Walther, *Zum Anderen Ufer: Vom Marxismus und Atheismus zum Christentum* (*Towards the Other Shore: From Marxism and Atheism to Christianity*) (Remagen: Otto Reichl Verlag, 1960), p. 201.

2  H.-G. Gadamer attributes this remark to Fyodur Stepun; see Gadamer, *Philosophical Apprenticeships*, trans. Robert R. Sullivan (Cambridge, Mass.: MIT Press, 1985), p. 35.

3  Walther, *Zum Anderen Ufer*, p. 211.

4  See Jan Kühndel, 'Edmund Husserls Heimat und Herkunft,' *Archiv für Geschichte der Philosophie*, 51 (1969), pp. 286–90, and Hans-Rainer Sepp, ed., *Edmund Husserl und die phänomenologische Bewegung: Zeugnisse in Text und Bild* (Freiburg and Munich: Karl Alber Verlag, 1988).

5  See *Briefwechsel*, 8: 235. On Husserl's Jewishness, see Sepp, ed., *Edmund Husserl und die phänomenologische Bewegung*, p. 119, and Bohuslav Eliás, 'Die

Judenstadt von Prostejov und die Familie Husserl (Einige Bemerkungen)', in *Zur Problematik der transzendentalen Phänomenologie Edmund Husserls* (Prague: Tschechoslowakische Akademie der Wissenschaften 1988), pp. 234–9.

6 Sepp, ed. *Edmund Husserl und die phänomenologische Bewegung*, p. 120. See Malvine Husserl, 'Skizze eines Lebensbildes von Edmund Husserl', ed. Karl Schuhmann, *Husserl Studies*, 5 (1988), pp. 105–25. See also *Chronik*, pp. 2–3, and Andrew Osborn, *The Philosophy of Edmund Husserl in its Development from his Mathematical Interests to his First Conception of Phenomenology in the* Logical Investigations (New York: International Press, 1934), p. 10.

7 E. Parl Welch, *The Philosophy of Edmund Husserl* (New York: Columbia University Press, 1941), p. xiii.

8 After *LU* was published, Husserl was extremely critical of Wundt's reaction to it in his Draft Preface for the 1913 revised edition; see Hua 20/1: 314–29. For some reason, Fink omitted this section from his edition of the Draft Preface.

9 Thomas Masaryk left school at the age of 12 to work as a blacksmith, but enrolled in the University of Vienna in 1872. His first thesis, 'Principles of Sociology' (1877) was rejected, largely because sociology was still a suspect discipline, but his second thesis on suicide in 1878 was eventually accepted through the support of Brentano. In 1880 he converted from Catholicism to Protestantism. An activist Czech nationalist, he eventually became President of Czechoslovakia, which post he tried to use to protect Husserl from the political changes in Germany. See P. P. Selver, *Masaryk* (London: Joseph, 1940), and also K. Schuhmann, 'Husserl and Masaryk', in J. Novak, ed., *On Masaryk* (Amsterdam: Rodopi, 1988), pp. 129–56.

10 Weierstrass was born in Ostenfelde, Bavaria, on 31 Oct. 1815, studied at Bonn University and Münster. He qualified as a teacher of mathematics and began publishing articles on mathematics in obscure teachers' journals. As a result of his papers, he was awarded an honorary doctorate by the University of Königsberg and was appointed to the Technische Hochschule in Berlin in 1856 and then to the University of Berlin, where, together with Kronecker and Kummer, he gave Berlin a world reputation in mathematics.

11 See Iso Kern, *Husserl und Kant* (The Hague: Nijhoff, 1964), p. 1. Welch, however, writes: 'Paulsen was instilling in him a desire to study philosophy. He seized upon Husserl's reflective capacities and directed his thinking into channels that were destined to prove productive of profound insights' (*Philosophy of Edmund Husserl*, p. xiv). Erdmann (1805–92) studied theology at Dorpat and Berlin, where he was influenced by Hegel.

12 M. Husserl, 'Skizze', p. 112, records Husserl as saying: 'from Weierstrass I gained my ethos for scientific striving'.

13 In his 1929 speech of acceptance of the *Festschrift* dedicated to him, Husserl emphasized the influence of Weierstrass and Brentano (*Chronik*, pp. 344–5).

14 *Chronik*, p. 9. Husserl confirmed this in a letter to Mahnke on 4 May 1933, *Briefwechsel*, 3: 500. M. Husserl, 'Skizze', p. 112, claims it was out of respect for the wishes of his father, a fervent Austrian.

15 See his letter to the theologian Rudolf Otto, *Briefwechsel*, 7: 205–8.

16 For Husserl's relation to religion, see Karl and Elizabeth Schuhmann's Introduction to *Briefwechsel*, 10 35–6. See also Eberhard Avé-Lallemant, 'Husserl zu Metaphysik und Religion', in H.-M. Gerlach and H. R. Sepp, eds, *Husserl in Halle: Spurensuche im Anfang der Phänomenologie* (Frankfurt: Peter Lang, 1994), esp. pp. 102–3.

17 Adelgundis Jaegerschmidt, 'Conversations with Edmund Husserl, 1931–1938', trans. M. Brainard, *The New Yearbook for Phenomenology and Phenomenological Philosophy*, (2001), p. 343.

18 See e.g. Husserl's comments on Heidegger's Kant book, in *Trans. Phen.*, p. 443.

19 See Louis Dupré, 'Husserl's Thoughts on God and Faith', *Philosophy and Phenomenological Research*, 29 (1968), pp. 201–15, and James Richard Mensch, *Intersubjectivity and Transcendental Idealism* (Albany, NY: SUNY Press, 1988), pp. 360–74.

20 See, e.g., *LU*, Prol. §40, I 93; Hua 18: 147, where Husserl cites Hegel as having denied the Principle of Non-Contradiction.

21 E. Husserl, 'Recollections of Franz Brentano', *HSW*, p. 343; Hua 25: 305.

22 As Husserl wrote, 'Brentano's pre-eminent and admirable strength was in logical theory' (*HSW* 345; Hua 25: 309).

23 See D. Moran, 'Husserl's Critique of Brentano in the *Logical Investigations*', *Manuscrito*, special Husserl issue, 33, 2 (2000), pp. 163–205, and *idem*, 'The Inaugural Address: Brentano's Thesis', *Proceedings of the Aristotelian Society*, suppl. vol. 70 (1996), pp. 1–27.

24 See H. Spiegelberg, 'On the Significance of the Correspondence between Franz Brentano and Edmund Husserl', in R. M. Chisholm and R. Haller, eds, *Die Philosophie Franz Brentanos* (Amsterdam: Rodopi, 1978), pp. 95–116.

25 Husserl's letter to Marvin Farber, 18 June 1937, trans. in Kah Kyung Cho, 'Phenomenology as Cooperative Task: Husserl–Farber Correspondence during 1936–37', *Philosophy and Phenomenological Research*, 50, suppl. (Fall 1990), pp. 36–43.

26 Bernard Bolzano, a contemporary of G. W. F. Hegel, was born in Prague in 1781. He studied philosophy, theology and mathematics at the University of Prague, and wrote a thesis on geometry in 1804. In 1805 he was ordained a Catholic priest, and in the same year was appointed professor of religion there until he was dismissed by imperial decree in 1819. From 1820 to 1830 he retired to Techobuz, where he worked on his main book, *Wissenschaftslehre*, published in 1837 now in *Gesamtausgabe*, Reihe I, Bd. 11–13, ed. Jan Berg (Stuttgart Fromman-Holzboog, 1985–92) (*Theory of Science*, ed. and trans. Rolf George (Oxford: Blackwell, 1972)). He was in obscurity at the time, due to his suspect religious heterodoxy and radical political liberalism. Husserl claimed that he chanced upon the work in a used bookshop (see *Chronik*, p. 463).

27 B. Bolzano, *Wissenschaftslehre*. For Bolzano's influence on Husserl, see EV, p. 37; Fink, p. 129; Hua 20/1: 298.

28 For the recent revival of interest in Bolzano, see W. Künne, M. Siebel and M. Textor, eds, *Bolzano and Analytic Philosophy*, *Grazer Philosophische Studien* 53 (1997).

29 See J. Benoist, 'Husserl entre Brentano et Bolzano', *Manuscrito*, 33, 2 (Oct. 2000), pp. 11–39; and his 'Qu'est-ce qu'un jugement? Brentano, Frege et Husserl', *Études Phénoménologiqes*, 27–8 (1998), pp. 169–92.

30 In citing Husserl's Draft Preface to *LU*, I have given the page number of the Fink edition (abbreviated: Fink) followed by the new Hua 20/1 edition.

31 Stumpf first studied law and then wrote his doctorate with Lotze and a *Habilitation* on the principles of mathematics. His *Über den psychologischen Ursprung der Raumvorstellung* had appeared in Leipzig in 1873, and the first volume of his *Tonpsychologie* in 1883. The second volume appeared in 1890 (Leipzig: Hirzel, 3/90). Husserl and he became lifelong friends, staying in touch even after Stumpf moved to Munich in 1889, and then, in 1894, to Berlin.

32 Brentano wrote to Stumpf on 18 Oct. 1886 recommending Husserl as a 'mathematician and for some years an enthusiastic student of philosophy' who was working on problems of the continuum; see Robin Rollinger, *Husserl's Position in the School of Brentano* (Utrecht: Department of Philosophy, Utrecht University, 1996), p. 68. Brentano, an ex-priest who subsequently got married, had been forced to resign his professorship in Vienna, for reasons connected with the concordat between church and state in Austria at that time. He was demoted to the status of *Privatdozent*, and thereby lost his legal right to participate in *Habilitation* committees.

33 For Husserl's years in Halle, see Hans-Martin Gerlach and Hans Rainer Sepp, eds, *Husserl in Halle: Spurensuche im Anfang der Phänomenologie* (Frankfurt: Peter Lang, 1994). On his financial situation there, see Karl Schuhmann, 'Introduction: Husserl's "Marperger Lecture" from July 6, 1898', *The New Yearbook for Phenomenology and Phenomenological Philosophy*, 2 (2002), p. 296.

34 See Husserl's letter to Cairns of 21 Mar. 1930; *Chronik*, p. 22.

35 Cantor wrote a letter to Husserl on 7 Apr. 1915, *Briefwechsel*, 7: 51, sympathizing with him on hearing of the wounding of his son. On Cantor and Husserl, see Claire Ortiz Hill, 'Abstraction and Idealization in Edmund Husserl and Georg Cantor Prior to 1895', *Poznan Studies in the Philosophy of the Sciences and the Humanities*, 20 (1998), pp. 1–27.

36 For a list of Husserl's lecture courses at Halle, see Gerlach and Sepp, eds, *Husserl in Halle*, pp. 35–9.

37 Husserl's attempts at the second volume are published in Hua 12: 340–429 and 21: 3–215, 252–61.

38 Letter to Stumpf; Hua 21: 244–51, trans. in *EW*, pp. 12–19.

39 In *LU* Husserl explicitly excludes James from his critique of psychologism (see *LU* II §39, Appendix, I 323–4; Hua 19/1: 211).

40 Hubert Dreyfus and Dagfinn Føllesdal accept the view that Frege influenced Husserl. But see J. N. Mohanty, *Husserl and Frege* (Bloomington, Ind.: Indiana University Press, 1982), which argues that Frege played little or no role in Husserl's change of mind, as the change is already evident from 1891.

41 See E. Husserl, 'Intentional Objects', *EW*, pp. 345–87; Hua 22: 303–48. See also the draft translated by Robin Rollinger in his *Husserl's Position in the School of Brentano*, pp. 195–222.

42 Bolzano, *Wissenschaftslehre*, bk 1, p. 304; trans. *Theory of Science*, pp. 88–9: 'It is true that most ideas have some, or even infinitely many, referents. Still,

there are also ideas that have no referent at all, and thus do not have an extension. The clearest case seems to be that of the concept designated by the word "nothing". It seems absurd to me to say that this concept has an object too, i.e. a something that it represents . . . The same holds of the ideas "a round square", "green virtue", etc.'

43 Husserl, in his *Selbstanzeige* (Author's Announcement) (1900), now Hua 18: 262, claims that some copies were available from the end of November 1899, but the Foreword is dated Halle, 21 May 1900. Karl Schuhmann thinks it unlikely that any copies were available to the author before May 1900. Husserl had originally contracted with another publisher, Verlag Veit & Co., Leipzig, which had already printed some sample copies before Niemeyer took over and brought out copies in July 1900 (see *Chronik*, p. 61).

44 These Halle lectures have now been reconstructed from Husserl's working notes; see E. Husserl, *Logik: Vorlesungen SS 1896*, ed. E. Schuhmann, *Materialenbände*, vol. 1 (Dordrecht: Kluwer, 2001). As E. Schuhmann has shown, these lecture notes show a strong dependence on Bolzano's *Wissenschaftslehre* both for their conception of logic and for the order of their treatment of the central issues.

45 Husserl, *Logik: Vorlesungen 1896*, p. 23 (my trans.).

46 Husserl, however, was unsatisfied with a certain 'psychologising of the universal' he detected in Lotze's *Logic* (1874) §316. See Husserl, 'Review of M. Palagyi, *Der Streit der Psychologisten und Formalisten in der Modernen Logik* (The Dispute between Psychologists and Formalists in Modern Logic)', *EW*, p. 201; Hua 22: 156. For his critique of Lotze, see *LU* II §10, I 322 n. 5; Hua 19/1: 138.

47 Paul Natorp reviewed Husserl's *Prolegomena* in *Kantstudien*, 6 (1901), pp. 270–83, trans. in J. N. Mohanty, ed., *Readings on Husserl's Logical Investigations* (The Hague: Nijhoff, 1977), pp. 55–66. He later reviewed *Ideen* I in *Logos*, 7 (1917–18), pp. 224–46.

48 William Ernest Hocking, 'From the Early Days to the "*Logische Untersuchungen*"', in H. L. Van Breda and J. Taminiaux, eds, *Edmund Husserl 1859–1959*, p. 1, and Wilhelm Schapp's 'Erinnerungen', ibid., p. 13.

49 See W. Wundt, 'Psychologismus und Logizismus', in *Kleine Schriften*, Erster Band (Leipzig: Engelmann, 1910), pp. 513–634, and Husserl's reply in his Draft Preface of 1913; 20/1: 314–29. Husserl is very critical of Wundt's misreading, exclaiming at one point: 'One cannot read the *Logical Investigations* like a newspaper' (20/1: 320).

50 Sepp, ed., *Edmund Husserl und die phänomenologische Bewegung*, p. 162.

51 David Hilbert was born in Königsberg and completed his doctorate in 1885 at the university there. Hilbert was *Privatdozent* until 1892, and became a full professor there in 1893. In 1895 he was appointed by Klein to the chair of mathematics in Göttingen.

52 See Claire Ortiz Hill, 'Husserl and Hilbert on Completeness', in J. Hintikka, ed., *Essays on the Development of the Foundations of Mathematics* (Dordrecht: Kluwer, 1995), pp. 143–63.

53 Weyl was born in Elmshorn, Germany, and studied in Munich and in Göttingen. He completed his doctorate with Hilbert in 1908, and taught there as *Privatdozent* from 1910 to 1913, before moving to the Technische Hochschule in Zurich (1913–30). He emigrated to the USA in

1933, and was at the Institute for Advanced Study at Princeton from 1933 to 1951.

54 See esp. H. Weyl, *Raum, Zeit, Materie: Vorlesungen über Allgemeine Relativitäts theorie* (Berlin: Springer, 1918).

55 See O. Ewert, 'Einfühlung,' in *Historisches Wörterbuch der Philosophie*, Band II (Darmstadt: Wissenschaftliche Buchgesellschaft, 1972, corrected 1995), cols 396–7.

56 Husserl refers to T. Lipps at *LU* §17, **I** 40; Hua 18: 64, and in the Foreword to the second edition, *LU* **I** 6; Hua 18: 12.

57 Reinach wrote his *Habilitation* on the theory of judgement with Husserl in Göttingen in 1909 and became *Privatdozent* there, where he was considered a much clearer exponent of phenomenology than Husserl himself. He assisted Husserl in revising *LU*; see Husserl's Foreword to the 2nd edn (*LU*, p. 50; Hua 18: B xvii). He wrote a number of important articles, including one on negative judgements for Lipps's *Festschrift*. Husserl published an *In Memoriam* for Reinach in the *Frankfurter Zeitung* on 6 Dec. 1917 and again in *Kant-Studien* in 1918; see Hua 25: 296–303.

58 See Jean Héring, 'Edmund Husserl: Souvenirs et reflexions,' in Van Breda and Taminiaux, eds, *Edmund Husserl 1859–1959*, pp. 26–8.

59 An elegant expression of this outlook can be found in Reinach's *Über Phänomenologie* (*Concerning Phenomenology*) essay of 1914 and in Roman Ingarden's later study, *On the Motives which led Husserl to Transcendental Idealism*, trans. Arnór Hannibalsson (Hague: Nijhoff, 1975).

60 See J. N. Mohanty, 'The Development of Husserl's Thought', in *Cambridge Companion to Husserl*, p. 57.

61 This work had not yet appeared in English.

62 See Karl Schuhmann, 'Husserl's Yearbook', *Philosophy and Phenomenological Research* 50, suppl. (Fall 1990), pp. 1–25.

63 A. Schütz, in Van Breda and Taminiaux, eds, *Edmund Husserl 1859–1959*, p. 88.

64 The appointment was somewhat informal. See Edith Stein, *Self-Portrait in Letters, 1916–1942*, trans. Josephine Koeppel (Washington: Institute of Carmelite Studies Publications, 1993).

65 Letter to Ingarden, 19 Feb. 1918, in Stein, *Self-Portrait in Letters, 1916–1942*, p. 22.

66 Letter to Ingarden, 28 Feb. 1918, in Stein, *Self-Portrait in Letters, 1916–1942*, p. 23.

67 Ibid., p. 23.

68 Letter to Fritz Kaufmann, 22 Nov. 1919, in Stein, *Self-Portrait in Letters, 1916–1942*, p. 37.

69 M. Merleau-Ponty, *Phénoménologie de la perception* (Paris: Gallimard, 1945).

70 See Husserl's letter to the Harvard philosopher Hugo Münsterberg in the latter's *The Peace and America* (New York: D. Appleton & Co., 1915), pp. 222–4; repr. *HSW*, p. 352; Hua 25: 293–4).

71 For Husserl's political views, see Karl and Elizabeth Schuhmann, 'Einführung in die Ausgabe', *Briefwechsel*, 10: 18–23, and K. Schuhmann, *Husserls Staatsphilosophie* (Freiburg and Munich: Alber, 1988).

72 See Husserl, 'Fichtes Menschheitsideal: Drei Vorlesungen', in *Aufsätze und Vorträge (1911–1921)*; Hua 25: 267–93, trans. James G. Hart, 'Fichte's Ideal of Humanity [Three Lectures]', *Husserl Studies*, 12 (1995), pp. 111–33. The lecture series was delivered on 8–17 Nov. 1917, and repeated on 14–16 Jan. 1918 and 6–9 Nov. 1918, just before the Armistice.

73 Walther, *Zum Anderen Ufer*, p. 209.

74 Ibid. p. 201, where she speaks of 'the famous sofa of black oil cloth'. Subsequent page references are given parenthetically in the text.

75 Husserl announced his interest in a system in a letter to Ingarden of 25 Nov. 1921 (*Briefwechsel* 3: 213) and in one to Winthrop Bell of 18 Sept. 1921 (*Briefwechsel*, 3: 26).

76 See Donn Welton's explication of genesis in his *The Other Husserl*, pp. 198–220.

77 These lectures have now been published in Hua 35: 311–40. See also H. Spiegelberg, 'Husserl in England: Facts and Lessons', *Journal of the British Society for Phenomenology*, 1, 1 (1970), pp. 4–17. For Husserl's synopsis see his 'Syllabus of a Course of Four Lectures on "Phenomenological Method and Phenomenological Philosophy," delivered at University College, London, June 6, 8, 9, 12, 1922', *Journal of the British Society for Phenomenology*, 1, 1 (1970), pp. 18–23.

78 See E. Husserl, 'Author's Preface to the English Edition' of *Ideas: General Introduction to Pure Phenomenology*, trans. W. R. Boyce Gibson (London: Allen & Unwin, 1931), p. 22, where he refers to *CM* as 'an extended elaboration of the four lectures which he had the pleasure of giving first in the spring of 1922 at the University of London'. In a letter to Winthrop Bell, he described his London Lectures as part of a new spirit of international co-operation.

79 The first Kaizo article 'Renewal: Its Problem and Method' (Hua 27: 3–13) has been translated in *HSW*, pp. 326–34.

80 See Herbert Spiegelberg, 'On the Misfortunes of Edmund Husserl's *Encyclopaedia Britannica* Article "Phenomenology"', in *HSW*, pp. 18–20. For a full discussion of the affair, see Thomas Sheehan, 'The History of the Redaction of the *Encyclopaedia Britannica* Article', in *Trans. Phen.*, pp. 36–59.

81 See Richard Palmer, 'Husserl's Debate with Heidegger in the Margin of *Kant and the Problem of Metaphysics*', *Man and World*, 30 (1997), pp. 5–33. For Husserl's comments on Heidegger's *Being and Time*, see *Trans. Phen.*, pp. 263–422, and for his *Kantbuch* marginalia, see *Trans. Phen.*, pp. 437–72.

82 See Husserl's letter to Alexander Pfänder, 6 Jan. 1931; *Briefwechsel*, 2: 180–4, trans. Burt Hopkins in *Trans. Phen.*, pp. 479–83.

83 Emmanuel Levinas, 'La ruine de la représentation', in Van Breda and Taminiaux, eds, *Edmund Husserl 1859–1959*, p. 73.

84 Although a German typescript of the lectures circulated among Husserl's students, the original manuscript from which Levinas translated got lost. A revised German version of the text was eventually published in 1950, as Hua 1.

85 For an excellent commentary on *CM*, see A. D. Smith, *Routledge Philosophy Guidebook to Husserl and the Cartesian Meditations* (London and New York: Routledge, 2003).

86 E. Fink, *VI. Cartesianische Meditation*, Teil 1: *Die Idee einer transzendentalen Methodlehre*, ed. Hans Ebeling, Jann Holl and Guy Van Kerckhoven (Dordrecht: Kluwer, 1988), trans. Ronald Bruzina, *Sixth Cartesian Meditation: The Idea of a Transcendental Theory of Method: With Textual Notations by Edmund Husserl* (Bloomington, Ind.: Indiana University Press, 1995).

87 For a copy of this letter see Sepp, ed., *Edmund Husserl und die phänomenologische Bewegung*, p. 384. Hermann Heidegger had claimed that Husserl's *Beurlaubung* had already been officially sanctioned by the previous Rektor, Sauer; see H. Heidegger, 'Der Wirtschaftshistoriker und die Wahrheit: notwendige Bemerkungen zu den Veröffentlichungen Hugo Otts über Martin Heidegger', *Heidegger Studies*, 13 (1997), pp. 177–92, see esp. p. 186.

88 The page is B II 7 of the bundle entitled 'Epoche Noten in der üblichen Zeit, etwa Mai 1933'. I thank the Husserl Archive in Leuven for allowing me to see this page.

89 These references to Husserl in the Nazi journal *NS-Frauenwarte*, 20 (1937/8), p. 625, are cited in Peter Prechtl, *Husserl: zur Einführung* (Hamburg: Junius, 1991), p. 14.

90 See Jaegerschmid, 'Conversations with Edmund Husserl, 1931–1938', p. 344.

91 Schütz, in Van Breda and Taminiaux, eds, *Edmund Husserl 1859–1959*, p. 88.

92 Only the first two parts appeared in 1936, and the Husserliana edition (Hua 6) appeared in 1950, with further material (Hua 29) in 1993.

93 See H. L. Van Breda, 'Le sauvetage de l'héritage husserlien et la fondation des Archives Husserl', in H. L. Van Breda and J. Taminiaux, eds, *Husserl et la pensée moderne* (The Hague: Nijhoff, 1959), for the exciting story of the smuggling of the manuscripts.

94 See Jean-François Courtine, 'Fondation et proto-fondation des Archives Husserl à Paris', in E. Escoubas and M. Richir, eds, *Husserl* (Grenoble: Millon, 1989), pp. 199–205.

95 See Dieter Lohmar, 'Zu der Entstehung und den Ausgangsmaterialen von E. Husserls Werk *Erfahrung und Urteil*', *Husserl Studies*, 13 (1996), pp. 31–71, for identification of the manuscripts used by Landgrebe.

# Chapter 2   Husserl's Conception of Philosophy

1 F. Brentano, *Die vier Phasen der Philosophie und ihr augenblicklicher Status* (first published 1895, then Leipzig: Meiner, 1926; repr. Hamburg: Meiner, 1968), trans. Stephen Satris, as 'The Four Phases of Philosophy and its Present Condition', *Philosophy Today*, 43, 1/4 (Spring 1999), pp. 14–28.

2 In his later writings Husserl employs a barrage of terms to express different aspects of humanity. He speaks of different traditions of human self-understanding as giving rise to different 'humanities' (*Menschheiten*). He also speaks of a universal 'humanness' (*Menschentum*).

3 R. Ingarden, 'Edith Stein on her Activity as an Assistant of Edmund Husserl', *Philosophy and Phenomenological Research*, 23, 2 (Dec. 1962), p. 160.

4 Already in PSW (1910/11) Husserl speaks of the 'Socratic–Platonic revolution' that inaugurated Western science (25: 6).

5 See Iso Kern, *Husserl und Kant: Eine Untersuchung über Husserls Verhältnis zu Kant und zum Neukantianismus* (The Hague: Nijhoff, 1964), p. 35.

6 Husserl greatly resented the Heideggerian accusation that his phenomenology was oriented to the theoretical and ignored or undervalued the practical nature of our being-in-the-world. In fact, Husserl lays great stress on the non-theoretical nature of the natural attitude. Yet it is only when we come to recognize the natural attitude for what it is, that we break with it and adopt the philosophical, theoretical attitude which, as Husserl says in *Vienna Lecture* (1935), is still a form of *praxis*.

# Chapter 3   The *Philosophy of Arithmetic* (1891)

1 The first four chapters of *PA* are a lightly reworked version of Husserl's 1887 *Habilitation* thesis.

2 See Claire Ortiz Hill, 'Husserl, Frege and the "Paradox"', *Manuscrito*, 23, 2 (Oct. 2000), pp. 101–32. We know from the mathematician Heinrich Scholz that Husserl wrote to Frege about 'the paradox', which most scholars have assumed is Russell's paradox concerning the class of all classes that are not members of themselves. Frege's own work was undermined by Russell's paradox about set theory in 1906.

3 See the note in *Ideen* I §1 where Husserl attempts to clarify what he means by origin and genesis.

4 Hermann Weyl is normally associated with the term *Grundlagenkrise*, but it is often used by Husserl in a broad sense, e.g. in 1934, Hua 27: 226.

5 Husserl speaks of the crisis of foundations affecting the sciences in many places, e.g. his first draft for the *Encyclopaedia Britannica* article (*Trans. Phen.*, p. 100; Hua 9: 252), where he speaks of it as affecting both the empirical and the a priori sciences.

6 See also the excellent dissertation of José Huertas-Jourda, *On the Threshold of Phenomenology: A Study of Edmund Husserl's* Philosophie der Arithmetik (New York University: Dissertations International, Feb. 1969).

7 Husserl, 'Personal Notes,' in *EW*; *CW* 5: 490–1; Hua 24: 442–3.

8 In the context of the discussion (a rejection of the view that number combinations emerge from the representation of space), he criticizes Lange for ignoring the acts involved in combination by treating them as unconscious, and thus misconstruing Kant. On the other hand, Husserl also criticizes Kant for thinking that all combinations of content require synthetic acts.

9 Formal ontology, as introduced by Husserl in *Ideen* I §10, means the study of the a priori laws governing objects in general, property, relation and so on. See also *ELE* §§21–2, *FTL* §24 and Hua 13: 129.

10 Husserl's account of the nature our authentic, genuine experiences of the smaller numbers in the first part of *PA* was retained essentially unaltered in later writings. It is at the very heart of his conception of intuition as either empty or full. Thus in *APS*, he speaks of the fact that the presented object is the same in the cases of both empty and full presentation (*APS*; Hua 11: 245). Emptiness means a potential towards fulfilment. Husserl remarks that this thinking 'in the mode of emptiness' (*im Modus der Leere*; Hua 11: 245)

is at the centre of linguistic and logical thinking. Higher logical operations are entirely symbolic, and thus the challenge is to give an account of their legitimacy and justification.

11 G. Frege, *Conceptual Notation*, in T. W. Bynum, ed. and trans., *Conceptual Notation and Related Articles* (Oxford: Clarendon Press, 1972), p. 83 (trans. modified).

12 In a footnote, Husserl refers to *PA* as one of the works which sought to carry out elementary investigations into the nature of the intuiting and representing which make possible such a transition to scientific knowledge based on signs and symbols.

13 The traditional view goes back to Aristotle and, indeed, was held by Bertrand Russell prior to his 1903 *The Principles of Mathematics* (London: Allen & Unwin, 1903; repr. 1956), ch. 11. Russell claims that we know basic numbers by a kind of acquaintance (p. xv). He originally held that numbers were indefinable, but changed to Frege's position in the *Principles*. I am grateful to Jim Levine for clarifying this point.

14 David Bell makes a similar point in his *Husserl* (London: Routledge, 1991), p. 61.

15 Though Claire Ortiz Hill has pointed out that Husserl thinks of the numerical abstractive process as actually different in kind from the type described by Aristotle, Locke and Mill; see her *Word and Object in Husserl, Frege and Russell* (Athens, Oh.: Ohio University Press, 1991), p. 68. See *PA*, pp. 89ff; 12: 85ff.

16 In a note (*PA*, p. 223, Hua 12: 210 n. 1), Husserl expresses regret that Ehrenfels's 1890 article, 'Über Gestaltqualitäten' ('On Gestalt Qualities') with its discussion of 'figural moments', arrived too late for him to take proper account of it. Husserl, however, does acknowledge the influence of Carl Stumpf's concept of 'fusion' (*Verschmelzung*) drawn from his *Tonpsychologie*, 2 vols. (1883, 1890). Husserl notes that Ehrenfels had been prompted to his analysis of the indirect grasp of totalities by the work of the physicist Ernst Mach, viz. his *Contributions to the Analysis of the Sensations* 1886, rev. 1905, trans. C. M. Williams and S. Waterlow (Chicago: Open Court, 1959).

17 The German word *Vorstellung* is often used to translate 'idea' in the Lockean or Cartesian sense. Frege stresses the term's subjective meaning, but Husserl used it more broadly, as did other German writers; see Claire Ortiz Hill and Guillermo E. Rosado Haddock, *Husserl or Frege? Meaning, Objectivity and Mathematics* (Chicago and La Salle, Ill.: Open Court, 2000), pp. 101–2.

18 See M. Dummett, *Frege: Philosophy of Mathematics* (London: Duckworth, 1991), p. 20. Even in *FTL*, Husserl continues to see the concept of *etwas* as fundamental (FTL §27, p. 87; Hua 17: 91).

19 Husserl, *PA*; 12: 83 n. 1, relying on a German translation of E. B. Tylor's 1871 study *Primitive Culture*, notes how primitive cultures employ this concept of indeterminate multiplicity once they count beyond 3 or 5.

20 See Bell, *Husserl*, pp. 55–6, for an excellent discussion of this point.

21 Gottlob Frege, 'Rezension von: E. G. Husserl, *Philosophie der Arithmetik I*', *Zeitschrift für Philosophie und philosophische Kritik*, vol. 103 (1894), pp. 313–32; repr. in Frege, *Kleine Schriften*, ed. I. Angelelli (Hildesheim: Georg Olms, 1967), pp. 179–92; trans. E. W. Kluge, 'Review of Dr. E. Husserl's *Philosophy*

*of Arithmetic'*, in F. Elliston and P. McCormick eds, *Husserl: Expositions and Appraisals* (Notre Dame, Ind.: University of Notre Dame Press, 1977), pp. 314–24. Hereafter cited *'Rezension'* followed by German page number and English pagination from the Elliston and McCormick translation.

22 See E. Husserl, 'Review of Ernst Schröder's *Vorlesungen über die Algebra der Logik'*, *EW*, pp. 52–91; Hua 22: 3–43. See G. Frege, 'Kritische Beleuchtung einiger Punkte in E. Schröders *Vorlesungen über die Algebra der Logik'*, *Archiv für systematische Philosophie*, 1 (1895), pp. 433–56; repr. in Frege, *Kleine Schriften*, pp. 193–210; trans. Peter Geach as 'A Critical Elucidation of Some Points in E. Schröder's *Vorlesungen über die Algebra der Logik'*, in Peter Geach and Max Black, eds, *Translations from the Philosophical Writings of Gottlob Frege* (Oxford: Basil Blackwell, 1966), pp. 86–106.

23 See 'Frege–Husserl Correspondence', in J. N. Mohanty, *Husserl and Frege* (Bloomington, Ind.: Indiana University Press, 1982), pp. 118–19.

24 G. Frege, 'On Concept and Object' (1892), in M. Beaney, ed., *The Frege Reader* (Oxford: Blackwell, 1997), p. 186. For a discussion of the reason why Frege regarded the sense/reference distinction as a distinction within the notion of *content*, see Michael Dummett, *Frege*, pp. 15–16.

25 See G. Frege, 'Reply to Cantor's Review of *Grundlagen der Arithmetik'*, in Frege, *Collected Papers on Mathematics, Logic and Philosophy*, ed. B. McGuinness, trans. Max Black et al. (Oxford: Blackwell, 1984), p. 122.

26 'Frege–Husserl Correspondence', p. 120.

27 See Claire Ortiz Hill, 'Husserl and Frege on Substitutivity', in L. Haaparanta, ed., *Mind, Meaning and Mathematics* (Dordrecht: Kluwer, 1994), pp. 113–40.

28 See Claire Ortiz Hill, 'Frege's Attack on Husserl and Cantor', *The Monist*, 77, 3 (1994), pp. 345–57, where she speculates that perhaps Frege's real target is not Husserl, but rather another Halle mathematician, Georg Cantor.

29 See Donn Welton, 'Husserl and Frege', *Journal of Philosophy*, 84, 10 (Oct. 1987), p. 522.

30 Claire Ortiz Hill has pointed out that the founder of set theory, Georg Cantor, was equally lax about discriminating between these terms in his own works; see her 'Abstraction and Idealization in Edmund Husserl and Georg Cantor prior to 1895', *Poznan Studies in the Philosophy of the Sciences and the Humanities*, 20 (1998), p. 16.

31 Frege concedes that Husserl does occasionally talk of number as the extension of a concept, but has a confused notion of extension.

32 The *locus classicus* for this position is Dagfinn Føllesdal's master's thesis, *Husserl und Frege, ein Beitrag zur Beleuchtung der Entstehung der phänomenologischen Philosophie* (Oslo: Aschehoug, 1958), trans. Claire Ortiz Hill, as 'Husserl and Frege: A Contribution to Elucidating the Origins of Phenomenological Philosophy', in Haaparanta, ed., *Mind, Meaning and Mathematics*, pp. 3–47.

33 See Husserl's review of Schröder, *EW*, pp. 52–91; Hua 22: 3–43, and Mohanty, *Husserl and Frege*, p. 2.

34 Husserl, 'Zur Logik der Zeichen', *EW*, pp. 20–51; Hua 22: 340–73; see esp. *EW*, p. 23; Hua 22: 343. See Guillermo E. Rosado Haddock, 'Remarks on Sense and Reference in Frege and Husserl', repr. in Hill and Haddock, *Husserl or Frege?*, p. 32.

35 I am grateful to Jan Wolenski for giving me his draft paper 'Twardowski and the Distinction between Content and Object', with its account of the distinction in Bolzano, Zimmermann, Twardowski, Höfler and Meinong in their *Logik* textbook, Marty, and others. Frege's semantic version, which distinguished *Sinn* from *Bedeutung*, was not well known until it was popularized by Bertrand Russell in his *Principles of Mathematics* (1903).

36 For a full account of the debate, see Mohanty, *Husserl and Frege*.

37 Dummett, however, in *Frege*, pp. 19–21, assumes that Frege did have an impact on Husserl.

38 Hermann Lotze, *Logik: Drei Bücher vom Denken, vom Untersuchen und vom Erkennen*, 2nd edn. (Leipzig: Hirzel, 1880). Husserl made these claims public in his 1903 review of Melchior Palágyi, *EW*, p. 201; Hua 22: 156. He repeats them in his letter of 17/21 June 1933 to E. Paul Welch, *Briefwechsel*, 6: 460.

39 The nature of Lotze's concept of objectivity is complex, as Michael Dummett has shown in his 'Objectivity and Reality in Lotze and Frege', *Inquiry*, 25, 1 (Mar. 1982), pp. 95–114.

40 For Brentano's remark, see W. Stegmüller, *Main Currents in Contemporary German, British, and American Philosophy* (Dordrecht: Reidel, 1969), p. 93.

41 'Frege–Husserl Correspondence', p. 122.

42 Ibid., p. 123.

43 For a discussion of these topics, see Michael Dummett, *Origins of Analytic Philosophy* (London: Duckworth, 1991).

44 For an excellent discussion of Husserl's concept of logic in the *Prolegomena*, see R. Bernet, 'Different Concepts of Logic and their Relation to Subjectivity', in Dan Zahavi and Frederick Stjernfelt, eds, *One Hundred Years of Phenomenology: Husserl's* Logical Investigations *Revisited* (Dordrecht: Kluwer, 2002), pp. 19–30.

45 See O. Wiegand, *Interpretationen der Modallogik: ein Beitrag zur phänomenologischen Wissenschaftstheorie* (Dordrecht: Kluwer, 1998).

# Chapter 4   Husserl's 'Breakthrough Work': *Logical Investigations* (1900/1901)

1 Husserl's 'zigzag' method probably inspired Heidegger's discussion of the hermeneutic circle as 'relatedness backward and forward' in *Being and Time*, §2 (*SZ* 8).

2 Husserl's later position is summarized in *EU*, where he writes: 'Despite all the Platonic turns of phrase by which we have described its relation to the particular, the ideality of the universal must not be understood as if it were a question here of a being-in-itself devoid of reference to any subject. On the contrary, like *all* objectivities of understanding, it refers essentially *to the processes of productive spontaneity* which belong to it correlatively and in which it comes to original givenness. The being (*Sein*) of the universal in its different levels is essentially a *being-constituted* (*Konstituiert-sein*) in these processes' (*EU* §82, p. 330; 397).

3 George Heffernan, 'A Study in the Sedimented Origins of Evidence: Husserl and his Contemporaries Engaged in a Collective Essay in the

Phenomenology and Psychology of Epistemic Justification', *Husserl Studies*, 16, 2 (1999), pp. 83–181.

4 See also *FTL* §§105–7, pp. 277–90; Hua 17: 283–95. See Dagfinn Føllesdal, 'Husserl on Evidence and Justification', in R. Sokolowski, ed., *Edmund Husserl and the Phenomenological Tradition* (Washington: Catholic University of America Press, 1988), pp. 107–29.

5 Brentano was also fond of the idea of 'fixing'; what is noticed in experience; see his *Descriptive Psychology*, trans. Benito Müller (London: Routledge, 1995), pp. 66ff.

6 Jocelyn Benoist has raised the interesting question of whether Husserl's determination of actuality in terms of temporal existence goes against the proclaimed ontological neutrality of *LU*.

7 See Kevin Mulligan, 'Husserl on States of Affairs in the *Logical Investigations*', *Epistemologia*, 12 (1989), special issue, pp. 207–34. The term *Sachverhalt* was used by Stumpf in his lectures, but first appears in print with Husserl in *LU*. It subsequently was made canonical by Wittgenstein in the *Tractatus*.

8 For an excellent discussion of this distinction, see J. N. Mohanty, *Edmund Husserl's Theory of Meaning* (The Hague: Nijhoff, 1976).

9 In fact, Husserl anticipates Alexius Meinong's *theory of objects* (*Gegenstandstheorie*), first formally laid out in his *Über Annahmen* (1902), trans. James Heanue, *On Assumptions* (Berkeley: University of California Press, 1983). However, he considered Meinong's theory as ill thought out, and even insinuated that Meinong was plagiarizing his own ideas. He saw his a priori 'rational ontology' of objects as the realization of an older philosophical idea found in Leibniz.

10 John Stuart Mill, *A System of Logic, Ratiocinative and Inductive, Being a Connected View of the Principles of Evidence, and the Methods of Scientific Investigation*, 2 vols, (London: Parker, 1843), vol. 1, Introduction §7, p. 13. Husserl cites Gomperz's translation of Mill.

11 Frege attacks psychologism in his *Conceptual Notation* (*Begriffschrift*, 1879), *Foundations of Arithmetic* (*Grundlagen der Arithmetik*, 1884), and *Basic Laws of Arithmetic* (*Grundgesetze*, 1893).

12 See M. Dummett, *Frege: Philosophy of Mathematics* (London: Duckworth, 1991), p. 14.

13 This becomes an issue for Derrida; see his *La Voix et le phénomène* (Paris: PUF, 1967), ed. and trans. David Allison, *Speech and Phenomena and Other Essays on Husserl's Theory of Signs* (Evanston, Ill.: Northwestern University Press, 1973).

14 In *LU* Husserl used the expressions 'state of affairs' (*Sachverhalt*) and 'situation' (*Sachlage*) more or less interchangeably. Later in *EU* §59, he will claim that they express different states of affairs based on the same situation (*Sachlage*). See Guillermo E. Rosado Haddock, 'On Husserl's Distinction between State of Affairs (*Sachverhalt*) and Situation of Affairs (*Sachlage*)', in T. M. Seebohm, D. Føllesdal and J. N. Mohanty, eds, *Phenomenology and the Formal Sciences* (Dordrecht: Kluwer, 1991), pp. 35–57.

15 See K. Mulligan and B. Smith, 'A Husserlian Theory of Indexicality', *Grazer Philosophische Studien*, 28 (1986), pp. 133–63.

16 Husserl, e.g., rejects the view of abstraction that says it picks out what is common to two entities. He remarks that a common wall between two houses would fit that definition (24: 294).

17 In *Ideen* I §12, Husserl speaks of 'eidetic singularities'.

18 John Locke, *An Essay Concerning Human Understanding*, ed. Peter H. Nidditch (Oxford: Clarendon Press, 1979), iv. vii. 9, p. 596.

19 Husserl's account of parts and wholes (or 'mereology' from the Greek word *meros*, meaning 'part') draws on two main sources: Brentano's lectures (*DP*, pp. 15–17), and Stumpf's investigation of sensory experiences, especially his *Tonpsychologie* (*Psychology of Tones*, vol. 1 (Leipzig: Hirzel, 1883), vol. 2 (1890); repr. Amsterdam: Bonset, 1965) and his *Über den psychologischen Ursprung der Raumvorstellung* (*On the Psychological Origin of the Presentation of Space*) (Leipzig, 1873; repr. Amsterdam: Bonset, 1965).

20 In *PA* Husserl conceived of the properties of an object as parts of a whole (Hua 12: 159), and adopts Stumpf's distinction between the dependent and independent contents of a psychological act (Hua 12: 94n.). But he is critical of Stumpf's account of fusion, in that Stumpf thinks that a simultaneous set of presentations is sufficient to produce a fusion, whereas for Husserl there must be, besides the 'part intuitions' (*Teilanschauungen*) of the individuals, an intuition of the whole row, pile or whatever (Hua 12: 23, 204). Here Husserl is distinguishing between the simultaneous presentation of parts and their fusion.

21 See R. Rollinger, *Husserl's Position in the School of Brentano* (Utrecht: Department of Philosophy Publications, Utrecht University, 1996), pp. 48–9.

22 Stumpf, *Über den psychologischen Ursprung der Raumvorstellung*, p. 109. See Rollinger, *Husserl's Position in the School of Brentano*, p. 82.

23 For a clear discussion of the project, see Peter M. Simons, 'Meaning and Language', in B. Smith and D. Woodruff Smiths, eds, *The Cambridge Companion to Husserl* (Cambridge: Cambridge University Press, 1995), esp. pp. 118–22.

24 See Elmar Holenstein, 'Jakobson's Contribution to Phenomenology', in David Armstrong and C. H. Van Schooneveld, eds, *Roman Jakobson: Echoes of his Scholarship*, (Lisse: De Ridder Press, 1977), pp. 145–62.

25 Husserl frequently contrasts 'real' parts (i.e. really existing, actual parts) with *reell* parts (i.e. immanent or 'internal' parts which make no reference to actuality).

26 Husserl's discussion of truth in *LU* VI provided Heidegger with the basis of his account of truth in *SZ* §44 with its distinction between truth as correctness and truth as disclosure. See Ernst Tugendhat, *Der Wahrheitsbegriff bei Husserl und Heidegger* (Berlin: de Gruyter, 1967).

# Chapter 5   The Eidetic Phenomenology of Consciousness

1 In 1910/11, Husserl speaks of the 'fundamental forms' (*Grundgestalten*) and 'fundamental composition' (*Grundverfassung*; Hua 13: 111) of consciousness. He speaks variously of 'the life of the soul' (*das Seelenleben*; 34: 5), 'the entire

concrete subjective life' (*das ganze konkrete subjective Leben*; 9: 43), the 'life of worldly consciousness' (*Weltbewusstseinsleben*; 34: 387), and so on.

2 Husserl offers his phenomenological descriptions in *LU* as a major advance over the descriptive psychologies of Brentano and Stumpf. He believes he has developed a far more rigorous and nuanced analysis of the elements of conscious processes and their inter-connecting unity (see, e.g., Hua 9: 36 for his criticism of Brentano's vision).

3 Husserl distinguishes 'states' (*Zustände*) from 'acts' (*Akte*). Positional acts have a belief component, but this is not an act of believing in the full sense (which Husserl reserves for judgement); see Hua 23: 458.

4 See Ullrich Melle, 'Husserl's Phenomenology of Willing', in James Hart and Lester Embree, eds, *Phenomenology of Value and Valuing* (Dordrecht: Kluwer, 1997), pp. 169–92.

5 The author who wrote under the pseudonym Max Stirner (1806–56) was a left-wing Hegelian. His best-known work appeared in 1844 as *Der Einzige und sein Eigentum* (repr. Stuttgart: Reclam, 1991), trans. by Steven T. Byington as *The Ego and His Own: The Case of the Individual against Authority* (London: Constable, 1973).

6 Of course, there are also gaps in consciousness, e.g. during sleep, and here the mystery is how the newly reawakened consciousness regains its mode of givenness, so that the 'I' can again recover itself as bearer of these habitualities, memories and so on.

7 Manuscript L I 15 2b, quoted in Dan Zahavi, *Self-Awareness and Alterity: A Phenomenological Investigation* (Evanston, Ill.: Northwestern University Press, 1999), p. 77.

8 See Husserl's draft *Encyclopedia Britannica* article, *Trans. Phen.*, p. 95; Hua 9: 247. Husserl repeats this criticism of Brentano in *CM* §17, *Krisis* §68 and elsewhere.

9 Noesis and noema are referred to briefly in the Amsterdam Lectures (9: 327) and in the *Encyclopedia Britannica* article (9: 283); see also *Trans. Phen.*, p. 185. In *APS* he talks of the correlation between thinking as sense-giving and the thought as the sense (*Sinn*; 17: 374). But the noema is a far less prominent theme in his philosophy than the extensive commentary on it would suggest.

10 See E. Husserl, *Briefe an Roman Ingarden*, p. 10.

11 Husserl unfortunately describes the noema both as a 'content' and as 'immanent' in the flow of consciousness. It is not, however, a real part of the *Erlebnis*; it is a purely phenomenological concept.

12 Of course, to be more precise, it belongs to the sense (*eidos*) of an *apple tree* that an apple tree is something that can be chopped up and burnt.

13 Rudolf Bernet in his 'Husserls Begriff des Noema', in Samuel Ijsseling, ed., *Husserl-Ausgabe und Husserl-Forschung* (Dordrecht: Kluwer, 1990), pp. 61–80, criticizes *Ideen* I for not distinguishing clearly the noema as individual appearing object and the noema as ideal sense. Bernet finds three separate meanings of noema in Husserl: as the appearance as such, the ideal meaning, and the constituted entity.

14 E. Fink has argued that the psychological attitude to the noema yields a meaning, whereas the transcendental attitude yields the thing itself; see his

'The Phenomenological Philosophy of Edmund Husserl and Contemporary Criticism', in R. O. Elveton, ed., *The Phenomenology of Husserl: Selected Critical Readings*, 2nd edn (Seattle: Noesis Press, 2000), pp. 70–139, esp. p. 117.

15 See Dagfinn Føllesdal, 'Husserl's Notion of Noema', *Journal of Philosophy*, 66 (1969), pp. 680–7.

16 Husserl, *Ideen* III §16, p. 76; Hua 5: 89. Generally speaking, although Husserl uses the terms *Sinn* and *Bedeutung* interchangeably in *LU*, in *Ideen* I he restricts the word *Bedeutung* 'meaning' to linguistic contents (see *Ideen* I §95) and speaks of liberating the word *Sinn* from its relation to linguistic expressions (*APS*; 17: 374).

17 See Robert Sokolowski, 'Intentional Analysis and the Noema', *Diacritica*, 38 (1984), pp. 113–29; John J. Drummond, *Husserlian Intentionality and Non-Foundational Realism: Noema and Object* (Dordrecht: Kluwer, 1990); and *idem*, 'An Abstract Consideration: De-ontologizing the Noema', in J. J. Drummond and L. Embree, eds, *The Phenomenology of the Noema* (Dordrecht: Kluwer, 1992), pp. 89–109.

18 For Husserl on time, see John Brough, 'The Emergence of an Absolute Consciousness in Husserl's Early Writings on Time-Consciousness', *Man and World*, 5, 3 (1972), pp. 298–326 and *idem*, 'Husserl's Phenomenology of Time-Consciousness', in J. N. Mohanty and William R. McKenna, eds, *Husserl's Phenomenology: A Textbook* (Washington: Center for Advanced Research in Phenomenology and University Press of America, 1989), pp. 249–89; Robert Sokolowski, 'The Inside of Time', in *Husserlian Meditations* (Evanston, Ill.: Northwestern University Press, 1974), pp. 138–68; and Zahavi, *Self-Awareness and Alterity*.

19 Zahavi, *Self-Awareness and Alterity*, p. 79 (citing Hua 10: 84), maintains that *Erlebnisse* understood as acts are not strictly speaking temporal objects in our pre-reflective experience of them, but become such when explicitly objectified in reflection. They are contents of consciousness. Husserl, however, many times comments on the fact that *Erlebnisse* are real occurrences in the world, as well as segments of immanent consciousness.

20 See A. D. Smith, *The Problem of Perception* (Cambridge, Mass.: Harvard University Press, 2002), pp. 117–18.

21 See Natalie Depraz, 'Hyletic and Kinetic Facticity of the Absolute Flow and World Creation', in John B. Brough and Lester Embree, eds, *The Many Faces of Time* (Dordrecht: Kluwer, 2000), pp. 25–35.

22 See Nam-In Lee, *Edmund Husserls Phänomenologie der Instinkte* (Dordrecht: Kluwer, 1993).

23 See Eugen Fink's comments on the naïveté of certain 'depth-psychological' discussions of the unconscious; *Krisis*; 6: 473–5.

24 See James Richard Mensch, 'Instincts', in *Postfoundational Phenomenology: Husserlian Reflections on Presence and Embodiment* (University Park, Pa.: Pennsylvania State University Press, 2001), pp. 35–52, and Lee, *Edmund Husserls Phänomenologie der Instinkte*.

25 Max Scheler, on the other hand, took notice of Freud and Nietzsche right from the start in his phenomenological analyses of moods, feelings and the affective life in general.

26 *EP* I; Hua 7: 262; see also *Trans. Phen.*, p. 217; Hua 9: 306; *Phen. Psych.*, p. 112; Hua 9: 147.

27 For a discussion of the nature of Husserl's account of self-awareness, see Zahavi, *Self-Awareness and Alterity*, pp. 52–62.

28 Although not quite in the Berkeleian sense, as its *percipi* does not give rise to its *esse*, but rather its being is so constituted that it is perceived immediately and without aspects.

29 This appears to be a development of the claim in *LU* I that no mental experience announces itself to us through an intimation, or *Kundgabe*; rather, it is directly experienced or lived through.

30 'We call an investigation "phansiological" that explores the *cogitatio* with respect to its real (*reellen*) composition' (*ZB*; Hua 10: 277n.).

31 See S. Luft, *Phänomenologie der Phänomenologie: Systematik und Methodologie der Phänomenologie in der Auseinandersetzung zwischer Husserl und Fink* (Dordrecht: Kluwer, 2002) p. 40.

32 For a thorough study of the neutrality modification in Husserl, see Marcus Brainard, *Belief and its Neutralization: Husserl's System of Phenomenology in Ideas I* (Albany, NY: SUNY Press, 2002), pp. 157–71.

33 It is not clear what he means by 'interpretation', except that it is an intuitive grasp or apprehension that does not involve inference or reasoning. Husserl emphasizes in *LU* VI §26 that there are different complex relations between interpretative grasp and its matter in the different forms of intuiting. For instance, purely sigmitive intending needs no relation between sensuous marks and an object to make the objective attribution, whereas in representational thinking some kind of internal relation (based on similarity and resemblance) is necessary.

34 For a discussion of Husserl's changing view of sensation, see Donn Welton, *The Other Husserl* (Bloomington, Ind.: Indiana University Press, 2001). p. 178.

35 Drummond, *Husserlian Intentionality and Non-Foundational Realism*, p. 157.

36 See also *Krisis* §28, p. 105; Hua 6: 107.

37 Indeed, interestingly, Edith Stein commented that Husserl expressed the perceptual presence of a transcendent thing in terms of the paradigm of the encounter with another person, present in the flesh, *in propria persona*, personally and so on (which presumably stimulated Levinas's interest in the face to face encounter).

38 Herman Philipse, 'Transcendental Idealism', in B. Smith and D. Woodruff Smith, eds, *The Cambridge Companion to Husserl* (Cambridge: Cambridge University Press, 1995), pp. 262ff, believes that this 'projective theory of perception' has idealist consequences, in that the thing that is experienced 'bodily' is constructed out of felt sensations and an interpretative act of projection.

39 The notion of a surrounding world may have come to Husserl through his reading of Avinarius, but he makes the concept his own and develops it into a central theme of phenomenology.

40 Merleau-Ponty and Stein both want to claim that we can see properties such as softness, hardness, brittleness and so on. According to Stein, I actually *see* the velvet softness of a fabric in a painting. For Merleau-Ponty, I actually hear the brittleness of the glass material when a glass shatters.

41 J.-P. Sartre, in *L'Imaginaire: Psychologie phénoménologique de l'imagination* (Paris: Éditions Gallimard, 1940), has a somewhat different reading of the nature of the suspension of the thetic act in imagination. For him the suspension of belief 'remains a positional act'.

42 Husserl has many interesting things to say concerning the relationship between original and reproduction, and makes the point that reproductions of paintings, etc., often serve as memory tools evoking the memory of the original. Husserl also recognizes that if reproduction is absolutely perfect, then the notion of original has no more than a sentimental value. This discussion anticipates, but is more systematic and detailed than, Walter Benjamin's famous essay 'The Work of Art in the Age of Mechanical Reproduction' (1935), published in *Illuminations*, ed. Hannah Arendt, trans. Harry Zohn (London: Fontana, 1973).

43 Like Wittgenstein, Husserl is interested in the perceptual shift, or 'conflict' (*Widerstreit*), which takes place when we see that the woman is actually a wax figure, a mannequin (see *DR* §15, e.g.).

44 For an illuminating discussion, see Richard Cobb-Stevens, 'Two Stages in Husserl's Critique of Brentano's Theory of Judgment', *Études Phénoménologiques*, No. 27–8 (1998), pp. 193–212.

## Chapter 6    Transcendental Phenomenology: An Infinite Project

1 New material on transcendental idealism has recently been published in E. Husserl, *Transzendentaler Idealismus: Texte aus dem Nachlass* (1980–1921), ed. R. Rollinger and R. Sowa, Hua 36 (Dordrecht: Kluwer, 2003).

2 E. Husserl, 'Fichte's Ideal of Humanity [Three Lectures]', trans. James G. Hart, *Husserl Studies*, 12 (1995), pp. 111–33; Hua 25: 267–93.

3 E. Husserl, 'Kant und die Idee der Transzendentalphilosophie', *EP* I; Hua 7: 230–87; trans. Ted E. Klein and William E. Pohl as 'Kant and the Idea of Transcendental Philosophy', *Southwestern Journal of Philosophy*, 5 (Fall 1974), pp. 9–56.

4 While the term 'idealism' does not appear in the text of *Ideen* I, it was included in the thematic index compiled by Gerda Walther and included in the 2nd edn (1922) with Husserl's approval; but it is clear from marks on his own copy of the Index that he was not entirely happy with it. This index was replaced with a new index by Landgrebe in the 3rd edn; see K. Schuhmann, *Die Fundamentalbetrachtung der Phänomenologie* (The Hague: Nijhoff, 1971), p. xxxv.

5 Most of Husserl's students, including Adolf Reinach, Edith Stein, Roman Ingarden, Hedwig Conrad-Martius, Gerda Walther and Martin Heidegger, rejected this idealist turn.

6 See Husserl's letter to Roman Ingarden of 31 Aug. 1923, in E. Husserl, *Briefe an Roman Ingarden*, ed. R. Ingarden (The Hague: Nijhoff, 1968), p. 26.

7 Letter of Husserl to Welch, 17/21 June 1933; *Briefwechsel*, 6: 459.

8 Husserl claims, e.g., that 'the history of psychology is actually only a history of crises' (*Krisis* §57, p. 203; 6: 207).

9 Edith Stein, *Life in a Jewish Family 1891–1916: An Autobiography*, trans. Josephine Koeppel, in *Collected Works of Edith Stein*, vol. 1 (Washington, DC: Institute of Carmelite Studies Publications, 1986), p. 250.

10 Brentano claimed in his *Descriptive Psychology* lectures that the only genuine perception was inner perception: 'all phenomena should be called "inner"' (*DP*, p. 137), and again, 'everything psychical falls under inner perception' (*DP*, p. 129). In *Psychology from an Empirical Standpoint* he writes: 'inner perception is the only perception in the true sense of the word' (*PES*, pp. 97–8). Indeed, even the assumption of the existence of an external world is 'initially hypothetical' (*DP*, p. 163). Stumpf too thought that the belief in an external world was based on a conscious or unconscious inference (see the quotation from his 1886/7 Lectures on Psychology in Rollinger and Sowa's Introduction, Hua 36: p. xiv n. 2).

11 E. Husserl, 'Author's Preface to the English Edition', in *Ideas: General Introduction to Pure Phenomenology*, trans. W. R. Boyce Gibson (New York: Collier Books, 1962), p. 5; the German text of this Preface has been translated as an Epilogue in *Ideen* II, p. 408; Nachwort Hua 5: 141.

12 However, he seems not to have read very much Hegel; so his rediscovery of German Absolute Idealism is largely inspired by his own critique of the transcendental tradition from Descartes to Kant and Fichte, and again through his reading of Dilthey. He does, however, refer to the Preface to Hegel's *Phenomenology of Spirit* in *Krisis* §57; 6: 204–5.

13 Frequently Husserl asserts that the goal of the human spirit is to become God. The essence of the divine is, as it were, incorporated into the goal of being human. God, moreover, is somehow split or divided into the plurality of egos; see James Richard Mensch, *Intersubjectivity and Transcendental Idealism* (Albany, NY: SUNY Press 1988), pp. 368–9.

14 Edmund Husserl in conversation with Adelgundis Jaegerschmid in 1935; see Adelgundis Jaegerschmid, 'Conversation with Edmund Husserl, 1931–1938', trans. Marcus Brainard, *The New Yearbook for Phenomenology and Phenomenological Philosophy*, 1 (2001), p. 338.

15 P. Natorp, *Platos Ideenlehre: Eine Einführung in den Idealismus*, 1st edn (1903); rev. 1921; (repr. Hamburg: Meiner, 1994), p. x, cites Herman Cohen for opening his eyes to Plato. Natorp sees Plato, not Berkeley, as the true originator of idealism.

16 For Husserl's engagement with neo-Kantianism, see Iso Kern, *Husserl und Kant: Eine Untersuchungen über Husserls Verhältnis zu Kant und zum Neukantianismus* (The Hague: Nijhoff, 1964), esp. pp. 321–420.

17 Husserl frequently comments on Kant's Letter to Herz; see, e.g., his 'Phänomenologie und Erkenntnistheorie' (1917); Hua 25: 143.

18 Kant wavered somewhat in the Third Critique, since aesthetic judgement precisely concerns the apprehension of the supersensible, albeit again in judgement.

19 E. Marbach, *Das Problem des Ich in der Phänomenologie Husserls*, Phaenomenologica 59 (The Hague: Nijhoff, 1974), p. 51.

20 But see his comment that the approach of 1907 contained errors; 8: 433.

21 See Iso Kern, 'The Three Ways to the Transcendental Phenomenological Reduction in the Philosophy of Edmund Husserl', in F. Elliston and P. McCormick, eds, *Husserl: Expositions and Appraisals* (Notre Dame: Univer-

sity of Notre Dame Press, 1977), pp. 126–49; John J. Drummond, 'Husserl on the Ways to the Performance of the Reduction', *Man and World*, 8, 1 (Feb. 1975), pp. 47–69; R. Bernet, I. Kern and Eduard Marbach, *An Introduction to Husserlian Phenomenology* (Evanston, Ill.: Northwestern University Press, 1993), pp. 58–77; and D. Welton, *The Other Husserl* (Bloomington, Ind: Indiana University Press, 2000), pp. 133–64.

22  This concern is expressed in a range of works; see *Phän. Psych.*, *Encyclopedia Britannica* article (e.g. *Trans. Phen.*, p. 95; Hua 9: 247), and *Krisis*.

23  See Charles Adam and Paul Tannery, *Oeuvres de Descartes*, 11 vols (Paris: Vrin, 1996), vol. VII, p. 25 (hereafter 'AT' followed by the volume and page number). English translation is from John Cottingham, Robert Stoothoff and Dugald Murdoch, eds, *The Philosophical Writings of Descartes* (Cambridge: Cambridge University Press, 1985), vols 1 and 2.

24  See the extended discussion in Hua 7: 78–140 and also 6: §22.

25  Husserl frequently accuses Locke of missing out entirely the nature of consciousness as consciousness-of. See the first draft of the *Encyclopedia Britannica* article, *Trans. Phen.*, p. 94; Hua 9: 246.

26  But even here the situation is complicated, because Husserl thinks of reasons as motivations, and these are essentially connected with human freedom. Indeed, the concept of freedom only makes sense within a context of motivation (see, e.g., *Ideen* I §56).

27  See Rollinger and Sowa's Introduction (Hua 36: pp. xxi and 73ff), which stresses that at this time (*c.*1915) Husserl uses the term to refer to the thesis that real objects cannot exist without an actual (as opposed to possible) consciousness.

28  Roman Ingarden, *On the Motives which led Husserl to Transcendental Idealism*, trans. Arnór Hannibalsson (The Hague: Nijhoff, 1975), p. 1 n. 1.

29  Ibid., p. 21.

30  I wish to acknowledge the important contribution of Rudolf Bernet's 'Husserl's Transcendental Idealism Revisited' paper presented to the 33rd Husserl Circle Annual Meeting in New York, June 2003. Bernet argues that Husserl's argument in *Ideen* I depends on the distinction between immanent and transcendent experience, whereas his explorations in 1913 depend on a contrast between the possibility of an object and the consciousness that represents it.

31  E. Husserl, 'Fichte's Ideal of Humanity [Three Lectures]', *Husserl Studies*, 12 (1995), p. 132; Hua 15: 386.

32  Ingarden, *On the Motives which led Husserl to Transcendental Idealism*, p. 21.

## Chapter 7   The Ego, Embodiment, Otherness, Intersubjectivity, and the 'Community of Monads'

1  I have greatly benefited from a number of studies, including Klaus Held, *Lebendige Gegenwart: Die Frage nach der Seinsweise des transzendentalen Ich bei Edmund Husserl, entwickelt am Leitfaden der Zeitproblematik* (The Hague: Nijhoff, 1966), and Eduard Marbach, *Das Problem des Ich in der Phänomenologie Husserls* (The Hague: Nijhoff, 1974), and more recent works by James Richard Mensch, *Intersubjectivity and Transcendental Idealism* (Albany, NY:

SUNY Press, 1988); James G. Hart, *The Person and the Common Life: Studies in a Husserlian Social Ethics* (Dordrecht: Kluwer, 1992); David Carr, *The Paradox of Subjectivity: The Self in the Transcendental Tradition* (Oxford and New York: Oxford University Press, 1999); Dan Zahavi, *Self-Awareness and Alterity: A Phenomenological Investigation* (Evanston, Ill.: Northwestern University Press, 1999); *idem, Husserl and Transcendental Intersubjectivity*, trans. Elizabeth A. Behnke (Athens, Oh.: Ohio University Press, 2001); Natalie Depraz, *Transcendance et incarnation: Le statut de l'intersubjectivité comme altérité à soi chez Husserl* (Paris: Vrin, 1995); Donn Welton, *The Other Husserl* (Bloomington, Ind.: Indiana University Press, 2000); and Sebastian Luft, *'Phänomenologie der Phänomenologie': Systematik und Methodologie der Phänomenologie in der Auseinandersetzung zwischen Husserl und Fink*, Phaenomenologica 166 (Dordrecht: Kluwer, 2002).

2  See Luft, *'Phänomenologie der Phänomenologie'*, pp. 119–20.

3  Both Sartre and Aron Gurwitsch similarly elaborated a non-egological account of consciousness in Husserl, on the basis that the ego is not experienced in our flowing psychic stream and that it becomes the object of judgements or assumptions.

4  In *LU*, Husserl is not a phenomenalist. Indeed, he thinks that F. A. Lange's project of a 'psychology without a soul' (*LU* V §7, **II** 90; Hua 19/1: 371) involves a commitment to phenomenalism.

5  Paul Natorp wrote two main works in this area: *Einleitung in die Psychologie nach kritische Methode* (Freiburg: Mohr, 1888), and *Allgemeine Psychologie nach kritischen Methode*, Band I (Tübingen: Paul Siebeck, 1912), both of which were in Husserl's possession. Husserl refers to Natorp's *Allgemeine Psychologie* as a 'new' work in his second edition Foreword to *LU* (Hua 18: 15). I am indebted to Sebastian Luft, 'Reduction and Reconstruction: On the Methodological Dispute between Natorp and Husserl regarding the Question of Subjectivity', paper read to 33rd Meeting of Husserl Circle, June 2003.

6  Of course, Husserl in turn was criticized by the neo-Kantians for objectivizing subjectivity.

7  Exchanges with Paul Natorp in particular influenced his shift in position.

8  From this discussion, and specifically from *Ideen* I, Jean-Paul Sartre took the ego to be an actual object of the *Erlebnis*, something transcendent, 'outside, in the world'. See J.-P. Sartre, *The Transcendence of the Ego*, trans. F. Williams and R. Kirkpatrick (New York: Octagon Books, 1972), p. 31. The ego is an object of consciousness for Sartre, and hence is never in consciousness. It is, for Sartre, a psychophysical object in the world. Pure consciousness for Sartre is not egological at all. Sartre famously distinguished between a pre-personal, non-reflective, non-egoistic *cogito* and a later, reflective *cogito*, and denied that a transcendental ego must be posited in order to account for either the unity or individuality of the stream of conscious experiences. But Sartre's account (and indeed Husserl's at this stage) seems to have serious problems, not least of which is that it leaves open the possibility that I can have somebody else's experiences.

9  See Eugen Fink's summary of Husserl's philosophy in Hua 27: 250.

10  See Elizabeth A. Behnke, 'Edmund Husserl's Contribution to Phenomenology of the Body in *Ideas* II', in T. Nenon and L. Embree, eds, *Issues in Husserl's Ideas II* (Dordrecht: Kluwer, 1996), pp. 135–60; Donn Welton, 'Soft,

Smooth Hands: Husserl's Phenomenology of the Lived Body', in D. Welton, ed., *The Body: Classic and Contemporary Readings* (Oxford: Blackwell, 1999), pp. 38–56; and James Dodd, *Idealism and Corporeity: An Essay on the Problem of the Body in Husserl's Phenomenology* (Dordrecht: Kluwer Academic Publishers, 1997).

11 Husserl also discusses the body in *APS* (Hua 11: 50ff). *EP* II (Hua 8: 60, 71, as well as 8: 60, 71 and 491–6), *Phän. Psych.* (Hua 9: §§15, 21, and 39; *CM* V §§44, 51–6), and *Krisis* (Hua 6: §§28, 47, and 62), as well as in the inter-subjectivity volumes.

12 Both Edith Stein and Merleau-Ponty develop and expand on Husserl's conception of the body.

13 The body is 'constantly perceived'; see M. Merleau-Ponty, *Phénoménologie de la perception* (Paris: Gallimard, 1945), p. 106, trans. C. Smith as *Phenomenology of Perception* (London: Routledge & Kegan Paul, 1962), p. 90.

14 In this respect, body practices or regimes such as physical exercise, yoga, tai-chi, ballet, etc. might be considered to be folk explorations of aspects of the somatological experience in the life-world.

15 In a text from 1921 Husserl recognizes the Leibnizian source of this concept of the person, quoting from the *Nouveaux essais*, ii. 27 §9 (Hua 14: 48).

16 See, e.g., Richard Cobb-Stevens, 'James and Husserl: Time-Consciousness and the Intentionality of Presence and Absence', in D. Zahavi, ed., *Self-Awareness, Temporality and Alterity: Central Topics in Phenomenology* (Dordrecht: Kluwer, 1998), pp. 41–57.

17 Quoted in D. Zahavi, 'The Fracture in Self-Awareness', in *Self-Awareness, Temporality and Alterity*, p. 29.

18 See Klaus Held, 'Heimwelt, Fremdwelt, die eine Welt', *Phänomenologische Forschungen*, 24/5 (1991), pp. 305–37; Bernhard Waldenfels, 'Homeworld and Alienworld', in Ernst Wolfgang Orth and Chan-Fai Cheung, eds, *Phenomenology of Interculturality and Life-World*, Sonderband (Freiburg and Munich: Karl Alber, 1998), pp. 72–88; and Anthony J. Steinbock, *Home and Beyond: Generative Phenomenology after Husserl* (Evanston, Ill.: Northwestern University Press, 1995).

19 Of course, conditions wherein one does not feel at home in one's body, including rare conditions such as believing a limb of one's body is an alien appendage, are modifications possible only because of the original feeling-at-home in the body which they disrupt.

20 For further discussion of this topic in Lipps, Scheler, Stein and Husserl, see my 'The Problem of Empathy: Lipps, Scheler, Husserl and Stein', in Thomas A. Kelly and Phillip W. Rosemann, eds, *Amor Amicitiae: On the Love that is Friendship: Essays in Medieval Thought and Beyond in Honor of the Rev. Professor James McEvoy* (Leuven, Paris and Dudley, Mass.: Peeters, 2004), pp. 269–312.

21 E. Husserl, *Urteilstheorie Vorlesung 1905*, ed. E. Schuhmann, Materialen-bände 5 (Dordrecht: Kluwer, 2002). Here *Einfühlung* is used to refer to the 'mode of consciousness relating, by a neutrality modification, to non-doxic, non-objectivating acts' (Hua 13: p. xxvi). He refers to the difference between an actual question and empathy in the question, an actual joy and empathy in the joy. At this point Husserl also uses the expressions *sich hineindenken* and *sich hineinphantasieren* (Hua 13: p. xxvi). But Husserl goes further in

these lectures and designates objectivating acts such as 'quasi-judgements' as empathies: mere presentation is an empathic modification of a judgement. This is close to Lipps, for whom aesthetic empathy is a 'quasi-judgement'. But Meinong, as we have seen, uses the term in a similar manner in *Über Annahmen*, ed. and trans. as *On Assumptions* by James Heanue (Berkeley: University of California Press, 1983), §54.

22 Dan Zahavi defends the irreducibly plural view of the transcendental subjectivity as always an intersubjectivity, and he interprets passages emphasizing uniqueness and individuality as simply explicating the phenomenological sense of an 'I' which can be experienced only in the first-person mode; see his *Self-Awareness and Alterity*, p. 165.

23 See Mensch, *Intersubjectivity and Transcendental Idealism*, p. 240, for a defence of the view that the absolute is 'pre-I', pre-individual.

24 Fink, *VI. Cartesianische Meditation. Teil 1: Die Idee einer transzendentalen Methodlehre*, ed. Hans Ebeling, Jann Holl and Guy van Kerckhoven (Dodrecht: Kluwer, 1988), trans. by Ronald Bruzina and Eugen Fink as *Sixth Cartesian Meditation: The Idea of a Transcendental Theory of Method* (Bloomington, Ind.: Indiana University Press, 1995).

25 Zahavi, *Husserl and Transcendental Intersubjectivity*, p. 71.

26 See Hua 13: 5–8. The term 'monad' appears both in his 1910/11 *GPP* lectures and in PSW (1910/11).

27 Edmund Husserl, 'Naturwissenschaftliche Psychologie, Geisteswissenschaft und Metaphysik (1919)', in Nenon and Embree, eds, *Issues in Husserl's Ideas II*, pp. 1–7, trans. Paul Crowe as 'Natural Scientific Psychology, Human Sciences and Metaphysics', ibid., pp. 8–13.

## Conclusion: Husserl's Contribution to Philosophy

1 As Husserl said in a letter to Ingarden of 10 July 1935, see *Briefe an Ingarden mit Erlauterunger und Erinnerungen an Husserl* (The Hague: Nijhoff, 1968), p. 93.

2 See Jacques Derrida, *Speech and Phenomena and other Essays on Husserl's Theory of Signs*, ed. and trans. David Allison (Evanston, Ill.: Northwestern University Press, 1973).

3 Tze-Wan Kwan, 'Husserl's Concept of Horizon: An Attempt at Reappraisal', *Analecta Husserliana* 31 (Dordrecht: Kluwer Academic Publishers, 1990), pp. 361–99; and Roberto J. Walton, 'World-experience, World-representation, and the World as an Idea', *Husserl Studies*, 14 (1997), pp. 1–20.

4 Derrida, *Speech and Phenomena*, pp. 26 and 108.

5 Here I am quoting the translation by James Richard Mensch in his *Intersubjectivity and Transcendental Idealism* (Albany, NY: SUNY Press, 1988), p. 208.

6 Derrida, *Speech and Phenomena*, p. 12.

7 Hans-Georg Gadamer, 'The Phenomenological Movement', in *Philosophical Hermeneutics*, trans. and ed. David E. Linge (Berkeley: University of California Press, 1977), p. 142.

8 See Dermot Moran, *Introduction to Phenomenology* (London and New York: Routledge, 2000).

9 Moritz Schlick, *Allgemeine Erkenntnislehre,* Naturwissenschaftliche Monographien und Lehrbücher 1 (Berlin, 1918; 2 edn 1925), trans. as *General Theory of Knowledge* by A. E. Blumberg and H. Feigl (Chicago: Open Court, 1985).

10 For a study of phenomenology in France, see Bernhard Waldenfels, *Phänomenologie in Frankreich* (Frankfurt: Suhrkamp, 1983).

# Bibliography

## Husserl Bibliography

Spileers, Steven, ed. *The Husserl Bibliography*. Dordrecht: Kluwer, 1999.
Lapointe, François. *Edmund Husserl and his Critics: An International Bibliography (1894–1979)*. Bowling Green, Oh.: Philosophy Documentation Center, 1980.

## Primary Sources

### Works by Edmund Husserl in German

The complete critical edition of Husserl's works is:

Husserl, Edmund. *Gesammelte Werke*, Husserliana. Dordrecht: Kluwer, now Springer, 1956– .

To date the following volumes have been published:

Volume 1: *Cartesianische Meditationen und Pariser Vorträge*, ed. Stephan Strasser. The Hague: Nijhoff, 1950; repr. 1991.
Volume 2: *Die Idee der Phänomenologie: Fünf Vorlesungen*, Nachdruck der 2. erg. Auflage, ed. W. Biemel. The Hague: Nijhoff, 1973.
Volume 3/1: *Ideen zu einer reinen Phänomenologie und phänomenologischen Philosophie*. Erstes Buch: *Allgemeine Einführung in die reine Phänomenologie*, 1. Halbband: *Text der 1–3. Auflage*, ed. K. Schuhmann. The Hague: Nijhoff, 1977.
Volume 3/2: *Ideen zu einer reinen Phänomenologie und phänomenologischen Philosophie*. Erstes Buch: *Allgemeine Einführung in die reine Phänomenologie*, 2. Halbband: *Ergänzende Texte (1912–1929)*, ed. K. Schuhmann. The Hague: Nijhoff, 1977.

Volume 4: *Ideen zu einer reinen Phänomenologie und phänomenologischen Philosophie*. Zweites Buch: *Phänomenologische Untersuchungen zur Konstitution*, ed. Marly Biemel. The Hague: Nijhoff, 1952; repr. 1991.

Volume 5: *Ideen zu einer reinen Phänomenologie und phänomenologischen Philosophie*. Drittes Buch: *Die Phänomenologie und die Fundamente der Wissenschaften*, ed. Marly Biemel. The Hague: Nijhoff, 1952; repr. 1971.

Volume 6: *Die Krisis der europäischen Wissenschaften und die transzendentale Phänomenologie: Eine Einleitung in die phänomenologische Philosophie*, ed. W. Biemel. The Hague: Nijhoff, 1962; repr. 1976.

Volume 7: *Erste Philosophie (1923/24). Erster Teil: Kritische Ideengeschichte*, ed. R. Boehm. The Hague: Nijhoff, 1965.

Volume 8: *Erste Philosophie (1923/24). Zweiter Teil: Theorie der phänomenologischen Reduktion*, ed. R. Boehm. The Hague: Nijhoff, 1965.

Volume 9: *Phänomenologische Psychologie: Vorlesungen Sommersemester 1925*, ed. W. Biemel. The Hague: Nijhoff, 1968.

Volume 10: *Zur Phänomenologie des inneren Zeitbewusstseins (1893–1917)*, ed. R. Boehm. The Hague: Nijhoff, 1966; 2nd edn 1969.

Volume 11: *Analysen zur passiven Synthesis: Aus Vorlesungs- und Forschungsmanuskripten (1918–1926)*, ed. M. Fleischer. Dordrecht: Kluwer, 1988.

Volume 12: *Philosophie der Arithmetik: Mit ergänzenden Texten (1890–1901)*, ed. L. Eley. The Hague: Nijhoff, 1970.

Volume 13: *Zur Phänomenologie der Intersubjektivität: Texte aus dem Nachlass. Erster Teil: 1905–1920*, ed. I. Kern. The Hague: Nijhoff, 1973.

Volume 14: *Zur Phänomenologie der Intersubjektivität: Texte aus dem Nachlass. Zweiter Teil: 1921–1928*, ed. I. Kern. The Hague: Nijhoff, 1973.

Volume 15: *Zur Phänomenologie der Intersubjektivität: Texte aus dem Nachlass. Dritter Teil: 1929–1935*, ed. I. Kern. The Hague: Nijhoff, 1973.

Volume 16: *Ding und Raum: Vorlesungen 1907*, ed. U. Claesges. The Hague: Nijhoff, 1973.

Volume 17: *Formale und transzendentale Logik: Versuch einer Kritik der logischen Vernunft: Mit ergänzenden Texten*, ed. Paul Janssen. The Hague: Nijhoff, 1974.

Volume 18: *Logische Untersuchungen. Erster Band: Prolegomena zur reinen Logik*. Text of 1st and 2nd edns, ed. E. Holenstein. The Hague: Nijhoff, 1975.

Volume 19: *Logische Untersuchungen. Zweiter Band: Untersuchungen zur Phänomenologie und Theorie der Erkenntnis*, in 2 vols, ed. Ursula Panzer. Dordrecht: Kluwer, 1984.

Volume 20/1: *Logische Untersuchungen: Ergänzungsband. Erster Teil: Entwürfe zur Umarbeitung der VI. Untersuchung und zur Vorrede für die Neuauflage der 'Logischen Untersuchungen' (Sommer 1913)*, ed. U. Melle. Dordrecht: Kluwer, 2002.

Volume 21: *Studien zur Arithmetik und Geometrie: Texte aus dem Nachlass (1886–1901)*, ed. I. Strohmeyer. Dordrecht: Kluwer, 1983.

Volume 22: *Aufsätze und Rezensionen (1890–1910)*, ed. B. Rang. Dordrecht: Kluwer, 1979.

Volume 23: *Phantasie, Bildbewusstsein, Erinnerung: Zur Phänomenologie der anschaulichen Vergegenwärtigungen: Texte aus dem Nachlass (1898–1925)*, ed. Eduard Marbach. Dordrecht: Kluwer, 1980.

Volume 24: *Einleitung in die Logik und Erkenntnistheorie: Vorlesungen 1906/07*, ed. Ullrich Melle. Dordrecht: Kluwer, 1985.

Volume 25: *Aufsätze und Vorträge (1911–1921)*, ed. H. R. Sepp and Thomas Nenon. Dordrecht: Kluwer, 1986.

Volume 26: *Vorlesungen über Bedeutungslehre: Sommersemester 1908*, ed. Ursula Panzer. Dordrecht: Kluwer, 1986.

Volume 27: *Aufsätze und Vorträge (1922–1937)*, ed. Thomas Nenon and H. R. Sepp. Dordrecht: Kluwer, 1989.

Volume 28: *Vorlesungen über Ethik und Wertlehre (1908–1914)*, ed. Ullrich Melle. Dordrecht: Kluwer, 1988.

Volume 29: *Die Krisis der europäischen Wissenschaften und die transzendentale Phänomenologie: Ergänzungsband: Texte aus dem Nachlass (1934–1937)*, ed. Reinhold N. Smid. Dordrecht: Kluwer, 1992.

Volume 30: *Logik und allgemeine Wissenschaftstheorie: Vorlesungen 1917/18, mit ergänzenden Texten aus der ersten Fassung 1910/11*, ed. Ursula Panzer. Dordrecht: Kluwer, 1996.

Volume 31: *Aktive Synthesen: Aus der Vorlesung 'Transzendentalen Logik' 1920/21*, ed. Roland Breeur. Dordrecht: Kluwer, 2000.

Volume 32: *Natur und Geist: Vorlesungen Sommersemester 1927*, ed. Michael Weiler. Dordrecht: Kluwer, 2001.

Volume 33: *Die 'Bernauer Manuskripte' über das Zeitbewusstsein (1917/18)*, ed. Rudolf Bernet and Dieter Lohmar. Dordrecht: Kluwer, 2001.

Volume 34: *Zur Phänomenologischen Reduktionen: Texte aus dem Nachlass (1926–1935)*, ed. Sebastian Luft. Dordrecht: Kluwer, 2002.

Volume 35: *Einleitung in die Philosophie: Vorlesungen 1922/23*. ed. Berndt Goossens. Dordrecht: Kluwer, 2002.

Volume 36: *Transzendentaler Idealismus: Texte aus dem Nachlass (1908–1921)*, ed. Robin Rollinger and Rochus Sowa. Dordrecht: Kluwer, 2003.

Volume 37: *Einleitung in die Ethik: Vorlesungen Sommersemester 1920 und 1924*, ed. Henning Peucker. Dordrecht: Springer, 2004.

Volume 38: *Wahrnehmung und Aufmerksamkeit: Texte aus dem Nachlass (1893–1912)*, ed. Thomas Vongehr and Regula Giuliani. Dordrecht: Springer, 2004.

***Other Editions and Selections of Husserl's Works***

*Allgemeine Erkenntnistheorie 1902/03*, ed. E. Schuhmann. Materialenbände 3. Dordrecht: Kluwer, 2001.

*Briefwechsel*, ed. Karl Schuhmann in collaboration with Elizabeth Schuhmann. *Husserliana Dokumente*, 10 vols. Dordrecht: Kluwer, 1994.
'Entwurf einer "Vorrede" zu den *Logischen Untersuchungen* (1913)', ed. Eugen Fink, *Tijdschrift voor Filosofie*, 1, 1 (Feb. 1939), pp. 107–33 and 1, 2 (May 1939), pp. 319–39.
*Erfahrung und Urteil: Untersuchungen zur Genealogie der Logik*, rev. and ed. Ludwig Landgrebe. Prague: Academia-Verlag, 1938; 7th. edn, Hamburg: Felix Meiner, 1999.
*Logik: Vorlesungen SS 1895 und SS 1896*, ed. E. Schuhmann. Materialenbände 1. Dordrecht: Kluwer, 2001.
*Méditations cartésiennes: introduction à la phénoménologie*, trans. G. Peiffer and E. Levinas. Paris: Almand Colin, 1931.
*Natur und Geist: Vorlesungen Sommersemester 1919*, ed. M. Weiler. Materialenbände 4. Dordrecht: Kluwer, 2002.
*Urteilstheorie Vorlesung 1905*, ed. E. Schuhmann. Materialenbände 5. Dordrecht: Kluwer, 2002.
*Vorlesungen WS 1902/03*, ed. E. Schuhmann. Materialenbände 2. Dordrecht: Kluwer, 2001.

**Works by Husserl in English Translation**
*Analyses Concerning Passive and Active Synthesis: Lectures on Transcendental Logic*, trans. Anthony J. Steinbock. *Collected Works*, vol. 9. Dordrecht: Kluwer, 2001.
*Cartesian Meditations*, trans. D. Cairns. The Hague: Nijhoff, 1967.
*The Crisis of European Sciences and Transcendental Phenomenology: An Introduction to Phenomenological Philosophy*, trans. David Carr. Evanston, Ill.: Northwestern University Press, 1970.
*Early Writings in the Philosophy of Logic and Mathematics*, trans. Dallas Willard. *Collected Works*, vol. 5. Dordrecht: Kluwer, 1994.
*Experience and Judgment: Investigations in a Genealogy of Logic*, rev. and ed. L. Landgrebe, trans. J. S. Churchill and K. Ameriks. London: Routledge & Kegan Paul, 1973.
'Fichte's Ideal of Humanity [Three Lectures]', trans. James G. Hart, *Husserl Studies*, 12 (1995), pp. 111–33.
*Formal and Transcendental Logic*, trans. D. Cairns. The Hague: Nijhoff, 1969.
*Husserl, Shorter Works*, trans. and ed. Frederick Elliston and Peter McCormick. Notre Dame, Ind.: University of Notre Dame Press, 1981.
*The Idea of Phenomenology*, trans. Lee Hardy. *Collected Works*, vol. 8. Dordrecht: Kluwer, 1999.
*Ideas Pertaining to a Pure Phenomenology and to a Phenomenological Philosophy, First Book*, trans. F. Kersten. Dordrecht: Kluwer, 1983.

*Ideas: A General Introduction to Pure Phenomenology*, trans. W. R. Boyce Gibson. London: Allen & Unwin, 1931.

*Ideas Pertaining to a Pure Phenomenology and to a Phenomenological Philosophy, Second Book*, trans. R. Rojcewicz and A. Schuwer. *Collected Works*, vol. 3. Dordrecht: Kluwer, 1989.

*Ideas Pertaining to a Pure Phenomenology and to a Phenomenological Philosophy, Third Book*, trans. T. E. Klein and W. E. Pohl. *Collected Works*, vol. 1. The Hague: Nijhoff, 1980.

*Introduction to the Logical Investigations: Draft of a Preface to the Logical Investigations*, ed. E. Fink, trans. P. J. Bossert and C. H. Peters. The Hague: Nijhoff, 1975.

'Kant and the Idea of Transcendental Philosophy', trans. Ted E. Klein and William E. Pohl, *Southwestern Journal of Philosophy*, 5 (Fall 1974), pp. 9–56.

*Logical Investigations*, trans. J. N. Findlay, ed. with a New Introduction by Dermot Moran and a New Preface by Michael Dummett, 2 vols. London and New York: Routledge, 2001.

*On the Phenomenology of the Consciousness of Internal Time*, trans. J. B. Brough. *Collected Works*, vol. 4. Dordrecht: Kluwer, 1990.

*The Paris Lectures*, trans. P. Koestenaum. The Hague: Nijhoff, 1970.

*Phantasy, Image-Consciousness, Memory*, trans. J. Brough. *Collected Works*, vol. 11. Dordrecht: Springer, 2005.

*Phenomenological Psychology: Lectures, Summer Semester 1925*, trans. J. Scanlon. The Hague: Nijhoff, 1977.

*The Phenomenology of Internal Time Consciousness*, ed. Martin Heidegger, trans. J. S. Churchill. Bloomington, Ind., and London: Indiana University Press, 1964.

*Philosophy as a Rigorous Science*, 1911, in Quentin Lauer, *Edmund Husserl: Phenomenology and the Crisis of Philosophy*, New York: Harper and Row, 1964.

*Psychological and Transcendental Phenomenology and the Confrontation with Heidegger (1927–31): The Encyclopaedia Britannica Article, The Amsterdam Lectures 'Phenomenology and Anthropology' and Husserl's Marginal Note in Being and Time, and Kant on the Problem of Metaphysics*, trans. and ed. T. Sheehan and R. E. Palmer. *Collected Works*, vol. 6. Dordrecht: Kluwer 1997.

'Syllabus of a Course of Four Lectures on "Phenomenological Method and Phenomenological Philosophy", Delivered at University College, London, June 6, 8, 9, 12, 1922', *Journal of the British Society for Phenomenology*, 1, 1 (1970), pp. 18–23.

*Thing and Space: Lectures of 1907*, trans. R. Rojcewicz. *Collected Works*, vol. 7. Dordrecht: Kluwer, 1997.

Welton, Donn, ed. *The Essential Husserl*. Bloomington, Ind.: Indiana University Press, 1999.

## Selected Secondary Literature

Bell, David. *Husserl*. London: Routledge, 1991.

Benoist, Jocelyn. *Intentionnalité et langage dans les* Recherches logiques *de Husserl*. Paris: PUF, 2001.

Bernet, Rudolf, Iso Kern and Eduard Marbach. *An Introduction to Husserlian Phenomenology*. Evanston, Ill.: Northwestern University Press, 1993.

Brainard, Marcus. *Belief and its Neutralization: Husserl's System of Phenomenology in* Ideas I. Albany, NY: SUNY Press, 2002.

Brough, John. 'Presence and Absence in Husserl's Philosophy of Time-Consciousness', in L. Langsdorf, S. Watson and E. M. Bower, eds, *Phenomenology, Interpretation and Community* (Albany, NY: SUNY Press, 1996), pp. 3–15.

Cairns, Dorion. *Conversations with Husserl and Fink*, Phaenomenologica 66. The Hague: Nijhoff, 1975.

Carr, David. *Interpreting Husserl: Critical and Comparative Studies*. Dordrecht: Kluwer, 1987.

Carr, David. *The Paradox of Subjectivity: The Self in the Transcendental Tradition*. Oxford and New York: Oxford University Press, 1999.

Cobb-Stevens, Richard. *Husserl and Analytic Philosophy*. Dordrecht: Kluwer, 1990.

Dastur, Françoise. *Husserl des mathématiques à l'histoire*. Paris: PUF, 1995.

DeBoer, Theodor. *The Development of Husserl's Thought*. The Hague: Nijhoff, 1978.

Depraz, Natalie. *Husserl*, Collection Synthèse. Paris: Armand Colin, 1999.

Depraz, Natalie. *Transcendance et incarnation: Le Statut de l'intersubjectivité comme altérité à soi chez Husserl*. Paris: Vrin, 1995.

Derrida, Jacques. *Edmund Husserl's Origin of Geometry: An Introduction*, trans. J. P. Leavey and D. B. Allison. Hassocks: Harvester Press, 1978.

Derrida, Jacques. *Speech and Phenomena and Other Essays on Husserl's Theory of Signs*, ed. and trans. David Allison. Evanston, Ill.: Northwestern University Press, 1973.

Dodd, James. *Idealism and Corporeity: An Essay on the Problem of the Body in Husserl's Phenomenology*. Dordrecht: Kluwer Academic Publishers, 1997.

Dreyfus, Hubert L., ed. *Husserl, Intentionality and Cognitive Science*. Cambridge, Mass.: MIT Press, 1982.

Drummond, John J. *Husserlian Intentionality and Non-Foundational Realism: Noema and Object*. Dordrecht: Kluwer, 1990.

Elliston, F. A. and P. McCormick, eds. *Husserl: Expositions and Appraisals*. Notre Dame, Ind.: University of Notre Dame Press, 1977.

Elveton, R. O., ed. *The Phenomenology of Edmund Husserl: Selected Critical Readings*. Chicago: Quadrangle, 1970; 2nd edn, Seattle: Noesis Press, 2000.

Escoubas, Elaine and Marc Richir, eds. *Husserl*. Grenoble: Millon, 1989.

Farber, Marvin. *The Foundation of Phenomenology*. Cambridge, Mass.: Harvard University Press, 1943.

Fink, Eugen. 'Operative Begriffe in Husserls Phänomenologie', *Zeitschrift für philosophische Forschung*, 11 (1957), pp. 321–7.

Fisette, Denis, ed. *Husserl's Logical Investigations Reconsidered*. Dordrecht: Kluwer, 2003.

Føllesdal, Dagfinn, 'Husserl's Notion of Noema', *Journal of Philosophy*, 66 (1969), pp. 680–7.

Haaparanta, Leila, ed. *Mind, Meaning and Mathematics: Essays on the Philosophical Views of Husserl and Frege*. Dordrecht: Kluwer, 1994.

Hart, James G. *The Person and the Common Life: Studies in a Husserlian Social Ethics*. Dordrecht: Kluwer, 1992.

Heidegger, Martin, *Being and Time*, trans. John Macquarrie and E. Robinson. New York: Harper & Row, 1962.

Held, Klaus. *Lebendige Gegenwart: Die Frage nach der Seinsweise des transzendentalen Ich bei Edmund Husserl, entwickelt am Leitfaden der Zeitproblematik*. The Hague: Nijhoff, 1966.

Hill, Claire Ortiz. *Word and Object in Husserl, Frege and Russell*. Athens, Oh.: Ohio University Press, 1991.

Holenstein, Elmar. *Phänomenologie der Assoziation: Zu Struktur und Funktion eines Grundprinzips der passiven Genesis bei E. Husserl*. The Hague: Nijhoff, 1972.

Hopkins, Burt C., ed. *Husserl in Contemporary Context*. Dordrecht: Kluwer, 1997.

Husserl, Malvine. 'Skizze eines Lebensbildes von Edmund Husserl', ed. Karl Schuhmann, *Husserl Studies*, 5 (1988), pp. 105–25.

Ingarden, Roman. *On the Motives which led Husserl to Transcendental Idealism*, trans. Arnór Hannibalsson. The Hague: Nijhoff, 1975.

Janssen, Paul. *Edmund Husserl. Einführung in seine Phänomenologie*. Freiburg: Karl Alber, 1976.

Kohák, Erazim. *Idea and Experience: Edmund Husserl's Project of Phenomenology in Ideas, II*. Chicago: University of Chicago Press, 1978.

Landgrebe, Ludwig. *The Phenomenology of Edmund Husserl: Six Essays*, ed. D. Welton (Ithaca, NY: Cornell University Press, 1981).

Lee, Nam-In. *Edmund Husserls Phänomenologie der Instinkte*. Dordrecht: Kluwer, 1993.

Levinas, E. *La Théorie de l'intuition dans la phénoménologie de Husserl*. Paris: Félix Alcan, 1930; repr. Paris: Vrin, 1963.

Levinas, E. *The Theory of Intuition in Husserl's Phenomenology*, trans. A. Orianne. Evanston, Ill.: Northwestern University Press, 1973.

Lohmar, Dieter. *Edmund Husserls 'Formale und transzendentale Logik'*. Darmstadt: Wissenschaftliche Buchgesellschaft, 2000.

Luft, Sebastian. 'Husserl's Theory of the Phenomenological Reduction: Between Life-World and Cartesianism', *Research in Phenomenology*, 34 (2004), pp. 198–234.

Luft, Sebastian. *'Phänomenologie der Phänomenologie': Systematik und Methodologie der Phänomenologie in der Auseinandersetzung zwischen Husserl und Fink*, Phaenomenologica 166. Dordrecht: Kluwer, 2002.

McKenna, William R. *Husserl's 'Introductions' to Phenomenology: Interpretation and Critique*. Dordrecht: Kluwer, 1982.

McKenna, William R., R. M. Harlan and L. E. Winters, eds. *Apriori and World: European Contributions to Husserlian Phenomenology*. The Hague: Nijhoff, 1981.

Marbach, Edouard. *Das Problem des Ich in der Phänomenologie Husserls*, Phaenomenologica 59. The Hague: Nijhoff, 1974.

Marion, Jean-Luc. *Reduction and Givenness: Investigations of Husserl, Heidegger, and Phenomenology*, trans. Thomas A. Carlson. Evanston, Ill.: Northwestern University Press, 1998.

Mensch, James Richard. *Intersubjectivity and Transcendental Idealism*. Albany, NY: SUNY Press, 1988.

Mensch, James Richard. *Postfoundational Phenomenology: Husserlian Reflections on Presence and Embodiment*. University Park, Pa.: Pennsylvania State University Press, 2001.

Merleau-Ponty, M. *Phénoménologie de la perception*. Paris: Gallimard, 1945.

Merleau-Ponty, M. *The Phenomenology of Perception*, trans. C. Smith. London: Routledge & Kegan Paul, 1962.

Mohanty, J. N. *Edmund Husserl's Theory of Meaning*. The Hague: Nijhoff, 1976.

Mohanty, J. N. *Husserl and Frege*. Bloomington, Ind.: Indiana University Press, 1982.

Mohanty, J. N., ed. *Readings on Edmund Husserl's* Logical Investigations. The Hague: Nijhoff, 1977.

Mohanty, J. N. and William R. McKenna, eds. *Husserl's Phenomenology: A Textbook*. Washington: Center for Advanced Research in Phenomenology and University Press of America, 1989.

Moran, Dermot. 'Heidegger's Critique of Husserl's and Brentano's Accounts of Intentionality', *Inquiry*, 43, 1 (March 2000), pp. 39–65.

Moran, Dermot. 'Husserl and the Crisis of the European Sciences', in M. W. F. Stone and Jonathan Wolff, eds, *The Proper Ambition of Science*, London and New York: Routledge, 2000, pp. 122–50.

Moran, Dermot. 'Husserl's Critique of Brentano in the *Logical Investigations*', *Manuscrito*, special Husserl issue, 33, 2 (2000), pp. 163–205.

Moran, Dermot. *Introduction to Phenomenology*. London and New York: Routledge, 2000.

Moran, Dermot. 'The Problem of Empathy: Lipps, Scheler, Husserl and Stein', in Thomas A. Kelly and Phillip W. Rosemann, eds, *Amor Amicitiae: On the Love that is Friendship: Essays in Medieval Thought and Beyond in Honor of the Rev. Professor James McEvoy* (Leuven, Paris and Dudley, Mass.: Peeters, 2004), pp. 269–312.

Mulligan, Kevin, ed. *Speech Act and Sachverhalt: Reinach and the Foundations of Realist Phenomenology*. Dordrecht: Nijhoff, 1987.

Mulligan, Kevin and B. Smith. 'A Husserlian Theory of Indexicality', *Grazer Philosophische Studien*, 28 (1996), pp. 133–63.

Natorp, Paul. *Allgemeine Psychologie nach kritischer Methode*, vol. 1. Tübingen: Paul Siebeck, 1912; repr. Amsterdam: Bonset, 1965.

Natorp, Paul. *Einleitung in die Psychologie nach kritischer Methode*. Freiburg: Mohr, 1888.

Natorp, Paul. 'Zur Frage der logischen Methode. Mit Bezug auf Edm. Husserls Prolegomena zur reinen Logik', *Kantstudien*, 6 (1901), pp. 270–83.

Osborn, Andrew. *The Philosophy of Edmund Husserl in its Development from his Mathematical Interests to his First Conception of Phenomenology in the Logical Investigations*. New York: International Press, 1934.

Prechtl, Peter. *Husserl: zur Einführung*. Hamburg: Junius, 1991.

Ricoeur, Paul. *Husserl: An Analysis of his Philosophy*. Evanston, Ill.: Northwestern University Press, 1967.

Rollinger, Robin. *Husserl's Position in the School of Brentano*. Utrecht: Department of Philosophy, Utrecht University, 1996.

Schérer, René. *Husserl, sa vie, son œuvre*. Paris: PUF, 1971.

Schérer, René. *La Phénoménologie des 'Recherches Logiques' de Husserl*. Paris: PUF, 1967.

Schuhmann, Karl. *Die Fundamentalbetrachtung der Phänomenologie: Zum Weltproblem in der Philosophie Husserls*. The Hague: Nijhoff, 1971.

Schuhmann, Karl. *Husserl-Chronik: Denk- und Lebensweg Edmund Husserls*. The Hague: Nijhoff, 1977.

Seebohm, Thomas and Joseph Kockelmans, eds. *Kant and Phenomenology*. Washington: Center for Advanced Research in Phenomenology, 1984.

Sepp, Hans Reiner, ed. *Edmund Husserl und die phänomenologische Bewegung: Zeugnisse in Text und Bild*. Freiburg and Munich: Karl Alber Verlag, 1988.

Smith, A. D. *Routledge Philosophy Guidebook to Husserl and the* Cartesian Meditations. London and New York: Routledge, 2003.

Smith, Barry and David Woodruff Smith, eds. *The Cambridge Companion to Husserl*. Cambridge: Cambridge University Press, 1995.

Smith, David Woodruff and Ronald McIntyre. *Husserl and Intentionality: A Study of Mind, Meaning and Language*. Dordrecht: Reidel, 1982.

Sokolowski, Robert. *The Formation of Husserl's Concept of Constitution*. The Hague: Nijhoff, 1964.

Sokolowski, Robert. *Husserlian Meditations: How Words Present Things.* Evanston, Ill.: Northwestern University Press, 1974.

Sokolowski, Robert. 'Husserl's Concept of Categorial Intuition', *Phenomenology and the Human Sciences,* supplement to *Philosophical Topics* (1982), pp. 127–41.

Sokolowski, Robert. *Introduction to Phenomenology.* New York: Cambridge University Press, 1999.

Soldati, Gianfranco. *Bedeutung und psychischer Gehalt, eine Untersuchung zur sprachanalytischen Kritik von Husserls früher Phänomenologie.* Paderborn: Schöningh, 1994.

Spiegelberg, Herbert, with Karl Schuhmann. *The Phenomenological Movement: A Historical Introduction,* 3rd edn. Dordrecht: Kluwer, 1994.

Stein, Edith. *On the Problem of Empathy,* trans. Waltraut Stein. *Collected Works of Edith Stein,* vol. 3. Washington: Institute of Carmelite Studies Publications, 1989.

Steinbock, Anthony J. *Home and Beyond: Generative Phenomenology after Husserl.* Evanston, Ill.: Northwestern University Press, 1995.

Ströker, Elizabeth. *Husserl's Transcendental Phenomenology.* Stanford, Calif.: Stanford University Press, 1993.

Tugendhat, Ernst. *Der Wahrheitsbegriff bei Husserl und Heidegger.* Berlin: de Gruyter, 1967.

Van Breda, H. L. and J. Taminiaux, eds. *Edmund Husserl 1859–1959: Recueil commémorative publié à l'occasion du centenaire de la naissance du philosophe.* The Hague: Nijhoff, 1959.

Welton, Donn. *The Origins of Meaning: A Critical Study of the Thresholds of Husserlian Phenomenology.* The Hague: Nijhoff, 1983.

Welton, Donn. *The Other Husserl.* Bloomington, Ind.: Indiana University Press, 2000.

Wiegand, Olav K., R. Dostal, J. N. Mohanty and J. J. Kockelmans, eds. *Phenomenology on Kant, German Idealism, Hermeneutics and Logic.* Dordrecht: Kluwer, 2000.

Willard, Dallas. *Logic and the Objectivity of Knowledge: A Study in Husserl's Early Philosophy.* Athens, Oh.: Ohio University Press, 1984.

Zahavi, Dan. *Husserl and Transcendental Intersubjectivity,* trans. Elizabeth A. Behnke. Athens, Oh.: Ohio University Press, 2001.

Zahavi, Dan. *Husserl's Phenomenology.* Stanford, Calif.: Stanford University Press, 2003.

Zahavi, Dan. *Self-Awareness and Alterity: A Phenomenological Investigation.* Evanston, Ill.: Northwestern University Press, 1999.

Zahavi, Dan and N. Depraz, eds. *Alterity and Facticity: New Perspectives on Husserl.* Dordrecht: Kluwer, 1998.

Zahavi, Dan and Frederick Stjernfelt, eds. *One Hundred Years of Phenomenology: Husserl's Logical Investigations Revisited.* Dordrecht: Kluwer, 2002.

# Index

98899475R00172

Made in the USA
Columbia, SC
02 July 2018